EVERYDAY
activism

a handbook for lesbian, gay, and bisexual people and their allies

edited by
Michael R. Stevenson, Ph.D.
& Jeanine C. Cogan, Ph.D.

Routledge
New York & London

Published in 2003 by
Routledge
29 West 35th Street
New York, New York 10001
www.routledge-ny.com

Published in Great Britain by
Routledge
11 New Fetter Lane
London EC4P 4EE
www.routledge.co.uk

10   9   8   7   6   5   4   3   2   1

Library of Congress Cataloging-in-Publication Data

Everyday activism : a handbook for lesbian, gay, and bisexual people and their allies / edited by
   Michael R. Stevenson and Jeanine C. Cogan.
      p. cm.
   Includes bibliographical references and index.
     ISBN 0-415-94481-3 (hardback) — ISBN 0-415-92668-8 (pbk.)
   1. Gay rights. 2. Gays—Political activity. I. Stevenson, Michael R. II. Cogan, Jeanine C.
HQ76.5 .E95 2003
305.9'0664—dc21   2002153069

CONTENTS

             Christopher J. Portelli

Chapter 7   **Ending Discrimination in the**   *145*
             U.S. Military
             Clinton W. Anderson and C. Dixon Osburn

PART III   CREATING EQUALITY

Chapter 8   **Honoring and Protecting Relationships**   *171*
             Robin A. Buhrke

Chapter 9   **Recognizing and Legitimizing Families**   *193*
             Beverly R. King

Chapter 10 **Debunking Myths About Child Abuse**   *211*
             Michael R. Stevenson

Chapter 11 **Making Schools Safe**   *229*
             Karen M. Anderson and Michael R. Stevenson

Appendix   **Web Resources**   *245*
             Jennifer M. Hoag and Lisa M. Schmidt

             Notes   *257*

             Biographical Notes   *299*

             Index   *303*

ACKNOWLEDGMENTS

First and foremost we wish to express our appreciation to our contributors. Without their commitment and their patient and persistent support, this volume would have been impossible to produce. This is indeed an unusual group of scholars/practitioners/advocates, who have intentionally and elegantly bridged the divide between those who gather and interpret data and those who use it as a basis for advocacy. We are grateful for their diligence, their expertise, and their commitment to everyday activism both literally and figuratively.

We wish to thank Nicole Bixler, Jennifer M. Hoag, Charity Schafer, and Lisa Schmidt for their tireless efforts on behalf of this book. In addition to hours of library research, they provided invaluable assistance with proofreading and fact checking in their role as assistant to the senior editor. We also wish to thank Ilene Kalish, Kimberly Guinta, and our team at Routledge for their belief in this project and their assistance in bringing our vision into reality.

We wish to acknowledge Charles W. Smith, The Gay Financial Network, and SIECUS (The Sexuality Information and Education Council of the United States) for granting permission to print excerpts from their publications in chapter 6, Obtaining and Maintaining Housing. We also wish to acknowledge Michelle M. Benecke, Esq., former Army officer and co-founder of Servicemembers Legal Defense Network, for her contributions to chapter 7, Ending Discrimination in the U.S. Military, and the series of reports that provided much of the basis for its conclusions.

INTRODUCTION

getting involved

Michael R. Stevenson and Jeanine C. Cogan

In the Introduction, you will

- *Learn how to use this book to advocate for equality.*
- *Learn the importance of public policy.*
- *Learn how persistence and hard work led to a national lesbian health agenda.*
- *Learn about international advocacy needs and efforts.*
- *Get a sneak preview of the remaining chapters.*

There is no doubt that the policy climate for lesbian, gay, and bisexual people (collectively referred to here as LGBs)[1] has improved over the course of history and that important policy strides have been made in the last 25 years. Consider that since 1974, the U.S. Senate has repeatedly introduced legislation to protect LGB employees from being fired simply for their sexual orientation. Although as of 2002 the bill has not yet passed, it came very close in 1996 and support remains strong and steady.[2] In the late 1980s, the U.S. Congress supported protections against antigay hate crimes. Under the leadership of Senator Arlen Specter, a devout Republican from Pennsylvania, Congress passed the Hate Crimes Statistics Act of 1990 and Republican president George H. W. Bush signed it into law. As a result, state and local law enforcement agencies are encouraged to collect data on anti-LGB hate crimes.

In the 1990s during the Clinton administration, an unprecedented number of openly lesbian and gay people were appointed to government positions. Some of these positions were high ranking and visible.[3] In addition, President Clinton signed an executive order banning discrimination against lesbians and gay men in federal agencies and was the first sitting president to attend an openly gay public event, a Human Rights Campaign fund-raiser. In 2000 Vermont passed the

Act Relating to Civil Unions, which created the legal status of civil union for same-sex couples.[4]

At a time when LGB communities have achieved such positive policies, there has been an equally powerful effort to deny the civil rights of LGBs. In 1998, as plans for this book were formulated, the majority leader of the U.S. Senate publicly characterized homosexuality as a sin comparable to alcoholism, kleptomania, and sex addiction. Senate Republicans blocked James C. Hormel's nomination as ambassador to Luxembourg simply because he is openly gay. The House of Representatives approved a measure to deny federal housing funds to San Francisco because of its support of domestic partnership laws for gay and lesbian couples. The U.S. House considered a bill that would have denied funds to implement President Clinton's executive order barring federal agencies from discriminating against gays and lesbians (an order that 70 percent of U.S. Americans favored). At the final hour, the House dropped a provision that would have barred unmarried couples in Washington, D.C., from adopting children. Conservative groups ran full-page ads in major newspapers featuring "ex-gays" and offering to "cure" gay men and lesbians.

As has been the case throughout history, when marginalized groups gain more rights there is a strong counterforce fiercely fighting to maintain the status quo. Clearly LGBs are experiencing a strong and consistent effort to squash the progress made in the policy arena. LGB civil liberties are constantly under siege and advocates for equality need to be well armed. This book offers strategies, information, and inspiration to those who wish to continue the fight for equality for LGB people. If you have never written a letter to Congress, pushed for LGB partner benefits, or participated in a LGB rally, *Everyday Activism* is for you. This book also has a lot to offer those who are already active LGB advocates. The information we present will prepare the novice to confidently engage in first-time advocacy as well as strengthen the old-timer's approach. In short, we believe there is something useful for everyone.

a unique contribution of this book

In addition to discussing advocacy on current issues, we offer a solid scientific foundation for the policy recommendations that appear throughout the chapters. We want you to know the facts and be able to separate myth from reality. Science has played and continues to play a significant role in advocating equality for LGBs. It has done so at least since 1972 when the American Psychiatric Association removed homosexuality from the *Diagnostic and Statistical Manual of Mental Disorders*. As a result of that decision, millions of people were no longer considered psychologically deviant. And this was in great part due to the work of established and respected scientists who consistently found that there were no notable differences in psychological well-being between homosexual and heterosexual people.[5]

For several decades, social scientists have been conducting research examining a range of issues important to the quality of life for LGBs, including parenting, maintaining loving relationships, violence, workplace and housing discrimination, and youth issues. Findings from this research are essential to the debates about LGB issues and can help to create a more informed policy agenda, rather than one fueled by bigotry or myth.

research as an important policy tool

In a political climate fueled by ideology, the information provided by opinion polls is not a sufficient basis for public policy. One problem in relying exclusively on data gathered in political polls is that ordinary people do not trust their results. According to a Shell Poll,[6] 49 percent of U.S. Americans believe that the Bible can predict the future and 21 percent believe in the predictions of astrologers, whereas only 10 percent believe pollsters can make accurate predictions. At least the pollsters do fare better than Ouija boards (3 percent) and the Magic Eight Ball (2 percent)!

Perhaps the public recognizes that "many polls are not objective tools to take the country's political pulse, but instruments to be used for political advocacy. After all, political-communications strategies are based on surveys designed to figure out how to change people's minds."[7] Harris Polls and studies conducted for the American Council on Education demonstrate that the general public has more confidence in college and university leaders than in journalists or most members of Congress.[8] So universities and their researchers need to play a larger role in informing policy makers and the voting public about how their scholarly work can be used in the development of sound public policy.[9]

We recognize a certain irony in using the results of one set of polls to demonstrate the limitations of data drawn from other polls. We do so, not to discredit pollsters or their findings. In fact, many of the contributors to this book (including the two of us) rely, in part, on data from polls. On the contrary, we raise this issue to emphasize that the quality of political polls and other forms of research can and should be evaluated in scientific terms, and to underscore our belief that good science is a better basis for public policy than personal ideologies and politically motivated polls.

Whether members of the U.S. Congress or individuals writing letters to the editor, savvy advocates need access to sound research data on issues facing LGBs. *Everyday Activism* provides realistic interpretations of the available research, set in a framework for understanding the process of public policy development. We believe this book has a great deal to offer any advocate. However, we recognize that the Internet is better suited for specific up-to-the-minute information on relevant court cases and legislative initiatives. As a result, within every chapter you will find links to the best LGB sites the web has to offer.

The contributors to this book are experienced in the intricacies of research and have specific expertise in areas that affect the lives of LGBs across the country. As you will note from their brief biographies, most have credentials as scholars and experience in advocacy and/or policy development, a rare combination in a world of narrow specialties. And, importantly, you will find more evidence than rhetoric in the chapters that follow. The contributors carefully document the most relevant research while drawing clear distinctions between this research and common misconceptions or faulty logic.

In doing so, we discuss the policy implications of widely held assumptions, concepts, and theories about sexual orientation. We describe what research has revealed, identify gaps in scientific knowledge, and suggest alternative approaches to policy development. In short, the resources provided in this volume can be used to inform public policy debates in order to promote policies sensitive to the interests of gay, lesbian, and bisexual people.

overview

Our book starts with a series of basic chapters that will provide you with solid footing. They will help you gear up to make a difference in the lives of LGB people. In chapter 1, Jeanine Cogan discusses how to establish relationships with members of Congress in order to effectively influence policy. Although the examples and strategies she describes are focused on federal-level activism, similar strategies can be used to effect change in policy at any level. This is the how-to chapter. Through it, Cogan offers tools for effective lobbying that can then be applied to the content-specific chapters that follow.

In chapter 2, Michael Stevenson considers some basic questions that are important to understanding the public policy issues discussed throughout the book. What does it mean to be LGB? What causes people to be LGB? How large are the LGB communities? Is it illegal to be LGB? Responses to these questions (though frequently distorted) are often at the root of antigay rhetoric and therefore need to be better understood. Although the questions appear simple on the surface, the answers are surprisingly complex.

At the heart of much anti-LGB rhetoric is the long-debunked notion that LGBs are psychological deviants. In chapter 3, Jessica Morris and Stacey Hart discuss the mental health of LGBs and the unfounded assumptions that underlie anti-LGB policy efforts. They continue the discussion, started in chapter 2, of how science is often misused in conflicts over policy decisions. Given its impact on LGB-affirming policy, Morris and Hart base their analysis on the rhetoric of the ex-gay movement.

With chapters 4 through 7, our focus shifts to explicit attempts to end discrimination and promote LGB-affirming federal policies. Based on her own work as an advocate on Capitol Hill, Jeanine Cogan describes the political landscape relevant to including sexual orientation in existing federal hate crimes laws. In the chapter that follows, David Sobelsohn provides readers with a basic understanding of antidiscrimination law and how it affects LGBs. Although there have been few attempts to develop LGB-affirming housing policy at the federal level and little empirical research is available, in chapter 6 Christopher Portelli describes the policy implications relevant to anti-LGB discrimination with respect to housing. Given that policy is less well developed in this area, Portelli also provides LGB readers with sound advice on how to protect themselves from discrimination in housing. In chapter 7, Clinton Anderson and C. Dixon Osburn provide an analysis of policy relevant to LGB people in the military. In addition to a concise history of relevant policy, they argue that "Don't Ask, Don't Tell, Don't Pursue, Don't Harass" should eventually be replaced with policies that ensure full equality. In the meantime, they demonstrate how the lives of all service members would improve if current policy was applied more effectively.

With chapters 8 through 11 our focus shifts again to creating equality for LGB youth and families. While some of the issues discussed in these chapters have gained national attention, others have not. For example, no U.S. jurisdiction allows marriage between same-sex couples. And while more and more employers are instituting domestic partner benefits, such benefits fall far short of the benefits, rights, and responsibilities that stem from legal marriage. In chapter 8, then, Robin Buhrke reviews policy as it relates to same-sex marriage and domestic partner benefits.

In chapter 9, Beverly King considers the role of public policy in the recognition of families headed by lesbians and gay men. In addition to providing an extensive summary of attempts to limit or curtail parenting by LGBs, she reviews the available research on the development of children with lesbian or gay parents. This research clearly shows that knowing a person's sexual orientation tells us very little about his or her potential as a parent.

In chapter 10, Michael Stevenson confronts the myth that LGB people are a threat to children. He describes how research findings have been misused in policy discussions as he evaluates the relevant scientific evidence. The data are clear. LGBs are not a threat to the well-being of children. Stevenson suggests further that arguments to the contrary serve as red herrings distracting policy makers from developing policies that would effectively protect children from harm.

In chapter 11, Karen Anderson and Michael Stevenson confront the prejudice and hate expressed toward LGB students and teachers in the schools. They begin with a discussion of local control of schools and describe how the federal government interferes, even when it provides few resources. They also describe the climate LGB students often face as they attempt to concentrate on learning. The picture they paint isn't pretty. Clearly many schools are not addressing the needs of LGB students. Although we must continue to defend against federal restrictions that prevent local schools from supporting LGB students, most of this work must be done at the state and local levels.

the need for further scholarship and policy analysis

One of the important findings of this book is that scholars need to conduct more methodologically sophisticated, policy relevant research on issues of particular concern to LGBs. Such research is important, even when it challenges the rhetoric currently being used by LGB-identified advocacy groups.

However, there are policy arenas that deserve special attention. As we planned this book, we had hoped to cover issues specific to transgendered people, LGB health policy, and LGB international policy. Unfortunately, we discovered that relevant research was just beginning in some areas and virtually nonexistent in others. As we discuss in the following sections, we hope that researchers and policy analysts will develop these areas further so that they can be discussed in depth in future editions of *Everyday Activism*.

Transgendered People

Despite recent (and laudable) efforts to include transgender issues within the broad umbrella of the LGB rights movements, the focus of virtually all the relevant social science research includes lesbians, gay men, and (sometimes) bisexuals to the exclusion of transgendered persons. As a result, this volume does not directly consider issues related to transgendered identity. Although these issues are being debated in the federal courts,[10] policy makers have rarely confronted them. Even though the Human Rights Campaign has chosen officially to include the rights of transgendered people in their mission,[11] only Rhode Island, Minnesota, and a few other local jurisdictions have transgender-inclusive nondiscrimination laws or have interpreted local ordinances to include the transgendered.[12] Unfortunately, some attempts to garner support for the rights of transgendered people in other parts of the world, including Britain[13] and Malaysia,[14] have faced considerable opposition. However, professional associations like the American Public Health Association[15] as well as the federal government[16] are actively encouraging research on transgendered individuals, as we note in the next section. As a result, we are hopeful that a body of relevant research will develop in the near future.

LGB Health Issues

Until very recently, policy makers and researchers[17] have given little attention to LGB health issues. As Andrea Solarz[18] explains in Box I.1, after many years of work by women's health advocates, the Institute of Medicine (IOM) released a historic report on lesbian health issues in 1999. In short, the report concludes that lesbians may be disproportionately likely to experience certain health problems and to encounter barriers to quality health care. Unfortunately, similar reports on the health of gay men and bisexuals have not been developed.

Although the federal government has funded some research on LGB health issues in recent years,[19] the IOM report calls for more federal funding for such research.[20] Support for more research will also result from the Department of Health and Human Services, which included LGB-related indicators in the agency's long-range plan on health and prevention.[21]

In 2001, following the historic federally supported meetings described in Box I.1, the National Institutes of Health announced a program encouraging researchers to apply for grants to study LGB and transgendered health issues. This was the first time the NIH formally invited research on LGB-related issues other than HIV and AIDS. The call for funding expires in June 2004. The announcement states:

> Current scientific evidence clearly indicates that the majority of LGBT people do not suffer from clinical disorder. . . . However, recent data from both national health surveys and targeted studies suggest that prevalence rates of affective disorders, tobacco addiction, alcohol abuse, certain forms of drug abuse, and possibly other dysfunctions are higher for LGBT populations (or particular segments of those populations) than for the general population. The data also suggest that LGBTs are more likely than the general population to seek mental health and substance abuse services. But LGBT clients may often fail to receive appropriate and effective services, because many service providers have limited knowledge of or experience in working with LGBTs.[22]

It is our hope that the research resulting from these federal programs[23] will be successful in clarifying our understanding of LGB health issues. In the meantime, you should encourage these federal agencies to continue to support new research efforts that address the health-related needs of LGB people.

Box I.1

ADVOCATING FOR LESBIAN HEALTH: THE STORY OF THE IOM REPORT

Andrea Solarz

In 1999, the prestigious National Academy of Sciences Institute of Medicine (IOM)[24] released its first-ever report on lesbian health issues. Entitled *Lesbian Health: Current Assessment and Directions for the Future*,[25] the report was met with great enthusiasm by the lesbian health community—it represented, for the first time, prominent mainstream scientific support for a national agenda on lesbian health research. The recommendations of the report, which focused on the conduct of lesbian health research, problems in the delivery of health care services to lesbians, and the health status of lesbians, presented a clear blueprint for future advocacy efforts. The story of how this report came about illustrates both how complex and challenging the process of changing the federal status quo can be, as well as how long-term persistence can pay off.

The IOM report on lesbian health research was a culmination of years of concerted effort by lesbian health advocates working to increase federal attention to lesbian health concerns. During the mid-1990s, lesbian health advocates, buoyed by the election of President Clinton, initiated a number of activities to advance support for lesbian health issues. Most importantly, efforts were mobilized to advocate for the development of a national lesbian health policy agenda. Coincident with the April 1993 gay rights march in Washington, D.C., representatives of national and local lesbian and gay health organizations met with Health and Human Services Secretary Donna Shalala to discuss ways the Department of Health and Human Services (DHHS) could increase its attention to, and better address, the needs of LGB and transgendered individuals.[26]

As a result of the meeting with Secretary Shalala, DHHS sponsored a Lesbian Health Roundtable meeting of lesbian and bisexual women's health activists in February 1994 in order to formalize recommendations to DHHS for a lesbian health agenda. At this meeting, the recommendations developed for the 1993 meeting with Secretary Shalala were refined and expanded. As part of the roundtable, meetings were scheduled between the attendees and high-ranking representatives of targeted DHHS agencies responsible for funding a variety of relevant research and service programs.[27]

A number of positive outcomes emerged from the roundtable meeting. Supplemental resources were quickly provided for researchers funded by the National Institutes of Health to support inclusion of lesbian and bisexual women in ongoing studies. In addition, following a letter-writing campaign initiated by national organizations in 1994, questions on sexual orientation were included in two national women's health assessments, the Women's Health Initiative and the Harvard Nurses' Health Study.[28]

Lesbian health activists continued to exert pressure on NIH after the conference to require that questions about sexual orientation be included in funded research studies. One of the barriers to achieving this goal was the significant number of methodological challenges that are involved in conducting research on lesbians (for example, the difficulty of obtaining representative samples of a "hidden" population). Recognizing that the methodological challenges in conducting lesbian health research presented problems both for researchers and for the federal program staff reviewing proposals, it was recommended that a methodology conference be held to discuss further these issues and identify appropriate strategies for addressing them. Convened by the NIH Office of Research on Women's Health (ORWH) in August 1994, the meeting was attended by lesbian health activists and researchers from around the country. Although well intentioned, the meeting did not resolve the concerns of the lesbian health community. It also brought to light differing political agendas among some of the lesbian health advocacy groups, which resulted in conflict and dissention at the meeting. In particular, there were different perspectives on how best to conduct lesbian health research and about the goals and format of the proposed methodology conference.[29]

Against this backdrop of conflict, lesbian health organizations continued to urge NIH to hold a conference that focused on the difficult methodological issues involved in conducting research on lesbian health. At various meetings that occurred following the methodology conference, including a January 1995 meeting of the DHHS interagency Coordinating Committee on Women's Health, the ORWH continued to express their interest in and support for identifying an effective mechanism for addressing the difficult methodological issues. Subsequently, the ORWH decided that the most effective way to review and assess the methodological issues involved in conducting lesbian health research would be to have the evaluation conducted by an independent organization outside the government and outside of the political context of the lesbian health community. As a result, the ORWH contracted in 1996 with the IOM to assess the strength of the science base regarding the physical and mental health of lesbians, review the methodological challenges involved in conducting research on lesbian health, and suggest areas for further research attention.

The findings from the final report have been used extensively by lesbian health advocates to call for additional federal support for lesbian health research, as well as support for addressing lesbian health issues in state and local programs.[30] In addition, the recommendations spawned several significant federal responses, including a 2-day conference on New Approaches to Research on Sexual Orientation, Mental Health, and Substance Abuse[31] and a Scientific Workshop on Lesbian Health convened to consider steps for implementing the recommendations in the IOM report.[32]

International Policy

Since we began work on this book, policy milestones have been achieved around the globe. To name only a few, the Netherlands became the first country in the world to legalize same-sex marriage.[33] Tokyo became the first jurisdiction in Asia to prohibit discrimination based on sexual orientation.[34] Discrimination based on sexual orientation was also banned in Romania,[35] and the European Union granted work protections for gay men and lesbians.[36] Same-sex couples in New Zealand were given the same property rights as married couples.[37] Two openly gay men, who are partners, were appointed to senior political positions in Norway.[38] And the Chinese Psychiatric Association unanimously agreed to stop classifying homosexuality as a pathological condition.[39]

In contrast, the climate for LGBs remains hostile in other parts of the world. For example, a Saudi Arabian court sentenced nine men to more than 2,400 lashes each (most likely with a bamboo rod or a whip with lead piping attached to its tips) doled out in 50 separate installments (to avoid killing the recipient) for engaging in same-sex sexual behavior. The Saudi government subsequently beheaded three additional men for engaging in homosexual behavior.[40] The Namibian government has called for the arrest, deportation, or imprisonment of gays and lesbians, banned visits by gay and lesbian foreigners, and reportedly encouraged the "elimination" of gays and lesbians "from the face of Namibia."[41] And accusations of sodomy were successfully used to imprison significant political leaders in Malaysia and Zimbabwe.[42]

Although it rarely does so, the U.S. government has the potential to influence positively the lives of LGBs worldwide. This could include, among many other things, recognizing the life partners of members of the U.S. American Foreign Service and making it easier for LGB foreign service members from abroad to bring their partners to the United States.[43] In Box I.2, we describe three issues relevant to U.S. international policy. As before, we encourage you to call for more research, analysis, and attention to LGB issues in international policy.

Box I.2

IMMIGRATION AND HUMAN RIGHTS

Although some progress has been made, researchers and policy analysts have paid far too little attention to LGB issues concerning international policy. In the following, we describe three recent efforts to confront LGB issues concerning immigration and human rights.

Immigration Policy Concerning Partners of U.S. Citizens
While a growing number of countries around the globe allow their citizens to sponsor a same-sex partner for immigration purposes, the United States currently has no such provision. A reader's poll taken by *The Advocate* showed that 74 percent of respondents would leave the United States if their partners were unable to obtain U.S. citizenship.[44] In an attempt to correct this problem, Rep. Jerrold Nadler (D-N.Y.) introduced the Permanent Partner Immigration Act in 2000 and again in 2001. This bill would put same-sex couples on equal footing with other-sex couples when dealing with U.S. immigration law.[45] Fourteen countries currently allow lesbian or gay partners of their citizens to become permanent residents: Australia, Belgium, Canada, Denmark, Finland, France, Iceland, Israel, the Netherlands, New Zealand, Norway, South Africa, Sweden and the United Kingdom.[46] Although Al Gore endorsed the idea during his bid for the U.S. presidency, Nadler's bill made little progress in Congress.[47]

San Francisco is the only jurisdiction in the United States to provide some protection for foreign partners of U.S. citizens. City employees are prohibited by city ordinance from aiding the Immigration and Naturalization Service in deporting foreign-born partners of gay and lesbian citizens of San Francisco, even if those partners are in the United States illegally.[48] In addition to the ACLU, the Human Rights Campaign, the National Gay and Lesbian Task Force, the Lesbian and Gay Immigration Rights Task Force, and the International Gay and Lesbian Human Rights Commission have been involved in efforts to educate policy makers on this vital immigration issue.[49] In addition to sound research data on binational same-sex couples, policy makers need to hear about the lives of couples whose lives are disrupted by these policies.[50]

LGB Internationals Seeking Asylum in the United States
Immigration law is at the heart of another LGB-relevant international policy question that deserves further research and analysis. Should the U.S. government grant asylum to LGB foreign nationals seeking refuge from prejudice and victimization abroad? Unfortunately, the answer from policy makers has not been the resounding "Yes!" we might expect. In fact, docu-

ments prepared by the U.S. Department of State, including the reports federal policy makers use to inform policy decisions, often exclude cases involving LGBs.[51] In 1994 with encouragement from U.S. Attorney General Janet Reno, Immigration and Naturalization Service officials began to include gay and lesbian people among those who could apply for asylum in the United States.[52] Between 1994 and 1999 fewer than 2,000 claims were made; given the confidentiality of these records, it is impossible to determine their outcomes.[53] Moreover, such cases can get caught up in the courts; they are not always successful, in spite of the evidence; and some courts have been more willing than others to rule in favor of LGB applicants.[54] Amnesty International, the Lambda Legal Defense and Education Fund, the Lesbian and Gay Immigration Rights Task Force, and the International Gay and Lesbian Human Rights Commission are involved in efforts to help those seeking asylum. As with immigration policy concerning binational couples, you can help to educate policy makers about issues concerning human right abuses abroad and encourage the development of additional resources and research.

Taking a Stand Against Violence and Harassment
In June 2001, shortly after the release of an Amnesty International report,[55] Rep. Tom Lantos (D-Calif.) introduced a resolution condemning persecution of gays by foreign governments. This was Lantos's second attempt to introduce such language in the U.S. House of Representatives. After offering 19 arguments in support of the resolution, it concludes

> [B]e it resolved [t]hat congress condemns all violations of internationally recognized human rights norms based on the real or perceived sexual orientation or gender identity of an individual; . . . [and] recognizes that human rights violations abroad based on sexual orientation and gender identity should be punished . . . and that such violations should be given the same consideration and concern as human rights violations based on other grounds in the formation of policies to protect and promote human rights globally.[56]

Although Lantos's bill has not yet become law, its introduction provided an opportunity to educate Congress and the general public about this issue. Furthermore, we believe there is reason for hope. The Department of State, for example, has officially recognized the value of scientific research by adding a Science and Technology adviser to the staff of the Secretary of State.[57] Thus, we are hopeful that the fruits of the behavioral sciences can be used to improve U.S. international policy, especially as it applies to LGBs. It is the responsibility of researchers and policy analysts to conduct, review, and disseminate research on binational couples and asylum seekers, as advocates document the impact of U.S. foreign policy on LGBs around the globe.

how to use this book

Although we encourage it, we do not expect you to read this book from cover to cover, at least not right away. The chapters are written such that each can stand on its own. When an issue is important in more than one context, as is often the case, we have inserted endnotes to refer readers to other relevant chapters.

In addition, each chapter includes a policy brief similar to documents that legislative aides develop for senators and members of Congress. Each brief highlights the most important points and is intended for wide distribution. When you arrange to meet with your state or federal representatives or choose to write your congressperson, we encourage you to provide a photocopy of the relevant brief as part of your lobbying effort. Each one includes a reference to its source so that recipients will be able to track down additional information should they find it useful.

Each chapter concludes with suggestions for further reading. So, readers who wish to become experts on a specific topic are encouraged to consult these resources. Endnotes associated with each chapter provide a variety of additional relevant information. Some provide further details on the topic at hand or refer readers to specific sites on the Internet. Other endnotes simply refer readers to primary and secondary source material available in print or online.

In addition to being better informed about important issues, we hope that this book inspires you to act. To facilitate effective advocacy, each chapter also includes a list of specific actions you can take to advocate for equality. These activities range from those that will keep you up to date on policy developments to those that can create opportunities for you to have a direct impact on the lives of LGBs across the country and around the globe. One simple way to participate is to support the advocacy groups who work diligently to promote LGB-positive policy. The largest of these organizations are listed in Box I.3.

You can also make use of the wealth of resources that can be retrieved via the internet. The appendix of this book, Web Resources, is not intended to be comprehensive. However, it does include descriptions and web addresses for many of the most useful electronic resources. Given the nature of the web, we will not be surprised if the quality and content of specific webpages changes over time. We have been as accurate as possible in providing specific web addresses. However, even during the writing of this book, some relevant resources have been withdrawn and are no longer available. The best sites frequently update information, so you may wish to consult the main webpage that produced the information for the most recent statistics or research findings.

Box I.3

TWELVE LARGEST NATIONAL LGB GROUPS FOR 2001*

Human Rights Campaign (HRC)
www.hrc.org

Lambda Legal Defense
www.lambdalegal.org

Gay and Lesbian Alliance Against Defamation (GLAAD)
www.glaad.org

Gay Lesbian Straight Education Network (GLSEN)
www.glsen.org

National Gay and Lesbian Task Force (NGLTF)
www.ngltf.org

National Latina/o Lesbian, Gay, Bisexual, and Transgender Organization
(LLEGÓ)
www.llego.org

Gay and Lesbian Victory Fund
www.victoryfund.org

Parents, Family, and Friends of Gays and Lesbians (PFLAG)
www.pflag.org

Servicemembers Legal Defense Network (SLDN)
www.sldn.org

National Youth Advocacy Coalition (NYAC)
www.nyacyouth.org

Gay and Lesbian Medical Association (GLMA)
www.glma.org

National Center for Lesbian Rights (NCLR)
www.nclrights.org

---

* Listed in descending order of budgets. Adapted from "The money behind the
movement." (2002, March 29). *The Washington Blade*, p. 20.

getting involved

By now, you may have wondered just whom we include among the people we wish to reach with this book. Put simply, we hope it means **you** and any number of other individuals who have an interest in advocating for equality. Potential allies include people in "official" advocacy roles, whether as a paid professional or student intern. More importantly, our list of potential advocates includes homemakers, religious leaders, and all manner of professionals, as well as parents, relatives, and friends of LGBs. The list is nearly endless. Whether you work in some official capacity as a policy analyst or simply wish to write a better letter to an editor or elected official, this book is for you. To become involved, the most important qualification is simply the desire to make a positive difference in policy that affects the lives of LGB people.

We offer readers good data, strategies, and inspiration in order to support LGBs in claiming a rightful place as equal citizens. This is not a book about special rights or requests for privilege. Rather, it is a book about ending discrimination. It is not about passively reading but about changing the social norms that relegate LGBs to second-class citizenship.

Building on the blood, sweat, and tears of so many others who have paved the way, we urge you to speak up, and to do so over and over again. We need to understand the policy process and recognize that there are many opportunities to exercise influence.[58] Write a letter to your senator. Schedule a meeting with your congressperson. Join an organization that supports LGB rights. Do it today. This is a book about doing. Doing means telling your stories and the stories of those you care about. It also means clarifying the misrepresentations that obstruct LGB-positive policy and defining the policy agenda. As a voting citizen and as a constituent, you have rights and power. So exercise those rights with vigor! Read a chapter or two—then act on what you have learned. The next chapter provides details on how to begin, so read on.

what you can do!

- Read this book and put what you learn into action.
- Join and support the advocacy groups that champion the issues you care about most.
- Keep abreast of important policy developments.
  - Monitor the websites of your favorite advocacy groups.
  - Read *The Washington Blade* (www.washblade.com) or other resources that cover LGB policy developments locally, regionally, nationally, and internationally.

- Monitor sources of local news for LGB content.
- Register on the Activist Alert Network sponsored by People for the American Way Foundation (http://www.pfaw.org) to receive e-mail alerts concerning relevant legislation.
- Call and write your elected officials. Include a policy brief from this book with your letter. The Take Action page on the NTLGF (www.ntlgf.org) website shows you how to contact your elected officials.
- Write letters to the editor of local papers correcting misrepresentations and praising LGB sensitive coverage. (See Box 1.7 for details.)
- Support efforts to increase funding for research on LGB relevant policy issues.
- Support efforts to end discrimination worldwide.
- Create opportunities to educate others.
- Find an opportunity to tell your own story.

for more information

- Adam, B. D., Duyvendak, J. W., & Krouwel, A. (1999). *The global emergence of gay and lesbian politics: National imprints of a worldwide movement.* Philadelphia: Temple University Press.
- The American Civil Liberties Union website (www.aclu.org) includes a variety of resources on lesbian and gay rights.
- *Healthy People 2010 Companion Document for LGBT Health* is available for downloading at the GLMA website (www.glma.org) or the National Coalition for LGBT Health website (www.lgbthealth.net).
- Human Rights Campaign (www.hrc.org) works for lesbian, gay, bisexual, and transgendered equal rights.
- Lambda Legal Defense Fund (www.lambdalegal.org) is dedicated to the civil rights of lesbians, gay men, and people with HIV/AIDS.
- Leonard, A. S. (Ed.). (1997). *Homosexuality and the constitution.* New York: Garland.
- The Lesbian and Gay Immigration Rights Task Force website (www.lgirtf.org/issues/html) includes a variety of useful resources.
- Silvestre, A. J. (Ed.). (2001). *Lesbian, gay, bisexual, and transgender health issues: Selections from the American Journal of Public Health.* Washington, DC: American Public Health Association.

Part I

gearing up to make a difference

CHAPTER 1

influencing public policy[1]

Jeanine C. Cogan

In this chapter, you will

- *Learn the importance of public policy in everyday life.*
- *Learn who makes public policy decisions.*
- *Find out how to influence policy on existing issues.*
- *Learn how to influence policy by creating support for an invisible issue.*
- *Learn to write informed letters to your senator, representative, governor, mayor, or anyone else!*

During my second week in Washington, D.C., starting my new policy career, I witnessed a political circus that resulted in a huge blow to the lesbian, gay, and bisexual civil rights movement. A bill that would for the first time in U.S. history federally define a marriage as a union between a man and a woman was being passionately debated and came to a vote on the Senate floor. According to the language in the Defense of Marriage Act (DOMA), "the word 'marriage' means only a legal union between one man and one woman as husband and wife, and the word 'spouse' refers only to a person of the opposite sex who is a husband or wife." DOMA was approved by the House on July 13, passed by the Senate on September 10, and signed into law by President Clinton on September 21, 1996.

This legislation was designed to preempt a pending court ruling in Hawaii that could have recognized same-sex marriages.[2] Passing this law meant that a marriage between two lesbians or two gay men in Hawaii (if the court ruled in that direction) could not be considered a legal union as defined by the federal government. DOMA is a striking exception to the Full Faith and Credit Clause of the U.S. Constitution, which requires that court judgments of one state be recognized in all other states.[3]

After passing DOMA, the Senate then voted on the Employment Non-Discrimination Act (ENDA), a bill that would prevent employers from using an individual's sexual orientation as the basis for adverse or different treatment in employment.[4] One vote—50 against, 49 in favor—defeated this bill, championed by Edward Kennedy (D-Mass.).[5]

The fate of both bills depended partly on the common rhetoric used by foes of the LGB community. The arguments used to successfully promote the antigay bill and to defeat the gay-positive bill were based on misinformation and flawed assumptions about LGBs. For example, opponents have argued, "ENDA would require schools to hire gay teachers who have a deleterious impact on children." Yet as you will see in Part III of this book, research does not support the assumption that gay adults are a threat to children. A central role of LGB advocates is to challenge directly such myths and misperceptions. Only then will these fictions start to unravel and cease to serve as an impetus for misguided policies.

the importance of LGBs' involvement in policy

Not only did the passage of DOMA and the defeat of ENDA reflect an inaccurate depiction of LGB lives, it likely reinforced existing negative attitudes toward LGBs.[6] As with anti-Semitism and racism, heterosexist attitudes are influenced by societal norms and values. Societal institutions, such as the government, communicate particular values and attitudes to their members. In addition to the specific impact of laws on individuals, statutes also serve a symbolic function by codifying the values of the society. Thus, laws that ignore or punish specific forms of sexual expression convey social disapproval of those behaviors to all citizens. In turn, laws reinforce hostility against the people who practice such behaviors—in this case lesbian, gay, and bisexual people.

Clearly, DOMA is only one example of the hundreds of laws and policies that affect the daily lives of LGBs. Government policies have immediate and direct consequences for the political and economic power, opportunities, and quality of life of lesbians, gay men, and bisexual. LGBs can facilitate social change through promoting public policies that directly challenge the roots of disempowerment and negative social conditions. Additionally, LGBs' involvement in policy development is crucial to correcting the inaccurate assumptions that many policy makers hold.

Yet federal and state politics are commonly portrayed as open only to a few select stakeholders, as too complex to maneuver, and/or as too big for an individual to have an impact on. One goal of this book is to correct these misperceptions with information on and tools for how to successfully influence policy. This chapter reflects my experience as a policy advocate at the federal level. However, the basic principles and strategies described here can be applied to other levels of government and policy development. This chapter considers three topics: the players in policy development, the lifestyle of policy makers, and how you too can influence policy.

the players in federal policy development

There are at least five central groups or stakeholders involved in influencing the legislative process: constituents, organizations or interest groups, coalitions, members of Congress, and congressional staffers. The role that each plays in the federal policy-making process is briefly described below.

Constituents

Anyone eligible to vote is a constituent. This probably includes you and many of the people you care about. As such, your primary mechanism for influencing the federal legislative process is through your members of Congress: senators and representatives. According to the American Psychological Association,[7] some members of Congress view their constituents as having the most influence on their voting decisions—more than lobbying groups, their colleagues, and party pressures. Because the people in their districts vote members of Congress into office, members are motivated to attend to constituent concerns. Indeed, constituent service is one of the most important aspects of congressional life.[8]

Constituents articulate their views and concerns to members through visits, letters, e-mail, and/or phone calls. In addition, grassroots activism, such as rallies and protests, is effective in mobilizing constituents within a community and to focus members' attention on specific issues. Constituents may also be a member of or become involved in organizations that work to influence policy.

Advocacy Organizations

There are numerous types of organizations and interest groups that advocate for specific policies. They cover a range of issues, including business and industry, science and technology, professional interests, labor, civil rights, public interest, and governmental interests.[9] Organizations often have a person or office responsible for advocating on behalf of their members' interests and concerns. Advocating on behalf of a large number of people across the nation can offer more political weight to a message than simply advocating on behalf of one's own interests as a constituent.[10]

Congressional staff often work closely with advocacy groups.[11] In order to move a bill forward, staffers may work with advocacy groups to identify members in key congressional districts who need to be contacted directly by their local constituents. Such grassroots support for a bill may help it gain active congressional consideration and increase its priority as an issue on the legislative agenda.

Box I.3 in the Introduction lists the largest national organizations involved in promoting gay positive policies. A more extensive list appears in the Appendix. To be able to exert more significant influence, advocacy groups may coordinate efforts and work together through coalitions.

Coalitions

Coalitions typically are composed of clusters of advocacy organizations that share common interests or political positions with the aim of developing strength in numbers in order to influence policy. The coalition is designed to bring diverse organizations together to lobby on national policies, promote grassroots activism, and educate the public.[12] Members of a coalition may establish personal relationships with staff and members of Congress, which can contribute to the success of a bill or other policy initiative. Coalitions vary significantly in their membership, structure, and missions. Their constituencies and agendas may shift and adapt according to the changing policy environment and legislative focus. Membership within a coalition is typically on a group, rather than individual, basis. Coalition activities include regular meetings, federal and local outreach efforts, the sharing of knowledge and resources, and strategizing about how to optimize their influence. Working in coalitions maximizes the likelihood of successfully influencing the legislative process by allowing a large number of people to express their opinion on an issue in a short period of time.

Members of Congress

Certainly, a legislator's colleagues, the other policy makers, are another important influence. Numerous factors contribute to the decisions legislators make.[13] Three primary considerations are key in members' political decisions: (1) to satisfy constituents, (2) to enhance their personal reputations within the political world, and (3) to create good policy. All three can be accomplished when members have the skill to successfully work with and influence one another.[14] Members influence each other through direct one-on-one interaction, legislation, briefings, hearings, speeches, and the press. The well-known "Dear Colleague" letter on Capitol Hill, in which members explain legislation to their colleagues and urge them either to become co-sponsors or to vote along similar lines, is a primary strategy for influencing other members.

Members also influence each other through party affiliation and loyalty. Party politics plays a significant role in members' policy decisions.[15] Party leadership may urge members to vote in a certain way on specific legislation. Partisan politics are most apparent in party "whipping." Whipping occurs when party leadership strongly encourages members to vote in a particular way with the implied assumption that doing so will result in rewards. For voting along party lines, members can be rewarded with positions on more powerful committees, among other things that give them more power and clout with colleagues. This influence with colleagues may translate into a greater likelihood of successfully addressing constituent concerns, thereby improving reelection possibilities.

Congressional Staff

Until the 1950s, the U.S. Congress was a part-time institution that worked for 9 of the 24 months of a congressional session. The congressional workload has doubled in the last 30 years.[16] Currently, members work 18 months per session. The increased workload resulted from a series of decisions that enlarged congressional staff assistance, beginning in 1946 with the Legislative Reorganization Act.[17] For example, in 1967 members of the House of Representatives employed 4,000 people as personal staff. By 1990 that number had doubled. Interestingly, some scholars have argued that the increase of staff has resulted in expanded staff autonomy. With larger staffs, members are able to take on more issues and expand their workload. In turn, members need to rely more on and increasingly delegate independent authority to their staff.

Consequently, staff play a critical role in determining policy. Members rely on staff to track specific issues, write speeches, educate them on a range of topics, advise them on legislation and policy decisions, and write legislation. The autonomy and influence of a staffer depends on a range of factors including their individual personalities, the structure of the office, and the members' style.[18]

the lifestyle of a policy maker

"To best understand the way in which federal policy is formulated, it helps to think of Capitol Hill as a community, or culture, with its own inhabitants, rules, norms, and social processes."[19] Only by understanding the culture of politicians can scientists, lobbyists, activists, or anyone else hope to influence the federal process and shape public policy.[20] Four central characteristics of congressional

Box 1.1

WRITE AN EFFECTIVE BRIEFING SHEET OR TALKING POINTS

1. *First identify the goal and state it clearly.* Why are you lobbying the member? What is the reason for meeting with the staffer?
2. *Summarize the research and main arguments using bullet points.*
3. *Stay focused on one topic.* If you wish to discuss more than one topic, prepare separate briefing memos (one per topic).
4. *Be concise.* Keep briefing memos to one page, if possible. If the message cannot be conveyed in a page or two, you will likely lose the opportunity to influence the staff.
5. *Make the briefing memo easy to read and visually appealing.*

offices are the rapid pace, the large workload, the valuing of direct experience over other data, and the need to compromise.

Political life is typically a lifestyle of unanticipated, urgent deadlines. Given these tight timelines, it is not uncommon for staffers to become "experts" on a specific topic in a few days or mere hours. Therefore, as they are searching for facts on a topic, staffers must rely on easily accessible, digestible resources—typically the Internet or talking points provided by advocates. The outcome of such quick research is often a blend of substantive and political information. Also, with the expanded congressional workload, staffers are typically stretched so thin that reading one-page summaries is all they have time to do. Extensive reports are often useless unless there is a one- or two-page summary (called talking points or briefing memo).[21] Boxes 1.1 and 1.2 explain how to prepare such documents.

Although some policy makers appreciate the importance and usefulness of considering scientific data in their decision-making process, they tend to place greater value on precedent and anecdotal evidence. It is not unusual for legislation to remain stagnant until an event occurs to galvanize members of Congress. For example, in 1998 the Hate Crimes Prevention Act received attention, with hearings in both the House and Senate, only after an African American man was brutally murdered in Jasper, Texas. Similarly, critical gun control legislation that had been introduced each session of Congress for a number of years was not seriously considered until after the Columbine High School shooting in Littleton, Colorado, in 1999. The palpable role of real-life stories in members' policy decisions may in part reflect that they are primarily motivated to address the needs of their con-

Box 1.2

AN EFFECTIVE BRIEFING MEMO[22]

GOAL: WE URGE YOUR BOSS TO SUPPORT THE HATE CRIMES PREVENTION ACT (HCPA)

Why We Need the HCPA

- According to community surveys, violence against individuals on the basis of their real or perceived race, ethnicity, religion, sexual orientation, gender, disability, and other social groupings is a fact of life in the United States.

- A civil rights statute, Section 245 of Title 18 U.S.C., gives federal prosecutors the authority to investigate allegations of hate violence based on race, religion, and national origin. This avenue for federal involvement is necessary in order to address cases where state and local authorities fail to properly respond to victims' allegations. Currently such federal investigations are minimal, with typically less than 10 prosecutions annually.

- This statute is critical for responding to the problem of hate violence, yet it does not include a broad definition of hate crimes in line with more recent legislation. In 1994 Congress passed the Hate Crimes Sentencing Enhancement Act as part of the Violent Crime Control and Law Enforcement Act of 1994. In this law, hate crimes were defined broadly as a crime committed against the person:

    "because of the actual or perceived race, color, religion, national origin, ethnicity, gender, disability, or sexual orientation of that person."

Purpose of the HCPA

- The main purpose of the HCPA is to bring Section 245 of Title 18 U.S.C. in line with this recent hate crimes definition so that federal officials can investigate and prosecute crimes motivated by hate based on the victim's real or perceived gender, disability, or sexual orientation.

- The Department of Justice (DOJ) receives inquiries from families of gay victims asking for their involvement when local authorities have failed to respond. Unfortunately, the DOJ does not have the authority to investigate such cases. The DOJ considers this bill an important measure in assisting them to properly respond to victims' concerns.

stituents and do so after hearing of their concerns and hardships. Additionally, research on persuasion shows that, depending on the audience, appealing to one's emotions, especially with fear-arousing messages, can be a powerful method of communication.[23] This lesson has not gone unnoticed by policy makers.

Given the nature of our two-party system of government, members must work with individuals who may have very different opinions and perspectives on an issue. As a consequence, to move a policy initiative forward one must have enough support, which often requires negotiation and compromise. This tendency to compromise may collide with the desires and expectations of constituents and advocacy groups.

Understanding the unique culture of policy makers allows you to be more effective in influencing federal policy. Given the rapid pace and heavy workloads, you can increase your effectiveness in working with congressional offices by interacting with staff in a way that shows respect for staffers' time and efforts. Additionally, when working with staff it is useful to offer both data and personal stories of affected individuals. Finally, you may be more successful working with staff if you have an understanding of the limitations of members of Congress due to the institutional tendency toward compromise.

influencing public policy

There are two basic avenues by which you can shape policy. In some cases, you will want to influence legislators on issues that are already on the public agenda. In others, you will want to create legislative support for an unknown or invisible issue.

Influencing Legislators on Existing Issues

As you already know, voting constituents are greatly valued in legislative offices. A constituent communicating concerns to members of Congress can play an influential role in the legislative process. The most common way in which individuals can influence policy is to register opinions on already existing bills. Interested constituents can communicate with members of Congress or work in coalitions to promote or prevent the passage of particular legislation.

Contacting Members of Congress. The first step in effective communication with Congress is to determine the best person to contact. Usually, contacting your own legislator—the person who represents your congressional district— is most effective. As your elected official, this is the person who represents you and therefore must be sensitive to your views and concerns. Occasionally, however, in order to achieve a certain goal it will be more appropriate to contact other members of Congress. For example, if a member is recognized as a leader on an issue in which you have expertise or interest, then contacting that member is appropriate, even if he or she does not represent your congressional district or state.

Constituents can contact members of Congress through phone calls, letter writing, e-mail, or a visit (see Boxes 1.3 and 1.4). The purpose of the communication often determines which mode of communication to use. For example, is the communication meant to register an opinion or to educate members of Congress on a particular issue? Is it designed to establish a relationship with the congressional office? Is an immediate response and action needed?

If a bill is currently being debated, it is controversial, and/or there are other time pressures, you may be more successful communicating with members by phone. Members of Congress may inquire from staff what their constituents are expressing and consider this when making policy decisions. Constituents inter-

---

Box 1.3

CONTACT YOUR LEGISLATORS

Federal level
When writing a letter to your member of Congress use the following congressional addresses:

(Your Congressperson) The Honorable First, Last Name
U.S. House of Representatives
Washington, DC 20515

(Your Senator) The Honorable First, Last Name
U.S. Senate
Washington, DC 20510

When calling your member of Congress, use the U.S. Capitol Switchboard at 202–224–3121. Constituents should ask for their representative and/or senator.

State and Local Level
Use GovSpot at *www.govspot.com/* to identify and contact your state and local leaders. GovSpot.com is a nonpartisan government information portal designed to simplify the search for relevant government information online. This resource offers a collection of top government and civic resources such as government websites and documents, facts and figures, news, political information, and how to locate state and local policy makers.

Box 1.4

ORGANIZE VISITS WITH ELECTED OFFICIALS[24]

One of the best avenues to equality for LGB Americans is through establishing a personal relationship with your elected officials. Like any relationship, these relationships require cultivation over time and will involve developing ties to the elected official as well as members of their staff. A personal visit can be key to this kind of interaction. For state and local officials, this may not be difficult. If a visit to Washington, D.C., is difficult, you can arrange to visit your members of Congress when they return to their district office.

When you schedule such a visit, it may be helpful to organize a small group of like-minded voters. Taking a delegation of interested persons with you will enhance your visit. If this is not possible, bring at least one other person with you for support.

Your meeting will be most effective by doing the following:
- Identify the "visit team" (no more than six individuals) from your state or district who are interested in LGB issues.
- If you are from a big state and you are meeting with your senator, you may want to include individuals from several points around the state. The same is true for congressional districts and for state and local officials.
- The official's political party doesn't really matter. However, it helps if you can get someone on your team who is politically well connected or has a good sense of the local political dynamic.
- Make sure members of your team are comfortable with the process. If they are truly uncomfortable, they may detract from the overall impression you want to leave with your elected official.
- Arrange the date, time, and place for a premeeting of the visit team. Use this meeting (or at least a conference call) to make sure everyone is on board. You do not want questions or disagreements within your group during the visit.
- Arrange the date, time, and place for a meeting by contacting the state, district, or local office of the elected official you wish to meet.
- Coordinate the participants in the meeting to make sure that the visit team "sings with one voice" in making points with the elected official.
- Use the material in *Everyday Activism* to arm the team with the facts. In addition, do some research on the local situation so that you can personalize your arguments.
- Visit-team leaders should be prepared to guide and direct the meeting. After assembling at the office, team members should introduce them-

selves and identify the organization or institution with which they are affiliated.

- The visit-team leader should then lay out the problem and briefly outline the impact of the issue on the official's constituency.
- An open discussion should follow, with each team member providing his or her input while maintaining as much of a conversational tone as possible.
- Above all **listen**. Try to ascertain where your official is coming from. Employ active listening techniques to show her or him that you understand the concerns being raised. Try to answer objections and concerns as appropriate but don't get into a fight. Be firm and assertive but **not** combative.
- Be sure that the elected official is asked at some point to take a certain action, to support a policy initiative, or vote in a particular way on current legislation. For example:

  "Will you please assist our efforts to overturn the ban on lesbian and gay men in the military? Specifically, we would like for you to sponsor legislation to repeal the ban."

  "Will you support efforts to end workplace discrimination against lesbian and gay men? Specifically, we would like for you to co-sponsor ENDA."

- If the official expresses uncertainty about the facts, offer to provide further information to document the facts. The policy briefs that appear in the chapters of *Everyday Activism* have been designed for this purpose.
- After the visit, send a follow-up letter thanking the official for his or her time and consideration. Include the information you offered to provide (e.g., a copy of the relevant policy brief) with your letter.

ested in calling members should call the U.S. Capitol Switchboard at 202–224–3121 and ask for their representative and/or senator.

If you are interested in receiving a response to an inquiry or educating members of Congress, then writing a letter or setting up a visit are preferable. (For help organizing and conducting visits to congressional offices, refer to Box 1.4.) The most effective letters are those that are concise and focused on one issue. (An example of a sample letter is shown in Box 1.5.) To write an effective letter, you should follow these three steps:

1. *State the purpose.* The first paragraph should include who you are and why you are writing this particular member of Congress. For example, "I am writing

Box 1.5

AN EFFECTIVE CONSTITUENT LETTER[25]

The Honorable John Doe
U.S. House of Representatives
Washington, DC 20515

Dear Representative John Doe:

I am a constituent and am writing to ask you to oppose the proposed amendment by Congressman Todd Tiahrt (R-Kan.) to the D.C. appropriations bill that would prevent unmarried couples from adopting children in Washington, D.C. This current bill is ill-conceived and based on a number of inaccurate beliefs about lesbians and gay men as parents.

As a lesbian mother, I live in constant fear of losing custody of my child even though I am a nurturing, committed parent. I participate actively in the school board and related activities. My ability to be a caring and effective parent has nothing to do with my sexual orientation. This current amendment further threatens my daily existence as a parent.

According to the American Psychological Association, research shows that lesbians and gay men are fit parents. Contrary to the belief that gay parents may have a negative influence on their children, when compared with children of heterosexual parents, children of gay men or lesbians show no marked difference in their intelligence, psychological adjustment, social adjustment, popularity with friends, development of sex role identity, or development of sexual orientation. Overall, the belief that children of gay and lesbian parents suffer deficits in personal development has no empirical foundation.

In sum, the characterization of homosexual parents as being a threat to children is inaccurate, therefore calling into question policy decisions based on this belief. I urge you to oppose this amendment. I look forward to hearing your perspective.

Respectfully,
Jane Smith

you as a constituent in your district." This is followed by the purpose of the letter. Bill names and/or numbers should be used if possible and applicable; for example, "I am writing to urge you to vote for the Hate Crimes Prevention Act."

2. *State the evidence/argument.* The purpose is followed by a rationale for the requested action. For example, "Given that so many states currently do not have

laws that allow crimes to be investigated as hate crimes, the passage of this bill is necessary." Personal experiences that support the stated position can be concisely summarized as well. If you would like to make a research-based argument, then a short summary of the research or the presentation of some data can be effective.

3. *Ask for a response.* To optimize the impact of a correspondence, you should conclude by specifically asking members to reply. Responding to constituent mail is a vital role of congressional offices. The last paragraph should reiterate your concern and request a response.[26]

Effective Advocacy. When interacting with policy makers, advocates may err by being overly critical without offering specific suggestions or alternatives. Making this mistake will limit your effectiveness. Most legislators and their staff want to write the best bills possible and implement effective policies. For this reason, you should view the staffer as a friend, not a foe. Many staffers will be open to your expertise and ideas (though they may not always implement them). Therefore, when possible, it is useful to offer particular strategies for implementing the goals or ideas you want to promote.

For example, if you support the overall purpose of a bill but think it has flaws, prepare talking points that outline the concerns and offer alternatives. When I served as a legislative assistant for Congresswoman DeGette, I wrote a bill that health consumers supported but health providers opposed. After introducing the bill, many provider groups were critical and some raised legitimate concerns. The groups who were most effective were those that offered alternative language for the bill. Even if they agree with your perspective, legislative staffers may not have the time or expertise to find a solution for your concern. However, you can play a unique role in the legislative process by offering specific solutions and assistance to the congressional staff.

Creating Congressional Support for an Unknown Issue

In addition to influencing important policy decisions about existing legislation and visible issues, you can also help set the legislative agenda. For example, hate crimes legislation grew out of a national coordinated movement that promoted this issue as an important policy priority. Individuals and organizations met with members of Congress urging them to recognize and address this growing problem.

Finding Members to Support and Promote an Issue. Members of Congress become known for their leadership in particular areas. You should research which member is likely to support and promote your issue. Given the continuing hostile environment toward LGBs, most members, even leaders on LGB-positive policies, will not showcase their work on LGB rights. So while information about members' policy priorities and accomplishments is available on their websites, you may have to look beyond their bios or issues of interest. For example, Rep. Christopher Shays (R-Conn.) has been a leading advocate for ENDA. However, his endless support for LGB protections against workplace discrimination is not obvious from his website under the heading "issues." Instead, you have to look under "press releases." Keep this in mind as you explore members' homepages and other information. The Internet address for members' homepages for the House of Representatives is www.house.gov. For the Senate, it is www.senate.gov. Members' biographies are also available by accessing the website on biographical directories of members of Congress at bioguide.congress.gov/. An excellent book, titled *Politics in America*, provides descriptions of the members of Congress and is published each year by the *Congressional Quarterly*.

Another useful avenue for learning the legislative priorities of members is to see what bills they introduced or co-sponsored through accessing the Thomas website at thomas.loc.gov. This site provides information about the bills members have introduced and/or co-sponsored, as well as the text of legislation, congressional records, committee information, and bill status and summaries.

Establishing Relationships With Congressional Staff

As you have learned already, congressional staff are critical in policy development and their influence can be substantial. Staffers serve as gatekeepers to members of Congress by deciding who receives entrée into the office. If staff advise the member of Congress to meet with a particular advocacy group, the member is likely to do so. Given this influence, advocates interested in making contact with their representatives should establish rapport with the legislative staff. To this end, you can seek an appointment by calling the legislative assistant currently working on the issue of interest. In order to increase the chances of success, you should offer an explanation for choosing this particular member and state the purpose of the proposed meeting. For example, "I am calling you because your boss is a leader on employment issues. I know she led the fight to save small businesses last year. I would like to schedule an appointment with you to discuss another important employment issue: the need for legislation to prevent work-related discrimination based on sexual orientation."

Educating Staff. The primary goal of working with congressional members is to increase their knowledge and understanding of a particular topic that can lead to congressional interest and action. Because advocates tend to hold detailed knowledge on a specific topic while staffers have a little information about many topics, staffers typically welcome information. Due to the workload constraints, you should present concise summaries and clearly outlined points and goals. To facilitate this process, prepare handouts for congressional staff with talking points or briefing memos that summarize the topic. Each subsequent chapter of this volume includes a policy brief that can be used for this purpose. As you have already seen, Box 1.1 provides guidelines for writing an effective policy brief and Box 1.2 contains an example.

Addressing Inaccurate Perceptions and Reaching a Broader Audience. Given that there is so much misinformation about the lives of LGBs, one of the most important roles you can play is to correct myths and stereotypes. This is where research is particularly helpful. The American Psychological Association (APA) has created many documents based on solid social science evidence. Summaries of research that clarify the truth about LGBs' lives and experiences are readily available by accessing the American Psychological Association Lesbian, Gay, and Bisexual Concerns Office website at www.apa.org/pi/lgbc/publications/pubsreports.html/.

In addition to educating the major players in the policy process, you may need to reach broader audiences with your efforts to raise awareness and correct misinformation. Writing letters to the editor of local, regional, and national publications is one way to do this. Most policy makers play close attention to the media in their districts, so such letters can also have an impact on policy making. In addition, many newspapers welcome well-written op-ed columns on issues of concern to their readers. The guidance provided in Boxes 1.6 and 1.7 may help you get your ideas into print.

conclusion

Every day, thousands of people are actively lobbying members of Congress in an effort to influence policy. In order to defend against anti-LGB policies and to advocate for policies that are proactive in improving the lives of lesbian, gay, and bisexual people, we must remain active participants in the legislative process. From writing letters to establishing more enduring relationships with congressional staffers, we all can and do influence policy.

To some this process may seem cumbersome and complicated. However, please remember that help is always available. If fact, if you have questions about

Box 1.6

WRITE A LETTER TO THE EDITOR[27]

- Make one point (or at most two) in your letter or fax. State the point clearly, ideally in the first sentence.
- Make your letter timely. If you are not addressing a specific article, editorial, or letter that recently appeared in the paper you are writing to, then tie your issue to a recent event.
- Familiarize yourself with the coverage and editorial position of the paper to which you are writing. Refute or support specific statements, address relevant facts that are ignored, but avoid blanket attacks on the media in general or the newspaper in particular.
- Check the letter specifications of the newspaper to which you are writing. Length and format requirements vary from paper to paper. (Generally, roughly two short paragraphs are ideal.) You also must include your name, signature, address, and phone number.
- Look at the letters that appear in your paper. Are the letters printed usually of a certain type?
- Support your facts. If the topic you address is controversial, consider sending documentation along with your letter. But don't overload the editors with too much information.
- Keep your letter brief. Type it.
- Find others to write letters when possible. This will show that other individuals in the community are concerned about the issue. If your letter doesn't get published, perhaps someone else's on the same topic will.
- Monitor the paper for your letter. If your letter has not appeared within a week or two, follow up with a call to the editorial department of the newspaper.
- Write to different sections of the paper when appropriate. Sometimes the issue you want to address is relevant to the lifestyle, book review, or other section of the paper.

the federal government, trained staff at the Federal Consumer Information Center will answer your questions about federal programs, benefits, or services. You can call their toll-free hotline at 800–688–9889 (TTY 800–326–2996) between 9 A.M. and 8 P.M. Eastern time or use their website (www.info.gov/).

Although this chapter has focused on advocacy at the federal level, the same basic principles and processes can be applied at any level. Whether you want to push for LGB-affirming legislation on Capitol Hill, in your state legislature, or

Box 1.7

WRITE AN OP-ED[28]

An op-ed gets its name because of its placement opposite the editorial page. It is longer than a letter to the editor—usually 500–800 words. Also often referred to as an opinion editorial, these are more difficult to get printed than a letter to the editor but can be very effective.

Getting It in Print

- *Pick the right author.* Many papers will only print an op-ed from a representative of an organization or from a noted authority. A meeting with the editor can also help to establish the author as credible. Using a local spokesperson increases the local perspective or interest, especially on issues with national significance.

- *Pitch the article ahead of time.* Ideally, pitch your idea to the editor about 2 weeks before you want it to run. If you are responding to an op-ed that has just been published, contact the op-ed page editor right away to ask about a response. Even if they don't ask, offer to send a draft for their consideration.

- *Follow the guidelines.* Call your paper to find out the preferred length for an op-ed, deadlines, and any other requirements. Unless guidelines say otherwise, submit the piece typed and double-spaced on white paper with 1-inch margins. Ideally, the first page should be on your letterhead. Have a header at the top of each additional page with your name, the date, and the page number. Fax, mail, e-mail, or hand deliver the piece to the op-ed page editor.

- *Have a specific point of view and something fresh to offer.* Try to be ahead of the curve in public discussion of an issue. Let friends and peers review the piece and offer comments.

- *Follow up.* Follow the mailing with a phone call to the op-ed page editor. Be polite and respectful of his or her schedule, but try to emphasize again, as feels appropriate, why the paper should run the piece. Remember—there is a lot of competition for space on the op-ed page. If you are not successful on your first try, don't give up. The media is increasingly receptive LGB voices.

with local elected officials, you will be most effective when you educate yourself and share that knowledge with those you wish to influence. Developing relationship networks can be an effective strategy for educating officials and members of their staffs regardless of the level of government. Well-crafted letters to the editor and op-ed columns can raise awareness of the issues locally, regionally, and nationally. As we suggested in the Introduction, this book is about taking action. So use the lessons you have learned from this discussion and make a difference.

what you can do!

- Stay informed through LGB publications, traditional newspapers, and weekly newsmagazines.
- Monitor the websites of LGB and LGB-friendly organizations. Most operate free listservs that provide legislative updates and/or up-to-date summaries of state and federal policy initiatives. For example:
  - The Human Rights Campaign (www.hrc.org) provides extensive information on civil rights, AIDS, lesbian health, gays in the military, the Employment Non-Discrimination Act, hate crimes and other policy issues.
  - The National Gay and Lesbian Task Force (www.ngltf.org) provides headlines in the news of gay policy issues, AND up to date information about state and federal policy initiatives.
  - Parents, Families, and Friends of Lesbians and Gays (www.pflag.org) provides advocacy, information, and resources for support and education.
  - Lambda Legal Defense and Education Fund (www.lambdalegal.org) provides information concerning current legal issues, nationally and state by state.
  - Queer Resources Directory (www.qrd.org) contains more than 20,000 files about queer issues including, families, youth, religion, health, electronic resources, media, events, politics, and organizations.
- Track LGB-relevant issues through policy-specific websites. For example:
  - Legislative Information on the Internet (thomas.loc.gov) provides information about legislation, the congressional record, committee information, and bill status and summary.
  - Congress.org (www.congress.org) allows you to identify and contact your federal and state elected officials by entering your ZIP code, and provides updates on current issues and action alerts.

- The Center for Information Law and Policy (www.infoctr.edu/fwl) offers the Federal Web Locator with information and links to the executive and judicial branches, and federal agencies.
- Contact your legislators on LGB relevant issues by e-mail, phone, or personal visit. Use the briefing sheets at the end of each chapter. Use the following to locate contact information for congressional leaders:
  - www.congress.org Identify and contact your federal and state elected officials by entering your ZIP Code.
  - www.senate.gov Senators' contact information as well as committee membership.
  - www.house.gov Contact information as well as committee membership for members of the House of Representatives.
- Hold the press accountable by writing a letter to the editor or op-ed columns correcting misperceptions about LGB lives and policy (see Boxes 1.6 and 1.7).
- Support national organizations promoting LGB-affirming policies (see the Introduction and the Appendix for suggestions).

for more information

- American Psychological Association. (1995). *A psychologist's guide to federal advocacy*. Washington, DC: Author.
- *Bernstein*, M., & Reimann, R. (Eds.). (2001). *Queer families, queer politics (between men–between women: lesbian and gay studies)*. New York: Columbia University Press.
- D'Emilio, J., Turner, W. B., & Vaid, U. (2000). *Creating change: Sexuality public policy, and civil rights*. New York: St. Martin's Press.
- Fahy, U. (1995). *How to make the world a better place for gays and lesbians*. New York: Warner Books.
- Greenberg, E. H. (1996). *The House and Senate explained: The people's guide to Congress*. New York: W.W. Norton.
- Harbeck, K. M. (1993). Invisible no more: Addressing the needs of gay, lesbian and bisexual youth and their advocates. *High School Journal, 77*, 169–176.
- Porter, C. (2000). *How to get a job in Congress (without winning an election)*. Arlington, VA: Blutarsky Media.
- Price, D. E. (2000). *The congressional experience*. Boulder, CO: Westview Press.
- Ross, B. H., Kerwin, C., & Fritschler, A. L. (1996). *How Washington works*. Englewood Cliffs, NJ: Thomas Horton & Daughters.

- Smith, R. A., & Haider-Markel, D. P. (2002). *Gay and lesbian Americans and political participation*. Santa Barbara, CA: ABC-CLIO.
- Wells, W. G. (1996). *Working with Congress: A practical guide for scientists and engineers*. Washington, DC: American Association for the Advancement of Science.

CHAPTER 2

answering basic questions

Michael R. Stevenson

In this chapter, you will

- *Discover what drives antigay policy.*
- *Learn the difference between sexual orientation and sexual behavior.*
- *Find out why policy makers debate the size of the LGB community.*
- *Get the facts on existing sodomy laws.*
- *Learn how to counter antigay arguments.*

Regardless of your knowledge of scientific theory or research, you probably already have opinions about why people are LGB, and whether governments should intervene in the sex lives of citizens. The same is true for our elected and appointed government officials! However, in contrast to personally held beliefs, the way government officials answer such questions can have wide-ranging impact. Two very different but simple examples illustrate the point. In regard to state law, the way Delaware senators answer the question "Is 'gay behavior' chosen?" could determine whether sexual orientation is added to the state nondiscrimination law.[1] On a different level, when gay foreign nationals ask for asylum in the United States, success for the applicant can depend on the Immigration and Naturalization Service officer's belief about the origins of sexual orientation.[2]

In general, advocates of antigay policy initiatives characterize homosexuality as a chosen behavior. They claim that the LGB community is either so small that it is irrelevant or so large that ensuring equal rights would be too costly. In doing so, they often misrepresent the complexity of human sexuality and research findings. The mischaracterization of what it means to be LGB is at the crux many antigay policies, such as the Defense of Marriage Act, opposition to employment nondiscrimination policies, and the maintenance of sodomy laws.

Correcting these misconceptions, among the voting public as well as law-makers, will foster nonbiased and evenhanded policy. To do so, however, we need to explore some provocative questions[3] that raise complicated scientific and political issues. For example, if a person has a sexual experience with someone of the same sex, is he or she homosexual? What does it mean to be gay or lesbian? What is sexual orientation? What causes it? What percentage of the population is LGB? And finally, how and when should government intervene in the sexual behavior of adults? Although academic scholarship rarely provides the simple answers policy makers seek, developing a basic understanding of the relevant research will inform the debate. It will also help you to participate more effectively in the process. To this end, this chapter highlights the arguments made on both sides of the debate. It also provides a sound basis for clarifying the questions when simple answers are not sufficient.

what is sexual orientation?

Among scholars, the term *sexual orientation* describes an enduring emotional, romantic, sexual, or affectional attraction to another person. Thanks in large part to the pioneering work of Alfred Kinsey, scientists often think of sexual orientation as a continuum that ranges from exclusive homosexuality to exclusive heterosexuality. Persons with a homosexual orientation are sometimes referred to as gay or as lesbian.[4] Heterosexual persons are often referred to as straight. People with a bisexual orientation are found around the midpoint of the continuum. They may experience sexual, emotional, and affectional attraction to either sex.[5]

Although there is a considerable amount of healthy discussion about how best to conceptualize the sexual interests of women and men,[6] drawing distinctions among sexual orientation, sexual identity, and sexual behavior is very useful, particularly in attempts to apply the findings of recent research to questions of policy.

Scientists[7] as well as nonscientists[8] often confuse sexual behavior with sexual orientation. In the past, researchers have routinely assumed that individuals who have ever engaged in same-sex sexual behavior were by definition *homosexual.* To some degree, this continues in public discourse about sexuality. However, to equate behavior with identity is no longer considered scientifically rigorous.[9] Sexual orientation refers to feelings of emotional, romantic, and affectional attraction and sexual interest, not simply sexual behavior. Persons may or may not express their sexual orientation in their behaviors and their sexual behaviors may or may not reflect their sexual feelings and identity.[10] In other words, some heterosexual people have had same-sex sexual experiences and many gay and lesbian people have had sexual experiences with the other sex.

Furthermore, contrary to assumptions made by the public and by antigay activists,[11] engaging in same-sex behavior is not synonymous with the adoption of a gay identity (being gay or lesbian). *Sexual identity* refers to the extent to which people recognize their sexual attractions and incorporate those interests into their sense of who they are as sexual people. For some, it is a reflection of their sexual attractions and behavior; for others, it is not. In a survey of sexual behavior among U.S. adults, researchers[12] interviewed 3,432 people who were carefully selected to represent the U.S. adult population. Over 9 percent of the men in this study reported engaging in a same-sex sexual behavior at least once since puberty, while only 2.8 percent reported some level of gay identity. Among those interviewed, men who experienced both same-sex desire and same-sex behavior were very likely to identify as gay. However, some men with adult same-sex experience continued to engage in same-sex behavior without identifying as gay. Similarly, other men in the sample experienced same-sex desire without identifying themselves as gay. In other words, some men do not adopt a gay identity in spite of the fact that they engage in same-sex sexual behaviors or experience sexual desire for other men.

These data show that it is inappropriate to make assumptions about an individual's sexual identity or desires solely on the basis of their sexual behaviors. Many men experience same-sex desire or engage in same-sex sexual behavior but do not claim a gay identity. For example, reports from men in the so-called ex-gay movement indicate that although they no longer act on their attractions to other men, they still experience same-sex desire.[13] Clearly, equating same-sex sexual behavior with gay identity seriously underestimates the complexities of what it means to be gay.[14]

The concept of being *out* about one's gayness, first to oneself and then more publicly, has been central to what it means to have a gay identity.[15] Unlike other groups where membership depends on publicly observable characteristics, LGBs have no such marker of group membership and often must be proactive if they wish to reveal their sexual identities to others.[16] This self monitoring can consume enormous amounts of time and energy and is not foolproof. In fact, one study showed that a person's sexual orientation can be judged by others at better than chance levels in some circumstances.[17] On the other hand, according to the National Coalition of Anti-Violence Projects, 30 percent of reported victims of antigay hate crimes are not gay, but are perceived to be so.[18] Put simply, it is inappropriate to assume that gay and lesbian people can pass as straight whenever they choose or that others can accurately perceive a person's sexual orientation only when it is revealed purposefully. Given these data, public policies based on assumption of invisibility (the military's "Don't Ask, Don't Tell" policy, for example) are illogical.

Box 2.1

IMPORTANT DISTINCTIONS FOR POLICY MAKERS

Sexual orientation refers to an enduring emotional, romantic, sexual, or affectional attraction to another person, which cannot be determined solely on the basis of one's sexual behavior.

Sexual identity refers to the extent to which people recognize their sexual attractions and incorporate those interests into their sense of who they are as sexual people.

Sexual behavior refers to erotic activity and is most broadly described in phrases like "men who have sex with men" or "women who have sex with women"; sexual behavior is not always consistent with the labels (straight, gay, lesbian, or bisexual) people choose to describe their sexual identities.

---

what causes a person to have a particular sexual orientation?

Nature and Nurture

The causes of sexual orientation have been central to policy debates that involve the rights of LGBs.[19] In addition to its moral condemnations, the Christian right characterizes homosexuality as a chosen behavior rather than a trait that cannot be easily changed. Instead of directly addressing the moral arguments, the public faces of the LGB rights movements have countered these assertions by citing evidence that sexual orientation is innate.[20]

The efforts of LGB activists undoubtedly have been encouraged by survey research. This work suggests that people who believe that LGB orientations are chosen tend to oppose LGB rights whereas beliefs in biological causes are related to support for LGB rights.[21] An increasing number of U.S. adults believe that homosexuality is something with which a person is born. In June 1977, 13 percent held this belief. By June 1998 the figure had risen to 31 percent. As expected, beliefs in environmental causes have dropped over the same period although much less dramatically. In 1977, 56 percent believed that homosexuality was due to upbringing or other environmental factors. The figure for 1998 was 47 percent.[22] (Rather than posing the question as if it had to be one or the other, it would be interesting to know how many people believe that sexual orientation is the result of both nature and nurture!)

Unfortunately, finding evidence of a relationship between beliefs in biological causes and support for gay rights tells us nothing about which factor is the cause and which is the effect. In fact, these data can be interpreted in at least three different ways. It is possible that (1) a belief in biological determinism could lead people to support gay causes. However, it is also possible that (2) support for gay causes leads people to believe in biological determinism or that (3) beliefs in biological causes and support for LGB rights both have some other common cause.[23]

Arguments claiming that sexual orientation is biologically determined may have been useful in changing the law.[24] However, establishing a biological explanation for sexual orientation will not guarantee improved legal status for LGBs.[25] Members of ethnic minorities, for example, continue to be subjected to varying degrees of discrimination, legal and otherwise,[26] even though their status as group members is assumed to be biologically determined.

Clearly, the origins of sexual orientation and identity are complex. However, research emphasizing genetic, neurological, and hormonal factors has gained considerable media attention. While the biological evidence accumulates, [27] geneticists continue to debate the roles genes play in these processes.[28] As with most other complex human characteristics, we are not likely to find unequivocal evidence of a single gene that controls sexual orientation—a *gay gene*. However, new studies continue to show that sexual orientation is related to a wide variety of biological markers for processes that affect prenatal development. To name just a few, recent findings demonstrate relationships between sexual orientation and specific aspects of auditory functioning, the likelihood of being left-handed, and finger-length patterns.[29]

Frankly, few policy makers care whether more gay men than straight men are left-handed or whether lesbians are in some way more similar to heterosexual men than heterosexual women. However, these findings are important because they suggest that the development of sexual orientation may begin before birth. Certainly, many LGB adolescents and adults report becoming aware of their same-sex sexual interests at an early age.[30] Taken together, these findings suggest that the development of sexual orientation begins early and is influenced in significant ways by biological processes.

One of the many difficulties scientists face in developing an adequate theory of sexual orientation is the absence of good longitudinal data on the normative development of sexuality with large representative samples of women and men.[31] Without such data, theories will continue to be contentious, fragmented, and misrepresented (whether deliberately or inadvertently). This is especially true of the ever popular but simple-minded *it's chosen* or *it's innate* theories bandied about in the media and by lobbyists.

In spite of the emphasis given to such arguments, in reality we know very little about the causes of any sexual orientation, heterosexual or otherwise. Although scientists espouse a variety of theories about its origins, most agree that sexual orientation and identity are complex and most likely the result of an interaction of environmental, cognitive, and biological factors.[32] These are lifelong developmental processes that are affected by the historical and cultural context in which a person lives. With *Undressed* on MTV, *Queer as Folk* on HBO, and *Will & Grace* on network television, not to mention gay/straight alliances in public schools, LGB youth coming of age in the United States in the early 21st century experience a far different environment within which to explore and understand their sexual identities than those who came of age in earlier eras. Given the individual differences in how biology, experience, and cognition interact over the life-course, the process will *not* be the same for everyone.[33]

But Is Sexual Orientation a Choice?

A related aspect of the debate about causes is the extent to which choice plays a role in *sexual orientation*. Researchers and activists who support anti-LGB causes[34] have attempted to convince the public as well as policy makers that LGBs consciously (and arbitrarily) choose to be gay. It follows that if LGBs choose their orientations, then they could just as readily choose to be heterosexual. Members of ex-gay movements are used as examples of people who have chosen to conform in this way.[35] Proponents of LGB-positive public policy counter by arguing that choosing to be gay or lesbian would be irrational because of the prejudice and discrimination experienced by LGBs and by reiterating the mantra that LGBs are "born, not made." It is important to point out the prejudice inherent in both sides of this debate. The question assumes that no healthy, well-adjusted person would choose to be gay or lesbian, and the response does little to address that assumption.

Brian McNaught, a well-known Irish-Catholic author and gay activist captured this quandary best in his essay *I Like It*:

> Wouldn't you really rather be straight? asked one Jewish talk-show host. Would you rather be Christian? I asked.
>
> Think of all the hostility you face, commented one black woman. Because of that, wouldn't you prefer being heterosexual?
>
> Who's telling who about hostility? I queried. How much would it take you before you wished you were white?[36]

McNaught's essay goes on to describe many of the positive consequences of identifying as gay. Without debating its causes, he ends with an affirmation.

I like being gay because it is an essential aspect of who I am . . . and I like myself.

Although it might make life less complicated, human beings do not have conscious control over their sexual attractions. We do not get to choose who sparks our sexual interest, toward who we have that WOW reaction across a crowded room, or who makes us turn our head or take a second look. Even after marriage, heterosexual adults can find themselves attracted to potential partners other than their spouse. Men identified with ex-gay organizations have admitted that even after years of heterosexual marriage, their sexual interest in men remains.[37]

Although people cannot control their attractions, they can control how they respond. This realization brings us back to the distinctions among sexual orientation, sexual identity, and sexual behavior (see Box 2.1). In U.S. culture, we encourage people of all sexual orientations to make choices about their sexual behavior. Although married heterosexuals do not always make choices consistent with traditional marriage vows, most of these adults are capable of choosing whether to engage in sexual behavior with a person other than their spouse. Although less effective than other approaches to preventing unintended pregnancy and the spread of sexually transmitted diseases,[38] the U.S. government funds sex education programs that expect adolescents to "just say no" to premarital sex. Clergy in some mainstream religious denominations are expected to keep their vows of chastity. Similarly, LGBs can and do make choices about their sexual behavior. But these choices are about behavior, not sexual orientations or feelings of attraction.

LGBs and non-LGBs also make choices about the labels they use to refer to their sexual interests. For example, some people who engage in same-sex sexual behavior choose to identify as LGB while others maintain their straight identity in spite of their behavior.[39] Some women who experience attraction to both men and women choose nonetheless to identify as lesbian. Over the course of their lives, still others change the label they use to describe their identity.[40] The primary point here is that as human beings, people make a lot of decisions about their behavior and the way that they understand their own identity. However, there is no evidence to suggest that we have control over when and toward whom we experience sexual interest. Furthermore, research on attempts to change those attractions suggests that LGBs can, with varying degrees of success, stop engaging in same-sex sexual behavior. However, they cannot stop the feelings of attraction to members of their sex and develop an orientation to members of the other sex.[41] To paraphrase Brian McNaught, the policy question becomes: Is it right for government to prohibit individuals from expressing such an essential aspect of who they are?

It is important to return, for a moment, to the question of why this issue of choice is relevant to public policy in the first place. The freedom to make choices is central to the U.S. psyche, whether those choices are religious, economic, or personal. Antigay activists claim sexual orientation is chosen and therefore LGBs should simply conform to the heterosexual majority and choose to be straight. As Didi Herman noted in *The Antigay Agenda*, the irony in this position is clear:

> Religious affiliation is clearly a chosen identity. For evangelical Protestants this is nowhere more evident than in the need to be born again, a freely chosen, adult (re)commitment to Jesus. . . . If the religious are rightly afforded constitutional protection, why must lesbians and gay men prove genetic causation to gain the same?[42]

how many LGBs are there and is this important?

For some, perhaps many, policy makers, the size of the LGB community is important for one primary reason: money. How much will it cost to extend health benefits to the domestic partners of same-sex couples? Similarly, how much will it cost if protections from employment discrimination are extended to LGBs? Without reasonably accurate estimates of the number of LGB people, LGB-affirming policy makers cannot accurately project the fiscal implications of their proposals and their less affirming colleagues can claim that these proposals would be too costly and cannot be justified. Conversely, without a clear understanding of the size of the LGB community, anti-LGB groups can claim that it is so small that its needs (and perhaps its rights) deserve little attention.

Until recently, the commonly cited 10 percent figure had long been touted among LGB rights activists. The Christian right, on the other hand, has claimed that only 1 percent of adults are gay, perhaps to minimize the importance of LGB rights and to claim that living as a gay or lesbian is truly deviant.[43] It is important to make clear that debating these numbers merely distracts us from more important pursuits. It is no less right to treat a group fairly whether they make up 1 percent or 10 percent or 51 percent of the population.[44]

Even if it was important, estimating the size of the LGB community is a complex task. As we have discussed, sexual orientation means different things in different contexts. Over the past several decades, researchers and pollsters have classified the sexual interests of the participants in their research in a variety of ways. Some have focused on behavior. Others have asked respondents to choose a label for themselves. Still others have opted for more complex classification systems.

Given the different methods for classifying people, it is not surprising that estimates of the size of the LGB community vary. For example, the proportion of the adult population who admit to engaging in same-sex sexual behavior will be different from the proportion who report same-sex desire, and that figure is likely to be different still from the proportion who identify themselves as gay, lesbian, bisexual, or even queer. Furthermore, it is difficult to determine how many people have had such experiences or feelings but are unwilling to divulge that information to a pollster, an interviewer, a computerized survey, the census taker, or even on an anonymous questionnaire. To complicate matters further, most of the available research has been carried out on samples from patrons of gay-identified publications and businesses, psychotherapy or medical clients, or Internet sites, or on other samples that are biased in one way or another.[45] Estimates like these, including the 10 percent figure attributed to Kinsey,[46] are clearly problematic.

To remedy this problem, researchers have begun to study the LGB community using samples drawn from well-known national surveys like the General Social Survey[47] and the U.S. Census.[48] Although no one can claim that the results generated by these surveys are perfectly accurate, at least they are better than earlier findings and they are generated from data sources that are used to inform all sorts of policy initiatives.

Most people agree that the 10 percent figure is an overestimate.[49] Unfortunately, the sample sizes in these more recent surveys of gay men and lesbians are small and in the U.S. Census data only same-sex couples can be studied.[50] As a result, these estimates represent only a fraction of the total LGB population.[51] Nonetheless, the results provided by these demographic studies will be widely cited in policy circles.

Research, like exit polls,[52] seems to converge on the conclusion that 5 to 6 percent of U.S. adults self-identify as gay.[53] Demographic surveys show that men and women report same-sex desire at similar rates (7.7 percent for men and 7.5 percent for women) although a smaller proportion are willing to label themselves gay or lesbian (2.8 percent and 1.4 percent, respectively).[54]

In addition, data from the National Opinion Research Center show large increases in the number of U.S. adults who are willing to report having engaged in same-sex sexual behavior (4 percent for men and 3 percent for women in 1998, as compared with 2 percent for men and 0.02 percent for women in 1988).[55] Interestingly, between April (when gay marriage became legal in the Netherlands) and December 2001, the Netherlands' Central Bureau of Statistics reported that 3.6 percent of all officiated marriages were between people of the same sex.[56]

government regulation of consensual sexual behavior

By now, you should have a better understanding of the policy implications of questions concerning the origins of sexual orientation and the proportion of

U.S. adults who identify as gay or straight. Now, we need to turn our attention to even stickier questions concerning government regulation of consensual sexual behavior.

Sodomy Laws

Regulating sexual behavior is, for the most part, within the purview of the state rather than the federal government. In general, so-called sodomy laws restrict or prohibit sexual behaviors such as oral and anal sex, even between consenting adults.[57] Each state's law(s) has its own definition(s) of what constitutes sodomy. While some states have laws prohibiting sodomy regardless of the sex or sexual orientation of the participants, other states have laws prohibiting these behaviors only when they occur between two people of the same sex.[58]

Historically, all of the original 13 states had laws against sodomy that were rooted in religious beliefs.[59] Subsequently, as other states joined the union, each passed its own law. At one time or another, each of the 50 states has had its own sodomy law. In recent years, laws regulating consensual, private sexual behaviors between adults have been seen as violations of the right to privacy. Box 2.2 describes the status (as of 2002) of sodomy laws.

The courts continue to play a significant role in shaping policy in this area. In 1986 the U.S. Supreme Court upheld Georgia's state sodomy law in *Bowers v. Hardwick*. Michael Hardwick had been arrested *in his own bedroom* for the crime of sodomy with a consenting adult male partner.[60] Even though the charges against Hardwick were eventually dropped,[61] the Court ruled that the U.S. Constitution allows states to have sodomy laws and, consequently, each state can create its own law and set whatever punishment it deems suitable.[62]

In July 2000 the Louisiana Supreme Court upheld that state's law. In contrast to decisions by courts in other states, the Louisiana ruling claims that the state's classification of oral and anal sex as crimes, even between consenting adults in their own homes, does not violate the privacy rights clause in the Louisiana constitution. Furthermore, Justice Chet Traylor, writing for the majority, declared, "Simply put, commission of what the legislature determines as an immoral act, is an injury against society itself." It is noteworthy that the case on which the ruling was based involved heterosexual oral sex! [63]

As in the Louisiana case, proponents of sodomy laws argue that sodomy statutes serve a great social interest in promoting their morals and the traditional family structure and are therefore constitutionally within states' rights. Proponents of sodomy laws also view their repeal as government endorsement of same-sex sexual behavior and an indication of the moral decline of society.

It is important to point out that these cases hinge on the distinction I raised

Box 2.2

CURRENT SODOMY LAWS

As of July 2002, in 26 states and the District of Columbia sodomy laws had been repealed through legislative action. In 9 additional states the courts had declared the laws unconstitutional or unenforceable. Four states (Kansas, Missouri, Oklahoma, and Texas) have sodomy laws that target only same-sex behavior. However, in Missouri and Texas a court has declared the law unconstitutional but the highest court has not ruled similarly. Eleven states have sodomy laws prohibiting the behavior of both same-sex and other-sex couples. These are Alabama, Florida, Idaho, Louisiana, Massachusetts, Michigan, Mississippi, North Carolina, South Carolina, Utah, and Virginia. However, as in Missouri and Texas, the current status of laws in Florida and Michigan is unclear.[64] Punishments range from a $500 fine in Texas to up to life in prison in Idaho.[65] In addition, 82 countries worldwide have laws prohibiting sodomy; 42 have laws pertaining only to same-sex couples whereas the remainder have laws that apply regardless of the sexes of the participants.[66]

earlier, namely the difference between sexual orientation (a status) and sexual behavior ("sodomy," in this case). Supreme Court decisions before *Hardwick* clearly established the principle that it was unconstitutional to criminalize a person's status. In this context, then, it is not illegal to be gay or lesbian, although some states continue to prohibit same-sex sexual intimacy.[67]

In addition to moral arguments, proponents of sodomy laws also make health claims. For example, materials produced by the Family Research Institute compare some of the sexual practices attributed to gay men to consuming raw human blood and claim that these activities are *far* more self-destructive than smoking.[68] The U.S. Supreme Court allows states to create laws that promote the health of their citizens. So, supporters claim that sodomy laws can be used to promote good health; that is, they help to control HIV transmission.[69]

LGB rights advocates should dispute the argument that sodomy laws help to control HIV. First, one of the highest rates of HIV transmission is through penile-vaginal contact. Second, some sodomy laws prohibit oral-genital contact, including that between women, even though lesbians have an especially low risk of contracting HIV. Third, the argument put forth by sodomy law proponents supports the stereotype that AIDS is a gay disease. Promoting this stereotype reinforces the perception among heterosexuals that they are immune to the disease. This in turn may promote unsafe sex and the spread of HIV.[70]

Sodomy laws also serve as a legal means to discriminate against LGBs. These laws literally punish a category of sexual behaviors but can be used in practice to punish a particular sexual orientation.[71] Unlike the recent Louisiana case, sodomy laws are typically enforced only against LGBs. Even though some state laws apply to both heterosexual and homosexual sex, they are used to discourage the expression of an LGB identity.[72] According to the American Civil Liberties Union, state courts have also used sodomy laws to strip LGBs of other rights. For example, children have been taken away from gay and lesbian parents based on these laws.[73]

Overall, the majority of sodomy laws are rarely enforced but, as the Louisiana case makes clear, their existence obstructs the right of privacy for all citizens. The laws also promote discrimination toward LGBs. Further, these laws may prevent LGBs from being tested for HIV for fear of identification and punishment under these laws.

Public Sex

In addition to sodomy laws, state governments also regulate consensual sexual behavior in "public" venues. Public sex is relevant to this discussion because it provides a good example of what happens when policies are based on unfounded assumptions about the connections between sexual identity and sexual behavior. Furthermore, criminalization of public sex relies on sodomy and public indecency laws[74] and may be related to laws that make it illegal to transmit a sexually transmitted disease. Public sex is regulated by the state via the police,[75] but what makes sex *public*?

Public can be understood in terms of the accessibility of state regulators, a point raised by the Louisiana Supreme Court decision. However, *public* more often refers to spaces where access is not restricted, as in public parks, public restrooms, or commercial establishments such as bookstores or health clubs. On the other hand, *private* is usually understood in terms of restricted access. Ordinarily, the general public does not have access to private clubs, private parties, or private homes without an invitation or a membership card.

The importance of this distinction becomes evident amid recurrent concerns about the resurgence of unsafe sexual practices among gay men. Periodically, policy makers propose increases in policing or closure of venues where men have sex with men. The idea that sexual behavior performed in so-called public venues is in itself harmful or more likely to include the risk of disease transmission has been popular even among some gay-identified social commentators.[76] In fact, research evidence suggests that same-sex sexual behavior is likely to be safer in public than in private settings, because participants are more likely to take appropriate precautions with the less familiar partners they encounter in public venues. In private, sex is more likely to occur between men who are already acquainted and this can lead to riskier sexual interactions.[77]

In spite of this evidence, some authorities have proposed attempting to lower the HIV infection rate by eliminating sites where men regularly engage in erotic behavior with other men. These proposals have erroneously assumed that such activities occur only in establishments catering to self-identified gay men.[78] It follows, then, that sites with explicit connections to the gay community are often targeted for closure. In contrast, venues without such connections (mainstream health clubs, for example) are rarely if ever targeted, even though the same behaviors occur in these settings.[79]

Tearoom Trade,[80] the first monograph exploring public sex between U.S. men, showed that most of the individuals engaging in anonymous same-sex sexual encounters in public lavatories were married, predominantly heterosexual men. Similarly, men who have sex with other men in public commercial establishments, like locker rooms and saunas at health clubs, often do not describe themselves as gay.[81] As shown in Box 2.3, observations of and interviews with patrons in health club locker rooms[82] have shown that men who identified themselves as gay perceived this as public space and both avoided and objected to on-site erotic activity. On the other hand, the men who engaged in same-sex sexual behavior on site insisted they were straight and defined the space as private.

In some ways, in those areas of the United States and the world where sodomy laws remain, *private sex* and *having sex in private* are fictions.[83] In Georgia, given the existing sodomy laws and the U.S. Supreme Court's ruling in *Bowers v. Hardwick*, the state can regulate consensual sexual behavior that occurs in a person's own bedroom, making such a bedroom a public place. The same is apparently true in Louisiana after the Louisiana Supreme Court decision in *State of Louisiana v. Michael Smith*. In short, if Michael Hardwick could be arrested for engaging in a consensual sexual act with a male partner in his own bedroom and Michael Smith can be convicted for engaging in oral sex with a woman in a private hotel room, then **all** sexual behavior (regardless of the genders of the participants) is public sex at least until the remaining sodomy laws are repealed.

what does it mean to be gay or lesbian?

The material presented in this chapter is intended to help clarify significant questions policy makers often pose during debates of LGB-related policy. Scholars, lawmakers, and the concerned public may continue to disagree on the

Box 2.3

THE POWER OF RESEARCH FINDINGS

In 1995 Washington, D.C., health authorities began objecting to risky sexual activities allegedly associated with a new for-men-only health club. The club, which explicitly catered to gay men, was committed to providing educational programs aimed at preventing the spread of sexually transmitted diseases. At the same time, there were other facilities in the city, upscale health clubs officially catering to heterosexual men, where the same behaviors regularly occurred but where no preventive educational programs were being offered. William Leap, a widely published anthropologist associated with American University in Washington, D.C., got involved because he thought the new club was being unfairly targeted by city authorities and he believed that the research he had carried out in a variety of venues in D.C. was relevant to the case.

After hearing about the charges, Dr. Leap introduced himself to the owners of the club and was quickly invited to write a detailed letter for the editorial page of *The Washington Post*. In the letter, Leap used his research to call into question the city's charges against the new club. After the *Post* declined to print it, the letter was widely circulated. Although the impact of the letter is difficult to determine, formal charges against the club were dropped shortly after its circulation!

Two years later, the club was again threatened by city officials because of reports of on-site, unsafe, male-centered sexual activities. This time, the club's defense attorneys asked Leap to serve as an expert witness and to describe his research at other health clubs throughout the city. The defense team filed his credentials with the city attorney's office and indicated what issues would be raised in his public testimony. According to Leap, "shortly thereafter, the City's public health authorities agreed to a second out-of-court settlement, and to refrain from any further attempts at litigation. I have subsequently learned from several insiders in D.C. government that my willingness to go public with the research findings was very instrumental in moving the City authorities to accept this compromise and refrain from further litigation. And the D.C. government has made good on that promise, since that time."[84]

answers. However, I hope it is clear that what it means to be gay, lesbian, or bisexual is a very complicated, personal, and individual question. I also believe that the answer should have less to do with good public policy than many people think. The development of an individual's sexual identity is a lifelong process that is influenced by a wide variety of biological, experiential, and cognitive factors and these factors may well influence different people in different ways. As a result, debates about the causes of sexual identity and the size of the LGB community serve only as distractions that prevent progress toward a more inclusive democracy. In the final analysis neither a person's sexual orientation nor their private consensual sexual conduct should be a basis for denying equal legal treatment.

what you can do!

- Create opportunities to educate your local community about the distinctions among sexual orientation, identity, and behavior.
  - Respond to misinformation in the media with accurate information.
  - Following the suggestions in chapter 1, write an op-ed column for a local publication focused on the issues discussed in this chapter.
- Support a local or national LGB rights organization as a member or an ally. Join their listservs and frequent their websites.
- Become a resource for your community.
  - Learn to recognize antigay discrimination and scapegoating (as described in Box 2.3) and respond accordingly.
  - Speak with members of your civic and social groups about LGB-affirming policy.
- Support the repeal of existing sodomy laws.
  - Dispute claims that sodomy laws promote public health.
  - Explain that these laws are a threat to the privacy of all adults, regardless of their sexual orientation.
- Monitor the website of the National Gay and Lesbian Task Force (www.ngltf.org).
  - Read their *Fight the Right* handbook.
  - Implement their suggestions for action.
- Contact your members of Congress (as outlined in chapter 1). Include a copy of *Answers About Sexual Orientation*.

for more information

- American Civil Liberties Union Freedom Network. *Lesbian and Gay Rights*. Available at www.aclu.org/issues/gay/hmgl.html
- APA Office of Lesbian, Gay, & Bisexual Concerns. (1998). *A selected bibliography of lesbian, gay and bisexual concerns in psychology: An affirmative perspective*. Available at www.apa.org/pi/lgbc/publications/bibliography.html

Antigay policy is based on common misunderstandings of homosexuality. Antigay advocates characterize homosexuality as chosen behavior rather than an immutable trait. They claim the lesbian, gay, and bisexual (LGB) community is too small to be concerned about, so there is no need to spend time on gay-affirming policies. Another antigay strategy is to misrepresent the complexity of human sexuality and research findings.

Clarifying what it means to be gay, lesbian, or bisexual.

Sexual orientation refers to a person's enduring emotional, romantic, erotic, or affectional attraction to another person. It is distinct from sexual identity, which involves willingly choosing and using a particular label (like lesbian or gay) to identify one's own sexual interests. Sexual orientation is *not* synonymous with one's sexual behavior. Some men and women who engage in consensual same-sex behavior maintain a heterosexual identity and/or do not have an enduring attraction to members of the same sex.

What causes people to be gay or lesbian?

We don't know for sure. Just as we do not know what causes a person to be heterosexual. Yet the research clearly suggests that sexual orientation is the result of a complex interaction of environmental, cognitive, and biological factors. There are multiple causes and these causes could be different for different people. Considerable recent evidence suggests biology, including genetic, neurological, and hormonal factors, plays a significant role in determining sexual orientation.

Is sexual orientation a choice?

No. Have you ever tried to control whom you are attracted to or whom you dream about? It is not possible. Clearly then, we do not choose our sexual orientation. We do, however, choose whether to engage in sexual behavior and with whom. Indeed, the research on conversion therapy shows that homosexuals cannot change their sexual attraction from one gender to the other.

How many people are lesbian or gay?

What this question often disguises is the fact that LGB people deserve the same rights and status under the law as heterosexuals, regardless of their numbers. Given this essential principle, estimates of the number of gay and lesbian adults vary depending on the source of the data and the method used to collect it. Exit polls suggest that 5–6 percent of voters in the United States openly identify as gay or lesbian.

Antigay rhetoric is used to maintain and/or promote antigay policies.

Much mischaracterization of what it means to be gay is at the crux of antigay policies, such as the Defense of Marriage Act, opposition to employment nondiscrimination policies, and the maintenance and enforcement of sodomy laws. Correcting inaccurate ideas about homosexuality is key for nonbiased and evenhanded policy.

How sodomy laws are harmful.

In some parts of the United States, it is illegal to engage in consensual sexual behavior with a member of the same sex, even when the behavior occurs in private. Although sodomy laws may appear to regulate the sexual behaviors of all people regardless of sexual orientation, the laws are often enforced only when both partners are of the same sex. These laws have been used to strip lesbian and gay people of their rights, including the right to be a parent. They may hinder efforts to curb the spread of HIV and other sexually transmitted diseases. These laws also promote discrimination toward LGBs, and their existence obstructs the right of privacy for all citizens.

---

* The material presented here is discussed in greater detail in *Everyday Activism: A Handbook for Lesbian, Gay, and Bisexual People and Their Allies*, edited by Michael R. Stevenson, Ph.D., and Jeanine C. Cogan, Ph.D., and published by Routledge in 2003.

- Badgett, M. V. L. (2001). *Money, myths, and change: The economic lives of lesbians and gay men.* Chicago: University of Chicago Press.
- Best, J. (2001). *Damned lies and statistics: Untangling numbers from the media, politicians, and activists.* Berkeley: University of California Press.
- Black, D., Gates, G., Sanders, S., & Taylor, L. (2000). Demographics of the gay and lesbian population in the United States: Evidence from available systematic data sources. *Demography, 37*(2), 139–154.
- Bohan, J. S., & Russell, G. M. (1999). *Conversations about psychology and sexual orientation.* New York: New York University Press.
- Cain, P. A. (2000). *Rainbow rights: The role of lawyers and courts in the lesbian and gay civil rights movement.* Boulder, CO: Westview.
- Herman, D. (1997). *The antigay agenda: Orthodox vision and the Christian right.* Chicago: University of Chicago Press.
- Lambda Legal Defense and Education Fund. (n.d.) *Issues: Criminal Law.* Available at www.lambdalegal.org/cgi-bin/iowa/issues/record?record=11
- Money, J. (1988). *Gay, straight and in-between.* New York: Oxford University Press.
- National Gay & Lesbian Task Force. (n.d.) *Issues: Sodomy.* Available at www.ngltf.org/issues/issue.cfm?issueID=11
- West, D. J., & Green, R. (1997). *Sociolegal control of homosexuality: A multinational comparison.* New York: Plenum.

CHAPTER 3

defending claims about mental health

Jessica F. Morris and Stacey Hart[1]

In this chapter, you will

- *Find out how the Christian right portrays homosexuality as a mental illness.*
- *Use research to counter the arguments of anti-LGB advocates.*
- *Evaluate claims about whether sexual orientation can be changed.*
- *Learn about the debate surrounding the origins of sexual orientation.*
- *Learn about the ex-gay movement.*

No matter what the specific public policy issue, much anti-LGB rhetoric can be traced to the underlying argument that lesbians and gays are deviant. Historically, gay, bisexual, and lesbian people have been portrayed as deviant by religion, law, and medicine. More recently, the Christian right has used the "ex-gay" movement as an opportunity to portray homosexuality as a conscious choice. In fact, one prominent study of anti-LGB tactics concluded: "The ex-gay movement offers a vehicle for publicly questioning the very sexual and social identity of homosexuals and, by extension, undermining their claim to civil rights legal protections."[2] Although the most visible antigay crusaders are often associated with extremist Christian religious denominations, their arguments are rarely made purely on moral grounds. Rather, the arguments imply that the "deviance" of lesbians and gays actually reflects mental illness.

Although no current public policy initiatives specifically concern mental health and sexual orientation, many anti-LGB initiatives—and the advertising campaigns that promote them—depend on a basic assertion of homosexuality as a psychological flaw. The ability to identify these assertions can provide opportunities to present the facts and to confront distortions throughout anti-LGB rhetoric. This chapter will outline the major assertions behind anti-LGB public policy that can be traced to the basic, but false, presumption of mental illness. The arguments, based on these assertions, used in antigay campaigns will be detailed—including examples from specific anti-LGB initiatives. Then these assertions will be critically examined in the context of the current psychological research.

homosexuality and mental illness

There are many ways in which anti-LGB proponents attempt to portray homosexuality as a mental illness. Some rely on ignorance and try to tap into fears people have about AIDS, sexual abuse, and addictions. For example, the conservative Christian Research Institute states: "Homosexuality is neither a normal nor a healthy lifestyle . . . homosexuality is anatomically aberrant, psychologically deviant, and morally bankrupt."[3] Other common themes include equating homosexuality with addiction or an emotional wounding. In addition, the use of the word *homosexual* is quite purposeful, as this term has been historically associated with psychopathology.

Another tactic used by anti-LGB proponents is to view homosexuality as an addiction. In 1999, Senate Majority Leader Trent Lott stated in a television interview that he believed homosexuality to be a sin and a problem "just like alcohol . . . or sex addiction . . . or kleptomaniacs."[4] In addition, the assertion that homosexuality is an illness is sometimes implied by statements that incorrectly link being LGB with a host of actual mental health problems like substance abuse, depression, or an inability to be a happy and fulfilled person.

Indeed, prior to 1973, homosexuality had been considered a diagnosable mental illness and was used to justify anti-LGB policies such as banning gays from the military. However, by the 1970s, there was already a large body of research showing that homosexuality was neither psychopathological nor associated with mental illness.[5] Based on this research, the American Psychiatric Association removed homosexuality from the *Diagnostic and Statistical Manual of Mental Disorders* (*DSM*) 30 years ago.

This body of scientific evidence started with Evelyn Hooker's research in the 1950s.[6] Hooker's landmark research demonstrated that experts could not distinguish gay men from heterosexual men based on the results of psychological testing. This was in direct contrast to the widely held view of homosexuality as a mental illness and the assertion by professionals that it was readily diagnosable. In contrast to Hooker's study, other studies of the day were often methodologically flawed. For example, much of that research compared gay men receiving mental health treatment with heterosexual men who were not. It is no wonder that gay men who were receiving therapy looked less mentally healthy than heterosexual men who were not. Eventually, Hooker's groundbreaking research led to numerous studies that demonstrated few, if any, significant differences in mental health between heterosexuals and gays and lesbians. Furthermore, when differences are found, they are often attributable to increased stress from societal prejudice, and it is well established that LGBs experience discrimination and victimization in multiple domains.[7] Thus, there is now a long-standing and large body of research demonstrating that being LGB is not a mental illness.

When the American Psychiatric Association removed the diagnosis of homosexuality in 1973, a diagnosis of ego-dystonic homosexuality was added. This meant that homosexuality was only a mental illness for lesbians and gay men who viewed their homosexuality as wrong and something that needed to be changed. With the fourth edition of the *DSM*, the diagnosis of ego-dystonic homosexuality was also removed. In a society where LGBs experience ongoing oppression, thoughts of not wanting to be a member of that oppressed group are not pathological. Thus, the diagnosis of ego-dystonic homosexuality described an understandable reaction to societal discrimination rather than a mental disorder.[8] Similarly, the American Psychological Association continues to support its 30-year-old resolution that "homosexuality per se implies no impairment in judgment, stability, reliability, or general social or vocational capabilities."[9] (Box 3.1 includes further statements about homosexuality from major national mental health organizations.)

politics and mental illness

There are a number of ways that anti-LGB proponents try to argue that homosexuality is a mental illness. Anti-LGB activists insist that homosexuality was removed from the *DSM* not because there was research that supported the removal, but rather that intense political pressure from the gay rights movement forced psychiatrists (who are responsible for such decisions) to remove the diagnosis. "It is clear that the change in the American Psychiatric Association designation was not due to new findings, but had everything to do with the lobbying pressure and tactics of the homosexual community . . . the change in the APA classification cannot be construed to mean that there is anything close to a consensus among mental health professionals regarding the normalcy of homosexuality."[10] One prominent anti-LGB psychoanalyst has called the removal "the medical hoax of the century."[11] (See Box 3.2 for details about types of mental health professionals.)

Opponents of LGB rights often falsely claim that LGB rights activists believe **all** mental health professionals agree that homosexuality is *not* a mental illness (when this is not the case). Then the opponents identify mental health

Box 3.1

OFFICIAL STATEMENTS ABOUT PSYCHOTHERAPY AND SEXUAL ORIENTATION

American Psychological Association (APA)
Resolution on Appropriate Therapeutic Responses to Sexual Orientation, adopted by the APA Council of Representatives, August 14, 1997.[12]

> . . . be it resolved that the APA opposes portrayals of lesbian, gay, and bisexual youth and adults as mentally ill due to their sexual orientation and supports the dissemination of accurate information about sexual orientation, and mental health, and appropriate interventions in order to counteract bias that is based in ignorance or unfounded beliefs about sexual orientation.

The APA Council of Representatives also adopted Guidelines for Psychotherapy with Lesbian, Gay, and Bisexual Clients on February 26, 2000.[13]

American Psychiatric Association (ApA)
ApA Position Statements on Homosexuality: Psychiatric Treatment and Sexual Orientation, December 1998.[14]

> The potential risks of "reparative therapy" are great, including depression, anxiety and self-destructive behavior, since therapist alignment with societal prejudices against homosexuality may reinforce self-hatred already experienced by the patient. Many patients who have undergone "reparative therapy" relate that they were inaccurately told that homosexuals are lonely, unhappy individuals who never achieve acceptance or satisfaction. The possibility that the person might achieve happiness and satisfying interpersonal relationships as a gay man or lesbian is not presented, nor are alternative approaches to dealing with the effects of societal stigmatization discussed. Therefore, the ApA opposes any psychiatric treatment, such as "reparative" or "conversion" therapy, which is based upon the assumption that homosexuality per se is a mental disorder or based upon the a priori assumption that the patient should change his/her homosexual orientation.

American Counseling Association (ACA)
Resolution on Sexual Orientation and Mental Health, passed by the Governing Council of the American Counseling Association, March 27, 1998.[15]

> The ACA opposes portrayals of lesbian, gay, and bisexual youths and adults as mentally ill due to their sexual orientation; and supports the dissemination of accurate information about sexual orientation, men-

tal health, and appropriate interventions in order to counteract bias
that is based in ignorance or unfounded beliefs about same-gender
sexual orientation.

National Association of Social Workers (NASW)

Position Statement of the NASW on "Reparative" and "Conversion"
Therapies for Lesbians and Gay Men, adopted by the NASW Board of
Directors, January 21, 2000.[16]

> Increased media campaigns, often coupled with coercive messages
> from family and community members, has created an environment in
> which lesbians and gay men often are pressured to seek reparative or
> conversion therapies, which **cannot and will not change sexual
> orientation**.

American Psychoanalytic Association (APsaA)

APsaA Position Statement on the Treatment of Homosexual Patients.[17]

> The APsaA affirms the following positions: 1. Same-gender sexual ori-
> entation cannot be assumed to represent a deficit in personality
> development or the expression of psychopathology. 2. As with any
> societal prejudice, anti-homosexual bias negatively affects mental
> health, contributing to an enduring sense of stigma and pervasive
> self-criticism in people of same-gender sexual orientation through the
> internalization of such prejudice. 3. As in all psychoanalytic treat-
> ments, the goal of analysis with homosexual patients is understand-
> ing. Psychoanalytic technique does not encompass purposeful efforts
> to "convert" or "repair" an individual's sexual orientation. Such
> directed efforts are against fundamental principles of psychoanalytic
> treatment and often result in substantial psychological pain by rein-
> forcing damaging internalized homophobic attitudes.

American Academy of Pediatrics

AAP Policy Statement on Homosexuality and Adolescence.[18]

> Confusion about sexual orientation is not unusual during adolescence.
> Counseling may be helpful for young people who are uncertain about
> their sexual orientation or for those who are uncertain about how to
> express their sexuality and might profit from an attempt at clarifica-
> tion through a counseling or psychotherapeutic initiative. Therapy
> directed at specifically changing sexual orientation is contraindicated,
> since it can provoke guilt and anxiety while having little or no poten-
> tial for achieving changes in orientation. The psychosocial problems of
> gay and lesbian adolescents are primarily the results of societal
> stigma, hostility, hatred, and isolation.

Box 3.2

UNDERSTANDING THE "PSYCHS"

There are a number of different terms all starting with *psych* that mean quite different things. Some indicate a job role, others educational degrees, and still others stand for a person's philosophy and theoretical orientation regarding human behavior. Because anti-LGB advocates use these terms in a way that can be confusing, we have provided some clarification below.

- **Psychotherapist** is the most general term. It describes a job, someone who does mental health counseling. Anyone can use this title to describe what she or he does, no matter what education she or he has.

- Both **psychologist** and **psychiatrist** are legal terms, regulated by government, and can only be used by someone who has been licensed. A **psychologist** has a doctoral degree (that is, a Ph.D., Ed.D., or Psy.D.). Those in clinical practice must be licensed by their state; other types of mental health professionals (for example, marriage and family therapists) may not call themselves psychologists even if they have a doctoral degree. A **psychiatrist** is a medical doctor (that is, an M.D.) who has specialized in psychiatry. A competent psychiatrist should be board certified.

- **Psychoanalysts** are a subset of psychotherapists (of any educational background) who identify with certain general philosophies—often referred to as a theoretical orientation—about human behavior and how to change it. Broadly speaking, psychoanalysts trace their understanding of the human psyche to Freud and his theories. Traditionally, psychoanalysts were the most likely group to see homosexuality as having an origin in childhood problems and as developmentally inferior to heterosexuality. However, the American Psychoanalytical Association has recently made an official statement, clearly stating that homosexuality is not "a deficit in personality development" or psychologically abnormal.

Individual psychologists and psychiatrists can have their license or certification revoked if they violate certain ethical codes or laws (in a sense, they are disbarred). In addition, membership in professional organizations can be terminated if an individual does not uphold standards. However, because psychotherapist is not a protected title, there is no way to regulate psychotherapists.

- The **American Psychiatric Association**, whose members are psychiatrists (M.D.s), is the organization that develops the diagnoses for mental illness and writes and publishes the *DSM*. The **American Psychological Association**, a much larger organization, does not contribute to the *DSM* but has made a number of official statements about the normality of homosexuality. The other professional organizations that are concerned with mental health have all made statements affirming that homosexuality is not a mental illness. These organizations include the **American Counseling Association, National Association of Social Workers, American Medical Association, American Association of Behavior Therapy, Association for Women in Psychology**, and **American Academy of Pediatrics**.

professionals who are willing to state that homosexuality is, indeed, an indication of mental dysfunction. Having disproved their original, misrepresented premise, they assert that LGB rights activists must be mistaken in their claim that homosexuality is not a mental illness and, therefore, homosexuality must be dysfunctional. The logic of this argument inappropriately attempts to infer that homosexuality must be a mental illness from the fact that some mental health professionals disagree with the official positions of mental health organizations. It also is an attempt to disprove a false statement. LGB rights activists know full well that some mental health practitioners cling to the belief that homosexuality is evidence of psychological disorder.

The bottom line is that the diagnosis of homosexuality was removed from the *DSM* decades ago. It was not a recent decision, as some have implied. Although the decision was not unanimous, diagnoses do not have to be unanimously agreed upon to be included in or to be removed from the *DSM*. In addition, the validity of assessments of illness does not depend on the absolute consensus of mental health professionals. Materials produced by the Christian right often support its anti-LGB views by quoting professionals—presented as important, influential, and well regarded—who disagree with the *DSM*. However, finding individual professionals who say that the removal of homosexuality from the *DSM* was wrong, and that homosexuality is a mental illness, cannot and does not change the fact that a large body of research has consistently found no increase in mental illness among lesbian, gay, and bisexual people.

Homosexuality is not the only diagnosis that has been surrounded by debate. In fact, many symptoms and diagnoses in the *DSM* have been questioned from time to time. For example, there was noticeable dissension about diagnoses, such as posttraumatic stress disorder, for those who have experienced ongoing childhood trauma. Some leaders in the field argue that the current criteria for posttraumatic stress disorder are not adequate.[19] As with any field, there is a plurality of views and the basic texts of the profession do not require absolute consensus. However, the decision to remove homosexuality from the *DSM* has rarely been questioned in subsequent decades. In fact, it has been continually reaffirmed by all major mental health organizations. For example, an American Psychiatric Association *FactSheet* released in February 2000 leaves no room for question:

> For a mental condition to be considered a psychiatric disorder, it must constitute dysfunction within an individual, cause present distress (for example, a painful symptom), disability (for example, impairment in one or more important areas of functioning), or a significantly increased risk of suffering death, pain, disability, or an important loss of freedom. A homosexual or bisexual individual may experience conflict with a homophobic society; however, such conflict is not a symptom of dysfunction in the individual.[20]

dueling "scientists"

An extremely important part of any public policy debate that involves mental health is the use of research and science to support arguments. Both pro- and anti-LGB advocates have tried to gain credibility through citing research. However, the science used by anti-LGB advocates is quite different from the science used to counter them. In political arenas such as civil rights and domestic partner debates, research is often referred to in brief sound bites or without substantiation. Only in certain situations, such as *amicus curiae* (friend of the court) briefs, is research reviewed more thoroughly. Anti-LGB briefs rely on a relatively small body of research, the quality of which is uneven at best. This research, conducted by supposititious experts, is presented as the truth about sexual orientation and mental health. However, the small body of research used to support anti-LGB claims is not accepted in the scientific community, due to its many methodological flaws. In fact, methodologically sound research has never supported the claims of anti-LGB advocates. For example, the public information provided by the American Psychological Association in *Answers to Your Questions About Sexual Orientation and Homosexuality* states: "Over 35 years of objective, well-designed scientific research has shown that homosexuality, in and of itself, is not associated with mental disorders or emotional or social problems."[21]

However, depending on how they are presented, sound and unsound research conclusions can look equally compelling. This is true whether the science behind the research supports the conclusions or not. Rather than trying to answer the research conclusions of anti-LGB advocates with specific appropriate research, it is often more helpful to move away from research. This avoids a no-win debate that becomes mired in the quality of specific research and dueling "expert" scientists. By falling into the dueling scientists trap, LGB rights advocates not only help their opponents, they also become distracted from the real issues. Research conducted on the effects of medicine and supplements may provide a useful example. When research is conducted on a medicine for FDA approval it is much more rigorous and methodologically sound than the research done by the makers of a nutritional supplement to promote their product. Although the claims about nutritional supplements and medicines look equally compelling, the standards to which the claims are held are different. Claims about medicines are subject to government oversight; claims about supplements are not.

A specific example of how anti-LGB advocates use unsound research to influence public policy and legal issues can be seen in how organizations present themselves differently depending on the situation. The Family Research Institute (FRI), run by the widely discredited psychologist Paul Cameron,[22] states that one of its goals is "to *inform* the American public and the mass media about the homosexual agenda and the scientific research of FRI, exposing its dangers."[23] In an *amicus curiae* brief against a lesbian mother, described as "living a defective lifestyle," FRI presents itself quite differently: "Family Research Institute, Inc., is committed to unfettered empirical examination of sexual and drug social policy from a traditional viewpoint."[24] However, by definition, "empirical examination" cannot stem from any viewpoint, "traditional" or otherwise. At the same time, FRI attempts to discredit widely accepted research results by attacking the "homosexual psychologists" as "biased investigators."[25]

attempts to "cure" homosexuality

Historically, there have been a number of psychotherapeutic approaches that purported to change a person's sexual orientation from lesbian or gay to heterosexual. Their practices are referred to with a variety of interchangeable labels including conversion therapy, reparative therapy, and reorientation therapy. In a religious context, they are sometimes called transformational ministries. Collectively, these therapies are the primary tools of the ex-gay movement. For example:

1. The executive director of the National Association for Research and Therapy of Homosexuality (NARTH), Joseph Nicolosi, claims: "A basic assumption of reparative therapy is that every man is, on a deeper level, heterosexual—even if he has been struggling with a homosexual *problem*."[26]

2. "Focusing on those homosexuals who want to change continues to emphasize the immorality and personal destructiveness of homosexuality."[27]

3. In a Family Research Council publication, Nicolosi also claims: "Compulsive, even addictive sexual patterns can be formed during youth. Later

in adult life, if this same person attempts to pursue a heterosexual lifestyle, he will find the transition very difficult."[28]

One approach to "curing" homosexuality is rooted in psychoanalysis. Interestingly, Freud, the founder of psychoanalysis, did not view homosexuality as an illness and therefore saw no need to develop a cure. Many years after Freud's death, a group of post-Freudian psychoanalysts developed techniques intended to change sexual orientation. These psychoanalytically based conversion therapies have been fully reviewed and widely criticized.[29] Psychoanalytically based conversion therapists believe that homosexuals have arrested psychological development. Their techniques typically consist of intensive individual treatment that explores childhood trauma and family-of-origin dynamics. Notably, the American Psychoanalytic Association has recently joined the other mental health organizations in their rejection of reparative therapy (see Box 3.1).

Another type of conversion therapy is behaviorally based, and its proponents assume that homosexuality is a learned behavior. Treatments vary and have included punishing same-sex desire and rewarding heterosexual desire. Methods used include electric shock, nausea causing drugs, and visualization of such aversive states. Behaviorally based conversion therapies sometimes include a social component in which the therapist gives advice about heterosexual dating and sexual relationships. A third type of conversion therapy is religiously based. Purportedly Christian in background, such treatments include support groups and intensive religious retreats that use prayer as the main form of therapy.[30]

There continues to be a fringe element among the mental health professions that advocates for curing homosexuality. These groups, which present themselves as professional organizations for academics and clinicians, are a distinct part of the ex-gay movement separate from the religiously based groups. Most prominent is the National Association for Research and Therapy of Homosexuality (NARTH) led by its president, Charles Socarides, M.D., and executive director, Joseph Nicolosi, Ph.D. Paul Cameron, Ph.D., who has served as chairman of the Family Research Institute and chairperson of the Institute for the Scientific Investigation of Sexuality, also advocates for anti-LGB policies from a mental health perspective. In the Family Research Institute's brochure, they advertise: "Acting as consultants in dozens of legal cases and ballot issues, FRI is a primary source for information on 'Homosexuals in the armed forces' and 'Effects of Homosexuality on public health.'"[31] There have even been suggestions that "cures" for homosexuality not be limited to psychotherapy but be expanded to include the use of medication. For example: "Although research on the use of medication to change homosexuality would be quite difficult to accomplish in the current environment, there are nonetheless some indications that such an approach might help."[32]

These groups are quite small; for example, NARTH claims about 800 members.[33] In contrast, the National Association of Social Workers has approximately 155,000 members and the American Psychological Association has approximately 151,000 members. Not one of the large national organizations representing mental health professionals has recognized the work of these anti-LGB advocates, or their organizations, as legitimate when issuing resolutions about reparative therapy (see Box 3.1).[34] Realizing this, Socarides, Nicolosi, and Cameron, and the organizations they represent, have publicly focused on conducting and publishing research. In contrast, a substantial body of work refuting the findings of such research has been published in respected academic forums.[35] Nevertheless, these organizations have been involved in public policy to an extent that is disproportionately large compared with the size and scientific acceptance of their research.

choice and change

Whether sexual orientation can be changed is a question that has profound public policy implications.[36] In fact, the foundation of the ex-gay movement depends on the notion that such change is possible. Leaders of the ex-gay movement claim: "Abandoning homosexual habits, like quitting drinking, can be done and is done by tens of thousands each year. Breaking homosexual habits without the assistance of religious involvement is more problematic, but even conventional psychotherapy claims about a 30% cure rate."[37]

However, *change* is only important in that it has been used as the ultimate and unquestionable proof that homosexuality is a *choice*. And the question of whether homosexuality is a choice has been at the core of every public policy issue. Despite warnings about the problematic implications, the argument that people are born gay or lesbian has been an important factor in the LGB civil rights movements. Anti-LGB advocates have, therefore, found themselves arguing that homosexuality is a learned behavior rather than an inborn quality. If the LGB-by-birth argument supports equal rights for gays, then, by using choice as the counterargument, antigay advocates can argue that gays do not need equal rights. The religious right and ex-gay movement claim that "the more the homosexual community can convince the general public that their homosexuality is beyond their or anyone else's control, the more tolerance or even preferential treatment they can gain in public policy."[38] As such, the ex-gay movement has stepped into this debate with an endless well of testimonials from ex-gays who have been "freed from the homosexual lifestyle."[39]

Anti-LGB advocates have a seemingly logical argument against LGB civil rights. The ex-gay movement, they argue, has proved that people can change from homosexual to heterosexual. Furthermore, if people can change, then homosexuality must be a choice and not an innately biological characteristic. Since civil rights should be granted only on the basis of innate characteristics, homosexuals do not deserve equal rights. One examination of the ex-gay movement's impact on equal rights claimed: "The ex-gay movement poses a significant new threat to efforts to secure civil rights for gay/lesbian/bisexual/transgender people. By using the ex-gay movement to convince people that lesbian, gay and bisexual people can become heterosexual, the Christian Right aims to foster the development of a restrictive legal environment in which only heterosexuals have legal rights."[40] The whole conceptualization of homosexuality as a lesser alternative to heterosexuality, or as some sort of developmental mistake, is in stark contrast to the understanding of sexual orientation accepted by mental health professionals in the United States.

One excellent recommendation for LGB rights activists who need to counter arguments from the ex-gay movement is: "Don't get caught up in the *nature vs. nurture* debate. The defense, 'we can't help it, we're born this way,' misses an important point—we all have the right to love whomever we choose."[41] It is easy to be distracted by the emotional impact that the ex-gay movement provides antigay advocates. We must not let this happen, but focus instead on the important fact that the appearance of change does not mean choice. The debate is often wrongly concentrated on the second part of the anti-LGB argument: something that is chosen does not warrant equal rights. The flaw is in the idea that the ex-gay movement's evidence of change leads to the conclusion that homosexuality is a choice. Overall, mental health professionals do not support the conclusions that the ex-gay movement's evidence of change is proof of choice. As with many aspects of mental health and human emotions, both nature and nurture have been rejected as the sole origin of sexual orientation. For example, the American Psychological Association says most scientists today agree that sexual orientation is most likely "the result of a complex interaction of environmental, cognitive, and biological factors."[42]

success of conversion therapy

Treatment to change sexual orientation from homosexual to heterosexual is not an accepted practice. However, a few therapists continue to offer this technique despite the findings that "reparative therapists attempt to teach gay men and lesbians to repress their sexual identity, yet have a dismal failure rate of 67% in trying to reach this goal, even by their own questionable standards."[43] Some of these therapists do have formal training in mental health, yet provide reparative therapy. Nonprofessionals also offer this type of therapy, often in what is presented as a Christian context. For example:

1. "Basically homosexuality is a neurosis. It's healable, it's treatable. We are ministering to 6,000 former homosexuals in the Exodus network. Basically, homosexuality is a stunting of psychosexual growth. They are children inside . . . spoiled, he'll keep coming at you . . . until you give him a whack on the bottom and say 'Enough!'"[44]

2. "Homosexual habits are learned and homosexuality can be unlearned."[45]

3. The Exodus International *Doctrinal and Policy Statements* puts forth a "message of liberation from homosexuality. . . . Exodus upholds heterosexuality as God's creative intent for humanity, and subsequently views homosexual expression as outside God's will. Exodus cites homosexual tendencies as one of many disorders that beset fallen humanity . . . promoting a message of freedom from homosexuality through the power of Jesus Christ."[46]

The academic and religious factions of the ex-gay movement both claim success but use different criteria to measure their results. The standards are more rigorous for less religiously based therapies, as the research results are presented in a more academic setting. However, this research has not been regarded as scientifically acceptable. According to the American Psychiatric Association: "There is no published scientific evidence supporting the efficacy of 'reparative therapy' as a treatment to change one's sexual orientation."[47]

One of the more problematic aspects of the research, according to the critiques, is the lack of proper outcome measures and the lack of follow-up with clients to examine whether changes in sexual orientation have been maintained over time.[48] Further, much of the research consists of case studies that detail the experience of a psychotherapist treating one client.[49] In contrast to methodologically sound measures of success, religiously based "cures" mark success through the testimonials of individual ex-gays.

One aspect of the criticism of the success claims of the ex-gay movement concerns the way success is marked. Some promise that successful ex-gay treatment can lead to heterosexual marriage and children. Others hold out celibacy as the measure of success. These differences are a controversial topic both within the ex-gay movement and among its critics. A strong argument against the treatment methods of ex-gay therapy is that while people may stop engaging in sexual behavior, their sexual orientation has not changed. The important issue is that the ex-gay movement is confounding and collapsing the complexities of human sexuality and sexual orientation. In fact, some people experience their sexual orientation as something intrinsic and unalterable, while others see themselves as having variations in their sexual orientation throughout their lifetime.[50]

The ex-gay movement first gained visibility through the so-called Truth in Love advertisements that appeared in national newspapers during July 1998. Sponsored and paid for by more than a dozen Christian right organizations, the full-page ads drew much attention. The headline of one ad read, "I'm living proof that Truth can set you free: Toward hope and healing for homosexuals."[51] No matter what psychology has to say about the failure of reparative therapy, the religious arm of the ex-gay movement holds out the promise that religious beliefs can alter sexual orientation. Not bound by scientific standards, the ex-gay movement relies on testimonials of individual who have been "freed from homosexuality." In contrast, equally powerful testimonials come from *former ex-gays*, people who participated in ex-gay treatments and subsequently rejected attempts to alter their lesbian or gay sexual orientation.[52] After the ad campaign, a number of former ex-gays spoke out, such as Tracey St. Pierre, who said: "for fifteen years I endured the mental torment of the 'ex-gay' movement. I did everything they told me to do. I prayed. I spoke to church counselors. They had me convinced I was going to hell. I finally realized that the hell the ex-gay ministries spoke of was the life I was living by pretending I was a heterosexual."[53] Furthermore, former ex-gay Darell Gingrich (Newt and Candace Gingrich's cousin) has stated: "I am here to say that these 'ex-gay' ministries don't work. Even though many of the people involved in these ministries might be well intentioned, they are causing pain in the lives of those who would be better off accepting how God created them."[54]

Ex-gay ministries set up a false dichotomy where being gay or lesbian and being religious are mutually exclusive. In fact, the vast majority of mainstream religious organizations do not support or agree with the views of the ex-gay movement. A 3-year examination of the ex-gay movement concluded, "Most mainstream religious leaders and religious organizations in the U.S. do not share the views of the ex-gay movement and the Christian Right about homosexuality."[55] An article in the *Journal of Psychology and Christianity* said that since "Christians are mandated, from Genesis to Revelation, to not oppress the weak or to not withhold justice, it is important for all Christians to be aware of the continued social and justice issues with which the gay community continues to struggle. . . . Whether the church will be identified with social justice or with persecution may well depend on whether and if Christians, lay and professional, will listen to the voices of gay and lesbian people."[56]

After careful examination of the Truth in Love ad campaign and the subsequent media storm, the media has been characterized as less than impartial. "For the most part, the media has been generous to the movement, covering it as a human interest story and neglecting to unmask the political and legal implications of the ex-gay movement's partnership with the Christian Right."[57] The media's method of covering the ex-gay movement as a nonpolitical human interest story was widespread, regardless of the fact that the connection between anti-LGB political groups and the ex-gay ministries has been well documented.

Although "Truth in Love" was presented as a mission with a mental health agenda, it was clearly an effort to influence public policy.[58] The ads ran the same week right-wing members of Congress launched antigay legislation. Even the ex-gay ministries are upfront about this: "Parents and Friends of Ex-Gays, or P-FOX, is here to begin the arduous task of pushing back the gay agenda."[59]

Despite the insistence of ex-gays that their homosexuality is "cured," even some of the figureheads of the ex-gay movement do not appear to remain cured. One such example is John Paulk, who served as an official with the antigay group Focus on the Family and as chairman of the board for Exodus North America. One of the most prominent and vocal ex-gays, Paulk had previously appeared on the cover of *Newsweek* in 1998 with his wife, an "ex-lesbian," as part of a feature story on the successes of reparative therapy. Despite his posture as an "ex-gay," Paulk was spotted in 2000 at a popular Washington, D.C., gay bar and photographed after spending an hour socializing with gay male patrons. He tried to claim he was just there to use the restroom, but then later admitted he had knowingly entered the gay bar. Because of this incident, Paulk was put on probationary status with Exodus North America, who said he had damaged the credibility of the ex-gay movement.[60] However, the Family Research Council claimed, "The Paulk incident does not invalidate the fact that more than 135 Exodus International ministries in 17 countries are helping people leave homosexuality every day."[61]

the ex-gay movement and civil rights

Ex-gay organizations portray themselves as concerned about the mental, physical, and spiritual health of lesbians and gay men, and as simply offering religious and peer counseling. However, there are many indications that the ex-gay organizations are funded by, and closely allied with, the political arm of the Christian right. According to political analysts, "the ex-gay movement provides political cover for a significant new phase in the Christian Right's long-running anti-gay campaign. The ex-gay movement is a potent tool for undermining the rationale for lesbian/gay/bisexual/transgender rights."[62]

One clear instance of the ex-gay movement's influence on lesbian, gay, and bisexual civil rights was the successful referendum in 1998 that rescinded Maine's antidiscrimination law (Question 6). This was the first time there had been such a reversal.[63] There are two clear examples of the ex-gay movement's involvement in the Maine referendum campaign. First, television commercials featured the testimonials of ex-gays who said they had been "saved by Christ."[64] Second, Anthony Falzarano, an ex-gay and head of Transformation Ministries and P-FOX, "toured Maine for a few days to spread the message: that homosexuality is a choice, a lifestyle which people can choose for themselves." He also stated that "politics has nothing to do with" his public tour of Maine.[65] However, the trail of money clearly supports a political connection. "Although claiming to be dedicated to non-political 'healing,' ex-gay organizations are strongly supported by political activists connected with the hard right wing of the Republican Party and the Christian Right."[66] The religious right has continued to financially support opposition to Maine's Question 6 and has used ex-gay movement rhetoric—for example, "oppose Question 6, Special Rights for Homosexuals, because . . . unlike genetic conditions such as race or skin color, when it comes to homosexuality, change is possible."[67] In addition to the Maine referendum, the ex-gay movement has been involved both in defending Colorado's Amendment 2 and in providing briefs for a number of legal cases. The debt from the costs of the Truth in Love ad campaign has been used to solicit donations in Christian right fund-raising letters.[68] The Church of Jesus Christ of Latter-Day Saints has also been heavily financially involved in "protection of marriage" initiatives, which now prohibit same-sex marriages in California (Proposition 22) and Nebraska (Initiative 416).[69] In dealing with the ex-gay movement in a public policy context, it is vital to focus on these connections. The ex-gay movement, with its Republican Party and Christian right financial backers, not individual ex-gays, are the forces trying to influence public policy.

suicidal behavior and substance abuse

Antigay activists alternatively embrace and deny that lesbian, gay, and bisexual youth have an increased risk of suicide attempts and substance abuse, depending on their agenda and the specific message they wish to promote. In some cases, they straddle both views within the same argument. For example:

1. A 1998 article in the Family Research Council's newsletter *Family Policy* stated that it was a "mythology that 30 percent of all teen suicides are committed by homosexual young people stressed out by 'homophobia.'" In the same article, the authors claim that "homosexuality is a risk factor for teen suicide . . . [which] is easily demonstrated."[70]

2. From Jane Boyer, board member of Exodus Ministries: "in areas that are most accepting of homosexuality, such as Hollywood and San Francisco and New York, there is the highest percentage of suicide, death from chemical dependency, drug addiction, alcoholism, and HIV amongst the gay community . . . Obviously in those areas that they are receiving the greatest acceptance, there is the highest percentage of death and despair amongst the gay community."[71]

In their arguments, which deny an increased attempted suicide risk, the Christian right has charged gay rights activists with manipulating the suicide statistics in order to promote a political agenda that "recruits" teens into gay life. Antigay activists often attack any school curricula or programs that would, in their opinion, "promote the gay lifestyle." Peter LaBarbera, who has served as a senior analyst in the cultural studies department of the Family Research Council, claims that gay school programs appeal to the public through the idea that "gay youth are victims in need of special protection by school administrators."[72] Programs like Los Angeles' Project 10, which offer a safe haven and support for LGB high school students, are accused of affirming homosexuality, "which will invariably ensnare vulnerable teens who might otherwise have avoided the destructive homosexual lifestyle."[73]

Findings from population-based, methodologically sound research do suggest that gay and bisexual male youths are three times as likely to *attempt* suicide as their heterosexual counterparts.[74] The results on attempted suicide rates for lesbian and bisexual female youth compared with heterosexual females have been mixed, with some studies finding lesbian and bisexual youth more likely to report suicide attempts, and others finding no differences.[75] Although the recent findings do suggest that a sizable minority of gay and bisexual male youth are at risk for attempting suicide, no information is currently available on youth who actually commit suicide. To date, there are no nationwide or statewide data on the frequency of *completed* suicide for lesbian, gay, and bisexually identified individuals.

Another implication of the statistic that 30 percent of gay youth report prior suicide attempts—and one that is rarely focused on by either pro- or anti–gay rights activists—is that 70 percent of gay youth consistently do *not* report suicide attempts. Researchers have cautioned against over-interpreting the higher rates of attempted suicide in gay youth to mean that *all* LGB youth are at serious risk for attempted suicide.[76] The Christian right has used these data to claim that the numbers of gay youth at risk are so small that this slice of the population is insignificant.[77] Therefore, they argue, gay-supportive programs in public schools are neither necessary nor a prudent use of sparse resources. Yet, simultaneously and contradictorily, they assert that these very programs are so powerful that they succeed in "converting" large numbers of "confused youth" to a lifestyle that will surely lead to suicide. These inaccurate and unfounded assumptions are not supported by the available research. However, they do feed directly into one of the Christian right's main tenets: Homosexuality causes unhappiness and a higher likelihood of suicide. It is important to stress here that scientific research does *not* imply that lesbian, gay, or bisexual self-identification *causes* a higher rate of suicide; such misinterpretations have been used by the Christian right to justify the use of reparative therapy as a way to save gay youth from this so-called destiny. In the 2000 elections, ex-gay movement propaganda was used to support Oregon's Measure 9, under which public schools would have been banned from providing instruction that might encourage, promote, or sanction homosexuality. A Christian right group, the Oregon Citizens Alliance, claimed that

> the common denominator in every suicide is a feeling of hopelessness. The last thing a suicidal person needs to hear is that there is no hope of recovery from his or her "homosexual orientation," . . . Yet, schools defiantly cling to a 'gay' dogma on this point, even in the face of substantial evidence that homosexuals can change."[78]

In their campaign materials, Oregon Citizens Alliance discrepantly stated: [H]omosexuality has not been shown to be a major factor in teen suicide. The Gallup organization interviewed almost 700 teenagers who knew a teen who had committed suicide; not one mentioned sexuality as a factor."[79] While the Christian right has produced several written documents trying to debunk what they called the "myth of gay youth suicide,"[80] they also seem solidly invested in using the increased suicide attempts statistic as proof that homosexuality inevitably leads to early death by suicide.

The Christian right has used similar misinterpretations of the data on alcohol and drug abuse to promote the tenet that sexual orientation causes destructive behavioral patterns. Although gay and lesbian youth appear to be more likely to use alcohol and drugs than heterosexual youth, not all lesbian and gay youth or adults use alcohol or drugs excessively.[81] Indeed, similar to the data for attempted suicide, only a select minority appear to be at risk for drug use. Moreover, lesbian and gay youth appear to use drugs and alcohol to escape from societal problems associated with sexual orientation (for example, to cope with victimization at home or school), as well as for the same reasons as do heterosexual youth (for example, rebellion or peer pressure).[82] Therefore, from the existing research, it cannot be concluded that LGB identification causes heavy use of alcohol, although the Christian right and the ex-gay movement are insistent in their claim that homosexuality causes a higher likelihood of suicide, drug and alcohol abuse, and other psychological problems.

The Christian right and ex-gay movement also downplay the effect of a homophobic society in the development of psychological distress in LGB individuals.[83] Social science research demonstrates that lesbian and gay youth are more likely to face certain stressors than their heterosexual counterparts. For example, up to one half of youth who are out as gay in high school have reported being verbally assaulted and ridiculed by their peers solely because they are LGB.[84] Further, LGB youth suicide attempts have been linked to experiencing violence at home related to their sexual orientation.[85] Importantly, one study found that the increased risk of suicide attempts among LGB youth no longer existed once the factors of levels of stress, poor social support, and amount of depression were taken into account.[86] These findings are extremely noteworthy because poor social support, depression, ability to cope with stress, and other such factors can be altered by improving the familial and social environments for LGB youth. In fact, a large population-based study found LGB youth who attended schools that did not provide gay-sensitive instruction were at greater risk for suicide attempts, threats to personal safety, pregnancy, and HIV infection.[87] These data strongly suggest that the focus should *not* be on changing sexual orientation, but rather on increased environmental and personal support systems for LGB youth.

services for youth

As previously discussed, anti–gay rights activists are particularly upset over public school programs that offer a safe haven and support for LGB students.[88] Nonetheless, LGB rights advocates successfully used research findings on attempted suicide as part of their lobbying for the well-known Gay and Lesbian Student Rights Law in Massachusetts, which was passed on December 10, 1993. This law prohibited discrimination on the basis of sexual orientation in Massachusetts public schools. The law also required that schools provide intervention and protection for students should they face unfair treatment or harassment based on sexual orientation. In addition, it ensured the right to form gay/straight alliance groups in school.[89]

Unfortunately, the Christian right has successfully blocked multiple efforts of LGB rights advocates to ensure safety for LGB public school students in several states. For example, the Florida Family Association (FFA) ran a massive mail-in campaign to protest Pinellas County's first high school gay and straight alliance. FFA President David Caton stated that his organization objected to the group "because it costs the school money to pay the counselor that oversees the group and because . . . it gives gay and lesbian students 'special rights.'"[90] In Clark County, Nevada, conservative Christian groups lobbied to delete any mention of specific types of harassment in a student harassment policy, solely for the purpose of not including sexual orientation.[91] Similar tactics were used at a Salt Lake City, Utah, high school where the school board voted to ban *all* extracurricular groups rather than allow the existence of a gay/straight alliance. Additionally, Christian right groups in Columbus, Ohio, propagated antigay rhetoric to oppose a Columbus Board of Education antiharassment policy that included sexual orientation, saying: "How can we continue to communicate that it is an inevitable and harmless 'orientation'? It [homosexuality] is one [road] that is extremely high for disease, dysfunction, and early death. Educators and parents deserve to know, and then be able to communicate these facts to every child."[92] Yet despite attacks on the policy claiming it "promoted homosexuality," the district passed the policy, which protects both employees and students.

conclusion

The Christian right and ex-gay movement play a critical role in creating and passing antigay legislation and preventing antidiscrimination laws for LGBs. Clearly, a central tenet of their campaigns is that gay, lesbian, and bisexual people are psychologically unstable, morally bankrupt, drug abusers and alcoholics, and dangerous to America's children.[93] These assertions form the cornerstone underlying antigay measures. Furthermore, the Christian right and ex-gay movement deliberately exploit the erroneous claim that LGB people can change if they really want to, and that reparative therapy is highly effective. However, not one of these assertions can be supported by the current accepted scientific research. LGB activists and public policy advocates can use research on mental health as an effective tool for exposing the Christian right.

what you can do!

- Understand that media campaigns that include testimonials by ex-gays often coincide with antigay political initiatives.
- Follow and support the work of the nonprofit organizations that monitor the ex-gay movement, such as
  - The National Gay and Lesbian Task Force (www.ngltf.org).
  - People for the American Way (pfaw.org).
  - Political Research Associates (publiceye.org).
  - Human Rights Campaign (www.hrc.org).
- Read the material written by these organizations, such as the annual publication *Hostile Climate* from People for the American Way and *Calculated Compassion* from Political Research Associates and the National Gay and Lesbian Task Force.
- Monitor the ex-gay movement and its supporters through the websites of groups like
  - The National Association for Research and Therapy of Homosexuality (www.narth.com).
  - Concerned Women for America (www.cwfa.org).
  - The Family Research Council (www.frc.org).
- Turn to the national professional organizations for accurate information (see Box 3.1). Use information they provide to counteract antigay activism.
- Know the common tactics of distortion used by antigay activists and academics.
- Be aware of the current ex-ex-gay (also referred to as former ex-gays) movement, as this is a new and evolving voice in the media and public policy debates.

THE TRUTH ABOUT SEXUAL ORIENTATION AND MENTAL HEALTH*

Most antigay rhetoric is rooted in the inaccurate characterization that lesbian, gay, and bisexual people (LGBs) are psychologically deviant. Correspondingly, antigay policies depend on the assertion that homosexuality is a psychological flaw. The truth, however, is that scientific research does not support these claims.

Is being lesbian, gay, or bisexual a mental illness?

No. A great deal of scientific research shows that homosexuals are no more likely to be mentally ill or have symptoms of pathology than heterosexuals. Based on this research the following national mental health organizations have clearly stated that homosexuality is not a mental illness:

- The American Psychological Association
- The American Psychiatric Association
- The American Counseling Association
- The National Association of Social Workers
- The American Psychoanalytic Association
- The American Academy of Pediatrics

Can homosexuality be "cured"?

No. The failure rate of conversion therapies aimed at changing sexual orientation is very high. No published scientific evidence in peer-reviewed journals exists supporting the claims that these therapies are effective. Testimonies from "ex-gays" claiming that they changed into heterosexuals through therapy do not scientifically demonstrate or prove the efficacy of such treatments.

Homosexuality portrayed as a destructive lifestyle.

Antigay advocates often exaggerate data on the high rate of suicide attempts and alcohol use among LGB youth as a strategy to equate homosexuality with unhappiness and suicidality. The truth is that while LGB youth do have higher rates of suicide attempts and alcohol use, the overwhelming majority does not attempt suicide or abuse alcohol.

Confusing homosexuality with a hostile, homophobic culture.

Antigay advocates present their data without a consideration of the homophobic culture in which LGB individuals live. The cause of the above-mentioned trends in suicide attempts and alcohol use is not homosexuality; however, it is the often negative cultural reactions to same-sex identification. Living in a homophobic society causes emotional stress.

---

* The material presented here is discussed in greater detail in *Everyday Activism: A Handbook for Lesbian, Gay, and Bisexual People and Their Allies*, edited by Michael R. Stevenson, Ph.D., and Jeanine C. Cogan, Ph.D., and published by Routledge in 2003.

- Find heterosexual allies, especially parents and children of LGB people and insiders like Christian psychotherapists.
- Challenge antigay policy initiatives by writing your state and federal legislators. Provide them with accurate information, including a copy of *The Truth About Sexual Orientation and Mental Health.*

for more information

- American Psychological Association. (2001). *Answers to your questions about sexual orientation and homosexuality.* Washington, D.C. Available at www.apa.org/pubinfo/answers.html
- Haldeman, D. C. (1999). The pseudo-science of sexual orientation conversion therapy. Angles, 4(1). Available at www.iglss.org/iglss/pubs/angles_4-1_p1.html
- Herek, G. M. (Ed.). (1998). *Psychological perspective on lesbian and gay issues: Vol. 4. Stigma and sexual orientation: Understanding prejudice against lesbians, gay men, and bisexuals.* Thousand Oaks, CA: Sage.
- Human Rights Campaign. (2000). *It's not about hope, it's about anti-gay politics: How to respond to anti-gay "change" ads in your community.* Washington, DC: Author. Available at www.hrc.org/publications/exgay_ministries/agpb.asp
- Human Rights Campaign. (2000). *Finally free: How love and acceptance saved us from the ex-gay ministries.* Washington, DC: Author. Available at www.hrc.org/publications/exgay_ministries/finallyfree.pdf
- Khan, S. (1998). *Calculated compassion: How the ex-gay movement serves the right's attack on democracy.* Somerville, MA: Political Research Associates. Available at www.ngltf.org/downloads/calccomp.pdf or www.publiceye.org/equality/x-gay/Calculated_Compassion_TOC.htm
- Marcus, E. (1999). *Is it a choice? Answers to 300 of the most frequently asked questions about gay and lesbian people.* San Francisco: Harper.
- Mills, K. I. (1999). *Mission impossible: Why reparative therapy and ex-gay ministries fail.* Washington, DC: Human Rights Campaign. Available at www.hrc.org/publications/exgay_ministries/change.asp
- People for the American Way. (yearly). *Hostile climate: An annual report on anti-gay bigotry in America.* Washington, DC: Author. Available at www.pfaw.org/hc
- Russell, G. M. (2000). *Voted out: The psychological consequences of anti-gay politics.* New York: New York University Press.

Part II

ending
discrimination

CHAPTER 4

combating hate crimes

Jeanine C. Cogan

In this chapter, you will

- *Learn how legislators have responded to hate crimes.*
- *Consider how hate crime policy development is influenced by homophobia.*
- *Find out why specific policy responses to hate crimes are important.*
- *Learn the arguments used to obstruct hate crime policies.*
- *Begin to advocate for the inclusion of sexual orientation in hate crime policies.*

In the last decade a number of high-profile and egregious antigay hate crimes and, in response, the aggressive advocacy of the LGB community have brought violence against gay men, lesbians, and bisexuals into the policy limelight. Though such violence has been a fact of life through most of our country's history, the term *hate crime* is a modern development. In the early 1980s, the gay rights, civil rights, and women's rights movements galvanized their communities to fight for an appropriate response to violence motivated by bigotry.[1] Activists influenced lawmakers to respond to what was perceived as an ever-growing pattern of violence targeted at minority communities with an original approach—the criminalization of bias-motivated intimidation and violence. As a result, hate crimes emerged as a new category of crime.[2] They were defined as violent acts against people, property, or organizations committed specifically because of the group to which the victim belonged or with which he or she identified.

The efforts of activists brought the problems of antigay and other bias-motivated violence to the forefront of American public policy. Government task forces and legislative campaigns emerged at all levels of government. Activists worked with police agencies to familiarize them with the dynamics of hate crimes and to encourage appropriate responses to various communities. The Federal Bureau of Investigation (FBI) developed training materials and programs for police agencies across the country to address the growing problem of hate crimes and how to properly identify and respond to them. In addition, both state and federal legislators responded by passing hate crimes laws.

state laws

All but four states have enacted some form of hate crimes law.[3] The most common state laws enhance penalties or provide for data collection. Other laws promote police training or prohibit cross burning, mask wearing, and/or paramilitary training camps.[4] While hate crime laws exist in most states, nearly half the states do not include sexual orientation–based crimes in their hate crime statutes. As such, gay men and lesbians are not protected against and lack legal recourse for antigay hate crimes in the majority of states. For this reason the federal government plays an important role in protecting all Americans. The overall lack of protection by states is also one argument in support of federal hate crime laws.

Box 4.1

STATES THAT INCLUDE SEXUAL ORIENTATION–BASED CRIMES IN THEIR HATE CRIME STATUTES[5]

Arizona	Kentucky	New Jersey
California	Louisiana	New York
Connecticut	Maine	Oregon
Delaware	Massachusetts	Rhode Island
District of Columbia	Minnesota	Tennessee
Florida	Missouri	Texas
Hawaii	Nebraska	Vermont
Illinois	Nevada	Washington
Iowa	New Hampshire	Wisconsin
Kansas		

federal response to hate crimes

The first federal hate crimes law in the United States, the Hate Crimes Statistics Act of 1990, was the culmination of years of collaboration between Congress and a broad-based advocacy group. Other activity followed and hate crime policy became an important priority for advocates and legislators alike.

What makes a crime a hate crime is the existence of bias or prejudice of the perpetrator against an individual based on the victim's real or perceived social grouping. Yet definitions differ in terms of which groups are included. Race, ethnicity, religion, and national origin are usually included. Gender, disability, and sexual orientation may not be. The legal definition of a hate crime depends on the hate crime law considered.

The Hate Crimes Statistics Act

The first hate crime law to pass was the Hate Crimes Statistics Act (HCSA) of 1990. In order for legislators to respond to hate crimes, they needed to know how widespread the problem was. The HCSA allowed the federal government to document the incidence of hate crimes. The law requires the U.S. Attorney General to collect data and publish an annual summary of hate crimes incidence across the country.

Hate crimes, as defined in the HCSA, were crimes that manifest evidence of prejudice based on *race, religion, sexual orientation,* or *ethnicity*, including crimes of murder, nonnegligent manslaughter, forcible rape, aggravated assault, simple assault, intimidation, arson, and destruction, damage, or vandalism of property. The category *disability* was added to the statute in 1994. The fact that sexual orientation was included in the first federal hate crimes bill was an important and hard-fought victory for the LGB community.[6] This set a precedent, making it difficult for legislators to exclude sexual orientation in future hate crimes bills. In addition, like all laws, the language served a symbolic function and communicated to the public that violence against gay men, lesbians, and bisexuals would not be tolerated.

Yet the fears and biases that pervade the halls of Congress led legislators, uncomfortable with including sexual orientation in the HCSA, to add the following sentence to the bill: "Nothing in this Act shall be construed, nor shall any funds appropriated to carry out the purpose of the Act be used, to promote or encourage homosexuality."[7] This language illustrates a common struggle activists encounter in promoting any LGB-positive policy: the misconception that LGB people are on a mission to recruit others or otherwise spread homosexuality.[8]

Although this law is important in recognizing hate crimes as a phenomenon that needs federal attention, the data it generates are imperfect. Rather than require the collection and reporting of hate crimes data, the HCSA merely encourages police agencies to report *voluntarily* the hate crimes data for their jurisdictions. As a result, many police departments did not provide any hate crimes data for the first few years. Or they provided data that were clearly inaccurate, such as zero hate crimes in the whole state of Alabama in 1996.[9] The usefulness of the data collected under the HCSA is contingent on the participation of police agencies and their provision meaningful data. After a number of years of FBI training regarding the importance and accurate identification of hate crimes, more reliable data are now available. Yet it remains widely recognized that the data from the HCSA underestimate the actual hate crimes that occur. For example, in 1998, the National Coalition of Anti-Violence Programs documented a total of 2,552 antigay hate crimes, while the FBI reported less than 1,300.

The Hate Crimes Sentencing Enhancement Act of 1994

The second federal law addressing hate crimes to pass Congress was the Hate Crimes Sentencing Enhancement Act of 1994. Passed as a part of the Violent Crime Control and Law Enforcement Act of 1994, this law directs the U.S. Sentencing Commission to provide sentencing enhancements of "not less than three offense levels for offenses that the finder of fact at trial determines beyond a reasonable doubt are hate crimes."

In this law, a hate crime is defined as a crime committed against a person because of *real or perceived race, color, religion, national origin, ethnicity, gender, disability,* or *sexual orientation.* Having sexual orientation included in the definition of hate crimes was a second success for gay activists. In fact, this law includes the broadest definition of hate crimes to date, and it serves as a precedent for definitions in future hate crimes laws.

The Hate Crimes Prevention Act

The public outcry over the brutal deaths of James Byrd and Matthew Shepard in 1998 intensified the pressure on Congress to address the growing problem of hate crimes in the United States. After more than 3 years of strong and broad-based advocacy, in the fall of 2000 the Republican-dominated House and Senate came close to passing the Hate Crimes Prevention Act (HCPA) as part of an omnibus spending bill. Unfortunately, efforts were thwarted, in part because of antigay fears.

Box 4.2

THE HATE CRIMES PREVENTION ACT (HCPA)

Background Information

- A civil rights statute, Section 245 of Title 18 U.S.C., gives federal prosecutors the authority to investigate allegations of hate violence based on
  race, religion, and national origin. This avenue for federal involvement
  is necessary in order to address cases where state and local authorities
  fail to properly respond to victims' allegations. Currently such federal
  investigations are minimal, with typically less than 10 prosecutions
  annually.

- This statute is critical for responding to the problem of hate violence,
  yet it does not include a broad definition of hate crimes that is consistent with more recent legislation. In 1994 Congress passed the Hate
  Crimes Sentencing Enhancement Act as part of the Violent Crime
  Control and Law Enforcement Act of 1994. In this law, hate crimes were
  defined broadly as a crime committed against the person:

  > Because of the actual or perceived race, color, religion, national ori-
  > gin, ethnicity, gender, disability, or sexual orientation of that person.

Purpose of the HCPA

- The main purpose of the HCPA is to add sexual orientation, gender, and
  disability to *existing* federal law regarding the authority of the federal
  government to investigate and prosecute crimes. This authority already
  exists for crimes committed because of the victim's race, color, religion,
  and national origin. HCPA thus brings more uniformity and fairness to
  existing law.

- The Department of Justice (DOJ) receives inquiries from families of gay
  victims asking for their involvement when local authorities have failed
  to respond. Unfortunately, the DOJ does not have the authority to
  investigate such cases. The DOJ considers this bill an important measure
  in helping them to properly respond to victims' concerns.

- The HCPA was first introduced in 1998 and included in a version of the
  Omnibus budget bill but was later dropped. In 1999 the bill was again
  introduced in both the House and Senate.

- In 2000 the Senate included the language of the HCPA in the defense
  authorization bill and the House voted to direct their conferees to

accept the language. During conference the hate crimes language was removed.

- In 2001 the HCPA was announced as the Local Law Enforcement Enhancement Act (LLEEA) and introduced in the House and Senate by Sens. Ted Kennedy (D-Mass.), Arlen Specter (R-Pa.), and Gordon Smith (R-Oreg.) (S. 625). At time of introduction the bill had 51 original co-sponsors in the Senate. On April 4, 2001, Rep. John Conyers (D-Mich.) introduced LLEEA (H.R. 1343) into the House. At the time of introduction the bill had 187 original co-sponsors in the House. The bill did not pass.

The purpose of the HCPA was to bring a civil rights statute, Title 18 U.S.C. Section 245, in line with more recent hate crimes definitions (see Box 4.2). The original statute gives federal prosecutors the authority to investigate allegations of hate violence based on race, religion, and national origin but not based on gender, disability, or sexual orientation. Provisions in the bill would extend these civil rights–era federal protections to violent crimes involving gender, disability, and sexual orientation and make it easier for the government to intervene in such cases.

The rationale behind the HCPA is that when people are attacked merely because of their real or perceived sexual orientation, gender, or disability, the law should be as tough on their perpetrators as it currently is on criminals who attack based on racial, religious, or ethnic bias.[10] Yet only in rare circumstances can the federal government investigate and prosecute hate violence against gays, lesbians, or bisexuals.

According to personnel in the Department of Justice (DOJ) there are times when antigay hate crimes are not properly addressed by local police agencies. Yet based on current law, the federal government has no authority to intervene. DOJ has received inquiries from families of gay victims asking for their involvement when local authorities failed to respond or when there are no state hate crimes laws available for recourse. Unfortunately, the DOJ does not have the authority to investigate such cases. The HCPA would expand the jurisdiction of Title 18 U.S.C. Section 245 so that federal officials could investigate and prosecute crimes motivated by hate based on the victim's real or perceived gender, disability, or sexual orientation. The DOJ considers the HCPA an important measure in helping them to properly respond to victims' concerns.

In the spring of 2000, after GOP leaders refused to bring up the bill on its own, the Senate, by an unexpectedly strong vote of 57 to 42, added the hate crimes language to the defense authorization. GOP leaders in the House prevented the bill from coming to the House floor for a vote, but after the Senate's action, the House voted 232 to 192 to instruct its conferees on the defense bill to go along with the Senate proposal. Unfortunately, during conference the Republicans stripped the language from the defense authorization bill.

Senate Majority Leader Trent Lott (R-Miss.) has taken credit for blocking the passage of the HCPA, couching his opposition as a concern over devaluing other crime victims: "It should not be made a matter of federal law to designate one group of crimes and its victims less important than others." While Lott's public comments have been along the lines of "all crimes are hate crimes," "murder is murder," and we should not divide people into categories, this is a disguise for his own antigay agenda. According to hate crime law advocates, Lott's reason for blocking the HCPA is that he does not want sexual orientation in the bill, and Lott has assured his extremely conservative constituents that he would not let a hate crimes bill with sexual orientation be passed into law.

fighting the resistance to hate crime laws

The concentration of activity on hate crimes over the last 15 years attests to the growing concern with the terrorist nature of violence motivated by hate or bigotry. The government response "reflects the acceptance of the idea that criminal conduct is different when it involves an act of discrimination."[11] This acceptance is tenuous at best and is laced with homophobia and heterosexism. As we can see in the ongoing battle over the HCPA, passing LGB-affirming policies in the current political climate is an uphill battle.

After the first decade of legislative activity on hate crimes, a growing number of people are challenging the validity of hate crimes as a category separate from other crimes. In addition to certain conservative legislators, more mainstream people and organizations such as opinion page editors and academics are resisting hate crimes policy.[12] Opponents have pursued the argument that it is wrong to designate one group of crimes and its victims as more important than others. A common complaint is, "If I am stabbed just for being in the wrong place at the wrong time, is my life valued any less than a gay man who is stabbed for being gay?" Often the efforts of oppressed groups to push for redress or civil rights protection are countered by the dominant group as an unfair push for "special rights." Indeed, Colorado's Amendment 2 passed, in large part, because its supporters framed this attack on gay civil rights as preventing LGB people from having "special rights." The position is that these crimes are already punishable by law and creating a separate category of crime based on those motivated by bigotry is unnecessary and creates special rights for those groups defined in hate crime laws.

Such arguments are a disguise for underlying heterosexism. Unfortunately, they are also often effective at killing potentially useful hate crime policies. Thus the question that LGB-affirming advocates need to address with policy makers is why hate crimes deserve a separate and unique policy response.

Hierarchy in Responding to Crime Is Not New

The first assumption that must be challenged in the common criticism of hate crimes legislation is the notion that all crimes are to be treated equally. Throughout criminal law there exists a hierarchy in crime from those considered most serious to least serious. A crime can be a misdemeanor, a minor crime with small consequence, or a felony, a more serious crime ranging from theft to first-degree murder. The circumstances and motive of the crime are always examined and considered as keys to how the courts should respond. A person who commits murder is treated more harshly than a person who commits a burglary. Premeditated murder is treated more seriously than a crime of passion. An arsonist who torches an apartment building with 500 occupants is treated differently from an arsonist who burns his doghouse. Are these described distinctions unfair or a sign of special rights assigned to certain communities the way hate crime policy is so typically characterized? Or is this a system of preference where crimes of larger magnitude and impact are logically treated with greater consequence? The criminal code is not flawless. However, the relevant point is that never have all crimes been treated equally and so this requirement should not be uniquely applied to hate crimes.

Impact on the Community

A general justification for hate crimes legislation is that crimes are more socially disruptive and harmful when motivated by bigotry. Hate crimes are damaging not only to the victim but also to the community at large. Hate crimes are message crimes, in that the perpetrator is sending a message to members of a certain group that they are despised, devalued, or unwelcome in a particular neighborhood, community, school, or workplace.[13] Thus, hate crimes serve as a form of intimidation not only for the victim but for all members of the targeted group. After the murder of Matthew Shepard, gay men and lesbians across the country felt victimized and feared for their safety. Members of gay and lesbian communities understood the perpetrators' message: "you are unworthy of life." Indeed, research shows that after hate crimes occur people have an increased sense of vulnerability in their communities.[14]

Box 4.3

A PARTIAL LISTING OF ANTIHATE NONPROFIT EDUCATIONAL AND NATIONAL ORGANIZATIONS

Anti-Defamation League—www.adl.org
Center for Living Democracy—www.livingdemocracy.org
Center on Hate and Extremism—/www.stockton.edu/~hate
Chicago Lawyers' Committee for Civil Rights Under Law, Inc.—
　　www.clccrul.org
Community United Against Violence—/www.cuav.org
Facing History and Ourselves National Foundation, Inc—www.facing.org
The Governors Task Force on Hate Crimes—www.stopthehate.org
Human Rights Campaign - http://www.hrc.org
Institute on Race and Poverty: Center on Speech, Equality, and Harm—
　　www.umd.edu/irp
Lambda Legal Defense and Education Fund—www.lambda.org
Leadership Conference on Civil Rights—www.civilrights.org/lcef/hate
National Gay and Lesbian Task Force—/www.ngltf.org
National Multi-Cultural Institute—www.nmci.org
The New York City Gay and Lesbian Anti-Violence Project—www.avp.org
Not in Our Town—www.igc.org/an/niot
Parents, Families, and Friends of Lesbians and Gays—www.pflag.org
Southern Poverty Law Center—www.splcenter.org
Stop the Hate—www.stop-the-hate.org
YWCA of the U.S.A—www.ywca.org

Impact on the Individual

An additional justification for hate crimes legislation is that such crimes have a disparate impact on the victim. Because the basis of attack is their identity, hate crime victims may suffer more severe consequences, such as rejecting the aspect of themselves that was the target of the attack, or associating a core part of their identity with fear, loss, and vulnerability. They may feel they have less control over their world and what happens to them, which is associated with lower self-esteem.

Indeed, research shows that when it comes to hate crimes, a crime is not simply a crime. A group of psychologists at the University of California at Davis found that hate crimes had a more serious impact on victims than did nonhate crimes. In a study of more than 2,000 gay men and lesbians in the greater Sacramento area, the researchers found that those who experienced a serious

Box 4.4

WHO TO CALL AFTER A HATE CRIME[15]

Your safety comes first. If you are injured or bleeding, or still in danger, call 911 or go directly to a hospital emergency room.

For emotional support and accessing resources:

- Call the national Hate Crime Hot Line staffed by LAMBDA at 800–686–HATE.
- LAMBDA is a nonprofit, gay/lesbian/bisexual/transgender agency dedicated to reducing homophobia, inequality, hate crimes, and discrimination by encouraging self-acceptance, cooperation, and nonviolence.
- You can also call the New York City Gay and Lesbian Anti-Violence Project (AVP) hotline at 212–714–1141. You can ask to speak with a male or female counselor and/or a Spanish- or English-speaking counselor. If you are located in a city where there is a local contact who can assist you, they will refer you to someone local. Otherwise AVP staff will offer support.
- If you're calling outside office hours, you need to be at a phone where AVP can call you back. If it's not safe for them to call you where you are, go to a safe place such as a friend's place, all-night diner, or hospital emergency room and call from there.
- You can call AVP's office at 212–714–1184 from 10:00 A.M. to 8:00 P.M. Monday–Thursday, 10:00 A.M. to 6:00 P.M. Friday (except major holidays) to speak with a staff counselor or schedule an appointment.

antigay crime had more severe psychological consequences than those who experienced a random crime of similar severity.[16] Hate crime victims suffered greater feelings of vulnerability, anger, and depression than those who were victims of random crimes. Additionally, the hate crime victims needed as much as 5 years to overcome the impact of their victimization. By contrast, victims of random crimes recovered from the consequences of the crime within 2 years. This is the largest and most extensive study examining the mental health consequences of any hate crimes.

Hate crime victims are not able to latch on to the typically used psychological defense of other crime victims: that they were simply in the wrong place at the wrong time, the victim of random violence. Instead, there is a purpose to the crime, and that purpose is to communicate that he or she is part of a group that is despised and devalued, that he or she deserves to be the victim of violence.

Box 4.5

WHAT TO KNOW IF YOU ARE A VICTIM OF A HATE CRIME[17]

There are many normal physical and psychological reactions to the trauma of victimization. Emotional reactions such as denial—trying to forget the crime or to pretend that it never happened—anger, isolation, fear, depression, and problems with concentration are common.

Survivors of violent crime may also experience physical problems that seem unrelated to an assault, such as head- or stomachaches. Insomnia, change in appetite, sexual difficulties, and general listlessness are also common physical changes suffered by crime victims. Ignoring these symptoms may lead to further complications.

You should also be aware of and consider the following:

- **Get medical attention.** Consult a physician or hospital emergency room, even if you do not believe that you have been seriously injured. Do this as soon after an assault as possible.

- **Document the incident.** Keep accurate records of an incident. Document physical injuries with photographs. Retain any written harassment you receive. Keep a log of the time and date of harassing phone calls. If harassing messages have been left on your answering machine, keep the tape or save the messages in the memory. Report it to AVP or LAMBDA (refer to box 4.4).

- **Take care of yourself.** Talking about the incident to supportive friends, lovers, or family members can be helpful. Accept your feelings and reactions to the trauma. You may find it helpful to discuss the incident with a counselor at AVP. Call AVP to find out about resources available to you.

- **Reporting crimes to the police.**
  1. There is no requirement that you report a crime to the police. The decision about filing a report is yours as the survivor of a crime. Do what is most comfortable for you. Keep in mind that police reports are public records and under most circumstances can be released to the media.
  2. In order to seek financial compensation from a state crime victim board for medical expenses or lost earnings, a police report is required.
  3. Many police departments have special departments that investigate bias incidents to handle your case.
  4. If you decide to report a crime, an advocacy and victim assistance organization may be able to provide assistance and support (e.g., AVP and LAMBDA).

- **Safety information.** You cannot ensure that you will never become a crime victim. No crime victim is to blame for the crime committed against them. Nevertheless, these few safety tips may be helpful:
  1. Find out about any local danger zones in the neighborhoods you frequent where lesbians and gay men may have been attacked. Avoid these areas, especially if you are alone.
  2. If you feel threatened or unsafe, trust your instincts and remove yourself from the situation as quickly as possible. Run. Bang garbage cans. Make noise. Yell "FIRE!" Call 911 for police assistance as soon as possible.
  3. Letting someone you do not know into your home or apartment may make you vulnerable to robbery and assault. If you leave a bar with someone you have just met, introduce him or her to a friend or bartender. Let other people know that you are leaving together. Exchange names and telephone numbers.
  4. Try to leave bars, community centers, and other LGB-identified facilities with people you know or trust. Assailants sometimes wait for potential victims outside of places where lesbians and gay men meet and gather.
  5. Carry a whistle. Consider taking a self-defense class.

- **What we can do as a community.**
  1. Violence against lesbians and gay men affects everyone in our communities. Every attack against one of us is in reality an assault against us all.
  2. The most effective way to deal with this violence is through community education and involvement.
  3. Learn about the nature and extent of anti-LGB violence and the services available through AVP, LAMBDA, and other social service agencies (see Box 4.6).
  4. Call organizations to document attacks, get help, or request a speaker for your organization or community group.

Hate Crimes Are Widespread

Hate crimes based on sexual orientation are underreported, yet the number of hate crimes that are reported already suggests a disturbing amount of bias-motivated violence against gays and lesbians. In the study mentioned earlier, more than one fifth of the 2,259 LGBs surveyed reported being the victim of a hate-motivated crime between age 16 and the time of the survey. More specifically, one in five women and one in four men had experienced an antigay hate crime.

Types of victimization included physical and sexual assaults, attempted assaults, robberies, thefts, vandalism, and assault with a weapon. This survey did not include any incidents from adolescence, which are quite common. The researchers also found that these hate crimes occur within an environment of overall antigay harassment. When respondents were asked about their experience with harassment in just the past 12 months, more than half (56 percent) said they were verbally abused, 19 percent said their lives were threatened, 17 percent said they were chased or followed, and 12 percent had objects thrown at them for being gay. Antigay violence and harassment are clearly facts of life for many people in the United States.

In addition to these research data, community-based watchdog groups find similarly disturbing rates of antigay violence. The National Coalition of Anti-Violence Programs, an umbrella group for approximately 25 local and state organizations serving victims of antigay hate crimes around the country, found that in 1998 there were 2,552 reported incidents of hate crimes in just 14 major cities across the United States.[18] In these 14 cities, this figure translates into seven antigay hate crimes a day or one hate crime every 3 hours.

According to data collected by the FBI's Uniform Crime Reporting Program, hate crimes reported on the basis of sexual orientation are increasing. Since the FBI began collecting statistics in 1991, hate crimes based on sexual orientation have nearly tripled. Between 1997 and 1998 reported hate crimes against gay men and lesbians increased by 14.3 percent. Whether this is a true increase in crime or an increase in reporting is unknown. If it is an increase in actual committed crime, this trend is particularly disturbing because, overall, serious crime continues to decrease nationally.[19]

Hate Crimes Are Underreported

As discussed earlier, data gathered under the Hate Crimes Statistics Act underestimate the actual number of hate crimes that occur nationally. The HCSA makes the reporting of hate crimes by state and local jurisdictions voluntary, so many jurisdictions do not participate. For example, in 1997 ten of the 100 most populous cities in the United States did not participate in the reporting of hate crimes data.[20]

Additionally, social science research shows that hate crimes are less likely to be reported to the police than random crimes.[21] One reason for this lack of reporting is the perception that police agencies are themselves homophobic and will not be responsive to the incident and/or may even further victimize the individual by a homophobic response. Another important factor causing the underreporting is that some victims may fear being outed in their communities or

Box 4.6

REPORTING AND DOCUMENTING HATE CRIMES

Why Should I Report Anti-LGBT Incidents?
When such incidents are invisible, it is harder to protect against them. Careful documentation and statistics are very important tools in fighting oppression and bigotry.

After an incident, help is often available—even if you wish to remain completely anonymous or choose not to report to the police. When we decline to report to law enforcement authorities or prosecute the offenders, we become passive victims who are at even greater risk for future victimization.

Survivors of bias incidents often say that they fear reporting to the police or that they simply don't know where to turn for help. So, they suffer in silence—feeling disconnected, helpless, and afraid.

Where Can You Report? Two Organizations That Document Hate Crimes
The National Coalition of Anti-Violence Programs (NCAVP) is a coalition of 25 lesbian, gay, bisexual, and transgender victim and documentation programs located throughout the United States. Before officially forming in 1995, NCAVP members collaborated with one another and with the National Gay and Lesbian Task Force (NGLTF) for over a decade to create a coordinated response to violence against our communities. Since 1984 members have released an annual report every March, promoting public education about bias-motivated crimes against lesbian, gay, bisexual, and transgender people.

The best way to contact NCAVP is through the New York City Gay and Lesbian Anti-Violence Project (AVP). Their office number is 212–714–1184, with hours from 10:00 A.M. to 8:00 P.M., Monday–Thursday, 10:00 A.M. to 6:00 P.M. Friday ET.

LAMBDA created the Hate-Crime Network, run by a team of experienced hate crime victim advocates who know the importance of hate crime laws, recovery services, and improved police response. But they also know that for the thousands of people affected by hate crimes each year, none of that matters if they can't tell anyone what happened.

Fortunately, there's the international Hate-Crime Network. It gives hate survivors a chance to tell someone what happened to them—regardless of where they live. And, among other things, it gives virtually anyone with e-mail or web access a chance to send personal messages to the victims, offering them compassion, encouragement, and hope.

LAMBDA is set up for you to report a bias incident online at hate-crime.website-works.com.

places of work. Lastly, researchers found that more severe forms of hate crimes were less likely to be reported to the police and concluded that this lack of reporting is in part due to the victim's fear that the perpetrators will seek revenge.[22]

Hate Crimes Warrant Government Intervention

One of the harshest critiques of hate crimes policy argues that since hate crimes are not increasing, they are not worthy of special protection.[23] This argument is flawed because it relies on FBI data gathered under the Hate Crimes Statistics Act, and as shown earlier those numbers underestimate the incidence of hate crimes. Besides, how many crimes does it take to qualify as an epidemic? There is ample evidence that hate crimes are a widespread and serious problem. Furthermore, does a criminal activity need to reach "epidemic" levels before laws are passed to address the problem? Finally, the construct of hate crimes evolved from social movements that were fighting crimes occurring against people within communities that held less social, political, and cultural power than the dominant group. A crime against a gay man or lesbian is a direct outgrowth of homosexuality being stigmatized and institutional discrimination that condones such stigmatization. Because hate crimes happen within the context of discrimination and stigma, any such crime warrants a policy response.

Responsibility of the Government

Hate crimes are a direct threat to some of the basic principles of American life. Each individual has the right to the pursuit of happiness without interference based on group identity or membership. Accordingly, a role of the federal government is to ensure equal treatment of all its citizens. The U.S. Constitution placed a special responsibility on the federal government to ensure that no citizen is subject to discriminatory treatment because of deeply rooted prejudice. To help carry out this duty, equal opportunity laws and civil rights protections have been passed and enforced. Thus the precedent exists for federal hate crime laws to ensure all members of society the freedom to exercise their civil rights without undue interference. The law remains an important avenue for stigmatized and minority groups to gain equality.

Hate Crimes Are Not Simply False Positives

Another complaint among critics of hate crime legislation is that victims who determine that they have experienced a hate crime may simply be inferring incorrectly. They may inaccurately perceive something as antigay due to their heightened awareness of their sexual orientation as a stigmatized status. Recently researchers have been interested in how people determine that a crime is based on their sexual orientation rather than just being random. In an attempt to shed light on the attribution processes that underlie self-reports of antigay and antilesbian victimization, researchers asked respondents why they believed that their victimization was based on sexual orientation.[24]

Respondents were asked, "What was it that made you realize or believe that the incident was related to your sexual orientation?" Results showed that two thirds of the explanations were based on unambiguous information: the perpetrators made explicit statements, the attack occurred in an LGB-identified location, or the crime was closely associated with behaviors by the victim that identified her or him as LGB. Only 16 percent of interviewees based their attribution merely on a hunch, and in many cases these reasons for believing that they were targeted because of their sexual orientation seemed highly plausible. These findings suggest that a victim's own evaluation that a crime is bias motivated is a good indicator that a bias crime did indeed occur.

Hate Crimes Can Be Documented

Another criticism of hate crime laws is that they introduce the impossible for prosecutors and the courts in requiring them to determine the motive of the perpetrator. Indeed it can be a challenge for law enforcement officials to decide whether a crime is a hate crime. Yet there is more rhyme and reason than often meets the critic's eye. The FBI worked with law enforcement to establish widely used bias crime indicators. These are objective facts, circumstances, or patterns attending a criminal act that standing alone or in conjunction with other facts or circumstances suggest that the offenders' actions were motivated in whole or in part by any form of bias. The more bias crime indicators evident in a particular crime, the more likely the crime was based on bigotry. Bias crime indicators include:

1. Racial, ethnic, gender, and cultural differences. If the victim and perpetrators differ in race, ethnicity, gender, or sexual orientation, then bias could be present. If the victim is a member of a group that is overwhelmingly outnumbered by members of another group in the area where the incident occurred, then bias could be present.

2. Overt language used—written statements or gestures.

3. Drawings, markings, symbols, and/or graffiti.

4. Representation of organized hate groups.

5. Previous occurrence of bias incidents.

6. Victim's perception.

> **Box 4.7**
>
> ## HATE CRIMES VS. HATE INCIDENTS: KNOWING THE DIFFERENCE[25]
>
> A hate incident is any act, whether consisting of conduct, speech, or expression, to which a bias motive is evident as a contributing factor, without regard for whether the act constitutes a crime.
>
> Hate incidents involve behaviors that, though motivated by bias against a victim's race, religion, ethnic/national origin, gender, age, disability, or sexual orientation, are not necessarily criminal acts. Hostile or hateful speech, for example, may be motivated by bias but is not illegal. Hate incidents become crimes only when they directly incite perpetrators to commit violence against persons or property, or if they place a victim in reasonable fear of physical injury.
>
> Police officers are trained to thoroughly document evidence in all bias-motivated incidents. Law enforcement can help to defuse potentially dangerous situations and prevent bias-motivated criminal behavior by responding to and documenting bias-motivated speech or behavior even if it does not rise to the level of a criminal offense.

7. Lack of other motives. If there is no clear economic (such as robbery) or other motive for the incident, then bias may be involved.

legitimate criticisms of hate crime legislation

Paradox in Enforcement

Preliminary analyses of how hate crimes sentencing enhancement laws are enforced reveal a potentially challenging paradox. According to Karen Franklin, a forensic psychologist in California, penalty enhancement policies raise an interesting question. They are enacted as a result of grassroots advocacy by minority group activists, but they are enforced by a criminal justice system—police, prosecutors, and judges—that is itself plagued with institutional racism, sexism, and homophobia. Thus, as with overall arrest rates for crime in general, FBI data show disproportionate arrest rates of African Americans for committing hate crimes. Additionally, Franklin highlights data in Florida, where whites were the largest category of hate crime victims, accounting for 50 percent of reported hate crimes. So the very groups who fought for protection against bigotry-motivated violence may well be the ones most likely to become convicted felons. The issue for advocates then is how to push for hate crime policies designed to protect marginalized groups in a well-documented racist, sexist, and homophobic judicial system.[26]

Problems With the Focus

Given that sentence enhancement is a popular response in the "get tough on crime" culture that has dominated U.S. policy for more than a decade, it is no surprise that hate crime activists' success has also been in the sentence enhancement arena. In addition to the paradox highlighted by Karen Franklin, this focus places peace activists, pacifists, anti–death penalty activists, and people committed to finding solutions other than further punishment in a quandary. Data on the death penalty show that harsh punishments do not serve as deterrents to crime. So although some activists are in support of hate crimes legislation, they have difficulty supporting efforts to pass hate crime sentencing enhancement bills.

prevention and education

You can now understand and appreciate the way in which hate crimes policy has evolved based on the political climate and negotiation. However, legislation that enhances penalties is not our only recourse to hate crimes and the attitudes and beliefs that provoke them. In addition to this hate crimes approach, it is important for advocates to focus more on prevention and education efforts. Boxes 4.8, 4.9, and 4.10 describe three such approaches.

what you can do!

- Contact your elected officials by mail, e-mail, phone, and personal visit.
  - Urge them to support hate crimes policies.
  - Provide a copy of *Why We Need Legislation on Hate Crimes* as a summary of the issues.
  - www.congress.org/ provides contact information for congressional leaders. Identify and contact your federal and state elected officials by entering your ZIP code.
- Contact your local police department.
  - Determine whether they collect and report statistics on hate crimes. If so, applaud their work. If not, encourage them to do so.
  - Encourage the department to provide ongoing training on appropriate responses to hate crime and its victims.

Box 4.8

SUPPORTING EFFORTS TO PREVENT HATE CRIMES

Social scientists have produced a vast amount of research examining antecedents, causes, and consequences of violent behavior. These studies show that violence is not random, uncontrollable, or inevitable. Many factors, both individual and social, contribute to an individual's propensity to use violence, and are within our power to change. There is overwhelming evidence that we can intervene effectively in the lives of people to reduce or prevent their involvement in violence.[27]

An important societal factor that contributes to violence among youth and is at the crux of hate crimes is prejudice. Prejudice, intolerance, and discrimination are demonstrated in countless acts of interpersonal behavior each day. Hate crimes are an extreme expression of this intolerance. Because hate crimes are rooted in intolerance and bigotry, addressing this bigotry can begin to prevent and eliminate the problem of hate crimes.

Clearly, an important avenue for hate crimes policy is advocating for prejudice prevention and education. Such efforts include the following:

- Urge the Department of Justice (DOJ) to offer more grants that allow communities to conduct prejudice prevention and education programs, particularly targeting youth, and support these programs.
- Urge the DOJ to continue its training with police officers and justice personnel to allow hate crimes policies to be implemented effectively and appropriately.
- Urge the Office of Juvenile Justice and Delinquency Prevention (OJJDP) to continue to fund important hate crimes prevention and other safe-community programs targeting youth, with a concentration on at-risk youth.
- Urge the Department of Education (DOE) to implement a prejudice reduction curriculum in the schools.

- Track hate crime policy through specific websites that provide current legislative highlights and other relevant information. Box 4.3 provides an extensive list. Start with www.adl.org.
- Write, e-mail, or call your federal policy makers urging them to support the Hate Crimes Prevention Act and other hate crimes bills. To call your representative and/or senator, you can use the Capitol switchboard at 202–224–3121.

Box 4.9

ADDRESSING ISOLATION

Much needless crime comes from people feeling isolated from others; lacking a sense of human connection; lacking a sense of belonging to a group or community. Raphael Ezekiel, an anthropologist who spent years talking with young men involved in neo-Nazi and Klan groups, concludes that most of the youth were drawn to these hate groups not out of hate but out of a desire to belong to a cause or a community.

He describes the relationships that emerged—he as a Jew with these self-declared anti-Semites. He realized that some of these youth's lives were being changed as he offered them interaction and connection, which they so craved. Ezekiel concludes that what these young men wanted most profoundly was to have close relationships and to feel that their lives mattered.[28]

In this culture of mass consumption, long hours of work, nonstop media, suburban isolation, and pervasive Internet use, the opportunities for human connection have dwindled for some. Youth are often searching for ways to have interaction with others and find meaning in their lives.

Both local and federal policy can be used to decrease social isolation and help promote and build community. For example, rather than pouring much of our government resources into policing and punishment efforts, more funds should be allocated toward programs and initiatives that build community.

Again, advocates can approach federal agencies such as the DOJ and DOE and urge them to fund community-building initiatives. In fact, the OJJDP included a commitment to creating positive opportunities for youth in its 1998 action plan for preventing youth delinquency.[29] Such initiatives need to be more actively promoted and supported by advocates.

Rather than being a touchy-feely liberal approach to crime, this strategy should be viewed as a cost-saving, proactive measure for building a sense of community that will prevent hate crimes as well as other forms of crime. This is evident from the after-school programs that have been popular in crime-fighting efforts.[30] These programs are successful in deterring crime by engaging young people in productive activity. This approach works, not only because planned activities keep youth busy but also because they offer them opportunities for social interaction rather than isolation.

Box 4.10

RAISING AWARENESS THROUGH FILM

Mediarights.org is a community website that helps media makers, educators, nonprofits, and activists use documentaries to encourage action and inspire dialogue on contemporary social issues such as hate crimes. This is a listing of documentaries that address hate crimes:

Ballot Measure 9 (1995). Winner of the Audience Award at Sundance and a Teddy Bear at the Berlin Film Festival, *Ballot Measure 9* tells a chilling story of intolerance, tracing a bitter election battle in Oregon.

The Brandon Teena Story (1998). When 20-year-old Brandon arrived in Falls City, Nebraska, in 1993, his look and charm won him several friends in town and even a pretty young girlfriend. But on Christmas Eve, Brandon was brutally raped and beaten and then, a week later, murdered, by two of his friends who became enraged when they discovered that he was actually a woman.

Kamikaze Summer (1996). A lesbian and a gay man from San Francisco, in an effort to discover why the religious right perceives homosexuality as a threat to civilization, embark on a road trip into the heartland of religious bigotry in America.

Licensed to Kill (1997). *Licensed to Kill* takes a riveting journey into the minds of men whose contempt for homosexuals led them to murder.

Lone Star Hate (1997). "The banality of evil" is one of the subjects of this Channel 4 documentary on the gruesome 1993 gay-bashing murder of Nicholas West in conservative Tyler, Texas.

Pink Triangles (1982). *Pink Triangles* was one of the first films to confront the pervasive homophobia in American life and served to alert audiences to the danger of scapegoating and violence that can occur in any society. It is a documentary film that challenges some of our most deeply rooted feelings: our attitudes toward homosexuality.

Tongues Untied (1989). This is the acclaimed account of black gay life by Emmy Award–winning director Marlon Riggs. Using poetry, personal testimony, rap, and performance, *Tongues Untied* explores homophobia and racism.

Treading Water (2001). *City Pages*, October 24, 2001: "Exploring queer life and history in northern Minnesota through the eyes of several locals."

Which Is Scary (1991). *Which Is Scary* is a documentation of seven individual stories of homophobia.

- Counter arguments against hate crime policies by writing a letter to the editor or an op-ed piece correcting misperceptions about hate crime policy. (For tips on how to do this, refer to Box 1.7.)
- Support the national organizations listed in Box 4.3 in their work to promote hate crime policies.
  - Become a member.
  - Subscribe to their legislative or media alerts.
  - Monitor their web sites.
  - Make a donation.
- Educate your community, family, and friends about antigay hate crimes.
  - Write a column for the newsletter of your church or civic organization.
  - Organize a screening and discussion of one of the documentaries listed in Box 4.10.
  - Organize a panel on preventing hate crimes for your local PTA.

for more information

- American Psychological Association. (1998). *Hate crimes today: An age-old foe in modern dress.* Washington, DC: Author.
- *Education Department, Office of Elementary and Secondary Education, Safe and Drug-Free Schools Program.* (1998). *Preventing youth hate crime: A manual for schools and communities.* Washington, DC: U.S. Government Printing Office.
- Herek, G. M., & Berrill, K. T. (1992). *Hate crimes: Confronting violence against lesbians and gay men.* London: Sage.
- Herek, G. M., Gillis, J. R., & Cogan, J. C. (1999). Psychological sequelae of hate crime victimization among lesbian, gay, and bisexual adults. *Journal of Consulting and Clinical Psychology, 67,* 945–951.
- Herek, G. M., Gillis, J. R., Cogan, J. C., & Glunt, E. K. (1997). Hate crime victimization among lesbian, gay, and bisexual adults: Prevalence, psychological correlates, and methodological issues. *Journal of Interpersonal Violence, 12*(2), 195–215.
- Jenness, V., & Broad, K. (1997). *Hate crimes: New social movements and the politics of violence.* Hawthorne, NY: Aldine de Gruyter.
- Jenness, V., & Grattet, R. (2001). *Making hate a crime: From social movement to law enforcement.* New York: Russell Sage Foundation.
- Johnson, S. E. (2002). *Standing on holy ground: The battle against hate crime in the deep south.* New York: St. Martin's Press.
- Kelly, R. J., & Maghan, J. (1998). *Hate crime: The global politics of polarization.* Carbondale: Southern Illinois University Press.
- Levin, J., & McDevitt, J. (1993, May). *Hate crimes: The tising tide of bigotry and bloodshed.* New York: Plenum Press.

What is the impact of hate crimes on the victims?

A crime is not simply a crime. Researchers have found that the experience of a serious hate crime has more severe psychological ramifications for the victim than a random crime of similar severity. Victims of hate crimes manifest higher levels of depression, stress, and anger than victims of a random crime. The negative effects of hate crimes are also longer lasting than those of other crimes.

What is the impact of hate crimes on the community?

Crimes are more socially disruptive and harmful when motivated by bigotry. Hate crimes are message crimes, in that the perpetrator is sending a message to members of a certain group that they are despised or unwelcome in a particular neighborhood, community, school, or workplace. Hate crimes serve as a form of intimidation not only for the victim but for all members of the targeted group.

How widespread are hate crimes?

Hate crimes based on sexual orientation are underreported, yet the number of hate crimes that are reported already suggests a disturbing level of bias-motivated violence against gays and lesbians. According to research with more than 2,000 gay, lesbian, and bisexual respondents, one in five women and one in four men has experienced an antigay hate crime since age 16. Crimes included physical and sexual assaults, attempted assaults, robberies, thefts, vandalism, and assault with a weapon.

What are the costs of hate crimes?

The increased enduring psychological stress of experiencing a hate crime may lead to increased financial costs for the individual or employer:

- *Health costs.* People are more likely to seek out and use mental health and physical health services after a traumatic event and during periods of great distress.
- *Work performance.* Certain types of hate crimes most commonly occur in public places, such as the workplace and schools. Hate crimes occurring in these environments may threaten the victim's sense of safety and in turn may affect work and school performance (for example, lower performance and greater absenteeism).

How often are hate crimes reported?

Research shows that hate crimes are less likely to be reported to the police than random crimes; overall, hate crimes are greatly underreported.

Why are hate crimes underreported?

Hate crimes are not only an attack on the individual. They are also an attack on that individual's community. As a result, hate crimes serve to threaten entire communities and fill them with fear. Fear plays a role in hate crimes reporting. More severe forms of hate crimes are less likely to be reported to the police. Researchers have concluded that this lack of reporting is due, in part, to the victim's fear that the perpetrators will seek revenge. Furthermore, the underreporting of hate crimes may be the result of a perception or concern that police agencies are biased against the group to which the victim belongs and will not be responsive to the incident.

---

* The material presented here is discussed in greater detail in *Everyday Activism: A Handbook for Lesbian, Gay, and Bisexual People and Their Allies*, edited by Michael R. Stevenson, Ph.D., and Jeanine C. Cogan, Ph.D., and published by Routledge in 2003.

CHAPTER 5

ending employment discrimination

David C. Sobelsohn

In this chapter, you will

- *Get the facts on job discrimination based on sexual orientation—it's legal!*
- *Learn the costs of job discrimination for LGBs and all Americans.*
- *Discover the available options if you have been discriminated against on the job.*
- *Be able to argue against claims regarding administrative costs, public health, and morality.*
- *Learn how you can help end job discrimination based on sexual orientation.*

A well-respected cook is abruptly dismissed. Her company explains that it will no longer employ lesbians. A married heterosexual can't get a teaching job. The principal thinks he has "homosexual tendencies." A black postal worker suffers verbal and physical harassment from bigoted co-workers. But they've targeted his sexual orientation, not his ethnicity. So his supervisors refuse to intervene.[1]

Cases like these hurt those directly involved as well as the overall economy. Furthermore, the majority of Americans support equal employment rights regardless of sexual orientation. Yet in most of the United States, the law makes job discrimination[2] based on sexual orientation *perfectly legal*. This chapter explains how this came to be true and what you can do to help change the law.

costs of discrimination

Job discrimination based on sexual orientation has profound effects both for its immediate victims and our entire economy. Like the majority of straight

Box 5.1

EXAMPLES OF EMPLOYMENT DISCRIMINATION

- From 1980 to 1984, Ernest Dillon worked quietly and without incident for the U.S. Postal Service in Allen Park, Michigan. Then, in 1984, another employee began to harass him, shouting out "fag" and obscene remarks when Dillon passed by. Dillon's supervisor refused to intervene. Eventually his harasser cornered Dillon and beat him unconscious. Although Dillon's attacker was fired, other employees kept up the harassment. Again management refused to intervene. Eventually, Dillon suffered an emotional breakdown. Under instructions from a therapist, he left work.
- In 1988 Vernon Jantz, a married heterosexual and father of two, applied for a job as a teacher and coach at a high school in Wichita, Kansas. The department director recommended Jantz for the job. But the principal's secretary told him Jantz reminded her of her ex-husband, who she thought was gay. So the principal hired someone else, explaining that he rejected Jantz because of his "homosexual tendencies."
- For 3 years, Cheryl Summerville worked as a cook at a Cracker Barrel restaurant in Douglasville, Georgia. She did her job well and her co-workers liked her. But in 1991, the company adopted a policy refusing to employ anyone "whose sexual preferences fail to demonstrate normal heterosexual values." Summerville's separation notice reads: "This employee is being terminated due to violation of company policy. The employee is gay." After her dismissal, Summerville had to take odd jobs and had problems making mortgage payments.
- In 1993 Jeffrey Blain started work at Golden State Container, a Phoenix-area manufacturer. In a few months he had earned a 37.5 percent raise and transfer to a new division. But his new supervisor spread rumors about Blain's sexual orientation. After Blain complained to Golden State's vice president, he was fired; the vice president explained only that Blain was "a fish out of water." Blain sued Golden State for wrongful discharge. But the court ruled "an employee is not wrongfully terminated if he is fired for being homosexual." Blain lost his case.[3]

Americans, most LGB Americans rely on their jobs for income to purchase necessities such as food, clothing, and shelter. Job discrimination also has serious psychological ramifications for LGBs. Experiences that reinforce a group's minority status can cause members of that group psychological harm.[4] Outside the workplace, gay men and lesbians, at least in large urban areas, can retreat to enclaves where their sexual orientation is the norm—such as bookstores, restaurants, and even whole neighborhoods. By contrast, nearly all workplaces have heterosexuality as the norm.

The need for a job, and the likelihood of minority status at work, affects all minorities. But job discrimination has unique effects on LGB employees.[5] Members of racial, ethnic, or religious minorities usually grow up in families with the same background. A sense of belonging, rooted in their upbringing, can sustain members of other minority groups in situations that reinforce their minority status. But lesbians and gay men typically grow up in predominantly heterosexual families and attend predominantly heterosexual schools, thus spending their formative years in relative isolation. As a result, discrimination in the workplace—the one place already almost certain to reinforce their outsider status—can cause unique psychological damage to gay men and lesbians.[6]

How extensive is job bias against LGB Americans? Answering this question with precision poses formidable challenges. Discovery of their sexual orientation can cost LGBs their jobs. For example, in one survey, 18 to 27 percent of employers admitted they would discriminate against a homosexual employee. Consequently, to protect themselves, many LGBs keep their orientation secret—even on anonymous surveys.[7] In addition, many victims of discrimination never learn the reasons for adverse actions taken against them. Still others may avoid claiming discrimination for fear of branding as a troublemaker. Taken together, these difficulties suggest that the available estimates understate the extent of job discrimination.

Surveys of the LGB workforce from the 1970s through the 1990s are consistent with the employer survey. In two early studies,[8] one fourth of all lesbians and nearly one third of all gay men reported incidents of job discrimination; 17 percent of all gay men reported lost jobs or rejected job applications. In two surveys from the early 1990s,[9] 37 percent of LBG graduates of the Harvard Business School and 26 percent of LGB student-affairs professionals reported having suffered job discrimination because of their sexual orientation. A synopsis of 20 different community-based surveys from 1980 to 1991 found that 16 to 44 percent of lesbian and gay workers reported having experienced some form of job discrimination because of sexual orientation.[10] A 1997 study of the general gay and lesbian community revealed that 14 percent had experienced job discrimination in the last year alone.[11]

Other studies demonstrate the effect of this discrimination on LGBs. Research has found significant associations between workplace discrimination and psychological damage, including damage accompanied by health-related problems such as severe headaches, exhaustion, and even ulcers.[12] In addition, a study of gay men suggests that fear of discovery drives them to enter occupations known for tolerance, at the expense of full use of their abilities and training.[13]

Underemployment and psychological stress take their toll on productivity. Gays and lesbians who hide their sexual orientation at work suffer in job performance, including reduced job satisfaction and organizational commitment.[14] Those gays and lesbians who suffer workplace discrimination have decreased job satisfaction, higher levels of lateness and absenteeism, and greater desire to quit.[15]

Not surprisingly, discrimination has serious economic effects. Census data show that, controlling for education, location, race, age, disability, and number of children, men with male partners had 26 percent lower incomes than married heterosexual men.[16] Controlling for the same variables, female same-sex couples had 18 to 20 percent lower incomes than heterosexual married couples.[17] Lee Badgett's groundbreaking 1995 study demonstrates that full-time working gay men earned 11 to 27 percent less than full-time working heterosexual men.[18] In addition, partnered gays and lesbians have significantly lower rates of home ownership than do married heterosexuals.[19]

Estimates of the percentage of gay men, lesbians, and bisexuals in the United States range from 1.3 to 12 percent, with most estimates between 3 and 6 percent.[20] Even accepting some of the lower estimates, and even assuming that only a portion of the income and wealth disparity results from discrimination, simple arithmetic indicates that, in a multitrillion-dollar economy, job discrimination based on sexual orientation costs billions of dollars each year. Simply put, a business whose employees feel safe from discrimination will have more productive workers. And a state or municipality whose workforce feels safe from discrimination will have a more productive, more affluent workforce.

public opinion and public ignorance

A substantial majority of the American public seems to understand the damage caused by job discrimination based on sexual orientation. In a national poll, 83 percent agreed that "gays should have equal rights in employment."[21] Yet the law clearly permits such discrimination. Why?

A partial explanation lies in widespread public ignorance of a basic principle of American labor law. Labor law started as part of the law of contracts. American contract law traces its origins to the law of England before American independence.[22] At first the province of English kings, disputes were eventually decided in Britain by judges with special training.[23]

Upon winning independence from England, American courts continued the British tradition of using judge-made law to resolve private disputes not covered by state or federal legislation.[24]

With the 19th century and the Industrial Revolution, an increasing percentage of legal disputes involved employment contracts, particularly their duration and the type of cause and notice required for termination. In 1877 an influential legal treatise declared the American rule "inflexible": either party to a employment contract, unless that contract expressly included specific protections, could dissolve their relationship at any time for any reason. This principle, the doctrine of employment-at-will, swept the United States until it was generally adopted.[25] It permits employees to quit whenever they like, without giving a reason. But it also permits employers to fire employees on the same basis.[26] So, for example, employers can fire workers for their taste in movies, the color of their eyes, or their political opinions.[27] Congress and nearly all the state legislatures have never overturned the employment-at-will doctrine.[28] As a result, the doctrine, for the most part, represents the state of American law today.

Most Americans do not realize their lack of job protection. Nearly two thirds of American workers think their employers cannot legally fire them without a "good reason."[29] Only one of four Americans knows that current federal law makes it legal to fire a worker just because he or she is gay or lesbian.[30] General ignorance of the law lends weight to the slogan often used to fight proposed antidiscrimination laws: "No Special Rights."[31] The slogan makes sense only on the false premise that workers already have the right to keep their jobs absent something related to job performance. If one misunderstands the law, and imagines that LGB workers already have some degree of protection,[32] agitation for an antidiscrimination law looks like an appeal for special status.[33]

Widespread public ignorance of the law on this issue probably results in part from widespread knowledge of contexts in which employees do have some job security.[34] First, the employment-at-will doctrine permits employers and employees to modify their rights by contract.[35] Some 16 percent of the American workforce has done just that through collective-bargaining agreements.[36] These agreements typically limit the grounds for firing union members to "just cause."[37] But just cause may or may not include sexual orientation,[38] and collective-bargaining agreements typically do not cover supervisory or managerial employees.[39]

Beyond express contractual provisions, some courts have found employer personnel codes to provide binding protection for employees.[40] But not all American workers have the protection of a personnel code covering sexual orientation; and even for those who do, many courts have yet to find personnel codes contractually binding.[41]

Finally, as with all common law, the doctrine of employment-at-will operates only in the absence of legislation. Both federal and state statutes limit the grounds on which employers can make employment decisions. On the federal level, the 1964 Civil Rights Act prohibits job discrimination based on race, color, sex, religion, or national origin. The 1990 Americans with Disabilities Act (ADA) limits employers' freedom to discriminate against individuals with disabilities.

The ADA expressly excludes sexual orientation from its coverage.[42] But one could make a compelling logical argument that the 1964 Civil Rights Act's ban on gender discrimination also outlaws discrimination based on sexual orientation. Discrimination based on the sex of a person's romantic interests is still discrimination based on sex.[43] In an analogous case, a federal court ruled that it violated a federal law against racial discrimination for an employer to discriminate based on the race of a job applicant's wife (the applicant was white, his wife black).[44] Similarly, it should violate federal law to discriminate based on the sex of a job applicant's partner. Nevertheless, federal courts have repeatedly refused to construe the 1964 Civil Rights Act to cover discrimination based on sexual orientation.[45]

Since 1972, when East Lansing, Michigan, became the first jurisdiction in the United States to enact a gay rights law, state and local governments have increasingly filled the gap left by the lack of federal legislation.[46] Slightly over one third of America's population now lives in towns, cities, counties, or states with statutes or ordinances that ban sexual orientation discrimination in both private and government employment.[47] These include 12 states (see Box 5.2), 100 cities, 18 counties, and the District of Columbia.[48] An additional 10 states (see Box 5.2), 41 cities, 18 counties, and the federal government have executive orders or administrative regulations covering government employment.[49] The U.S. Constitution also provides government workers some protection against job discrimination.[50] The proposed federal Employment Non-Discrimination Act (ENDA) would extend those protections to workers in the private sector (see Box 5.3).[51]

But executive orders and administrative regulations depend on support from each new administration. For example, in 1999 Ohio governor Robert Taft III (R) compelled the removal of sexual orientation from a long-standing antidiscrimination executive order.[52] A future U.S. president could unilaterally withdraw the current executive order banning sexual-orientation discrimination in federal agencies.[53] And executive orders, as well as the U.S. Constitution, only provide protection for government workers.[54] More than 96 percent of the American labor force works in private industry.[55] As a result, two thirds of the American workforce remains unprotected from job discrimination based on sexual orientation—despite widespread belief to the contrary.

The common misconception that current law already requires equal employment opportunities, combined with overwhelming opposition among Americans to job discrimination, points to a clear strategy for enacting job discrimination laws. Activists must educate legislators, legislative staff, and the general public about the incidence of job discrimination and the true state of the law. The Human Rights Campaign, through its Documenting Discrimination project, has identified exam-

Box 5.2

STATE PROTECTION AGAINST SEXUAL ORIENTATION JOB DISCRIMINATION

States That Ban Sexual Orientation Job Discrimination in Both Private and Government Employment

California	Massachusetts	New Jersey
Connecticut	Minnesota	Rhode Island
District of Columbia	Nevada	Vermont
Hawaii	New Hampshire	Wisconsin
Maryland		

States That Protect Only Public Employees From Sexual Orientation Job Discrimination

Colorado	Maryland	New York
Delaware	Montana	Pennsylvania
Indiana	New Mexico	Washington
Iowa		

ples of job discrimination around the country. Some of those cases, including three of the four summarized in Box 5.1, went to court, only for the court to dismiss them as having no basis in law.[56] The more such cases come to light, the greater the public awareness of the inadequacies of current law and the need for reform. When communicating with legislators and legislative staff, the more an activist can publicize cases in a legislator's own district, the more that legislative office will realize the impact of job discrimination based on sexual orientation.

costs of protection

Opponents of job discrimination laws typically make two types of empirical arguments.[57] First, they claim such a law will bring little benefit, because job discrimination based on sexual orientation takes place so seldom and because it already violates current law.[58] Earlier sections of this chapter considered these arguments and showed the costs of job discrimination and the inadequacy of current law. Opponents also argue that a job discrimination law will bring substantial costs.[59] These threatened costs fall into three general categories: administrative, health, and moral.

Box 5.3

THE EMPLOYMENT NON-DISCRIMINATION ACT OF 2001[60]

Under current law in 38 states, workers can lose their jobs simply because they are gay or lesbian. Twelve states prohibit job discrimination based on sexual orientation (see Box 5.2). Most of these state laws prohibit private sector and government employers, employment agencies, and labor unions from discriminating based on sexual orientation in hiring, firing, promoting, or compensating employees. Although these laws provide important protections, a 2000 Government Accounting Office report reveals they have not generated significant litigation.

The proposed federal Employment Non-Discrimination Act (ENDA) would prohibit private sector and government employers, employment agencies, and labor unions from discriminating, based on sexual orientation, in hiring, firing, promotion, or compensation. It explicitly prohibits preferential treatment and quotas. In addition, it exempts small businesses, religious organizations, and the military, and it does not require benefits for the same-sex partners of employees. A civil rights bill covering sexual orientation has been introduced in every session of the U.S. Congress since 1974. ENDA was first introduced on June 23, 1994.

ENDA has diverse, bipartisan support in Congress. The 2001 Senate bill's lead cosponsors were Sens. Edward M. Kennedy (D-Mass.), Arlen Specter (R-Pa.), Joseph Lieberman (D-Conn.), and James Jeffords (I-Vt.), In the House, the lead co-sponsors were Reps. Christopher Shays (R-Conn.), Mark Foley (R-Fla.), Barney Frank (D-Mass.), and Ellen Tauscher (D-Calif.).

ENDA also enjoys strong support from the general public and corporate America. According to a 2001 Gallup study, 85 percent of Americans believe gay and lesbian people should have equal job opportunities. A 2001 Harris Poll found that 58–61 percent of Americans favor a federal law banning job discrimination based on sexual orientation. The same poll revealed that only 25 percent realize no such law exists. Well over half of the Fortune 500 companies have implemented nondiscrimination policies that include sexual orientation, and 59 corporations and small businesses have explicitly endorsed ENDA.

Administrative

An antidiscrimination law could bring two types of administrative costs: preventive costs and remedial costs.[61] Preventive costs include, for example, retraining of workplace-diversity staff and the loss of productive but heterosexist employees.

A large portion of the general public still holds negative attitudes toward lesbians and gay men. At work, these attitudes are manifested in a range of behaviors, from verbal slurs (such as "fag" and "dyke" jokes) to violence. Just as avoiding liability under the 1964 Civil Rights Act means employers must make efforts to combat workplace harassment based on race and sex, so employers would have similar responsibilities under a job bias law covering sexual orientation.

Critics expressed analogous concerns about the costs of the Americans With Disabilities Act, which requires employers to make "reasonable accommodation" for workers with disabilities. They warned that accommodation costs would be "onerous" and "overwhelming," especially for smaller businesses.[62]

It hasn't turned out that way. As a 1995 study indicates, the average cost of accommodation has proved less than $1,000, with $200 more typical. Accommodation has actually saved employers an average of $10,000 in increased productivity and reduced costs of workers' compensation, other insurance, and finding and training new employees.[63] For the same reason, employers will likely see a net savings from elimination of sexual orientation discrimination in the workplace—without having to make any structural changes.

Remedial costs represent a second category of potential costs of an anti-discrimination law. Remedial costs include increased budgets for civil rights agencies and courts, and increased litigation costs for employers, all forced to deal with a new category of complaints. In 1996 Senate opponents claimed that ENDA "virtually guarantees an avalanche of costly litigation."[64] One opponent of the Massachusetts gay rights bill predicted: "We spend a million dollars a year now at the MCAD [Massachusetts Commission Against Discrimination]. If we have to deal with fags and lesbos [*sic*], you can bet we'll be spending ten million dollars a year."[65]

As with preventive costs, opponents of the American with Disabilities Act voiced similar concerns about remedial costs.[66] Again, these concerns have proved groundless.[67] With both the Justice Department and the federal Equal Employment Opportunity Commission stressing education and conciliation, the ADA's first 5 years saw only 650 lawsuits filed nationwide.[68]

As under the ADA, under a sexual orientation job bias law compliance and conciliation will likely keep litigation to a minimum. Moreover, one can expect proportionally less litigation about sexual orientation discrimination than about discrimination on other, more visible traits. Filing a sexual orientation complaint requires complainants to publicly disclose their orientation. Even under a job bias law, the requirement of public disclosure will keep many potential plaintiffs in the closet and out of court.[69] For many LGBs, the risk will remain too great—especially in jurisdictions with no protection against discrimination in other areas such as housing, education, and public accommodations.[70]

Indeed, the results under existing state laws demonstrate the fallacy of fearing a flood of litigation from a job bias law. In the first 4 years of the comprehensive Vermont antidiscrimination law,[71] the state attorney general initiated only 14 investigations; 7 were closed for inadequate evidence or unrelated administrative reasons, 1 was settled, and 6 remained pending as of late 1996.[72] Other states have had a similar experience.[73] For example, in 1999, of all pending job discrimination lawsuits in California, sexual orientation complaints made up less than 1 percent. New Hampshire that year saw only eight cases filed.[74] On the local level, in a study of 65 cities and counties with regulations covering sexual orientation government-job discrimination, less than a third reported even one complaint or grievance based on sexual orientation.[75] Clearly, concerns about the costs of administering a sexual orientation job-discrimination law have been greatly exaggerated, which is partly why ENDA was defeated when it came to the Senate floor for a vote (see Box 5.4 for the voting record)!

Health

Opponents of the comprehensive Massachusetts gay rights law[76] made two arguments related to public health. First, they argued that civil rights protection for gay men and lesbians would increase the spread of AIDS and HIV. In the mid-1980s, this argument succeeded in delaying enactment of the Massachusetts gay rights law for at least one legislative session. Second, opponents raised the hobgoblin of sexual abuse of children.[77] Activists may still hear these claims in the context of a proposed job discrimination law.[78] Neither has any basis in reality.

Medical science has known for well over a decade that those infected with HIV cannot transmit the virus through the kind of casual contact common among co-workers. Even in work environments such as hospitals or emergency medical teams that might expose co-workers to infected blood, the risk of transmission is tiny. With most HIV cases now occurring among heterosexuals, AIDS has become an increasingly irrational basis for antigay discrimination.[79]

False accusations of child sexual abuse have haunted stigmatized groups throughout history; LGBs share this smear with Catholics, Jews, and African Americans.[80] Studies have shown repeatedly the lack of evidence for this accusation.[81] Most cases of child sexual abuse involve heterosexuals, and gay men do not perpetrate this crime at any higher rate than do straight men.[82] The frequency of sexual activity between lesbians and children approaches zero.[83]

Box 5.4

HOW SENATORS VOTED ON THE EMPLOYMENT NON-DISCRIMINATION ACT

YEAS—49		NAYS—50	
Akaka	Kennedy	Abraham	Helms
Baucus	Kerrey	Ashcroft	Hutchison
Biden	Kerry	Bennett	Inhofe
Bingaman	Kohl	Bond	Kassebaum
Boxer	Lautenberg	Brown	Kempthorne
Bradley	Leahy	Burns	Kyl
Breaux	Levin	Byrd	Lott
Bryan	Lieberman	Campbell	Lugar
Bumpers	Mikulski	Coats	Mack
Chafee	Moseley-Braun	Cochran	McCain
Cohen	Moynihan	Coverdell	McConnell
Conrad	Murray	Craig	Murkowski
D'Amato	Pell	DeWine	Nickles
Daschle	Reid	Domenici	Nunn
Dodd	Robb	Exon	Pressler
Dorgan	Rockefeller	Faircloth	Roth
Feingold	Sarbanes	Ford	Santorum
Feinstein	Simon	Frahm	Shelby
Glenn	Simpson	Frist	Smith
Graham	Snowe	Gorton	Stevens
Harkin	Specter	Gramm	Thomas
Hatfield	Wellstone	Grams	Thompson
Hollings	Wyden	Grassley	Thurmond
Inouye		Gregg	Warner
Jeffords		Hatch	NOT VOTING—1
Johnston		Heflin	Pryor

Moral

At the core of opposition to protecting LGBs under a job discrimination law lies the claim that such a law would encourage behavior many people consider immoral.[84] Surveys on the morality of behavior commonly associated with homosexuality vary in their wording.[85] Still, for well over a quarter century, half or more of the U.S. adult public has agreed that "sexual relations between two adults of the same sex" are "always wrong."[86] Various polls put the current figure at between 46 and 59 percent.[87]

Opponents argue that a job bias law could increase the incidence of same-sex sexual or romantic behavior in several related ways. First, law expresses a society's values, and so has great symbolic power. Protection from discrimination based on sexual orientation will inevitably affect our culture. On this point supporters and opponents agree. By removing sexual orientation from the legally permissible criteria for employment decisions, a job bias law suggests the moral irrelevance of sexual orientation in a major area of daily life.[88] More concretely, job bias protection would reduce the costs of a same-sex sexual or romantic relationship. It could thus increase the number of people willing to form such relationships.[89] Finally, a job bias law would reduce the risk to LGBs of revealing their sexual orientation at work. So, opponents conclude that, when that work involves children, knowledge of the homosexuality or bisexuality of an adult in a leadership or mentoring position could inspire same-sex sexual behavior among the children.[90]

This differs from the claim that gay teachers will molest students. Rather than assume any direct sexual contact between adults and children, this argument stresses adults' power as role models. For example, Senator Hatch on the floor of the U.S. Senate repeatedly warned that the proposed federal Employment Non-Discrimination Act (ENDA) would require schools to respond equally to public displays of physical affection for their romantic partners by gay and straight teachers.[91] Under ENDA, a school would have no power to fire a male teacher for kissing his boyfriend in sight of his students—unless the school would also fire a male teacher for kissing his girlfriend in the same situation.[92] Senator Ashcroft expressed alarm at the effect on adolescents just beginning to experience feelings of sexual attraction, "unsure of themselves when they are in transition."[93]

To refute the moral argument, one must first clarify it. The argument just outlined stresses behavior. It has, as its premises, the immorality of same-sex sexual or romantic behavior, and the prediction that such behavior would increase under a job bias law covering sexual orientation.

Opponents sometimes seem to make a different argument, one about identity. Its premises are the inherent immorality of LGB people[94] and the prediction that the incidence of homosexual or bisexual orientation would increase under a job discrimination law.[95]

It is important to separate these two arguments: one claims immoral behavior, the other immoral identity. An effective response depends on the argument. Not surprisingly, LGB rights opponents often conflate the two. For example, on the floor of the U.S. Senate, opponents claimed that the proposed Employment Non-Discrimination Act—a bill drafted in terms of sexual orientation—really protects sexual conduct.[96] This claim assumes sexual orientation means what a person does, not who he or she is.[97]

But research demonstrates the difference between sexual orientation and sexual behavior.[98] The word *orientation* comes from the verb *orient*, which originally meant "cause to face or point toward the east," and now means "set or arrange in any determinate position." Accordingly, *orientation* means "alignment" or "direction."[99] It is the way something points, not where it goes. A compass may point north yet remain stationary. Thus, rather than a pattern of behavior, *sexual orientation* means a direction or proclivity—not action but attraction—toward people of a particular gender.

A major study of sexual behavior and sexual identity highlights the discontinuity. Researchers interviewed a carefully constructed representative sample of 3,432 American men. Over 9 percent had engaged in same-sex sexual activity at least once since puberty. But less than one third of those—only 2.8 percent— identified themselves as gay or bisexual.[100] Thus, engaging in same-sex sexual behavior does not necessarily mean one identifies as having same-sex sexual orientation. Likewise, identifying as gay or bisexual can have little bearing on one's sexual practices. As with heterosexual relationships, even intimate same-sex relationships do not always include sex.[101] A man can identify as gay or bisexual and not have sex with other men.

By covering only sexual orientation, job bias laws actually ignore sexual behavior and focus on attraction or inclination. Moreover, in covering orientation rather than any particular behavior, these laws protect heterosexuals,[102] despite perceived differences between heterosexual and homosexual behavior.

Once one separates the two morality-based arguments into "immoral identity" and "immoral behavior," one can develop effective responses to each. Social science readily refutes each premise of the immoral identity argument.

First, the notion that sexual orientation by itself has moral implications flies in the face of both traditional western ethical standards and repeated studies of sexual orientation.[103] In western ethical tradition, involuntary acts have no moral status. Moral sanction requires choice.[104] Americans intuitively understand this: Those who believe people are "born with" their sexual orientations tend to express greater support for lesbian and gay rights.[105] Conversely, dislike of gay men and lesbians rises among those who believe that sexual orientation is learned or chosen.[106] Science has yet to determine the origins of sexual orientation. But research demonstrates that sexual orientations are not arbitrarily chosen.[107] Without choice, sexual orientation by itself should not trigger moral condemnation.

The foregoing analysis may help explain the correlation between positive attitudes toward LGBs and awareness that one has a lesbian or gay acquaintance, friend, co-worker, or relative.[108] Perhaps knowledge of a particular friend or relative's homosexuality brings home the disconnect between sexual orientation and moral behavior, or between sexual orientation and personal choice.[109] Perhaps, too, knowing a gay man or lesbian shows a heterosexual that sexual orientation makes up only a part of who people are. The successful efforts to enact gay rights laws in Massachusetts and Hawaii rested, in part, on convincing heterosexual lawmakers that, in every relevant way, LGBs live lives identical to those of heterosexuals.[110]

Even assuming the immorality of certain sexual orientations, and even assuming that a job bias law would increase, for instance, the number of children taught by an openly gay teacher, such a law would have no effect on the percentage of people identifying as LGB. Same-sex attraction does not result from the known proximity of a gay or lesbian adult. Study after study shows that the sexual orientation of the most important role models in a child's life—his or her parents—has no effect on the child's orientation.[111] In supporting the right of California's gay teachers to keep their jobs, former president Ronald Reagan put the point succinctly: "Whatever else it is, homosexuality is not a contagious disease like the measles."[112]

On the morality of homosexual behavior, opinion surveys provide reason for hope. Over time, the percentage disapproving of same-sex romance has dropped, slightly in some studies, sharply in others.[113] And the next generation—those now 18 to 29—have an even less negative attitude.[114] A time may soon arrive when a majority of Americans reject any link between morality and sexual orientation.[115]

In general, however, direct attempts to change people's moral views on same-sex romance will prove unsuccessful. They are also unnecessary.[116] People who express moral disapproval of lesbians, gay men, and bisexuals can also support legal protections. For example, a coalition of clergy, including the head of Honolulu's Roman Catholic diocese, helped secure enactment of Hawaii's job bias law. Consistent majorities simultaneously find homosexuality immoral and support equal employment rights.[117] Moreover, the minority who see sexual orientation as morally neutral tend not to oppose a job bias law. Enacting such a law requires the support of at least some of the majority that considers same-sex sexuality immoral.

For those who consider same-sex sexual activity immoral, one can argue, as did advocates in Massachusetts, that an antidiscrimination law has minimal potential for increasing the number of same-sex sexual relationships. After all, the law protects identity rather than behavior.

But suppose one assumes that a job bias law will somewhat increase same-sex experimentation by people primarily heterosexual, or public displays of same-sex affection by LGBs, or both. A hate crimes law, by deterring violence against real or perceived gays and lesbians, could have the same effect.[118] In each case, legislators must weigh the costs of documented discrimination and violence against a speculative increase in behavior thought sexually immoral.

This way of looking at things helped persuade enough undecided legislators to enact the Massachusetts gay rights law.[119] It has also persuaded a majority of the American public to support the hiring of gay and lesbian elementary school teachers.[120] Americans recognize that quality education for our children and basic fairness for teachers matters more than the negligible risk that an LGB teacher will inspire his or her students to be gay. It is simply more important to combat discrimination based on a trait people cannot control, and that has no relation to their abilities, than to avoid the speculative risk of a slight increase in behavior some people find immoral.

what you can do!

- Report job discrimination to elected officials and to the Human Rights Campaign.
- Add your story to the Human Rights Campaign project Documenting Discrimination. Call 202–628–4160 or fill out the form at www.hrc.org/cgiforms/report/ddform.asp.
- Urge elected officials to support legislation that will end employment discrimination. Letters, telephone calls, and especially personal conversations have impact. Call the legislator's office, voice your support for antidiscrimination legislation, and ask when you can meet your representative.
  - Ask members of Congress to support the Employment Non-Discrimination Act.
  - Urge your state and local legislators to support state and local job bias laws.
  - Make sure your representatives know the true state of the law.
  - Do the same with candidates for local, state, and federal office.
  - Attach a copy of *Why We Need Legislation Prohibiting Employment Discrimination Based on Sexual Orientation* to your letter.
- Volunteer for the campaigns of candidates who support ENDA or a state or local job bias law. Box 5.4 shows how senators voted on ENDA. Above all, register and vote.

- When you read a newspaper or magazine article about antigay discrimination, write a letter to the editor. Use the material in this chapter to explain why we need a job bias law. Letters get printed—even if they disagree with the publication's point of view.
- Advocate with your employer.
  - Ask that your company join the dozens of companies that have publicly expressed support for ENDA.
  - Contact the human resources department. Ask if your personnel policy includes an antidiscrimination provision covering sexual orientation. If it doesn't, ask why.
- Advocate with your union.
  - Ask if your collective-bargaining agreement includes an antidiscrimination provision covering sexual orientation. If it doesn't, ask why.
  - Remind them that the AFL-CIO strongly opposes job discrimination based on sexual orientation.
- Join the national organizations working to protect LGBs from job discrimination:
  - The Human Rights Campaign, 202–628–4160, www.hrc.org;
  - The National Gay and Lesbian Task Force, 202–332–6483, www.ngltf.org; and
  - The Lambda Legal Defense and Education Fund, 212–809–8585, www.lambdalegal.org
  - Join your state LGB rights organization. Contact the National Gay and Lesbian Task Force for a complete list.
- Spread the word. Only one of every four Americans understands that the law does not protect LGBs from discrimination.
- Come out. If you are gay, lesbian, or bisexual, let people know, especially (if you feel safe) at work. Support for job bias laws increases among people who know they have a lesbian or gay acquaintance, friend, co-worker, or relative.

for more information

- Badgett, L. (1997). Vulnerability in the workplace: Evidence of anti-gay discrimination. *Angles, 2*(1). Available at www.iglss.org
- Badgett, M. V. L. (2001). *Money, myths, and change: The economic lives of lesbians and gay men.* Chicago: University of Chicago Press.
- *Employment discrimination against gays and lesbians: Employment Non-Discrimination Act (ENDA).* http://www.religioustolerance.org/hom_empl2.htm

WHY WE NEED LEGISLATION PROHIBITING EMPLOYMENT DISCRIMINATION BASED ON SEXUAL ORIENTATION*

Employment discrimination is a common occurrence.
Discrimination based on sexual orientation is widespread. Surveys report that 6 to 44 percent of lesbian and gay workers have experienced some form of job discrimination.

Currently, employment discrimination based on sexual orientation is legal.
Federal law prohibits job discrimination based on age, disability, race, color, sex, religion, and national origin. Federal law permits job discrimination based on sexual orientation. Some states have laws against such discrimination. Most do not. Two thirds of the U.S. workforce could lose their jobs simply because of their sexual orientation.

Workplace discrimination hurts employees and costs money.
Job discrimination based on sexual orientation results in psychological and physical damage. Gay men and lesbians who suffer workplace discrimination report health-related problems—such as severe headaches, ulcers, and exhaustion—decreased job satisfaction, higher rates of lateness and absenteeism, and greater desire to quit. These effects of discrimination reduce productivity and cost employers money.

Most Americans support protections against workplace discrimination.
In a 2000 poll, 83 percent agreed that "gays should have equal rights in employment." This percentage has remained consistently high over the years, with 83 percent supporting employment nondiscrimination in 1998, 85 percent in 1996.

Employment nondiscrimination laws are not costly.
States with job discrimination laws have not faced a flood of lawsuits. In the first 4 years of Vermont's law, the state attorney general initiated only 14 investigations and pursued only 7. In 1999, of all pending job discrimination lawsuits in California, sexual orientation complaints made up less than 1 percent.

Job discrimination based on sexual orientation has enormous costs for individuals, communities, and society. It should be illegal.

---

* The material presented here is discussed in greater detail in *Everyday Activism: A Handbook for Lesbian, Gay, and Bisexual People and Their Allies*, edited by Michael R. Stevenson, Ph.D., and Jeanine C. Cogan, Ph.D., and published by Routledge in 2003.

- Friskopp, A., & Silverstein, S. (1996). *Straight jobs, gay lives: Gay and lesbian professionals, the Harvard Business School, and the American workplace.* New York: Touchstone.
- General Accounting Office. (2000, April 28). *Sexual-orientation-based employment discrimination: States' experience with statutory prohibitions since 1997* (GAO/OGC-00-27R). Washington, DC: Author.
- Gore, S. (2000). The lesbian and gay workplace: An employee's guide to advancing equity. In B. Greene & G. L. Croom (Eds.), *Education, research, and practice in lesbian, gay, bisexual, and transgendered psychology: A resource manual* (pp. 282–302). Thousand Oaks, CA: Sage.
- Human Rights Campaign. (2001). Documenting discrimination. Washington, DC: Human Rights Campaign. Available at www.hrc.org/publications/pdf/docdis.pdf
- Laumann, E. O., Gagnon, J. H., Michael, R. T., & Michaels, S. (1994). *The social organization of sexuality: Sexual practices in the United States.* Chicago: University of Chicago Press.
- National Gay and Lesbian Task Force Policy Institute. (2000). *Legislating equality: A review of laws affecting gay, lesbian, bisexual, and transgendered people in the United States.* Available at www.ngltf.org
- Stein, E. (2001). *The mismeasure of desire: The science, theory, and ethics of sexual orientation.* New York: Oxford University Press.
- *The Employment Non-Discrimination Act of 2001, H.R. 2692 & S. 1284.* Available at thomas.loc.gov/ or from your senator or representative.
- Yang, A. (1998). *From wrongs to rights: Public opinion on gay and lesbian Americans move toward equality* (NGLTF Policy Institute, May 29, 1998). Available at www.ngltf.org

obtaining and maintaining housing

Christopher J. Portelli

In this chapter, you will

- *Discover the discrimination LGBs face when attempting to rent or own a home.*
- *Learn what LGBs must do to jointly own a home with a domestic partner.*
- *Get the facts on retirement and housing issues for the aging LGB baby boomers.*
- *Learn about homelessness and the lack of adequate housing for LGB youth.*
- *Learn about the positive influence of LGB communities.*

Over the course of the last 30 years, gay men and lesbians have fought ignorance and intolerance in our efforts to create homes free from government intrusion, public acts of prejudice, and private forms of antigay harassment. The impact of HIV-related discrimination further compounded housing issues in the 1980s, as AIDS-phobic, heterosexist landlords sought to evict ill gay men and their caregivers from their homes.

Activists and legal scholars differ on whether the courts or the legislature should be the focus for change in the housing policy arena. A tension between judge-made law and legislation has developed within states where definitions of *family*, *spouse*, and *relationships* affect people's rights to rent, own, and occupy a home of their choice, with a person of their choice, and in a location of their choice. Still, both courts and legislatures have been slow to recognize the rights of lesbians and gays in the housing market.

Unfair housing practices in the real estate rental and sales markets constitute only part of the problem. Many housing discrimination disputes are a consequence of the lack of legal recognition of same-sex marriage. Same-sex couples and surviving partners are often discriminated against by landlords, brokers, realtors, co-op boards, homeowners' associations, and state, city, and county taxing authorities whose rules protect only legally married, widowed, or divorced heterosexual spouses from displacement after the death or departure of a partner. In addition, LGBs face unique housing issues when aging. The question of where to find gay-friendly retirement communities, nursing homes, and home care facilities is one that was raised only recently by the aging gays and lesbians of the baby boom generation.

Lack of housing—even homelessness—is also a growing issue for the lesbian and gay community as more and more urban centers swell with youth forced to leave their homes due to the rejection (or outright violence) of their families, friends, schools, and social service agencies when they disclosed their sexual orientation.

All of these issues have led public policy theorists to begin to develop the notion of "queer space" in society. The "gay" or "lesbian" neighborhood is not new, but the idea that it is a vital force that urban planners and urban policy analysts should harness and preserve is recent. Controversies surrounding this idea have developed, especially when the power of LGB space is revealed to be the power of community development, the power of political change, the power of individual expression (both sexual and otherwise), and the power of all persons who engage in nonconforming relationships, regardless of sexual orientation, to live their lives freely and openly. In this chapter, I will cover five issues related to housing for lesbians and gay men: discrimination in the rental and/or purchase of a home, joint home ownership for same-sex couples, retirement and aging issues related to housing, homelessness and young people, and current public policy theory and trends in housing and urban development.

discrimination

Discrimination in housing takes several forms. Some of the most common are

- A landlord, apartment broker, or realtor refuses to show an apartment, condominium, co-op, or home to an individual or same-sex couple if he or she suspects the prospective tenant or buyer is lesbian, gay, or bisexual.
- A landlord rejects the rental application of a same-sex couple based on his or her so-called religious objections to homosexuality.
- A landlord evicts the surviving partner of a same-sex couple because the lease contained only the name of the deceased partner.

Other factors may also contribute to discriminatory housing practices against LGBs. Some local zoning laws, for example, restrict the occupancy of living units in certain delineated geographic areas of towns and cities to persons who are related by blood, adoption, or marriage. This would prevent two or more students, a group of nonmarried professionals, or a same-sex couple from sharing a home in certain neighborhoods. The U.S. Supreme Court has held that these zoning laws are permissible for the most part under the U.S. Constitution.[1] State courts have dealt with instances of sexual orientation discrimination in housing in a variety of ways. Not all are in favor of the injured gay or lesbian tenant or home owner.

Some of the most favorable developments relating to housing laws and lesbian and gay individuals have come from the New York and California courts. This probably can be attributed to several factors. The housing markets in the urban areas of both states—particularly Manhattan and San Francisco—are extremely tight. Rents are high, and rent-controlled apartments are scarce. Both Manhattan and San Francisco boast large and visible lesbian and gay communities, and both cities were hard-hit with the first wave of HIV and AIDS cases among gay men in the early 1980s. These communities have since reestablished themselves as a source of political and legal power, but by no means do they represent the entire diversity of LGB communities. Legal and legislative frontiers carved by these places, however, continue to provide strength for arguments against discriminatory housing practices on the basis of sexual orientation.

The following section looks at the housing victories achieved through the courts and the regulatory and legislative processes of these states and cities.

Antigay Discrimination in Apartment Leases

In 1989, in a state case called *Braschi*, a gay man who resided in New York City with his same-sex partner in a rent-controlled apartment faced eviction when his partner died of AIDS-related complications. Only the deceased partner's name was on the lease. In a surprising reversal of earlier decisions, the New York Court of Appeals found that the provision in the New York rent control laws which protects families against sudden eviction should not be restricted to blood relatives or married heterosexual couples. The court held, instead, that in the context of eviction, a more realistic and equally valid view of a family includes "two adult lifetime partners whose relationship is long term and characterized by an emotional and financial commitment and interdependence." Because Braschi was able to show that he and his partner of 9 years met this definition of family, he was able to succeed his partner on the lease and keep his home. This case is hailed as a great victory for the LGB community, both in New York and in other localities where attempts are made to evict the surviving partner of a same-sex relationship. By citing the court's reasoning in this case by way of analogy to New York's housing laws, *Braschi* can be used to argue on behalf of a more realistic view of family. The *Braschi* decision supports the principle that a surviving partner of a same-sex couple has the same rights as a married different-sex couple under the law.[2]

Braschi originally applied only to rent-controlled apartments. Such apartments in New York number only about 100,000. The city has, however, more than a million rent-stabilized apartments. Despite failed attempts by some state legislators to overrule the *Braschi* case, the New York State Division of Housing and Community Renewal expanded the scope of the ruling. It adopted regulations codifying *Braschi* and applying its definition of family to rent-stabilized apartments as well.[3]

It is important to note that the *Braschi* decision did not overturn New York law allowing landlords and co-op boards to add clauses to leases limiting occupancy to persons who are related by blood, adoption, or marriage. Several other states have similar laws allowing these discriminatory practices.[4]

Student Housing and the Levin Case

Not all decisions since the *Braschi* case regarding housing have been favorable in New York courts. Legal scholars have since suggested that *Braschi* may represent the upper limit on the rights and privileges that state courts will recognize with respect to lesbian and gay families.[5] Ten years after the *Braschi* decision, at least one case has held that *Braschi* did not change the law in New York to the extent where it eliminated all instances where landlords may treat married and non-married couples differently. This case, *Levin v. Yeshiva University*, was brought by two lesbian medical students in committed relationships (whose partners were not students themselves) who sought to gain the same access to low-cost married–graduate student campus housing as their legally married counterparts. They were rebuffed by the trial court, which held that *Braschi* did not apply.[6] The court reasoned that there were still some instances where a landlord had the right to explicitly restrict certain housing to legally married couples, and that so-called university housing was one of them.[7]

Some universities have responded affirmatively to requests by lesbian and gay students for campus residential housing on a par with other recognized subgroups within the university system, such as racial and ethnic minority students or common interest student groups. A study of gay-friendly campus housing indicates that several campuses, including Rutgers University, the University of California–Santa Cruz, the University of Maine at Orono, the University of Massachusetts–Amherst, and Wesleyan University in Connecticut, have established residence hall space for students interested in gay, lesbian, bisexual, and transgender issues.

University policy makers ought to heed the voices of lesbian and gay student advocates and those that support them regarding the need for LGB-friendly student housing. In an era when university students freely admit to rampant overt and covert homophobic attitudes and actions,[8] LGB students and those who identify with and support them ought to be afforded safe and comfortable housing that is equivalent to the accommodations made for other student groups.

Discrimination Against Tenants Based on Religious Objections

In several recent cases, landlords have raised First Amendment religious freedom issues to avoid renting apartments to LGB couples or unmarried straight couples. These landlords cite religious objections to justify their discriminatory rental practices. *Smith*, a California case, raised the question of whether a religious freedom defense can justify violation of antidiscrimination laws. The landlord in this case, Evelyn Smith, refused to rent an apartment to an unmarried, straight couple, claiming she would be "facilitating fornication" if she did so, and that this would be sinful according to her beliefs. In defending against a housing discrimination claim brought by the couple, Smith asserted that California's law prohibiting housing discrimination based on marital status interfered with her right to exercise her religious beliefs. In 1996 the California Supreme Court ruled that landlords renting apartments to the general public have no constitutional or statutory exemption from California's antidiscrimination laws. In 1999, the U.S. Supreme Court denied review in this case.[9]

Despite the U.S. Supreme Court's refusal to take up the matter in *Smith*, court decisions have proved inconsistent in dealing with the so-called religious freedom defense. For example, in a separate case in 1999 in Alaska, a panel of federal judges of the Ninth Circuit Court of Appeals found for the landlord in similar circumstances.[10] In the *Thomas* case, the judges decided that fair housing laws prohibiting discrimination on the basis of marital status were an unnecessary burden on the landlord's right to free exercise of religion. The dissent strongly objected, and a petition for rehearing, requesting the entire court hear arguments again for both sides and reconsider its decision, was filed. Meanwhile, the Michigan Supreme Court reached the opposite conclusion and found for the unmarried tenants in a case where a landlord cited religious objections to renting to an unmarried couple. But in light of the Ninth Circuit's *Thomas* decision, the Michigan Court vacated its original opinion and sent the case back to the lower court for reconsideration.[11]

Given the tenuous nature of these court decisions, LGBs who suspect that landlords in their community may have religious objections to their sexual orientation or other sexual conduct should take several steps to protect themselves when seeking a home. First, be aware of any pending cases in your area or surrounding areas where landlords may be in court using this religious objection defense. Usually, a LGB attorneys' group or the local chapter of the ACLU (or one in the nearest large city) will have this information. Then, seek advice of a local landlord/tenant lawyer before home hunting. He or she may have advice about where to look, what landlords to avoid, or how to proceed cautiously but in a way that preserves your rights in the event of a problem with a particular landlord or home owner.

Discrimination Against Gays Based on HIV Status

Lesbians and gay men are not always subject to housing discrimination based on sexual orientation alone. They are also discriminated against based on their real or perceived HIV status. Landlords have tried to evict tenants living with HIV or AIDS for a variety of reasons, including fear that property values will decrease because of the presence of a person or persons living with HIV or AIDS (referred to as PWA), fear of casual HIV transmission by the tenant to others on the premises, or the misperception of an opportunity to evict a tenant from a rent-controlled or rent-stabilized dwelling and charge higher rent to a new tenant.[12]

Under federal law, PWAs are considered disabled and are protected from housing discrimination under the Fair Housing Amendments Act of 1988 (FHAA).[13] They may also be protected under individual state antidiscrimination laws protecting people with disabilities from housing discrimination. The Americans With Disabilities Act of 1990 (ADA),[14] which protects people with HIV and AIDS from discrimination in employment and public accommodations, does not cover housing discrimination. Nor does the federal Rehabilitation Act of 1973,[15] except in the rare instance where the landlord is receiving federal funds. The FHAA is the only federal law that specifically protects PWAs, and those perceived as HIV positive or living with AIDS (whether they actually are or not), from discrimination in housing. Under the FHAA, an aggrieved tenant may sue in federal court in a private civil action and obtain injunctive relief (an order stopping eviction), and recover damages and attorney's fees if successful. The tenant may also seek administrative relief from the U.S. Department of Housing and Urban Development. However, this is not a requirement before filing a lawsuit in court.[16]

Despite these legal protections, according to the AIDS Action Council in Washington, D.C., in late 1999, at any given time a third to a half of all Americans with AIDS are either homeless or in imminent danger of losing their homes, and 60 percent of all PWAs will face a housing crisis at some point during their illness because of illegal discrimination resulting in loss of housing, wages, or medical coverage that makes them unable to pay their rent or mortgage.[17]

Box 6.1

LAMBDA SUES LANDLORD, BROKER FOR REFUSING TO RENT TO SAME-SEX COUPLES[18]

In Park Slope, a "disturbing pattern" of discrimination against lesbian and gay renters (*Beaton, et al. v. Vinje Realty Corp., F. J. Kazeroid Realty Group, Inc.*)

(NEW YORK, February 16, 2000)—Lambda Legal Defense and Education Fund has filed suit against a Brooklyn landlord and a real estate agent for refusing to rent a Park Slope apartment to two men because they are gay. According to the lawsuit filed in Kings County Supreme Court late Tuesday, the property owner, Harold Vinje of Vinje Realty, and the broker, F. J. Kazeroid Realty Group, rejected the gay couple's application for a vacant one-bedroom apartment, and then, during an investigation by the Open Housing Center, repeatedly turned away others posing as gay prospective renters.

"A prejudiced landlord and a complicit realtor turned away qualified applicants solely on the basis of sexual orientation. This disturbing pattern of discrimination is illegal and must not be tolerated," said Lambda Staff Attorney Marvin C. Peguese, who represents the plaintiffs in *Beaton, et al. v. Vinje Realty and F. J. Kazeroid Realty Group*. The lawsuit charges the landlord and realtor with violating the New York City Human Rights Law, which prohibits, among others, housing discrimination on the basis of sexual orientation. The plaintiffs, 21–year-old Gabriel Beaton and 24–year-old Philip Alberti, were the first to respond to the apartment's listing posted last October on the window of the F .J. Kazeroid office. Shortly after seeing the apartment, the couple filled out an application and left a $1,800 deposit with the broker. But the landlord abruptly canceled the lease-signing appointment, and the agent later told Beaton and Alberti that the landlord was unwilling to rent the one-bedroom apartment to two men.

"Our credit was good, we were the first to apply, and we put up the deposit. The only reason we were rejected is because we're gay," said Beaton. He added, "This kind of thing isn't supposed to happen in Park Slope and shouldn't be tolerated anywhere else. The broker even had the nerve to ask us not to take the landlord's homophobia as a reflection on her agency."

After the couple's application was denied, the Center, which investigates complaints of housing discrimination, sent several people to inquire about the same apartment. Those posing as same-sex couples were told the space was too small for two people, while those applying as non-gay couples were enthusiastically shown the apartment. The broker even told one woman inquiring as part of a different-sex couple that the landlord would not mind a couple, or even a couple with a child. The Center is also named as a plaintiff.

"Gay and lesbian people need to know that, like all New Yorkers, they are protected from housing discrimination under the New York City Human Rights Law, especially when there are landlords and brokers out there who think they can get away with unlawfully picking and choosing renters," said the Center's Executive Director Karen Webber. The Center is a fair housing agency promoting equal housing opportunity in the New York metropolitan area.

Beaton and Alberti eventually found another apartment in the neighborhood. Lambda is seeking compensatory and punitive damages on behalf of the couple as well as a permanent injunction to prohibit the landlord and broker from discriminating against other lesbian and gay couples.

Lambda is the nation's oldest and largest gay legal group, headquartered in New York and with regional offices in Los Angeles, Chicago, and Atlanta.

Two federal statutes help fund residential housing for PWAs. These are the Housing Opportunities for People with AIDS program (HOPWA)[19] of the U.S. Department of Housing and Urban Development, and the residential treatment program provisions of the Ryan White CARE Act[20] administered by the U.S. Health Resources Services Administration (HRSA). HOPWA is the only federal program that provides states and cities with resources to meet the local housing needs of PWAs. It allows local communities to devise housing strategies (group homes, apartment complexes, hotel/motel conversions, shelters, and so forth) to best accommodate the housing needs of PWAs and their families within their communities. Communities receiving HOPWA funds usually realize a savings to taxpayers through the decreased reliance on acute and emergency medical care services by homeless people with AIDS. According to AIDS Action Council, HOPWA dollars reduced the use of emergency health care services through 1998 by an estimated $47,000 per person per year.[21]

The residential treatment provisions of the Ryan White CARE Act provide funding to allow community health centers and public hospitals to designate residential treatment facilities specifically for PWAs who need daily medical care.

Both HOPWA and the Ryan White CARE Act were originally conceived as emergency legislation in the early 1990s. They were meant only to stem the tide of HIV until a cure or affordable treatment was made available that would render such "emergency" legislation unnecessary. It was generally thought that a cure would be found within 5 or 10 years of enactment of these emergency provisions. Unfortunately, we have entered the third decade of the HIV and AIDS pandemic with no cure in sight, and housing and treatment issues are still at crisis proportions.

Every year federal appropriations battles become more difficult as nonprofit advocates demand more AIDS funding and a conservative U.S. Congress fights to cut back or severely limit funds. In 1996 the Republican majority in Congress nearly succeeded in eliminating HOPWA. Every 5 years, renewal and reauthorization of the Ryan White CARE Act is hotly debated in the House and Senate. Thanks to the efforts of countless advocates (many of whom are LGB), and the Clinton White House, these federal AIDS housing and treatment programs have managed to survive with large annual increases. How long this trend will continue, especially in light of the public's misguided perception that the AIDS crisis is over, is yet to be seen.

To preserve housing programs and funds for PWAs, policy advocates need to work with lawmakers, using the facts to demonstrate the constant threat of homelessness faced by hundreds of thousands of Americans who are HIV positive. Grassroots organizers can play a significant role in this effort by acting as resources for the work of national organizations doing research in the field. Community efforts to bring statistics regarding housing problems faced by PWAs to the attention of Congress during Ryan White reauthorization and HOPWA appropriations hearings are crucial to the survival of these programs.

Fair Housing Regulations

As of the end of calendar year 1999, there were no federal statutes expressly protecting LGBs from antigay discrimination in the rental or purchase of housing, even though 11 states (and the District of Columbia) and many local governments have enacted laws banning discrimination based on sexual orientation.[22] The states with legal provisions in their civil rights laws banning such discrimination in housing are California, Connecticut, Hawaii, Massachusetts, Minnesota, Nevada, New Hampshire, New Jersey, Rhode Island, Vermont, Wisconsin, and Washington, D.C. According to a 2000 report by the National Gay and Lesbian Task Force (NGLTF), the laws in these states alone protect 65.2 million Americans.[23]

As recently as 1999, California formally added sexual orientation discrimination to its list of prohibited housing practices in its state civil rights statute, the Fair Housing and Employment Act, after a 19-year battle in the courts and in the legislature. Prior to this legislative action, the law prohibiting discrimination in housing on the basis of sexual orientation had been developed by the courts and codified in the state's labor laws. Until the change, the law did not have the enforcement authority of the California State Department of Fair Housing and Employment. California State Assembly Speaker Antonio Villaraigosa, who sponsored the bill, said when it passed, "Gays and lesbians will finally see their protections clearly spelled out in California civil rights law; they will enjoy the full application of anti-bias protections just like every other group. It is finally true equality under the law."[24]

Many cities, counties, and other even smaller residential jurisdictions like villages and towns have civil rights ordinances that cover housing discrimination against LGBs. The 2000 NGLTF report states that over 100 million Americans are now protected under these local laws banning discrimination on the basis of sexual orientation.[25]

Another public policy concern is the availability of public housing for LGB families. Such public housing rules are set by the U.S. Department of Housing and Urban Development (HUD) and are subject to approval by local housing authorities. As early as 1977, HUD attempted to open public housing to families of "two or more persons, sharing residency, whose income and resources are available to meet the family's needs, and who are related by blood, marriage or operation of law, or have evidenced a stable family relationship."[26] The last clause was meant to include both LGB and unmarried straight couples. Congress immediately eliminated this provision, primarily to eliminate eligibility for same-sex couples.[27] Unmarried straight couples have since argued and won access to public housing through the courts, but same-sex couples have not yet challenged this discriminatory law in court.[28]

Attorneys and advocates working for LGB equality in housing continue to fight through the legislatures and the courts to establish the rights of tenants and home buyers to the freedom and sanctity of their homes. Policy makers ought to include stiff penalties on landlords, realtors, and sellers for acts of antigay discrimination in housing, on par with federal fair housing laws protecting racial and ethnic minorities.

joint home ownership by LGB couples

Because LGB couples lack the protections of legal marriage, they are forced to use other provisions in the law to protect their joint ownership of property. This usually involves contacting lawyers, drawing up papers, and writing down the details of one's relationship in legal form. Such activities are often costly, in time, money, and self-education about the issues. Thus, securing legal rights for LGBs is often prohibitively expensive. Public policy needs to address these issues. Legal recognition of same-sex marriage, or at least the extension of all marriage rights and benefits to same-sex couples on both the state and federal level, appears to be the only way to resolve these inequities.

In the absence of legal recognition of same-sex marriage or the extension of these rights and benefits to LGB couples, however, LGB couples need to find a way, either through self-help, legal clinics, or the hiring of fee-for-service lawyers, to protect themselves and their property legally. Without such protections, current laws and policies of intestate succession (having no will) in most states would hand all of the deceased partner's real property to their next of kin, which may include a sibling, parents, or an ex-spouse. The partner would have no rights to the property. Similarly, if an LGB relationship dissolves, an ex-partner with no legally cognizable rights to a property, regardless of how much money or resources he or she may have invested in the home, relinquishes all his or her rights in that property. In fact, as of this writing, no court in the United States has awarded a same-sex ex-partner property rights based on the facts of their relationship alone, without formal agreements between them providing for joint ownership or division of property upon dissolution of the relationship.[29]

On top of all this, as insidious as it may sound, any provision in a will or in a contract that, on its face, may appear to be an agreement for property in exchange for the promise of sexual acts between the parties may, as a matter of law and policy, be unenforceable in court. A poorly drafted clause may mean the loss of property rights despite the best intentions of the couple or the drafter.

This means that LGB couples should address several important considerations when contemplating joint home ownership. Unlike legally married couples, they have no automatic inheritance by the surviving partner of a home in the deceased partner's name. And the ownership of joint property does not legally extend to nonmarried couples unless certain agreements embodied in proper legal documents are formalized.

For example, the LGB couple must decide whether to buy a home in one or both partners' names. More often than not, lawyers will advise that both names be on the title, deed, and mortgage of the home. In the case where partners have significantly different incomes or where one is purchasing the home for the benefit of both (but only that partner needs or desires the full tax benefits of the transaction), they will need ownership agreements and provisions in their wills to ensure inheritance by the surviving partner. These precautions are essential for providing safety and security of the couple regarding their property.

An attorney knowledgeable in real estate law and the special needs of same-sex couples is recommended for any LGB couple considering home ownership. A good attorney can provide for the particular needs for their families and relationships.

Box 6.2

GAY-SMART ESTATE PLANNING[30]

One partner owns a $200,000 home individually, and his new partner moves in. After a time, the home owning partner decides that the relationship has a good future and he wants to be sure that his partner gets title to the house in the event that he predeceases his partner.

The problem is, he also wants to be sure that his parents get $50,000 from his estate if he should predecease his parents. He has very little cash in the bank, but $130,000 equity in his home.

By using his will to transfer title to his partner he can (1) retain total control over the property (2) change the provisions of his will without anyone's knowledge or permission (3) provide for his parents by requiring his partner to execute a $50,000 mortgage to his parents before he can receive title to the property and (4) transfer title and provide security for his partner upon his death.

This is just one example of how important it is to get good gay-friendly and gay-knowledgeable legal advice before you purchase property with your partner.

Although real estate law varies from state to state, there are some basic principles LGB couples must consider before speaking to an attorney. Owning property as joint tenants means that both individuals own the property in its entirety. Both have use of the whole property at any time and a right of survivorship exists. This is an equal partnership arrangement; no possibility exists for each partner to own the home in different percentages. The right of survivorship means automatic transfer of the entire property to the surviving partner immediately upon the death of the other.

Holding title as tenants in common means that there is no right of survivorship; when a tenant in common dies, that partner's share of the property is left to a beneficiary in a will or, in the absence of a will, to next of kin according to the state's laws of intestate succession. Partners can own the land in unequal percentages under this arrangement.

Gay-friendly mortgage companies, real estate brokers, home inspectors, and insurers are now found in almost any major metropolitan area as well as in many LGB-welcoming towns and suburbs. Organizations dedicated to advocating on behalf of these include the National Lesbian and Gay Law Association in Washington, D.C., and local lesbian and gay bar associations found in large cities.

retirement and aging issues in housing for lesbians and gays

The aging baby boomers in the late 1990s have presented many challenges for policy makers, especially regarding issues of personal identity and sexuality. According to a jointly authored report released by the Kinsey Institute and the Sexuality Information and Education Council of the United States, serving the needs of aging LGB populations presents many difficult public policy issues.[31] The exact number of LGBs reaching retirement age in the year 2000 in the United States is not known. However, at least one commentator has estimated that in 1998 about 115,000 lesbians and gays over 50 resided in the state of California alone.[32] According to the Brookdale Center on Aging at Hunter College in 2000, more than 75,000 gays and lesbians over the age of 65 live in New York City.[33] As these individuals enter retirement and face chronic illnesses and disabilities associated with aging, important housing issues arise.

Many LGBs in their 60s and 70s lived during a time when disclosure of sexual orientation would almost certainly result in the loss of housing, job, career, and family. The issues currently faced by this population still include many hurdles, especially those related to accessing housing and home care services. These include when (or whether) to come out to a provider, how to ascertain whether a facility is gay friendly, and how to speak out against discrimination based on sexual orientation at a time in life when most people are vulnerable to abuses and discrimination based on age alone. Organizations such as Senior Action in a Gay Environment (SAGE) and the Gay and Lesbian Association of Retiring Persons (GLARP) were founded to help seniors with these issues. They can address these problems and circumstances in a variety of ways. They help LGB seniors access gay-friendly retirement communities and learn about advocacy organizations and community center programs that focus on their needs. They also advocate and support the development of lesbian and gay retirement homes and assisted living facilities.

Retirement communities for lesbians and gay men are now being developed throughout the United States.[34] They range from gated trailer park communities catering to older lesbians in Arizona to leisure estates with townhouses, assisted living facilities, and recreational complexes for retired LGB clientele in California.[35] "Part of what's driving this, as lesbians and gays are getting older, they're looking for community," said Terry Kaelber, director of SAGE, which also runs a New York City social service agency for seniors. "Community is important."[36]

These developing communities primarily use gay-targeted marketing techniques or legal set-asides to attract LGBs. In an ironic twist given the housing problems faced by LGBs, these communities could not prohibit heterosexuals from living in LGB retirement communities in areas with nondiscrimination statutes that protect against sexual-orientation discrimination in housing.

LGB community services centers also serve to assist LGB seniors with housing issues. According to the National Association of Lesbian and Gay Community Services Centers, almost every member center has advisers, advocates, programs, or other forms of assistance to help elder gays with housing questions.[37]

homelessness among lesbian and gay youths

Lack of housing—or homelessness—is another issue with significant impact on the LGB community. There is growing concern about the problems faced by scores of LGB and questioning youths who leave abusive environments at home or school. The National Lesbian and Gay Task Force has estimated that as many as 26 percent of all lesbian and gay youths are forced to leave their homes because of conflicts with their families over sexual orientation.[38] More often than not, these youths become homeless or wards of the state. Most live primarily on city streets. Although the actual numbers are not known, some national estimates suggest that one in four youths living on the streets is lesbian or gay. Local estimates are even higher. Agencies serving street youth in Los Angeles estimate that 25 to 35 percent of homeless youths are lesbian or gay, and agencies in Seattle estimate that 40 percent of their homeless youths are lesbian or gay.[39]

Cities like Austin, Texas; Seattle, Washington; San Francisco, California; Portland, Oregon; and Boston, Massachusetts, swell each year with a growing number of homeless gay youths. These cities have, for one reason or another, garnered reputations as liberal and welcoming, despite the inability of state agencies and the LGB communities at large to provide them with adequate shelter and housing. Most of these young people are teenagers fleeing homophobic homes, churches, school systems, social service agencies, foster care programs, and other environments in their native states where they were made to feel unwelcome.

Youths seeking shelter in mainstream service agencies or public programs are often met with harassment, discrimination, and even violence if they come out as LGB, reveal that they are transgendered, admit they are questioning their sexuality, or manifest identity traits inconsistent with stereotypical notions of gender or sexual orientation. According to one commentator, lesbian and gay youths looking for services are often met with the same homophobia and heterosexism that they had found in society at large: these youths are rejected and disenfranchised by the very agencies that should be serving them.[40]

Gay-friendly housing programs that shelter and care for these youths are few and far between. In fact, there are only two residential housing programs in the

Box 6.3

COMING OUT IN CONVALESCENCE[41]

Unfortunately, nursing homes, home care services, housekeeping, and senior centers are not currently in place for gay and lesbian seniors who cannot afford to pay. As a result, many retreat back into the closet when they are faced with dependency on public agencies and services. Even those who had open relationships, who were active in the community, and who were comfortable with their identity are often unwilling to open themselves up to the additional vulnerabilities that accompany coming out publicly.

Older gays and lesbians may decide to keep their sexual identity to themselves in regard to new doctors, home attendants, social workers, hospital staff, and visiting nurses. They may not feel safe opening up and may rationalize that retaining a gay identity is not important. They may fear that they will receive biased or inferior service if their sexual identity is exposed.

A few months ago, one of my clients was transferred from a hospital to a nursing home for temporary rehabilitation. At my first visit to this Brooklyn [New York] nursing home, I asked to meet with the social worker who would set up a discharge plan for my client, Lydia. I ended up meeting with the director of social services who was covering for the social worker that week. I introduced myself as Lydia's social worker from SAGE. "What is SAGE?" he asked. As I felt my anxiety surge at the thought of outing Lydia, I answered obliquely that SAGE was an agency in the city that assists senior citizens. "What does SAGE stand for?" he continued. "Senior Action in a Gay Environment," I answered as I handed him my card while attempting to mask my anxiety with a smooth transaction. "Why is Lydia involved with your agency?" he responded. "Because she's a lesbian and she needs social work assistance," I heard myself answer.

Panic struck as I reflected that Lydia had probably not come out to her home attendant for fear that the attendant would be uncomfortable, and, in turn, might not treat her well. I quickly explained to the director of the nursing home that I could not hide my identity in terms of my credibility in advocating for Lydia but that I was uncomfortable with the fact that I had outed her as a result of our conversation. I requested that he be sensitive about disclosing this information in the nursing home. The director said he appreciated my providing him with this information and that it would help in conducing an intake interview with Lydia in preparing her treatment plan. He said he would be sensitive in terms of disclosure to other staff, understanding that not everyone is gay affirming. Fortunately, in this instance, I found that each staff person was more helpful than the next. I do not always encounter this in under-funded and under-staffed facilities.

Lydia was eventually discharged in an extremely timely manner and received increased home care, which she had badly needed even before her hospitalization. As much as I can think it best for everyone to be out to all their providers, I know it is clearly frightening for a person to be in a vulnerable position when they are sick, healing, dependent, and uncertain about the provider's treatment if the provider knew they were gay or lesbian.

United States that provide shelter for gay and lesbian homeless youths. These are Gay and Lesbian Adolescent Social Services (GLASS) in Los Angeles, with space for 36 youths, and Green Chimney Gramercy Residence in New York City, with space for 25 youths.[42] There are other programs that provide temporary respite from life on the streets—like showers, lounges, free meals, medical and dental clinics, and peer support groups—for some gay and lesbian youths. These include programs like those at the Callen-Lourde Health Center in New York City, the Los Angeles Lesbian and Gay Community Services Center in Hollywood, the Sydney Borum Jr. Health Center in Boston, the Sexual Minority Youth Assistance League in Washington, D.C., and the North Carolina Lesbian and Gay Youth Network in Durham, North Carolina.

Advocates on behalf of lesbian and gay youth, like the National Youth Advocacy Coalition, OutProud, Boston's BAGLY (Boston Alliance for Gay and Lesbian Youth), and San Francisco's LYRIC, are all working to address these issues,[43] but funds for housing this population are almost nonexistent at the federal level, and extremely limited at the state level. The availability of state or federally funded HIV and AIDS housing may be another option, especially given the high numbers of HIV-positive youths among the homeless. At least one study has found as many as 47 percent of homeless young people between the ages of 10 and 21 are HIV positive.[44] But eligibility for AIDS housing assumes that a young person can access the health care or welfare system in his or her city or state. Many street youths fall outside the reach of these public safety nets. Programs providing housing assistance for people with AIDS are currently stretched to their limits, and specifically youth-oriented AIDS housing programs are currently nonexistent.

As homelessness plagues many sectors of American society with no clear national programs to offer relief, marginalized communities like LGB youth are often in an even more difficult situation. The few programs and services that do exist to assist the homeless generally are not gay welcoming or friendly. In fact, they offer nothing to LGB youth. Policy makers and youth advocates sensitive to the needs of lesbian, gay, bisexual, and questioning youths need community support at the national and local levels to address these youth housing issues. Large, well-established national and local LGB advocacy organizations need to hear the message that LGB youth are a priority for housing advocacy. Only by the actions of individuals volunteering, contributing funds, and demanding action on the part of these groups will any inroads be made into the issue of homelessness and gay youth.

neighborhoods and urban development

Since the turn of the 19th century, many lesbians and gay men have chosen to live in America's urban areas where the relative anonymity of big cities allows individuals to meet, engage in relationships, and congregate socially in safety.[45] The rise of "Boston marriages," or lesbian couples living together openly in East Coast urban areas in the 1900s, was one such indicator of quiet social acceptance by metropolitan society of unconventional living arrangements. Over time, cities became the place for LGBs to organize and exchange ideas about identity and society. This led to the development of political networks and the building of communities with common concerns and goals: namely, overcoming societal prejudices against people on the basis of their sexual orientation. At the turn of the 21st century, cities are the focal point of LGB life, and this fact has profound implications for urban politics, development strategies, and housing issues.[46]

In cities across the United States, distinct communities serve the housing and social needs of LGBs. New York and San Francisco are well known for their lesbian and gay neighborhoods. Pine Street in Philadelphia, Mount Vernon in Baltimore, the Halstead in Chicago, Capitol Hill in Seattle, Montrose in Houston, Dupont Circle in Washington, D.C., South Grand Street in St. Louis, the Chessman area of Denver, and Liberty Hill and the North Side area of Cincinnati, to name a few, are also neighborhoods that have a lesbian and gay identity.[47] "These urban domains of sexual identity are the most conspicuous expressions of the change brought by the cultural and political movement of city-dwelling lesbians and gay men."[48]

The impact LGBs have had on the revival of cities and neighborhoods is finally garnering the attention and focus of public policy analysts and urban scholars. Not enough research has focused on the contributions LGBs have made to cities over the past 30 years, but this is changing. For example, Mitchell Moss, professor of urban planning at New York University, has observed that many revitalized urban centers in the United States today owe a debt of gratitude to LGB communities. "Housing purchases and real estate investments by gays and lesbians have led to the rejuvenation of neighborhoods and the creation of new businesses. Nowhere is this trend more apparent than in the South Beach area of Miami Beach, a community that declined when its elderly population diminished. Thanks to an increase in its gay and lesbian population, South Beach has evolved into an international hot spot, featuring hotels, housing, nightclubs, shops, modeling agencies, and industries, such as the Latin American headquarters for both MTV and Sony."[49]

As a matter of policy, Moss recommends that cities use tax incentives, low-interest mortgage loans, and strengthened antidiscrimination laws in housing and employment to attract LGBs into transitional neighborhoods to foster the development of improved housing and creative entrepreneurship by our diverse communities.

Public policy expert Robert Bailey sums up the significance of LGBs living in urban centers this way: "The struggle toward self-empowerment by lesbians and gay men . . . has contributed to change in the political language of our cities, influenced electoral coalitions, altered public policy, and introduced its values and vocabularies into the social organization of urban governance."[50] His book, *Gay Politics, Urban Politics*, is a landmark effort capturing the spirit and power of lesbians and gays living in urban communities.

But not all observations about urban gay life by scholars have been positive or supportive. The neoclassical law and economics perspective of such scholars as Richard Posner implicitly refer to the so-called traditional occupations of gay men as the driving force of gay neighborhoods. In this view, gay men (in particular) and lesbians fleeing the scrutiny and criticism of mainstream society choose occupations best suited to their "lifestyles," and seek refuge in commercial neighborhoods. Simply put, gays live where the hair salons, florists, interior design firms, antique shops, and "creative arts" that employ them spring up, in Posner's words, "where their presence will not grate on heterosexual sensibilities."[51] Urban geographers like Paul Knox have characterized gay and lesbian neighborhoods as essentially isolationist strongholds of illicit sexual activity, "where openly homosexual behavior can take place." In his view, gay neighborhoods are "spaces of resistance to the dominant social order,"[52] and as such are important in understanding why minorities cluster for "attack," that is, to form political power bases from which to fend off government intrusion. These are rather simplistic and dim views of the myriad complex urban issues faced by lesbian and gay urban communities.

conclusion

Lesbians and gay men continue to encounter problems in obtaining and maintaining housing because of societal bias and prejudice. Individuals are denied housing, couples are denied benefits of a secure home, students have fewer options, our youth are homeless, our elderly limited in their choices of housing. The law does not always address these issues in a sweeping and efficient way. Public policy needs to respond to these issues with greater concentration of resources and efforts on the youngest and eldest in our communities. In the meantime, as LGBs build communities and transform towns and cities through organizing, lobbying, exercising economic power, and empowering the most disenfranchised to secure housing, LGB communities will continue to thrive.

Housing issues affect every segment of LGB communities. Not unlike the housing issues faced by African American civil rights leaders in the 1960s, these housing discrimination problems will take much time, money, energy, and effort by community advocates and activists working on several fronts before they are eliminated nationwide. Without federal protections against housing discrimination for lesbians and gays, and without the legal recognition of same-sex marriage, these issues will continue to affect us all. An even longer process involves the education of a country and the healing of a community. As long as public policy advocates, scholars, and activists continue to pursue these issues and increase awareness of the housing realities of lesbians and gays, progress will continue to be made. LGB neighborhoods and spaces will continue to grow and affect the development of cities, suburbs, and towns everywhere.

what you can do!

- Check the laws in your area for protections against housing discrimination based on sexual orientation, gender, and HIV status. Note the laws, their provisions, and who enforces them. Notify the appropriate authority if you are being treated unfairly.
- Advocate for local provisions for registering same-sex relationships as domestic partnerships or civil unions. Urge your employer to provide comprehensive employee benefits for their employees and their same-sex partners.
- Hire a gay or gay-friendly realtor or attorney to help with your search for a new home. Referrals may be available through
  - Homelounge.com (www.Homelounge.com).
  - The Gay and Lesbian Yellow Pages (www.glyp.com).
  - The Pink Pages (www.pinkweb.com).

- Your local gay legal organization.
- Realtor listings in the classifieds of your LGB community newspaper.
- Put both names on the lease when renting a home with a partner. When buying a home, discuss all the options with your partner *and your lawyer* beforehand, including
  - Whether both names will be on the title and mortgage.
  - The estate-planning documents needed to protect both partners' property interests.
  - The tax ramifications of the new home purchase.
  - How the property will be divided if the relationship ends.
- If you are a *student* looking for university housing, inquire about housing for LGB students. Find out whether policies concerning couples' housing apply to same-sex and different-sex unmarried cohabiting couples. If LGB students are being treated differently from straight students, contact
  - The LGB legal organization in your area.
  - The local chapter of the ACLU.
  - The Lambda Legal Defense and Education Fund (www.lambdalegal.org). The legal help desks at Lambda regional offices provide valuable information about how to find appropriate legal help.
- For information concerning LGB-friendly *retirement communities* and residential facilities that provide *convalescent care*, contact
  - Senior Action in a Gay Environment (SAGE) (http://www.sageusa.org) for a list of community-based service organizations in your area or SAGE at national headquarters at 212–741–2247.
  - The Sexuality Information and Education Council of the United States (SIECUS) (www.siecus.org) for resources on sexuality and aging.
- If you are under the age of 21 and concerned that your parent or guardian may turn you out of their home or become abusive if they were to find out you are lesbian, gay, or bisexual, seek help before you leave home.
  - Contact the National Youth Advocacy Coalition (NYAC) toll-free at 800–541–6922 (www.nyacyouth.org) for a list of community-based service organizations in your area.
- Organizations fighting against housing discrimination need your help and support. Contact them regarding becoming active through their local chapters, volunteer opportunities, legislative action campaigns, cash and in-kind donation programs, and other ways to help the cause. These organizations include
  - The Lambda Legal Defense and Education Fund (www.lambdalegal.org).
  - The National Gay and Lesbian Task Force (www.ngltf.org).
  - Senior Action in a Gay Environment (www.sageusa.org).

- The National Youth Advocacy Coalition (www.nyacyouth.org).
- The Human Rights Campaign (www.hrc.org).
- The American Civil Liberties Union (www.aclu.org).
- Your local LGB organization.
- Come out as a gay or gay-friendly landlord, home seller, real estate attorney, or real estate professional. This will raise awareness of the needs of LGB home buyers and renters and provide them with the needed services. It may also boost your business! To do so
  - Advertise in LGB community newspapers.
  - List your services with on-line resources like the Gay and Lesbian Yellow Pages (www.glyp.com) or the Pink Pages (www.pinkweb.com).
  - Register at HomeLounge.com as a gay or LGB-friendly realtor (www.homelounge.com).
- Contact your elected government officials and urge them to address housing discrimination based on sexual orientation. Provide a copy of *Why We Need Policy Prohibiting Housing Discrimination Based on Sexual Orientation.*

for more information

- Bailey, R. (1999). *Gay politics, urban politics: Identity and economics in the urban setting.* New York: Columbia University Press.
- Bell, D., Binnie, J., et al. (2001). *Pleasure zones: Bodies, cities, spaces.* Syracuse, New York: Syracuse University Press.
- Blasius, M. (1994). *Gay and lesbian politics: Sexuality and the emergence of a new ethic.* Philadelphia: Temple University Press.
- E'milio, J. (2000). *Creating change: Sexuality, public policy, and civil rights.* New York: St. Martin's Press.
- Fincher, R., & Jacobs, J. (1998). *Cities of difference.* New York: Guilford.
- Herman, D. (1997). *The anti-gay agenda: Orthodox vision and the christian right.* Chicago: University of Chicago Press.
- Riggle, E. D. B., & Tadlock, B. L. (1999). *Gays and lesbians in the democratic process: Public policy, public opinion, and political representation.* New York: Columbia University Press.

WHY WE NEED POLICY PROHIBITING HOUSING DISCRIMINATION BASED ON SEXUAL ORIENTATION*

As of 2002, no federal law protects lesbians and gay men from housing discrimination on the basis of sexual orientation. Due to inconsistent state and local policies, currently only 100 million Americans live in areas where laws protect them from housing discrimination based on sexual orientation. Gay, lesbian, and bisexual renters, home buyers, elderly, students, and teenagers remain targets for anti-LGB housing policies and practices.

Is there legal recourse for gays and lesbians whose rental applications for apartments are denied because of their sexual orientation?
In those states, cities, towns, counties, and other jurisdictions throughout the United States where antidiscrimination laws have been passed that expressly protect individuals from housing discrimination on the basis of sexual orientation, there may be some legal recourse. A lesbian or gay man whose rental application has been denied on the basis of her or his sexual orientation has no recourse outside of these jurisdictions.

Is an apartment renter who is the surviving partner of a same-sex couple protected from eviction by a homophobic landlord?
No, because the law generally does not recognize same-sex couples as having the same rights and benefits as legally married different-sex couples, the surviving partner of a same-sex relationship does not have the right to remain in an apartment where he or she is not a signatory on the lease. In New York, however, the courts have upheld the right of a same-sex surviving partner to remain in an apartment in such circumstances under that state's law protecting widowed "spouses" from eviction from rent-controlled and rent-stabilized apartments.

Are same-sex couples entitled to the same graduate student housing that their married different-sex counterparts are?
No, in the only case on the issue, the state courts in New York determined that graduate student housing could be restricted to legally married different-sex couples. Some universities voluntarily provide equal or alternative housing for lesbian and gay students, but even those programs have recently been called into question by administrators.

Are cohabitating same-sex couples entitled to the same property rights as legally married heterosexual couples?
No. State laws of intestate succession and joint or marital property provisions that extend the same property rights to both partners in a legal marriage generally do not apply to same-sex couples, no matter how long they have been involved in a committed relationship.

Are there retirement communities and nursing homes that serve the needs of elderly gay men and lesbians?
Yes, but most such places and programs are few in number, fairly new, or only recently under development. Decisions about when and whether to come out to home care workers, service providers in retirement communities, and primary care givers are difficult ones for members of the aging lesbian and gay population. These difficulties are compounded by the negative experiences many of our elderly had to endure in their youth because they were gay in an era that was not as accepting as ours is today.

Are there shelters for homeless gay youths?
Yes, but they are few and far between. Only two housing programs for lesbian and gay youths—one in New York and one in Los Angeles—could be located from around the entire country. This is troubling considering that social service agencies serving youths estimate that at least one third to one half of all homeless young people in the United States are lesbian or gay. Add this to the fact that most social service agencies tend not to welcome LGB youths, and it becomes clear that our communities currently face a crisis of homelessness among our youth.

---

* The material presented here is discussed in greater detail in *Everyday Activism: A Handbook for Lesbian, Gay, and Bisexual People and Their Allies*, edited by Michael R. Stevenson, Ph.D., and Jeanine C. Cogan, Ph.D., and published by Routledge in 2003.

CHAPTER 7

ending discrimination in the U.S. military

Clinton W. Anderson and C. Dixon Osburn

In this chapter, you will

- *Learn about the "Don't Ask, Don't Tell, Don't Pursue, Don't Harass" policy of the U.S. military.*
- *Discover the origin and history of the military policy on homosexuality.*
- *Learn LGB-positive arguments against "Don't Ask, Don't Tell."*
- *See how to put these arguments to use in improving implementation of the current policy.*
- *Learn how to work long term for repeal of "Don't Ask, Don't Tell."*

On July 5, 1999, U.S. Army Private Calvin Glover brutally beat Private First Class Barry Winchell to death with a baseball bat as Winchell slept on a cot outside his barracks room at Fort Campbell, Kentucky. According to Glover, Specialist Justin Fisher goaded him to his fatal attack on Winchell. Fisher was Winchell's roommate and the owner of the murder weapon. According to a number of witnesses, Fisher tormented Glover for having lost a fight the night before Winchell's murder to "a fucking faggot." Yet, in the initial reports, the Army attributed the murder simply to "an altercation between soldiers."[1]

Soldiers later testified, however, that Winchell had faced daily antigay harassment for months prior to his murder. The harassment, initiated by rumors started by Fisher, spread until it involved many of the men in their company. Rather than stopping the harassment Winchell experienced, his military superiors contributed to it by starting an investigation to determine whether the rumors were true. Winchell confided in two close friends that he was profoundly troubled by the harassment, but he believed that he could do nothing for fear he would be kicked out of the Army he loved.[2]

Earlier tragedies such as this had led LGBs to initiate a national effort to end harassment in and their exclusion from military service in the United States. This effort was ultimately successful in making "gays in the military," as the issue was known in the mass media, an important news topic, a focus of university student activism, and an issue during the 1992 presidential election campaign. In an effort to cement LGBs' support, Democratic Party presidential candidate Bill Clinton pledged that, if elected, he would sign an executive order lifting the ban on military service by gay men and lesbians.

Shortly after his inauguration, having won the election with very strong support from LGB communities, President Clinton redeemed his campaign promise and charged the Department of Defense (DOD) with revising the policy. During the first 6 months of the new administration, the controversy over gays in the military was one of the most visible and politically challenging issues faced by the Clinton administration.

Opposition to the president's plans was very strong among the military leadership, political conservatives, and many members of Congress. During the same time period as that in which the DOD was undertaking to develop its policy, the U.S. Senate Armed Services Committee held well-publicized hearings on the proposed policy change.[3] Although the DOD did ultimately revise the policy, the revision was strongly influenced by the formula "don't ask, don't tell" that was the theme of the Senate Armed Services Committee's deliberations. Ultimately, Congress took matters into its own hands and wrote into law the same grounds for discharge that had existed in policy since 1981—that service members would be discharged from military service if they stated that they were gay, engaged in affectional or sexual conduct with a person of the same gender, or attempted to marry someone of the same gender.[4] The primary rationale for the law was to preserve "the armed forces' high standards of morale, good order, discipline, and unit cohesion that are the essence of military capability."[5]

Notwithstanding its similarity to earlier regulations, the new law and its implementing regulations[6] promised a significant change from prior policy in three respects. First, in the process of developing the new law and policy in 1993, congressional and military leaders acknowledged for the first time that LGBs do serve honorably in the U.S. military.[7] Second, the policy also states that sexual orientation is no longer a bar to military service.[8] Third, the President, Congress, and military leaders agreed that the military would implement a number of measures intended to protect LGB service members in the military from the injustices to which they had previously been subjected. These promised measures gave the DOD regulations implementing the law their name: Don't Ask, Don't Tell, Don't Pursue. Thus, although LGBs were still prohibited from homosexual conduct, including statements of their sexual orientation (Don't Tell),[9] the military was supposed to (1) implement the law with due regard for the privacy rights and rights to association of service members (Don't Ask),[10] (2) stop its infamous investigations (witch hunts) to ferret out suspected LGBs (Don't Pursue),[11] (3) treat LGBs evenhandedly in the military criminal justice system (for example, they would not be criminally prosecuted under circumstances in which heterosexual service members were not prosecuted),[12] and (4) take steps to prevent antigay harassment.[13] In February 2000, in the wake of the murder of PFC Winchell, the Secretary of Defense officially added "Don't Harass" to the title of the policy.[14]

Unfortunately, the promises of the new policy have not been fulfilled. Reported violations of the policy[15] have greatly increased over the years since 1994, when Congress enacted it into law (see Table 7.1). Asking, pursuing, and harassing continued even though the Pentagon announced new training programs and guidelines on antigay harassment.[16] Discharges under "Don't Ask, Don't Tell, Don't Pursue, Don't Harass" remain alarmingly high (see Table 7.2). The U.S. military loses, on average, three to four persons every day because of its anti-gay policy—a total of 1,231 in 2000. Many more dedicated, competent service members have left at the end of their terms, fed up with constant fear, dissembling, and antigay harassment.

Both senior military leaders and the Pentagon's civilian leadership have simply failed to effectively implement the law and regulations. Until very recently, in the wake of Winchell's murder and the public outcry surrounding the case, military leaders utterly failed to address command violations of "Don't Ask, Don't Tell, Don't Pursue, Don't Harass." Despite survey results indicating that antigay harassment and other violations were a serious problem[17] and an action plan to address antigay harassment,[18] military leaders have done little to address the problems or to implement the plan. They failed to distribute guidance against antigay harassment, to implement the privacy protections promised under the policy, or to enforce the policy's limits on investigations. Leaders have held few officially accountable for asking, pursuing, or harassing service members and have provided no means of recourse for service members who are targeted. Military leaders have even instructed medical and mental health providers, law enforcement personnel, and others to turn in LGB service members who seek their help.

In this context, we must pursue two primary policy goals: (1) improve the implementation of the current policy to redeem the promises made with its adoption; and (2) advocate formulation of a new policy that eliminates discrimination against LGBs in the U.S. military.

The prospects of success in either domain are uncertain. In the 2000 election campaign "Don't Ask, Don't Tell, Don't Pursue, Don't Harass" reached its highest level of public debate since it was first implemented.[19] However, the election of President George W. Bush, who opposed repeal of the law, makes it

Table 7.1

INCIDENTS REPORTED TO THE SERVICE MEMBERS LEGAL DEFENSE NETWORK*

Year	Don't Ask	Don't Tell	Don't Pursue	Don't Harass	Total
1994	37	18	65	62	182
1995	77	18	141	127	363
1996	89	31	191	132	443
1997	124	22	235	182	563
1998	161	23	350	400	934
1999	194	52	471	968	1,685
2000	159	30	412	871	1,472
Total	841	194	1,865	2,742	5,642

* The Servicemembers Legal Defense Network is an independent legal aid and advocacy organization devoted to the protection of the civil rights of LGBs in the U.S. military. It reports on its cases in its annual reports, e.g., Sobel, S. L., Cleghorn, J. M., & Osburn, C. D. (2001). *Conduct unbecoming: The seventh annual report on "don't ask, don't tell, don't pursue, don't harrass."* Washington, DC: Servicemembers Legal Defense Network. The data presented in Tables 7.1 and 7.2 were obtained from those reports.

Table 7.2

DOD DISCHARGES OF SERVICE MEMBERS FOR HOMOSEXUALITY

Fiscal year	U.S. Armed Forces				
	Air Force	Army	Navy	Marines	Total
1991	151	206	545	47	949
1992	111	138	401	58	708
1993	152	156	334	40	682
1994	180	136	245	36	597
1995	234	182	260	46	722
1996	282	206	302	60	850
1997	309	197	413	78	997
1998	414	312	345	77	1,148
1999	352	271	315	97	1,035
Total	2,185	1,804	3,160	539	7,688

unclear how the Pentagon will respond to advocacy for improving its implementation. Congress seems unlikely to overturn the policy at this time, but the election of a more moderate Congress could change the likelihood of repeal. To date, Democrats in Congress have been far more outspoken against the law than their Republican counterparts, and the Democratic Party platform in 2000 called for repeal as well. Short of repeal, the election of a Democratic president has the potential to at least improve the implementation of the policy.

the history of military policy on homosexuality

A Policy Based on an Outdated Rationale

The law and regulations on homosexuality in the U.S. military have their historical source in a now obsolete psychiatric understanding of same-gender sexual orientation.[20] In the U.S. military's mobilization for World War II, psychiatrists worked to develop screening devices to identify inductees with mental illness. The psychiatrists' efforts were intended to avoid the high incidence of mental illness or "shell shock" service members experienced during World War I. Because psychiatry at that time considered same-gender sexual orientation to be a mental disorder, one component of the psychiatric screening was aimed at homosexuality. The original rationale for the new policies was that to define homosexuality as a mental disorder was a more humane basis for screening recruits and separating persons already on active duty than charging them under the sodomy statute in the Uniform Code of Military Justice (UCMJ), the criminal law code that governs uniformed military personnel. This new approach was also thought to be less costly to the government because the process was administrative, thus avoiding the rigorous procedures of the criminal justice system. Furthermore, identification of homosexual recruits during induction physicals was seen as a psychiatric contribution to the U.S. war effort that could benefit the profession's prestige.[21]

Rationalizing an Irrational Policy

Although the policy on homosexuality originated in a psychiatric context, the military distanced itself from the illness rationale early on and replaced it with other rationales justifying the ban on known LGB service members. One rationalization used by the military for nearly 30 years was the claim that LGB people were a security threat.[22] The security rationale fell into disfavor in the 1950s when the Pentagon published the Crittenden Report, which concluded that LGB people posed no national security threat. In the early 1990s, the military officially acknowledged that the security rationale was insupportable.[23] Ultimately, the

President issued an executive order in 1995 barring discrimination in the issuance of security clearances on the basis of sexual orientation.[24]

In 1981, motivated by an increase in court cases challenging discharges under the old policy, the DOD created a new policy asserting that LGB people were unfit for military service, period, and mandated, without exception, the discharge of all identified LGB service members.[25] Embedded in the 1981 policy was the assertion that "homosexuality is incompatible with military service."[26]

During the debate on gays in the military in 1993, the Pentagon and members of Congress backed away from the "fitness" rationale. Individuals like General Powell, Senator Nunn (D-Ga.), and Senator Thurmond (R-S.C.) all stated that gays served well in the armed forces.

In 1992 the U.S. General Accounting Office (GAO) characterized the military's rationale for this policy as assuming that heterosexual service members' prejudices against LGBs would harm the cohesion of military combat units and thus reduce their combat performance.[27] In formulating "Don't Ask, Don't Tell," Congress also abandoned the incompatibility rationale. The new policy, however, retained the rationale that openly LGB service members would harm unit cohesion.

arguments against "don't ask, don't tell"

There are many arguments against the current "Don't Ask, Don't Tell" policy. Criticisms of current policy include that it harms the military and its most important asset—its people; public opinion opposes the "Don't Ask, Don't Tell" policy; it is costly; the military as an institution is capable of successfully implementing change; and experience shows that LGBs can successfully serve openly.

"Don't Ask, Don't Tell" Hurts the Military and Its People

"Don't Ask, Don't Tell" is itself highly detrimental to unit cohesion. The policy hinders the performance of LGB service members, it erodes the bonds of trust between service members, it erodes faith in military standards by promoting a double standard, and it fosters an environment of hostility by tagging LGB service members as second-class citizens, unworthy of the uniform.

The policy has a negative impact on individual service members. Every phone call brings a fear that the phone is being tapped. Every car parked in the front of one's apartment building brings the fear that someone is watching. One never knows if one's commander has called you in to tell you about a commendation for a job well done or that you are about to be fired from the job you love. While many LGBs have had distinguished careers, placing this special burden on their service deprives the armed forces of members serving at their very best.

Because "Don't Ask, Don't Tell" enforces silence and secrecy as a condition of service, it requires LGB service members to lie, hide, evade, and dissemble among colleagues, commanders, and even military doctors. Coming out to anyone, anywhere, anytime carries the risk of expulsion. Thus, LGB service members cannot bring partners to social events. They cannot join freely in conversations about weekend plans or loved ones. When on deployment, LGB service members cannot even e-mail their life partners for fear of discovery and discharge. The inevitable result is that the bonds of trust and familiarity so important for effective units are diminished by the policy.

The policy forces commanders into the unsavory position of policing the private lives of service members. This leads to investigative excesses and distractions from important issues of mission readiness. Investigators often seize and analyze diaries, computer disks, address books, and e-mail searching for information about an individual's sexual orientation or conduct. Commanders and inquiry officers may ask dozens of other service members about someone's private life in an attempt to determine if they are LGB. Some cases that exemplify what LGB service members face are presented in Box 7.1. These examples belie the assertions of military leaders that "Proper implementation of the policy has been a priority and that the policy has, for the most part, been properly applied and enforced."[28]

Finally, because the policy pits "us" versus "them," it sends the unmistakable signal that treating LGBs as less than others is permissible. The policy itself creates a climate of hostility that, in the worst cases, leads to brutal explosions of violence, such as that which claimed the life of PFC Barry Winchell.

Five months after Winchell's murder, the Secretary of Defense ordered the Department Inspector General to investigate antigay harassment.[29] Between January 24 and February 11, 2000, 75,000 troops from randomly selected units at 38 randomly selected installations worldwide and from selected ships and submarines were surveyed. Eighty percent of the 71,570 respondents reported that they had heard offensive speech, derogatory names, jokes, or remarks about homosexual people in the previous year. Eighty-five percent believed such comments were tolerated to some extent. Thirty-seven percent of the respondents had witnessed or experienced harassment based on homosexuality. About 5 percent reported toleration of the harassment within their chain of command and 10 percent reported toleration of harassment within their unit. Nearly half reported that the current policy concerning homosexuality was only slightly effective or not effective at preventing or reducing harassment.[30]

The institutionalized discrimination suffered by LGBs in the U.S. military must be stopped. The government socializes young people in the military to treat LGBs as second-class citizens, encourages their harassment, and perpetuates

Box 7.1

EXAMPLES OF ANTIGAY HARASSMENT AND BREACHES OF MILITARY POLICY REPORTED TO THE SERVICEMEMBERS LEGAL DEFENSE NETWORK

"Faggot, Faggot Down the Street, Shoot Him, Shoot Him 'til He Retreats."
Shortly after the murder of PFC Barry Winchell in July 1999, one of Private Javier "Cortland" Torres's supervisors forced his unit to loudly sing this chant during a training run at Fort Campbell. This is one of a number of incidents in which supervisors referred derisively to gay people in front of Torres's unit. Other soldiers derisively dismissed the murder, saying, "So what if he [Winchell] was killed. He was gay." And, "Who cares? He was just a fag." After he expressed concern about PFC Winchell's murder, rumors about Torres's sexual orientation became prevalent. A straight friend warned Torres that he was in danger, after overhearing soldiers speculate about Torres's sexuality and make threatening comments. When some soldiers asked him if he was gay, too, Torres disclosed his sexual orientation to superiors in order to protect his safety. He was discharged.

Marine Officer Mocks PFC Winchell's Murder and Instructions Against Harassment.
In the course of forwarding an e-mail that instructed military leaders not to tolerate antigay harassment to his subordinates from his commander, Lieutenant Colonel Edward Melton mocked Winchell's murder, writing, "Due to the hate crime death of a homo in the Army, we now have to take extra steps to ensure the safety of the queer who has 'told.' . . . Commanders now bear responsibility if someone decides to assault the young backside ranger. Be discreet and careful in your dealings with these characters. And remember, little ears are everywhere."

Soldier Accused of Being a Lesbian After Reporting Attempted Rape
A young private first class, away from home for the first time, was attacked and nearly raped in her barracks hallway in Korea. When she reported the attack, the perpetrators retaliated by falsely accusing her of being involved in a lesbian relationship. The unit commander pressured her to accuse other women of being lesbians and, when she refused, sent her to a court-martial based on the false allegations. When a military judge threw out the charges for lack of evidence, the commander tried instead to discharge her. The commander dropped the charges only after substantial outside intervention.

Supervisor Threatens Marine Who Was Gay-Bashed With Criminal Investigation

When Marine Lance Corporal Kevin Smith was gay-bashed by civilians in San Angelo, Texas, his supervisor threatened him with an investigation into his private life rather than helping him bring his assailants to justice.

Commander Fails to Help Airman Who Received Death Threat

Then airman Sean Fucci woke up 2 days before Christmas to find the note, "Die Fag!" next to his bed. This was the second threat Fucci had received. When Fucci reported the threats, his commander responded with a written memorandum telling him there was nothing he could do to protect Fucci.

Sailors Threatened With Death or Assault

Four sailors aboard the *U.S.S. Eisenhower* reported being assaulted or threatened with their lives because they were perceived as being gay. Their supervisors did nothing to protect them. When they came out and sought discharge due to the threats, their supervisors instead accused them of trying to avoid their military duties and launched an investigation into their private lives.

Federal Judge Says Navy Launched "Search and 'Outing' Mission"

The Navy pursued Master Chief Petty Officer Timothy McVeigh based on an anonymous America Online profile containing the word "gay." A federal judge ruled in McVeigh's favor, stating, "Although Officer [sic] McVeigh did not publicly announce his sexual orientation, the Navy nonetheless impermissibly embarked on a search and 'outing' mission."[31] Ultimately, the Navy permitted McVeigh to retire at the rank he had earned, but Navy leaders maintained they did nothing wrong in pursuing McVeigh.

Air Force Cuts Deal With Felon to Get Names of Suspected Gay Men

Prosecutors at Hickam Air Force Base in Hawaii reduced the sentence of a convicted felon from life to 20 months on the condition that he accuse others of being in gay relationships. He named 17 men in all services. The Navy jailed one sailor. The Air Force pursued and discharged all Air Force members identified. Air Force investigators also questioned dozens of co-workers of one of the identified men in an effort to identify other gay service members.[32]

The Okinawa Witch Hunt

Corporal Craig Haack and 10 other marines were questioned at length about their sexual orientation during a witch hunt in Okinawa. A criminal investigator, Agent Jose Abrante, banged on Haack's door and loudly announced that he was under investigation for being gay so that the entire barracks could hear. Agent Abrante overturned Haack's bed, ransacked his belongings and seized his computer, computer disks, and address book, looking for any indication of Haack's sexual orientation.

Career Officer Court-Martialed After Witch-Hunt

The Air Force criminally prosecuted Major Debra Meeks based on allegations that she was in a relationship with a civilian woman, just as the major approached retirement. Air Force criminal investigators at Lackland Air Force Base solicited the allegations against her in the course of a witch hunt against Meeks and 11 other women named in the report of investigation. Meeks, who faced up to 8 years in prison and forfeiture of her entire pension, was acquitted at trial in a widely publicized case.[33]

Airman of the Year Discharged Although Accuser Recants

The Air Force discharged then airman Sonya Harden based solely on an allegation later recanted by her accuser. The accuser admitted she lied about Airman Harden being in a lesbian relationship in retaliation for a financial dispute between the two women. Airman Harden had presented ex-boyfriends to testify on her behalf at the discharge board, to no avail.

Psychiatrist Turns in Marine Who Asks About Homosexuality

A Navy psychiatrist turned in then Marine corporal Kevin Blaesing for merely asking what it meant to be gay. The psychiatrist testified at his discharge board that Blaesing never, in fact, revealed his sexual orientation. Blaesing's commander, Lieutenant Colonel Martinson, nevertheless pursued his discharge.[34] When Blaesing successfully sought, with outside help, to overturn his discharge, his commander retaliated by foreclosing his opportunity to reenlist.

West Point Seizes Cadet's Diary

The Army pursued and disenrolled Cadet Nikki Galvan of West Point based on statements she made in her personal diary. Galvan's commander, Lieutenant Colonel Abraham Turner, seized her diary and 3 years' worth of e-mail messages after Galvan filed a complaint against him for questioning her about her sexual orientation and private life. Galvan had started keeping her diary at the suggestion of West Point counselors, who felt it would help her deal with the grief of her mother's death.

Women Threatened With Prison During Witch Hunt

Investigators on board the *U.S.S. Simon Lake* directly questioned then seaman Amy Barnes and other women about their sexual orientation. Investigators threatened them with prison if they did not confess or accuse others of being lesbians, according to sworn affidavits the women later submitted in federal court. The Navy forced Seaman Barnes into court when Navy officials, apprised of the illegal investigation, refused to intervene to stop it. The Navy ultimately settled this case, although Seaman Barnes lost her career.

Navy Uses "Homosexual/Bisexual Questionnaire" to Ferret Out Gay Sailors
The Navy discharged two sailors after asking them 50 questions about their sexual orientation and activities, in part from a document titled "The Homosexual/Bisexual Questionnaire." The questionnaire appears to be a standard form used on the sailors' ship to investigate suspected gay personnel.

their rejection. Federal law on homosexuality in the U.S. military continues to put the full resources of the government to the task of creating and maintaining prejudice, discrimination, and violence against LGBs. "Don't Ask, Don't Tell, Don't Pursue, Don't Harass" is the only U.S. law that authorizes the firing of an American for being LGB, and it is the only law that punishes disclosure of one's sexual orientation to another.

In thinking about the injustices involved, one must also keep in mind that LGBs are recruited. There is no reason to assume that the military is any less appealing to LGBs than to others. As they enter the military, these young men and women are reaching a stage of their lives during which their well-being depends on their ability to build social support. These healthy support networks depend, at least in part, on their ability to disclose their sexuality to others. But this is exactly what the military prohibits.

Public Opinion Supports Military Service by LGBs

Although public opinion can be volatile from poll to poll, since the issue was first assessed in 1977 polls have consistently found that a majority of Americans support gays in the military and this majority has been increasing.[35] Independent public opinion polls released in 1999 and 2001 by Gallup and in 1999 by *The Wall Street Journal*/NBC[36] found that 70 percent or more of Americans support gays in the military. Major national and regional newspapers have repeatedly called for repeal of "Don't Ask, Don't Tell, Don't Pursue, Don't Harass," as did the Democratic Party platform in the 2000 presidential election.[37]

Similar beliefs have also been found among those in military service. One poll of soldiers indicated a dramatic decrease in strong opposition to gays in the military from 63 percent in 1993 to 36 percent in 1998.[38] In public statements, dozens of leading military figures have dismissed the notion that gay men and lesbians in any way impair the functioning of the services and urged an end to restrictions on service by LGB personnel.[39]

The Policy Is Costly

The military loses hundreds of trained personnel each year because of the current policy, and this loss is very costly (see Table 7.3). Based on estimates supplied to the General Accounting Office by the Pentagon in 1992, the cost of recruiting and training service members to replace those discharged for homosexuality was $28,226 for each enlisted individual and $120,772 for each officer.[40] These esti-

Table 7.3

LOWER BOUND ESTIMATES OF COSTS OF REPLACING SERVICE MEMBERS DISCHARGED UNDER POLICY CONCERNING HOMOSEXUALITY IN THE ARMED FORCES USING DOD ESTIMATES FOR FY 1990*

Fiscal year	Total discharged	Estimated replacement cost
1991	949	$26,786,474
1992	708	19,984,008
1993	682	19,250,132
1994	597	16,850,922
1995	722	20,379,172
1996	850	23,992,100
1997	997	28,141,322
1998	1,149	32,403,448
1999	1,034	29,213,910
2000	1,231	34,746,206
Total	8,962	251,747,694

* DOD reported to the Governmental Accounting Office (GAO) in 1992 that FY 1990 costs for recruiting and initial training of enlisted personnel to replace those discharged for homosexuality were $28,226 per person. Further, the GAO reported that 99 percent of those discharged were enlisted personnel. In the estimates in this table, we have assumed that all personnel discharged are enlisted and used the enlisted personnel cost estimate. The figures are clearly lower bounds. Some discharged personnel are officers, whose recruitment and initial training costs are much higher ($120,772 in FY 1992). Furthermore, the cost estimates do not include the costs of administering the policy concerning homosexuality in the armed forces, including the costs of investigations and administrative discharge hearings.

mates do not take into account the administrative costs of investigations and discharge proceedings, nor do they include costs related to the loss of service members who leave at the end of their enlistment terms or resign their commissions because they are tired of harassment and of the necessity to lie to their parents, medical professionals, and friends about who they are.

Military leaders can ill-afford to lose the valuable contributions of LGB service members. In fiscal year 2000, the Pentagon spent approximately $11,000 per recruit on advertising and recruitment in an effort to meet its recruitment goals.[41]

The Military Is Capable of Successfully Implementing Change

Although the U.S. military has been described as conservative, oriented toward tradition, and resistant to change, it also has a long history of successfully implementing change. Change has been accomplished with the support of scientific evidence, the help of professional experts and consultants, and a serious commitment to learn from mistakes. Examples include the integration of ethnic minorities and Native Americans during World War I, despite strong anti-immigrant, anti–Native American, and anti-Semitic sentiments at the time; the integration of Japanese Americans during World War II, despite the animosity toward and even internment of Japanese American civilians; the integration of African Americans since 1948;[42] the integration of Korean Americans during the Korean War; and the inclusion of women in noncombatant occupational fields since 1973.[43] The military also implemented policies to accommodate single-parent families and dual-career couples in the 1970s and early 1980s as these types of families increased among the all-volunteer force.[44]

It is important to understand that the military has the power of a total institution.[45] It provides its personnel with transportation, housing, food, clothing, medical services, education (both for military personnel and their dependents), and much more. Thus, perhaps more than any other institution, the U.S. military has the authority to implement change among its members. Furthermore, the U.S. military has the resources and infrastructure to develop and implement psychological technologies, as it did to reduce racial prejudice in the 1960s and 1970s.

The military has played an important role in broadening the sociocultural perspectives of the U.S. population. By deploying men, women, and their families throughout the world, it has exposed millions of U.S. citizens to diverse cultures with varied mores, beliefs, diets, and political systems. It has played a critical role in modeling for society the integration of African Americans, the broadening of occupational roles for women, and the expansion of gender and family roles of both men and women. Military personnel have had a long history of interracial and intercultural marriages. While the institution is conservative, its personnel have often been socially nontraditional.[46]

Experience Shows LGBs Have Served and Do Serve Openly

Many LGBs served more or less openly in the U.S. military during World War II. Their sexual orientation was known to many of their heterosexual comrades, and they served effectively in combat with the respect and admiration of those comrades.[47] Since World War II, published works and legal challenges to DOD policy have demonstrated that many LGBs have served with distinction in the U.S. military with their peers and superiors knowing of their sexual orientation.[48]

The United States and Turkey are the only original NATO countries banning service by openly LGB people. Furthermore, other military and quasi-military institutions have made the change to including openly LGB people.[49] Most recently among U.S. allies, Britain lifted its ban in January 2000, in response to a ruling by the European Court of Human Rights. According to a *New York Times* report, the British Defense Ministry has found "'widespread acceptance of the policy' and 'no reported difficulties of note concerning homophobic behavior.'"[50] Recent studies of the effects of lifting bans on LGB service in the military in Canada, Australia, and Israel have all concluded that the repeals have been nonevents. Some studies have even noted a correlation between lifting the ban and reduction in gender discrimination and sexual harassment in the military. LGBs have also been allowed to join US quasi-military organizations such as police and sheriffs' departments.[51] In summary, historical data and experience in other contexts show that heterosexuals can work with openly LGB people in military environments without the dire consequences that U.S. military leaders have predicted.

debunking the current rationale for the policy

Rather than being vulnerable to problems resulting from change, in reality, the military is highly capable of change. We need to leverage this fact to change the terms of the debate over "Don't Ask, Don't Tell" from the negative consequences that the supporters of the policy have claimed would follow from change to the positive consequences that would result—improving military readiness, reducing harm and injustice, and making policy consistent with the wishes of the American people.

The Military's Argument About Unit Cohesion Is Flawed

The military argues that the presence of openly LGB people in the services would be harmful to unit cohesion by disrupting the bonds of trust between service members. It argues that perceived differences between service members, including those due to variations in sexual orientation, would reduce social cohesion and thereby diminish performance. We have already discussed how the policy itself hurts unit cohesion, and how lifting the ban on known LGB service members would ameliorate anti-LGB sentiments to the extent they exist. To take this argument further, even if one accepts the unit cohesion rationale at face value as framed by ban advocates, the argument is not supported by social science research.

The military has defined *unit cohesion* in relation to combat:

> Cohesion exists in a unit when the primary day-to-day goals of the individual soldier, of the small group with which he identifies, and of unit leaders, are congruent—each giving his primary loyalty to the group so that it trains and fights as a unit with all members willing to risk death and achieve a common objective.[52]

Social scientists, in contrast, define *cohesion* in terms of the strength of the influences that keep members of a group together. These influences include the members' liking for the activities of the group, other group members, and the prestige associated with group membership.[53] The first of these three influences has been labeled *task cohesion*, and the second and third have been jointly labeled *social cohesion*.

The difference between the military definition of *unit cohesion* and the social science definition of *cohesion* is important. The first focuses on outcomes—primary loyalty to the group, willingness to risk death, and commitment to achieving a common purpose—whereas the second defines cohesion in terms of the three factors that produce it. The military has simply assumed that cohesion is based on interpersonal relationships and that it leads to better combat performance. The factors that produce the outcomes—loyalty, risk taking, and common purpose—are not defined in the military version of cohesion.

According to the military's own officials, whether a service member contributes to the cohesion of his or her unit depends not on what is known or believed about that service member, but primarily on whether the service member possesses the characteristics that soldiers value, such as "[f]ighting skill, physical fitness, stamina, and self-discipline, teamwork, duty or selfless service, and loyalty to unit and leaders."[54] As one witness testified before Congress, unit cohesion rests upon a "shared organizational structure and values" and "primary identity as soldiers."[55]

We must contest the military's assumptions about unit cohesion. The military must be challenged to prove that openly LGB people will harm unit cohesion. Social science research does not support the idea that perceived differences between service members within their combat units have a detrimental impact on task cohesion or performance. Indeed the evidence suggests that "Don't Ask, Don't Tell, Don't Pursue, Don't Harass" itself undermines unit cohesion.

Privacy Arguments Fall Short

Consistent with the history of evolving rationalizations we reviewed earlier, opponents of military service by known LGB people are increasingly emphasizing a new rationale—that heterosexual military personnel would be so resistant to living in close quarters with LGB people that forcing them to do so would be a violation of their expectations of privacy. To justify this rationale, a parallel has been drawn between sexual orientation and gender: Just as men and women are provided privacy from one another, heterosexuals deserve privacy from homosexuals.[56] This is the "showers" argument—men and women should not shower together; LGBs and heterosexuals should not shower together.

First, the days of open bay barracks have, by and large, ended in the military, a fact that takes the steam out of much of this argument. Service members no longer find themselves in mass living situations with the accompanying lack of privacy. Today, housing arrangements for most personnel, even junior enlisted members, are similar to college dormitories. On shore or in garrison, two or, at most, three people typically share a room with a private restroom and shower. Current conditions provide service members with a fairly large degree of privacy. The presence of known LGB service members would not, therefore, disrupt an entire unit. Any problems that arise from individual roommate assignments could be handled on an ad hoc basis, much as they currently are. Greater education and leadership about tolerance, including tolerance of homosexual orientation, combined with the experience of living and working with openly LGB people may reduce the climate of rampant homophobia and harassment in the armed forces and actually increase unit cohesion and performance.

Second, the comparison between gender and sexual orientation is inaccurate. Whereas males and females are segregated from an early age in public toilets and locker rooms, LGBs have grown up sharing such facilities with heterosexuals of their same sex. Of necessity, they have developed the same behavioral patterns generally used by heterosexuals in such settings (such as gaze aversion and other behaviors that scholars have called *civil inattention*).[57] The suggestion that any time an openly LGB person looks at another person, it is sexually motivated, whereas any time a heterosexual person looks, it is not, is simply wrong. This suggestion, with its implication that gay men, lesbians, and bisexuals are incapable of controlling their sexual impulses, is based on the myth that LGBs find all individuals of their same sex to be sexually attractive. The reality is that LGBs are no more likely than others to act on sexual impulses. In fact, fear of violence or harassment makes LGB people even less likely to act.

The military already has a framework for dealing with misconduct, in the form of the Uniform Code of Military Justice and its sexual harassment policy.

Any sexual misconduct, whether homosexual or heterosexual, can be most appropriately and most efficiently handled through these channels.

Attitudes and Behavior Can Be Changed

LGB military personnel often encounter individual incidents of anti-LGB prejudice, discrimination, and violence. Such incidents present a problem for which the military has solutions available.

Sexual prejudice[58] refers to heterosexuals' negative attitudes toward LGBs. Psychologists have found that sexual prejudice manifests the same psychological dynamics as racial and ethnic prejudices. One central factor in the reduction of prejudice and intergroup hostility is personal contact between members of different groups in situations in which they have similar status and are involved in the pursuit of shared goals. Research shows that contact in such situations leads to a reduction of prejudice.[59]

Several studies of prejudice against LGBs suggest that intergroup contact may likewise reduce prejudice based on sexual orientation. Having close relationships with LGB peers with whom one has discussed their sexual orientation is strongly associated with lowered sexual prejudice.[60] The positive relationship between interpersonal contact and attitudes has also been found in the military.[61] As the research on social cohesion shows, just being part of a group makes people like one another. Thus, the open presence of LGBs in the military will itself change attitudes.

Attitudes are not, however, the only factors that determine behavior. Another important influence is the perception of social norms.[62] Thus, if service members perceive that treating LGBs without prejudice is the social norm of the military, they are likely to act accordingly. If the military opposes prejudice, it will recede. If the military continues to endorse prejudice through exclusionary policies, prejudice will continue. As a hierarchical institution, one advantage the military has in dealing with heterosexuals who might seek to abuse their colleagues is the military chain of command. The military chain of command works, when leaders want it to, but it will necessitate leadership from the military.

Another important influence on behavior is the degree to which people believe that they are capable of acting effectively.[63] One way for the military to express institutional support for LGB service members and at the same time increase service members' beliefs in their personal efficacy in accepting LGB people is to provide training. The Dutch military has proactively implemented educational programs to counter sexual prejudice.[64] In the United States, some police and sheriffs' departments with openly gay members have encountered negative attitudes among some heterosexual personnel. In response, they have developed training programs for their officers.[65] The active involvement and leadership of high-ranking officers have been perceived to be important in the success of such programs.[66]

LGBs serve in the military despite the policy, as they have done since we have had a military. By forbidding LGBs from revealing their true selves to their friends, "Don't Ask, Don't Tell, Don't Pursue, Don't Harass" denies heterosexuals the knowledge and experience that is likely to reduce their prejudice, discrimination, and violence against LGB people.

improving the implementation of the current policy

Although the policy adopted in 1994 still prohibits LGB service members from engaging in homosexual conduct, including statements about their sexual orientation to others,[67] the policy is supposed to be implemented with due regard for the privacy rights and rights to association of service members. Furthermore, witch hunts against LGBs are not permitted under the policy, LGBs are not to be criminally prosecuted under circumstances in which heterosexual service members would not be, and harassment and violence are not to be tolerated.[68] None of these promises has been kept. So advocates should also seek to improve the current policy's implementation along the lines of those initial promises.

The Military Must Proactively Address Anti-LGB Harassment and Violence

In the aftermath of Barry Winchell's murder, the Pentagon issued stronger guidelines on antigay harassment, including more explicit language regarding nontolerance of antigay epithets such as "faggot," "fag," "queer," and "dyke." In addition, the Secretary of Defense and the chiefs of the services have issued statements denouncing anti-LGB harassment. The DOD even added "Don't Harass" to its description of the current policy.[69] The Army has issued the most comprehensive system of guidance and training to date. The other services have not. We must press the Pentagon, Navy, Marine Corps, and Air Force to ensure that appropriate guidance and training are implemented and to ensure that every service member, from recruit to flag officer, receives and understands the guidelines and leadership messages from the Secretary of Defense and chief of each service against anti-LGB harassment.

LGBs Must Be Provided Sufficient Privacy to Protect Their Well-Being

Military personnel must be able to report anti-LGB harassment and crimes without fear of being outed and discharged. Inspectors general, law enforcement personnel, equal opportunity representatives, chaplains, health care providers, commanders, and other personnel who deal with harassment-related issues should be given clear instructions to respect the privacy of those who consult them and maintain their confidentiality. They should be trained to handle service members' complaints of anti-LGB harassment and crimes appropriately. Service members—straight, gay, and bisexual—go to these sources for help, not to make public statements of their sexual orientation. These are private contexts and should remain so.

The Pentagon should also inform health care providers that there is no requirement to turn in LGB clients, and should further clarify that conversations with health care providers are not a basis for investigation or discharge under "Don't Ask, Don't Tell, Don't Pursue, Don't Harass." An executive order signed by President Clinton, providing for a limited psychotherapist privilege, prevents use of conversations with psychotherapists as incriminating evidence in criminal trials. The rule, however, does not address the fact that some psychotherapists continue to turn in LGB service members who are then administratively discharged under "Don't Ask, Don't Tell, Don't Pursue, Don't Harass."

Ensure Full and Appropriate Training on Investigative Limits

In 1999 the Secretary of Defense ordered mandatory training for all service members on the investigative limits of "Don't Ask, Don't Tell, Don't Pursue, Don't Harass."[70] The Pentagon should ensure that the services train all personnel on the policy's investigative limits and intent to respect service members' privacy. Leaders must set the proper tone and be involved in the training. If the training is to have positive effects, leaders must make a commitment to treat it seriously.

Hold Officers Accountable for Failures to Follow the Policy

Military leaders have held few people publicly accountable for asking, pursuing, or harassing. With the new guidelines on "Don't Ask, Don't Tell, Don't Pursue, Don't Harass," the Pentagon should remind commanders that there are specific consequences for violations, from letters of counseling to court-martial, depending on the offense. Senior leaders should set the example by holding those who violate the policy accountable, starting with requiring military leaders to demonstrate their commitment to stopping anti-LGB harassment. Leaders must show through their own actions that they take anti-LGB harassment seriously, and they should specifically inform service members that epithets such as "faggot," "dyke," and "queer" will no longer be tolerated.

Stop Improper Investigations

Under the current policy, military commanders have the right to conduct a "limited inquiry," based on "credible evidence" of homosexual conduct. Too often, commanders engage in far-reaching inquiries that include asking service members about issues not in question, interrogating family members and friends, and subjecting the service member under investigation to dozens if not hundreds of intrusive questions. Service members should have the opportunity to show why an inquiry should not be initiated in the first place to avoid the time, pain, and embarrassment an improper inquiry would produce. Service members should be able to obtain and consult with a military defense attorney before an inquiry is initiated, a right they are currently denied, and have an opportunity to demonstrate that no credible evidence exists. The Pentagon should also require commanders to state in writing the reasons for an investigation. This step would further safeguard against improper investigations.

Train Investigators and Adopt an Exclusionary Rule

Criminal investigators and law enforcement personnel need training to recognize and appropriately document and investigate possible anti-LGB hate crimes. The Pentagon should also adopt an exclusionary rule, as exists in the civilian world, so that improperly or illegally obtained evidence against service members can be excluded at administrative discharge board hearings. Service members deserve this procedural protection.

conclusion

The information provided here will help you to pursue change in the U.S. military policy on homosexuality in two different ways: (1) improving implementation of "Don't Ask, Don't Tell, Don't Pursue, Don't Harass"[71] and (2) the eventual repeal of the policy. These goals are neither inconsistent nor mutually exclusive. Although the policy should eventually be repealed, this will require a very careful and concerted effort to obtain the needed documentation, change the terms of the debate, and build support in the Pentagon, in Congress, and in grassroots constituencies. As of this writing, the political will does not exist in Congress to push for repeal; indeed, such efforts might well produce even greater harm. However, providing legal assistance now and pushing for better policy implementation not only improve LGB service members' lives today, they also lay the necessary groundwork for the policy's eventual repeal.

what you can do!

- Keep up to date on the latest news, information, and policy developments regarding the military's antigay policies.
  - Join the Servicemembers Legal Defense Network (SLDN).
  - Monitor the SLDN website and join the Front Line E-mail Action Alert Network. (www.sldn.org, click on "Join the Fight").
  - Monitor the website for the Center for the Study of Sexual Minorities in the Military (CSSMM) (www.gaymilitary.uscb.edu).
- If you, or someone you know, is the target of antigay harassment or discrimination in the armed forces, contact the Servicemembers Legal Defense Network (SLDN) (202–328–3244 or legal@sldn.org).
- Write your members of Congress asking for their support in repealing "Don't Ask, Don't Tell." Attach a copy of *"Don't Ask, Don't Tell" Should Be Repealed* to your letter.
  - Call your U.S. senators and representatives. The congressional switchboard can be reached at 202–224–3121. Let your elected leaders know that we can ill-afford to lose the talents of qualified, trained men and women simply because of their sexual orientation.
- Use Western Union (800–325–6000) to send the following public opinion message to your elected representatives in Congress. Use a similar strategy to contact the White House (202–456–1414).
  - *I (We) urge that you work to overturn the ban on lesbians and gay men in the military.*
  - Organize others in your area to make similar contacts.
- Visit with your senators and representatives in Washington or in their offices in your district.
- Make contributions to SLDN, CSSMM, or other organizations that are working to change the policy.

for more information

- Bérubé, A. (1990). *Coming out under fire: The history of gay men and women in World War II.* New York: Free Press.
- Center for the Study of Sexual Minorities in the Military (CSSMM). http://www.gaymilitary.uscb.edu.
- Halley, J. E. (1999). *Don't: A reader's guide to the military's anti-gay policy.* Durham, NC: Duke University Press.
- Herek, G. M. (2000). The psychology of sexual prejudice. *Current Directions in Psychological Science, 9*(1), 19–22.

The U.S. policy concerning homosexuality in the armed forces, 10 U.S.C. § 654, causes great harm to military discipline and good order, and to lesbian, gay, and bisexual service members who are targeted by its provisions. The U.S. Congress should repeal this harmful law.

Provisions and Intent.
Adopted by the Congress at the conclusion of major public debate over gays in the military, 10 U.S.C. § 654 mandates administrative discharges for service members who engage in homosexual conduct, including making statements that they have a homosexual sexual orientation or marrying someone of their biological sex. The policy was intended to balance concerns for military readiness with concerns that the previous policy unfairly targeted lesbian, gay, and bisexual service members for criminal prosecution, investigation, and punitive discharges.

Why 10 U.S.C. § 654 Should Be Repealed.
The policy hurts innocent people. In its implementation, the policy has failed to achieve its purpose and continues to harm both military discipline and the lesbian, gay, and bisexual people targeted by its provisions. In the debate surrounding the adoption of the policy, all participants agreed that lesbians, gay men, and bisexual people currently serve honorably and competently in the military and the unfair targeting of those individuals for discharge should stop. The policy unjustly excludes qualified individuals from serving in the military and fosters prejudice, discrimination, and violence against lesbian, gay, and bisexual service members.

Public opinion supports military service by gay, lesbian, and bisexual people. Public opinion polls have consistently shown that a majority of the American public supports the service of gay, lesbian, and bisexual people in the U.S. military.

The policy is costly. Based on 1990 dollars, American taxpayers paid more than $250 million for this policy during the years 1991–2000. There is no useful purpose served by spending millions each year to investigate and discharge patriotic Americans who wish to serve their country.

*Close relationships are **not** crucial in combat performance.* Supporters have claimed that heterosexual service members will be unable to establish close interpersonal relationships with homosexual service members. Regardless of the validity of this claim, social science research has shown that performance is related to shared commitment to the military goals of the unit, rather than close relationships, and that shared commitment to goals is strongly influenced by leadership.

Prejudice and discrimination can change. Contact between heterosexual and homosexual service members in situations where they are peers and share goals has been shown to lead to reduction in prejudice. Further, behavior change is influenced not only by attitudes. Establishing clear norms through leadership and providing training to increase confidence in dealing with the integration of openly gay, lesbian, and bisexual personnel will also influence behavior, perhaps even more strongly than prejudicial attitudes.

The U.S. military is capable of successfully implementing change. The military has proved itself willing, able, and effective in attacking prejudice and stereotypes within its ranks based on race and gender. This experience can and should inform efforts to eliminate barriers based on sexual orientation. Likewise, the experience of foreign militaries or of those American police and fire departments that hire lesbian and gay officers can be drawn upon in implementing the change.

Implementation.
The following principles should guide implementation of the repeal of the policy:

1. Sexual misconduct should be prohibited for all service members.
2. Sexual misconduct should be prosecuted equally regardless of sexual orientation.
3. Education and training programs should be undertaken to establish behavioral expectations and confront attitudinal barriers.
4. Research and evaluation should be undertaken to guide the implementation process.

The military can reduce antigay prejudice by fostering heterosexual and LGB personnel's development of shared commitments to the goals of military service, and by establishing norms that prejudice, discrimination, and violence will be negatively sanctioned. One norm to be promulgated is that everyone should be judged on her or his own merits, and that sexual orientation is irrelevant to performing one's duty. Another is that sexual harassment is unacceptable and will be punished, regardless of the gender of the people involved. A third norm is that intimate situations (such as sleeping quarters and the latrine) are not sexual.

---

* The material presented here is discussed in greater detail in *Everyday Activism: A Handbook for Lesbian, Gay, and Bisexual People and Their Allies*, edited by Michael R. Stevenson, Ph.D., and Jeanine C. Cogan, Ph.D., and published by Routledge in 2003.

- Herek, G. M., Jobe, J. B., & Carney, R. M. (Eds.). (1996). *Out in force: Sexual orientation and the military.* Chicago: University of Chicago Press.
- Leonard, A. S. (Ed.). (1997). *Homosexuality and the constitution: Homosexuals and the military* (vol. 4). New York: Garland.
- Mitchell, C. G. (2000). *Marching to an angry drum: Gays in the military.* Lincoln, NE: Writers Club.
- Servicemembers Legal Defense Network (SLDN). www.sldn.org
- Shawver, L. (1995). *And the flag was still there: Straight people, gay people, and sexuality in the U.S. military.* New York: Harrington Park Press.
- Shilts, R. (1993). *Conduct unbecoming: Gays and lesbians in the U.S. military.* New York: St. Martin's Press.
- Sobel, S. L., Cleghorn, J. M., & Osburn, C. D. (2001). *Conduct unbecoming: The seventh annual report on "don't ask, don't tell, don't pursue, don't harass."* Washington, DC: Servicemembers Legal Defense Network.
- Zeeland, S. (1993). *Barrack buddies and soldier lovers: Dialogues with gay young men in the U.S. military.* New York: Harrington Park Press.

Part III

creating equality

CHAPTER 8

honoring and protecting relationships

Robin A. Buhrke

In this chapter, you will

- Learn the definitions and legal benefits of marriage in the United States.
- Discover how the federal government has restricted access to marriage.
- Learn how Vermont became the first state in the United States to allow same-sex civil unions.
- Find out how governments around the world deal with the rights of same-sex couples.
- Master the basics concerning domestic partner benefits.

Conservative estimates indicate that at any given time, 40 to 71 percent of gay men and 45 to 80 percent of lesbians are involved in a steady relationship.[1] According to the 2000 U.S. Census, there were 1,202,418 lesbians and gay men in committed relationships.[2] These relationships can last over decades, and breakup rates are comparable to those of heterosexual relationships.[3] Indeed, "research has shown that most lesbians and gay men want intimate relationships and are successful in creating them. Homosexual partnerships appear no more vulnerable to problems and dissatisfactions than their heterosexual counterparts."[4] Some researchers have even suggested that heterosexual couples may have something to learn from gay and lesbian couples.[5] Moreover, "these non-marital relationships share principal elements of the marital relationship."[6]

As of early 2003, no jurisdiction in the United States allowed or recognized marriages between partners of the same sex. The Netherlands was the first European country to allow same-sex couples to marry.[7] Belgium passed a similar proposal in January 2003.[8] Several other countries allow same-sex relationship registration. While registration grants a number of rights and responsibilities, it stops short of the full benefits accorded heterosexual, married couples. Because same-sex couples cannot marry, some jurisdictions and employers have created a new category—domestic partners—to recognize and protect same-sex partnerships. Clearly domestic partner benefits fall far short of the rights and benefits accorded by marriage—domestic partner benefits are only available in certain jurisdictions or from some employers, and they do not represent the same type of legal contract as does marriage. In the absence of marriage, however, domestic partner benefits are an important step in the direction of recognizing the importance of same-sex relationships.

The purpose of this chapter is to review policy as it relates to same-sex, committed relationships—same-sex marriage (including the so-called Defense of Marriage Act) and domestic partner benefits. You will be much more effective in working for changes in policy in your jurisdiction or workplace if you are familiar with such efforts, both successful and unsuccessful, elsewhere.

same-sex marriage

In most jurisdictions in the United States, lesbians, gay men, and bisexuals are denied many basic protections against discrimination (for example, on the job and in the workplace, with regard to housing and public accommodations).[9] One of the more fundamental rights denied lesbians, gay men, and bisexuals is the right to enter into a civil, legal union with—that is, to marry—the partner of their choice. It is ironic that members of the lesbian, gay, and bisexual community are often unjustly accused of having unstable, short-lived relationships while at the same time are prohibited from establishing sanctioned, committed, legal relationships.

Regardless of whether you agree with the concept of marriage, the tangible benefits of legal marriage are many. In addition to social approval and increased relationship security, the U.S. General Accounting Office established that there are more than 1,049 federal rights, benefits, and responsibilities available to married couples. In addition, depending on the state, there are another 170 to 250 state laws prescribing rights and responsibilities for married spouses. Benefits include the ability to file joint tax returns, Social Security benefits, Veterans benefits, access to Medicare, automatic inheritance, the right to claim immigrant status by non-citizen spouses, the right to visit a spouse in the hospital, the right to make medical decisions for each other, guardianship, the right to visit a spouse in jail, the right to refuse to testify in court against a spouse, and the right to designate inheritance without challenge. While some benefits can be achieved by creating various legal documents, many benefits cannot be accomplished in this way. Automatic inheritance, automatic housing lease transfer, bereavement leave, child custody, crime victim's recovery benefits, domestic violence protection, exemption from property tax upon the death of a spouse, immunity from testifying against a spouse, insurance reductions, joint adoption and foster care, joint bankruptcy, joint parenting, medical decisions on behalf of a spouse, and visitation of a spouse in the hospital or in prison are benefits that cannot be provided for via legal documentation. Thus, the benefits available to married couples are simply not available to unmarried couples.

history

Laws restricting marriage have been modified and updated over the years as attitudes and beliefs have shifted. For example, laws prohibiting African Americans from marrying whites arose during slavery times, Asian Americans were prohibited from marrying whites beginning in the mid-19th century, and over time, more than 30 states adopted laws prohibiting "mixed-race" marriages.[10] It wasn't until 1967 that the Supreme Court struck down antimiscegenation laws.[11] And while rendered unconstitutional, several states continue to have such laws on the books. These so-called traditions were once thought to be wise restrictions, but in time were seen as unfair and discriminatory.

Legal challenges to the prohibition of same-sex marriage are not new. During the 1970s, a number of cases challenged same-sex marriage prohibitions in Minnesota,[12] Kentucky,[13] Washington,[14] Ohio,[15] Arizona,[16] and other states. Several other cases are on hold pending the outcome of current court cases.

Hawaii

In December 1990 three same-sex couples applied for marriage licenses in Hawaii. After their applications were turned down, they filed suit against the State of Hawaii in May 1991, claiming that the denial was based on sex discrimination.[17] The case later became known as *Baehr v. Miike* and then *Baehr v. Anderson*. In October 1991 the trial court dismissed the suit, and the case was appealed to the Hawaii Supreme Court. The Hawaii Supreme Court ruled that denying the marriage licenses was discriminatory, remanding the case back to the trial court for a hearing where the state was required to show it had a "compelling interest" for restricting marriage to other-sex couples.

In September 1996 the circuit court judge ruled that, under the state constitution, it was illegal to prevent people of the same sex from marrying. At that time, it was expected that the state supreme court would approve same-sex marriage the next year. On December 4, 1996, the state attorney general deputy filed—and was granted—a motion to stay the decision, stopping the issuance of marriage licenses to same-sex couples until after the state's appeal of the decision. In early 1999 the Supreme Court of Hawaii conducted a supplemental hearing and in August ruled that no more arguments would be made.

As the case was winding its way through the court system, the Hawaii State Legislature was divided over the prospect of same-sex marriage becoming legal in Hawaii. As a result, the 1994 Hawaii legislature passed a law prohibiting same-sex marriage and creating the Commission on Sexual Orientation to review which rights and benefits would be denied if same-sex marriages were not allowed. After being reconstituted the following year, the Commission recommended that the 1996 legislature legalize same-sex marriage. However, the 1995 legislature amended Hawaii marriage law to specify that marriage is between a man and a woman. In May 1997 the Hawaii State Legislature passed a constitutional amendment to be placed on the November 3, 1998, ballot that the "legislature may limit marriage to between a man and a woman." Voters approved the amendment by a 2–1 margin, thus changing the state constitution.

On December 9, 1999, the Hawaii Supreme Court dismissed the case, ruling that the issue had been made moot by the 1998 constitutional amendment. That is, because the Hawaii constitution now specified that marriage is between one man and one woman, denying marriage to same-sex couples was no longer unconstitutional. While the ruling did not overturn the 1993 decision that denying same-sex couples the right to marriage was sex discrimination or the 1996 decision that the state had no compelling reason to prohibit same-sex marriage, it effectively shut the door on same-sex marriage in Hawaii.

The Defense of Marriage Act (DOMA)

According to the U.S. Constitution's Full Faith and Credit Clause, states must recognize certain obligations, such as marriage, established in another state. "Full Faith and Credit shall be given in each State to the public Acts, Records and judicial Proceedings of every other State." Full faith and credit is based on the notion that because people are free to travel from state to state, the states must recognize each other's laws. Thus, if one state were to allow same-sex marriages, other states would be required to recognize them because of the Full faith and credit clause. In addition, those states would have to provide the same legal protections and benefits accorded to married, heterosexual couples to married, same-sex couples.

In response to the Hawaii case, the Defense of Marriage Act (DOMA) was introduced into Congress in May 1996 and passed the House of Representatives by a vote of 342–67 and the Senate by 85–14. (Box 8.1 shows how members of Congress voted.) President Clinton signed DOMA into law on September 21, 1996. DOMA contains two major provisions: it allows states the right to refuse to recognize legal same-sex marriages performed in other states, and it creates federal definitions of the terms *marriage* as the "legal union between one man and one woman as husband and wife" and *spouse* as referring "only to a person of the other sex who is a husband or wife." Thus, under DOMA, if one state establishes same-sex marriage, partners would only be married in that state (and those states that have not passed "other-sex only" marriage provisions), and they would not be considered legally married by the federal government. Thus, legally married, same-sex couples would not be eligible for Social Security benefits, inheritance rights, joint filing status for federal income taxes, and other benefits.

Prior to DOMA, the regulation and administration of marriage had always been handled at the state level. Domestic relations have always been the purview of the states, not the federal government. Proponents of DOMA claim that it does not prohibit same-sex marriage, it simply allows each state to decide for itself whether it wants to recognize same-sex marriages rather than have it forced on them by another state and the Full Faith and Credit Clause. In other words, without DOMA, if one state legalized same-sex marriage, every other state and the federal government would be required to recognize and accept those marriages performed in that state, even if those marriages were prohibited in the other state.

In addition to the challenge to the Full Faith and Credit Clause, a major problem with DOMA is that it creates the potential for two classes of legal marriage: those that are between heterosexuals and recognized across all states, the District of Columbia, and the federal government, and those that are between same-sex couples and recognized only by the state in which the marriage took place. Thus, a situation could easily arise where a same-sex, married couple vacations in a state where their marriage is not recognized, and therefore, their family health benefits or their rights to make medical decisions for one another are no longer recognized. Or a company having branches in more than one state may have employees whose marriages are legal in one state and not in another, creating chaos for benefits programs and making employee transfers much more complicated. Further, lawfully married, same-sex partners could file state tax returns as "married," but must file as "single" for their federal returns.

By 2002 at least 36 states had passed DOMA-like legislation restricting marriage to other-sex couples only, and each year more states introduce such legislation into their legislatures. Many legal scholars believe that DOMA will ultimately be ruled unconstitutional after challenge when one state allows same-sex marriage.

Vermont

In July 1997 three couples filed suit against the State of Vermont,[18] claiming that the "refusal to issue marriage licenses to them violates both state marriage laws

Box 8.1

HOW MEMBERS OF CONGRESS VOTED ON THE DEFENSE OF MARRIAGE ACT

The Senate Vote on the Defense of Marriage Act

YEAS—85	Domenici	Kyl	Thomas
Abraham	Dorgan	Lautenberg	Thompson
Ashcroft	Exon	Leahy	Thurmond
Baucus	Faircloth	Levin	Warner
Bennett	Ford	Lieberman	Wellstone
Biden	Frahm	Lott	
Bingaman	Frist	Lugar	NAYS—14
Bond	Glenn	Mack	Akaka
Bradley	Gorton	McCain	Boxer
Breaux	Graham	McConnell	Feingold
Brown	Gramm	Mikulski	Feinstein
Bryan	Grams	Murkowski	Inouye
Bumpers	Grassley	Murray	Kennedy
Burns	Gregg	Nickles	Kerrey
Byrd	Harkin	Nunn	Kerry
Campbell	Hatch	Pressler	Moseley-Braun
Chafee	Hatfield	Reid	Moynihan
Coats	Heflin	Rockefeller	Pell
Cochran	Helms	Roth	Robb
Cohen	Hollings	Santorum	Simon
Conrad	Hutchison	Sarbanes	Wyden
Coverdell	Inhofe	Shelby	
Craig	Jeffords	Simpson	NOT VOTING—1
D'Amato	Johnston	Smith	Pryor
Daschle	Kassebaum	Snowe	
DeWine	Kempthorne	Specter	
Dodd	Kohl	Stevens	

The House Vote on the Defense of Marriage Act

[Roll No. 316]	Armey	Ballenger	Barton
	Bachus	Barcia	Bass
YEAS—342	Baesler	Barr	Bateman
Allard	Baker (CA)	Barrett (NE)	Bentsen
Andrews	Baker (LA)	Barrett (WI)	Bereuter
Archer	Baldacci	Bartlett	Bevill

Bilbray	Coleman	Fields (TX)	Herger
Bilirakis	Collins (GA)	Filner	Hilleary
Bishop	Collins (IL)	Flake	Hilliard
Bliley	Combest	Foley	Hobson
Blumenauer	Condit	Forbes	Hoekstra
Blute	Cooley	Fowler	Hoke
Boehlert	Costello	Fox	Holden
Boehner	Cox	Franks (CT)	Horn
Bonilla	Cramer	Franks (NJ)	Hostettler
Bonior	Crane	Frelinghuysen	Houghton
Bono	Crapo	Frisa	Hoyer
Borski	Cremeans	Frost	Hunter
Boucher	Cubin	Funderburk	Hutchinson
Browder	Cummings	Furse	Hyde
Brown (FL)	Cunningham	Gallegly	Inglis
Brownback	Danner	Ganske	Istook
Bryant (TN)	Davis	Gekas	Jacobs
Bryant (TX)	de la Garza	Gephardt	Jefferson
Bunn	Deal	Geren	Johnson (CT)
Bunning	DeLauro	Gilchrest	Johnson (SD)
Burr	DeLay	Gillmor	Johnson, E. B.
Burton	Deutsch	Gilman	Johnson, Sam
Buyer	Diaz-Balart	Gonzalez	Jones
Callahan	Dicks	Goodlatte	Kanjorski
Calvert	Dingell	Goodling	Kaptur
Camp	Doggett	Gordon	Kasich
Campbell	Dooley	Goss	Kelly
Canady	Doolittle	Graham	Kennelly
Cardin	Dornan	Green (TX)	Kildee
Castle	Doyle	Greene (UT)	Kim
Chabot	Dreier	Gutknecht	King
Chambliss	Duncan	Hall (TX)	Kingston
Chapman	Durbin	Hamilton	Kleczka
Chenoweth	Edwards	Hancock	Klink
Christensen	Ehlers	Hansen	Klug
Chrysler	Ehrlich	Hastert	Knollenberg
Clayton	English	Hastings (WA)	Kolbe
Clement	Evans	Hayes	LaHood
Clinger	Everett	Hayworth	Largent
Clyburn	Ewing	Hefley	Latham
Coble	Fawell	Hefner	LaTourette
Coburn	Fazio	Heineman	Laughlin

Lazio	Nethercutt	Rush	Torkildsen
Leach	Neumann	Salmon	Torricelli
Levin	Ney	Sanford	Traficant
Lewis (CA)	Norwood	Sawyer	Upton
Lewis (KY)	Nussle	Saxton	Vento
Lightfoot	Oberstar	Scarborough	Visclosky
Linder	Obey	Schaefer	Volkmer
Lipinski	Ortiz	Schiff	Vucanovich
Livingston	Orton	Schumer	Walker
LoBiondo	Oxley	Seastrand	Walsh
Lowey	Packard	Sensenbrenner	Wamp
Lucas	Parker	Shadegg	Ward
Luther	Pastor	Shaw	Watts (OK)
Manton	Paxon	Shays	Weldon (FL)
Manzullo	Payne (VA)	Shuster	Weldon (PA)
Martini	Peterson (FL)	Sisisky	Weller
Mascara	Peterson (MN)	Skeen	White
McCarthy	Petri	Skelton	Whitfield
McCollum	Pickett	Smith (MI)	Wicker
McCrery	Pombo	Smith (NJ)	Wilson
McHale	Pomeroy	Smith (TX)	Wise
McHugh	Porter	Smith (WA)	Wolf
McInnis	Portman	Solomon	Wynn
McIntosh	Poshard	Souder	Yates
McKeon	Pryce	Spence	Young (AK)
McNulty	Quillen	Spratt	Zeliff
Menendez	Quinn	Stearns	Zimmer
Metcalf	Radanovich	Stenholm	
Meyers	Rahall	Stockman	NAYS—67
Mica	Ramstad	Stump	Abercrombie
Miller (FL)	Reed	Stupak	Ackerman
Minge	Regula	Talent	Becerra
Moakley	Richardson	Tanner	Beilenson
Molinari	Riggs	Tate	Berman
Mollohan	Roemer	Tauzin	Brown (CA)
Montgomery	Rogers	Taylor (MS)	Brown (OH)
Moorhead	Rohrabacher	Taylor (NC)	Collins (MI)
Morella	Ros-Lehtinen	Tejeda	Conyers
Murtha	Rose	Thomas	Coyne
Myers	Roth	Thornberry	DeFazio
Myrick	Roukema	Thurman	Dellums
Neal	Royce	Tiahrt	Dixon

Engel	McDermott	Slaughter	Dunn
Eshoo	McKinney	Stark	Ensign
Farr	Meek	Stokes	Fields (LA)
Fattah	Millender-	Studds	Flanagan
Foglietta	McDonald	Torres	Ford
Frank (MA)	Miller (CA)	Towns	Gibbons
Gejdenson	Mink	Velazquez	Greenwood
Gunderson	Moran	Waters	Hall (OH)
Gutierrez	Nadler	Waxman	Johnston
Harman	Olver	Williams	LaFalce
Hastings (FL)	Pallone	Woolsey	Lincoln
Hinchey	Payne (NJ)		Longley
Jackson (IL)	Pelosi	ANSWERED	McDade
Kennedy (MA)	Rangel	"PRESENT"—2	Meehan
Kennedy (RI)	Rivers	Jackson-Lee (TX)	Roberts
Lantos	Roybal-Allard	Owens	Thompson
Lewis (GA)	Sabo		Thornton
Lofgren	Sanders	NOT	Watt (NC)
Maloney	Schroeder	VOTING—22	Young (FL)
Markey	Scott	Brewster	
Martinez	Serrano	Clay	
Matsui	Skaggs	Dickey	

and the state Constitution." The court dismissed the case 5 months later, ruling that "same-sex marriage is not a fundamental right," "homosexuals are not a suspect class," and the state was justified in using marriage to promote procreation in spite of issuing licenses to couples who do not procreate. The case was appealed to the Vermont Supreme Court in January 1998. Briefs were filed the following March, and the case was argued November 18. As Vermont had no statute banning same-sex marriages, it was thought by many to be the most likely state to legalize same-sex marriage.

On December 20, 1999, the Vermont Supreme Court ruled that same-sex couples are entitled to the same benefits and protections as married couples. The court left the decision to the legislature whether to legalize same-sex marriage or to create a "separate but equal" domestic partner status to ensure the rights of same-sex couples and to provide the benefits and protections accorded through marriage.

On April 26, 2000, "An Act Relating to Civil Unions" was signed into law. The act, which went into effect on July 1, 2000, created the legal status of civil union that is parallel to civil marriage. Same-sex couples who enter into a civil union became eligible for the same rights and responsibilities accorded to married couples. Since the law institutes domestic partner benefits rather than expanding eligibility for marriage, the Full Faith and Credit Clause does not apply, and benefits are restricted to Vermont residents only. It is likely that the courts will be left to wrestle with the constitutionality of the "separate but equal" treatment of same- and other-sex couples.

Since the law went into effect there have been a number of attempts at repeal. In the two subsequent legislative sessions after the law went into effect, bills that would repeal the civil union law were introduced into either the Vermont House of Representatives or Senate. It is clear that the issue of civil unions is not settled, even in Vermont.

International Jurisdictions

Denmark first offered same-sex relationship registration in 1989, followed by Norway in 1993, Greenland in 1994, Sweden in 1995, Iceland in 1996, Finland in 1997, the Netherlands in 1998, and France in 1999. As of June 25, 1999, the Dutch Cabinet approved the filing of bills that would open marriage and adoption to same-sex partners. Finally, in 2001, the Netherlands became the first country with full same-sex marriage rights.[19] Registration establishes a legal bond between partners and typically offers same-sex couples many of the same rights as heterosexual, married couples in the areas of housing, pensions, inheritance, deaths, and divorce.[20] However, same-sex partner registration is not identical to marriage. Contrary to their heterosexual counterparts, partners in same-sex registered relationships are not allowed to adopt children and cannot have "official" church weddings. In addition, one of the partners must be a citizen of the country in which the relationship is registered, and the relationship is not recognized outside of that country.

Other countries are making progress in recognizing same-sex relationships as well. Since 1995 common law marriage statutes have covered Hungary's same-sex couples. In 1999 a Namibian court ruled that same-sex couples have the same rights as other-sex couples. Two decisions have changed the status of same-sex relationships in Canada: Quebec Law 21, unanimously approved by Quebec National Assembly, changed the definition of spouse in 39 provincial laws and regulations giving same-sex spouses the same benefits and responsibilities as other-sex common law spouses. Shortly thereafter, the Supreme Court of Canada ruled that Ontario's Family Law Act other-sex definition of the word *spouse* was unconstitutional and that protections for "spouses" must be available to same-sex partners.[21]

Box 8.2

COMMON ARGUMENTS USED AGAINST SAME-SEX MARRIAGE

Argument: Marriage is by definition between one man and one woman.
Counterargument: What has constituted marriage has changed over time. At one time, women were little more than the legal property of their husbands, and interracial marriage was illegal until 1967.[22] All of these so-called traditions of marriage have changed as the courts have come to deem them unfair, arbitrary, and/or discriminatory.

Argument: Marriage is for procreation.
Counterargument: Marriage licenses are not denied to heterosexual couples who don't want children, infertile couples, or women past menopause. Many married, heterosexual couples do not have children and many unmarried, same-sex couples do.

Argument: A one-man, one-woman marriage is best for children.
Counterargument: There are no restrictions on heterosexuals having children, regardless of their ability to raise and care for children. For example, the vast majority of child molesters are heterosexual, and there are no restrictions on their right to marry and bear children. In addition, there is no empirical evidence that lesbians and gay men are unfit to be parents or that the psychosocial development of children of lesbian and gay parents is compromised in any way.[23]

Argument: Same-sex marriage opens the door to a Pandora's box, including polygamy, sibling marriage, and pedophilia.
Counterargument: Marriage promotes stability, commitment, and responsibility in heterosexual relationships, and it would do so for same-sex relationships as well. Allowing same-sex couples to marry does not alter restrictions other than gender and would not allow or encourage transgressing bloodlines or age restrictions.

Argument: Lesbians and gay men are not denied the right to marry, they just have to meet the legal requirements of a one-male, one-female union.
Counterargument: Lesbians, gay men, and bisexuals are denied the right to marry if their partners are of the same sex. Over the course of history, the courts have struck down prohibitions against certain groups from marrying as discriminatory, arbitrary, and/or unfair.

Common Arguments Used Against Same-Sex Marriage

Box 8.2 contains a list of the more common arguments used against same-sex marriage along with their counterarguments. These arguments generally boil down to a handful of concerns that have little basis in fact or research.

domestic partner benefits

Although falling far short of providing the responsibilities and benefits of marriage, many jurisdictions and employers have begun recognizing the same-sex partners of their LGB citizens and employees.

Domestic partner policies are based on several arguments. First, domestic partner benefits are based on the notion of equal pay for equal work. Approximately 40 percent of employee compensation is composed of benefits.[24] Many employer policies use marriage to determine eligibility for some benefits, thus making some benefits unavailable to employees in same-sex relationships. That is, married employees' benefit packages are worth more than those employees whose partners are not eligible. For example, if John Smith is married to Mary Smith, his benefit package would include a premium paid by the employer covering Mary's and any children's benefits. If Bob Smith is in a committed but unmarried relationship with Mark Brown, Bob's benefit package would not include that premium and, therefore, Bob would be earning less.

Second, the workplace has become more competitive. Employers want to attract and keep qualified and competent employees, some of whom will be in significant same-sex relationships. Domestic partner benefits attract new employees and provide incentives for existing employees to remain. When employees leave for reasons unrelated to poor job performance, it is a waste of resources.

Definitions: Domestic Partners and Types of Benefits

Although defined by each employer, the term *domestic partnership* generally refers to two same- or other-sex adults, not otherwise legally married, in an ongoing, committed relationship. Approximately two thirds of domestic partner benefits policies cover both same- and (unmarried) other-sex couples.[25]

There are two classes of benefits, so-called hard and soft benefits. Hard benefits, such as health and dental insurance, education and tuition assistance, and pension benefits, are cost-intensive and carry a direct cost to the organization. Soft benefits engender less direct costs and vary by workplace. Examples of soft benefits include family and bereavement leave, sick leave, participation in credit unions, and access to library and recreational facilities. Soft benefits are easier and less expensive for employers to extend to domestic partners, but they are often seen as less important. In fact, the Human Rights Campaign includes only employers extending health or medical insurance in their lists of entities offering domestic partner benefits.[26]

History

Domestic partner benefits were first offered in 1982 to the employees of New York's *Village Voice*.[27] The next year, the American Psychological Association Insurance Trust began offering benefits to domestic partners, followed over the next few years by the California cities of West Hollywood and Berkeley, Ben & Jerry's Ice Cream Company, the City of San Francisco, and Montefiore Medical Center. In 1991 Lotus Development Corporation became the first private corporation to offer domestic partner benefits and Levi Strauss, the first Fortune 500 company.

Within the past decade, more and more employers in both the private and public sectors have adopted domestic partner policies. As of March 2002, the Human Rights Campaign (HRC) identified 4,438 entities, including state and local governments, colleges and universities, and private companies, offering domestic partner health benefits.[28] Some level of domestic partner benefits can be found in 130 local governments, eight states, 165 colleges and universities, and 3,992 private sector entities (including for-profit and not-for-profit businesses and unions), including 163 Fortune 500 companies.

More than 2,100 employers instituted domestic partner benefits in order to comply with the San Francisco Equal Benefits Ordinance. The ordinance, passed in 1996 and instituted in 1997, requires companies doing business with the city or county to offer the same benefits to employees' domestic partners as offered to legal spouses. Subsequently, Seattle and Los Angeles passed similar laws. Marriott International, Boeing, and Honeywell added domestic partner benefits in 1999, and United Airlines, after unsuccessfully fighting San Francisco's Equal Benefits Ordinance, began offering them in 2000. American Airlines and USAirways followed suit. Also in 2000, automakers DaimlerChrysler, Ford, General Motors, and Subaru added domestic partner benefits, as did Coca-Cola and General Mills.

For the first time in history, domestic partner benefits bills were introduced into both houses during the 105th Congress. On October 29, 1997, Rep. Barney Frank introduced H.R. 2761, the Domestic Partnership Benefits and Obligations Act of 1997. The bill had 23 co-sponsors and would have extended benefits to same- and other-sex domestic partners of federal employees. The bill was referred to the House Government Reform and Oversight Committee and the House Ways and Means Committee. A few months later, on February 12,

1998, Sen. Paul Wellstone introduced S. 1636, the Domestic Partnership Benefits and Obligations Act of 1998. The Wellstone bill would have made benefits available only to same-sex couples and was referred to the Committee on Finance. Both bills expired at the end of the session without further action. The House bills were reintroduced in each of the next two sessions and subsequently referred to the House Government Reform Committee and the House Ways and Means Committee. It is unlikely that domestic partner benefit legislation will pass both the House and the Senate as long as a Republican majority controls Congress and until the Employment Non-Discrimination Act has passed. In fact, in 2001 a coalition of religious leaders and "family"-policy advocates began lobbying for an amendment to the U.S. Constitution that would bar gay people from gaining the legal right to marry.[29] Although attempts to amend the Constitution rarely succeed, we must continue to monitor such efforts.

The Issues

Three major questions often arise in considering domestic partner benefits policies: who is eligible and how one documents eligibility; how much it will cost to provide the benefits; and what the tax ramifications are.

Eligibility and Documentation. Although domestic partner policies vary, employers who offer domestic partner benefits generally require the employee and his or her partner to establish that they are each other's sole domestic partner and intend to remain so indefinitely; would marry should same-sex marriage be legalized; have a common residence, and intend to continue the arrangement; are at least 18 years of age and mentally competent to consent to contract; share responsibility for a significant measure of each other's common welfare and financial obligations; are not married to or domestic partners with anyone else; and are not related in a way that, if the two were of differing sex, would prohibit legal marriage in the state in which they reside.

Waiting periods. A handful of employers require a waiting period between when the couple becomes a domestic partnership and when they are eligible for benefits. Waiting periods range anywhere up to a year, with the average being 6 months. Requiring a waiting period imposes an unfair burden on same-sex couples that is not required of married couples. In fact, of 50 states and the District of Columbia, 21 require no waiting periods or blood tests for marriage, 5 require a blood test but no waiting period, 21 require no blood tests but a waiting period of from 1 to 6 days (average = 3 days), and 4 require both a blood test and a waiting period. There is no required waiting period between the end of one marriage and the beginning of another, or for qualifying for benefits for a new spouse.

> **Box 8.3**
>
> ## TYPICAL REQUIREMENTS FOR DOCUMENTING DOMESTIC PARTNERSHIPS
>
> **One or more of the following may be required:**
> - Evidence of joint purchase of home
> - A copy of a lease for a residence identifying both parties as responsible for payment of rent
> - Evidence of a joint checking account
> - Evidence of a joint savings account
> - A title for a car showing joint ownership
> - Evidence of joint liability for credit cards
> - A copy of the form specifying that the domestic partner is the beneficiary of life insurance
> - Evidence that the domestic partner is the beneficiary of the employee's deferred compensation
> - Evidence of durable powers of attorney for property or health
> - Wills specifying the domestic partner as the major recipient of the employee's financial assets, or other forms of evidence depicting significant joint financial interdependency
> - Evidence of current domestic partner registration with a governmental entity

Affidavits and evidence. Generally, partners must sign affidavits affirming their commitments to care for one another and each other's debts for the duration of the partnership. In addition, although married couples are rarely asked to provide proof of their relationships, an employee applying for domestic partner benefits is often asked to sign an affidavit attesting to his or her relationship and to provide accompanying documentation. Typical documents required are listed in Box 8.3.

Cost of Benefits. The overall cost of domestic partner benefits is determined by two factors: the number of employees enrolling in benefits plans, and the cost per enrollee of the benefits themselves.

Enrollment. Enrollment rates for same-sex domestic partner benefits are consistently very low, averaging 2 percent or less.[30] Many employees don't utilize domestic partner benefits for a number of reasons. First, many partners may be already covered under their own policies. Second, as described below, because of tax laws, domestic partner benefits are costly to the individual employee. Finally, many LGB employees fear discrimination, and enrolling in domestic partner benefits programs requires the willingness to have their sexual orientation known to their employers.

Costs of benefits themselves. The costs of providing domestic partner benefits are very low. If benefits are extended to same-sex couples only, the average cost increase is 0.3 percent. If both same- and other-sex couples are eligible for benefits, costs increase anywhere from 1 to 3.4 percent.[31] Most organizations show no increase in cost.[32] On several occasions, *The Wall Street Journal* has stated, "Same-sex partner benefits are cheaper for the organization than benefits for traditional families."[33]

Tax Ramifications. There are no tax liabilities to the employer for domestic partner benefits. There are, however, in most cases, significant tax liabilities to employees utilizing domestic partner benefits. While employees do not have to pay tax on the benefits received for legal spouses, employees generally must pay tax on the fair market value of the benefits they receive for domestic partners. That is, if the employer pays $1,800 per year for a domestic partner's benefits, the employee would be taxed on that amount. In addition, because in most cases domestic partners do not qualify as dependents, the cost of benefits must come from pretax dollars.

Common Arguments Used Against Domestic Partner Benefits

As with same-sex marriage, the common arguments against domestic partner benefits have little basis in fact or research. Box 8.4 contains a list of the most common arguments and their counterarguments.

conclusions

Marriage is a basic, civil right, and it is only a matter of time before same-sex marriage will be legalized. Changes are occurring: over time who can legally marry has evolved; increasing numbers of jurisdictions and employers have recognized the importance of same-sex relationships and have instituted domestic partner benefits in recognition of same-sex relationships; and legal and policy gains have been made in a number of arenas, as detailed in other parts of this volume. Ultimately, the courts will determine whether Vermont's "separate but equal" domestic partnership plan is constitutional. And once one state legalizes same-sex marriage, the U.S. Supreme Court will, in all likelihood, address the constitutionality of the Defense of Marriage Act. It is only a matter of time before legal marriage becomes an option for same-sex couples, and lesbian, gay, and bisexual Americans will no longer be treated as second-class citizens.

Box 8.4

COMMON ARGUMENTS USED AGAINST DOMESTIC PARTNER BENEFITS

Argument: Domestic partner benefits mock the idea of commitment, since most domestic partner laws allow for easy dissolution of the relationship and the registry of several partners (consecutively) a year.

Counterargument: Domestic partner policies do not mock the idea of commitment. Indeed, in most policies, domestic partners must demonstrate an ongoing relationship, and in most cases, employees are not allowed to sign up new domestic partners for 6 months, and sometimes until 1 year, after the dissolution of a domestic partner relationship. There are no such requirements for married couples.

Argument: Domestic partner benefits cost too much.

Counterargument: Employers who have enacted domestic partner benefits, public and private entities alike, have reported no more than a 1 percent increase in costs, and most have incurred no increase.

Argument: Domestic partner benefits will raise insurance costs due to an increase in HIV/AIDS-related claims.

Counterargument: First, HIV/AIDS-related illness is not limited to same-sex domestic partners. HIV/AIDS is associated with risk behaviors, not sexual orientation. Second, while gay men are in the highest risk group for contracting HIV, lesbians are in the lowest risk group; the incidence of HIV is currently increasing more in the young, heterosexual population. Third, most providers of domestic partner benefits have reported no significant number of HIV/AIDS-related claims. Finally, the average lifetime cost of medical care for HIV/AIDS-related illness, $119,999, is equal to or less expensive than the cost of treating many cancers. Costs for a premature birth can reach as high as $1,000,000.[34] Surely one wouldn't decide to deny coverage for the premature birth of a baby simply because it would cost too much.

Argument: Unlike marriage, domestic partner relationships are easy to create and to dissolve.

Counterargument: First, the criteria for establishing a domestic partner relationship are "much more restrictive" than those necessary for marriage.[35] Partners often must reside together, may have had to have done so for a specified period, must have joint finances, and upon dissolution of the agreement, must wait before being allowed to form a new domestic partnership with another person. None of these criteria are required for marriage. Second, while it may be easier to dissolve a domestic partnership because it is necessarily not equivalent to marriage, it is not easy. Furthermore, as with a marriage, dissolution does not imply that a partner is no longer responsible for joint debts. Debts, property ownership, adoption, and so on are generally treated as contractual obligations and remain, regardless of the current status of the partnership. For traditionally incurred major debt (e.g., mortgage, lease, or car loan), partners are still responsible for the debt — both names remain on the loan note. In some cases, individuals may no longer be liable for their former domestic partner's personal credit card debt, but generally for major debt, lenders would consider both partners still responsible for repayment. Because state law covers marriage and divorce, each state may handle the situation a bit differently.

Argument: Domestic partner benefits policies will open the door to widespread fraud.
Counterargument: There is no evidence that domestic partners cheat in any greater proportion than anyone else. Many of the first enrollees to a health plan when it opens to domestic partners are unmarried heterosexual employees who have previously listed their partners as spouses. Most employers never ask for verification of marriage.

Argument: Domestic partner benefits provide all of the benefits of marriage, and none of the obligations.
Counterargument: In addition to the social benefits of marriage (e.g., the positive assumptions people make about married people), there are tangible benefits and legal rights accorded to married couples that are not covered by domestic partner policies, and therefore not available to domestic partners. Such benefits and rights include the right to inherit if your spouse doesn't have a will, the right to make medical and other decisions for a disabled spouse, the right to file joint income tax returns, deductions from inheritance taxes if a spouse dies, property tax breaks if a spouse dies, continuing Social Security pensions, and the right for one spouse to keep a jointly owned home even though the other is receiving Medicaid payments on the basis of poverty. There are many benefits available to married spouses for which domestic partners are ineligible.

In terms of obligations, marriage has two kinds of obligations:[36] the obligation to provide basic support to each other and marital property. In most states, married people are obligated to provide for the basic needs, including food, shelter, clothing, and medical care, if their spouses are unable to do so themselves. In most states, married people are obligated to share in each other's earnings. This is both an obligation and a right. As such, marital property or community property is an even swap of rights and obligations. Domestic partner policies do not require the sharing of earnings; nor do they provide the right to do so.

In short, both the burdens *and* the benefits are lighter for domestic partners than for marriage—federal law (via DOMA) has mandated that this be so. It makes no sense to have all the burdens of marriage and no benefits, or the other way around.

what you can do!

- Keep abreast of developments on same-sex marriage, civil unions, and domestic partner benefits by monitoring the following websites. Contribute to their work by becoming a member, making a donation, or volunteering your time.
  - The Human Rights Campaign (www.hrc.org).
  - The Lambda Legal Defense and Education Fund (www.lambdalegal.org).
  - The National Gay and Lesbian Task Force (www.ngltf.org).
- Determine whether your employer offers benefits for domestic partners. If not, use the materials provided by the Human Rights Campaign (*How to Achieve Domestic Partner Benefits in Your Workplace*: www.hrc.org/worknet/dp) to encourage them to do so.
- Determine whether your state has passed laws that limit access to marriage for same-sex couples. The HRC webpage lists states with antigay laws (www.hrc.org/issues/marriage/background/statelaws.asp).
- Oppose limitations on the right of gay and lesbian individuals to marry; oppose state legislation limiting the legal definition of family to blood and marital relationships; and fight to have antiquated laws taken off the books, such as antisodomy laws, which are disproportionately used to discriminate against lesbians and gay men.
- Support access to the benefits of marriage for same-sex couples. Use the material provided by
  - Vermonters for Civil Unions Legislative Defense Fund (www.vtmarriage action.org).
  - The Vermont Freedom to Marry Task Force (www.vtfreetomarry.org).
- Call and write your elected officials expressing your support for local, state, and federal policies that honor and protect couples in committed relationships, regardless of their sexual orientation. Include a copy of *Why We Need Domestic Partner Benefits*.

WHY WE NEED DOMESTIC PARTNER BENEFITS*

Background.
Within the past decade, more and more employers in both the private and public sectors have adopted domestic partnership policies. Among companies with at least 20,000 workers, over a third offered domestic partner benefits as of 2001. By April 2002 the Human Rights Campaign listed eight state governments, 130 local governments, 163 Fortune 500 companies, 165 colleges and universities, and 3,992 other private companies, nonprofits, and unions that offered such benefits.

Who are domestic partners?
The term *domestic partnership* generally refers to two, same- or other-sex adults, not otherwise legally married, in an ongoing, committed relationship.

What are domestic partner benefits?
Domestic partner benefits parallel those accorded to married couples. There are two classes of benefits, so-called hard and soft benefits. Hard benefits, such as health and dental insurance, are cost-intensive and carry a direct cost to the organization. Soft benefits, such as family and bereavement leave and spousal access to library and recreational facilities, engender few costs and vary by workplace.

Why do we need domestic partner benefits?
1. *Equal pay for equal work*. Domestic partner benefits represent the equalization of employee benefits. Forty percent of employee compensation comes in the form of benefits, and many employer policies use marriage to determine eligibility for some employee benefits.
2. *Workplace competition*. The workplace has become more competitive. That is, employers want to attract and keep the most qualified and competent employees, some of whom will be gay men and lesbians in significant relationships. Domestic partner benefits are an important recruiting tool.

How do we establish eligibility?
Typically, employers require that employees file an affidavit of eligibility for benefits with the personnel department certifying that the employee and the domestic partner of the employee
- Are each other's sole domestic partner and intend to remain so indefinitely.
- Have a common residence, and intend to continue the arrangement.
- Are at least 18 years of age and mentally competent to consent to contract.
- Share responsibility for a significant measure of each other's common welfare and financial obligations.

- Can provide evidence to support the request, which may include but is not limited to
  1. Evidence of joint purchase of home
  2. A copy of a lease for a residence identifying both parties as responsible for payment of rent
  3. Evidence of a joint checking account
  4. Evidence of a joint savings account
  5. A title for a car showing joint ownership
  6. Evidence of joint liability for credit cards
  7. A copy of the form specifying that the domestic partner is the beneficiary of life insurance
  8. Evidence that the domestic partner is the beneficiary of the employee's deferred compensation
  9. Evidence of durable powers of attorney for property or health
  10. Wills specifying the domestic partner as the major recipient of the employee's financial assets
  11. Or other forms of evidence depicting significant joint financial interdependency
  12. Evidence of current domestic partner registration with a governmental entity.
- Are not married to or domestic partners with anyone else.
- Understand that willful falsification of information within the affidavit may lead to disciplinary action, including termination, and the recovery of the costs of benefits received related to such falsification.
- Are same-sex domestic partners, and not related in a way that, if the two were of opposite sex, would prohibit legal marriage in the state in which they reside.

How many employees typically enroll in domestic partner benefits plans?
Enrollment rates for same-sex domestic partner benefits are consistently very low, averaging 2 percent or less. If other-sex couples are included, the rates average 3 to 4 percent.

What are the costs of providing domestic partner benefits?
The costs are very low. If benefits are extended to same-sex couples only, the average cost increase is 0.3 percent. If both same- and other-sex couples are eligible, costs increase 1 to 3.4 percent. Most organizations show no increase in cost.

---

* The material presented here is discussed in greater detail in *Everyday Activism: A Handbook for Lesbian, Gay, and Bisexual People and Their Allies*, edited by Michael R. Stevenson, Ph.D., and Jeanine C. Cogan, Ph.D., and published by Routledge in 2003.

- Write letters to the editor of local papers praising LGB-positive policies of major employers in your area.
- Support efforts to extend the benefits of marriage to same-sex couples by private employers and state and municipal governments.
- Network with other individuals and groups, locally and nationally, who have an interest in promoting same-sex marriage, civil unions, and domestic partner benefits. These might include clergy, parents, educators, campus organizations, civil rights groups, and gay/lesbian organizations.
- Support organizations and businesses that support the rights of gay- and lesbian-headed families (for example, those that have nondiscrimination policies and domestic partner benefits).

for more information

- Badgett, L. (1996). For richer, for poorer: The freedom to marry debate. *Angles, 1*(2). Available at www.iglss.org
- Badgett, L. (2000). Calculating costs with credibility: Health care benefits for domestic partners. *Angles, 5*(1). Available at *www.iglss.org*.
- Coles, M. A. (1996). *Try this at home: A do-it-yourself guide to winning lesbian and gay civil rights policy*. New York: New Press.
- Curry, H., Clifford, D., & Hertz, F. (2002). *A legal guide for lesbian and gay couples* (11th ed.) Berkeley, CA: Nolo.
- Eskridge, W. N., Jr. (2002). *Equality practice: Civil unions and the future of gay rights*. New York: Routledge.
- Herrschaft, D., & Mills, K. I. (2000). *The state of the workplace for lesbian, gay, bisexual and transgendered Americans 2000*. Washington, DC: Human Rights Campaign Foundation.
- Kohn, S. (1999). *The domestic partnership organizing manual for employee benefits*. Washington, DC: National Gay and Lesbian Task Force.
- Office of the Secretary of State. *The Vermont guide to civil unions*. Available at www.sec.state.vt.us/pubs/civilunions.htm
- Sullivan, A., & Landau, J. (Eds.). (1997). *Same-sex marriage: Pros and cons*. New York: Vintage.
- Vermont Department of Health. *Civil unions in Vermont: Questions and answers to help you plan your Vermont Civil Union*. Available at www.state.vt.us/health/civilunion.pdf
- Winfeld, L., & Spielman, S. (2000). *Straight talk about gays in the workplace* (2nd ed.). New York: American Management Association, Harrington Park Press.

CHAPTER 9

recognizing and legitimizing families

Beverly R. King

In this chapter, you will

- *Find out how LGBs are becoming parents.*
- *Learn how the legal system influences potential parents.*
- *Discover why it is difficult for LGB individuals and couples to have and adopt children.*
- *Learn how children with gay or lesbian parents are similar to and different from and those with heterosexual parents.*
- *Learn how to make the system friendlier for lesbian- and gay-headed families.*

There is no one typical family structure in contemporary American society. According to the most recent U.S. Census (2000), about half of all first marriages end in divorce,[1] and only 52 percent of all households are married-couple families.[2] The percentage of births to single women has held steady since 1994 at about 33 percent[3] and almost a quarter of U.S. children live with only one parent.[4] Between 1990 and 2000, the percentage of unmarried-partner households rose from 3.5 to 5.2 percent of all households in the United States,[5] and the number of acknowledged gay- and lesbian-headed families grew 314 percent in the same time period.[6] In fact, gay and lesbian couples reside in 99.3 percent of all counties in the United States.[7] Societal changes continue to bring about a rise in or increased recognition of nontraditional family arrangements, including a variety of blended family configurations and same-sex couples with or without children.

With all this familial diversity, it would seem unlikely that any one group would be targeted and singled out as a threat to the family. The Christian and secular right, however, has done just this with regard to lesbians and gays.[8] Their argument is that the basis for social order is the heterosexual nuclear family and

that if lesbian and gay individuals form family ties or have existing ones acknowledged, the prevailing social order will collapse.[9] A corollary of this argument is
that not only should LGBs not have families (including children) of their own,
but also that they should be kept as far away from other families (and children) as
possible for fear of contamination or conversion.[10] Representatives from conservative organizations such as Washington, D.C.'s, Family Research Council, the
Liberty Legal Institute in Plano, Texas, and the Pennsylvania Family Institute
repeatedly emphasize that it is in the best interest of children to be raised by a
mom and a dad, and that society will benefit from maintaining the definition of
family as consisting of a father, a mother, and their children.[11] As stated by Robert
H. Knight and Daniel S. Garcia, of the Family Research Council:

> The mom-and-dad family has long been recognized as the bedrock of civil society
> around the world. No institution is more important in shaping children than the
> family. Children need and deserve the best environment possible in which to learn
> and grow. The traditional mom-and-dad family provides this, while homosexual
> relationships do not. Homosexual relationships are not the equivalent of marriage,
> and children should not be placed in homosexual households.[12]

As they promote this belief, religious right groups are at the forefront of state
and federal efforts to ban gay marriage as well as to portray gay men and lesbians
as dangerous to children and prevent them from being parents. One of the most
insidious and perhaps dangerous of persons affiliated with the religious right is
Paul Cameron, founder and chairman of the Family Research Institute. Cameron
has published a number of pamphlets[13] that portray homosexual individuals as
much more likely than heterosexuals to commit a variety of crimes such as child
and partner abuse, child molestation, pedophilia, incest, and murder (including
sexual serial killings). He paints a picture of gay men and lesbians as promiscuous, psychologically unstable, excessively violent, destructive, and provocative of
crimes committed toward them. He seeks to associate sensationalized crimes and
other negative images with homosexual individuals and gay rights issues. To
quote from his pamphlet, *The Psychology of Homosexuality*:

> The "gay life" is short, lonely, and filled with cheating, insecurity, disease, and dan-
> ger. Although held captive by sexual addiction rather than brick and bars, homo-
> sexuals exhibit many of the same psychological traits as those imprisoned in death
> camps. The pathologies of homosexuals fit the traditional social-psychiatric view:
> Happiness and well-being are earned through social and sexual productivity, not
> "sexual freedom."

Cameron's studies, conclusions, and statistics are frequently cited by antigay
activists despite the fact that they have been denounced as inaccurate and decep-

tive by numerous professionals,[14] including those whose work he has misrepresented.[15] Complaints about his research methods and interpretation of research led to the termination of his membership in the American Psychological Association[16] and denouncement by the American Sociological Association.[17] Cameron has been discredited as an expert witness in at least two courtrooms as well—once in Colorado[18] and again in Texas, where his "expert" testimony on gay and lesbian parenting was rejected as being full of fraud and misrepresentation and contradicting all respected scientific research in the field.[19]

Such antagonism to gay and lesbian parenting has led to mind-boggling situations. In Massachusetts in the mid-1980s, then-governor Michael Dukakis enacted a policy that placed a ban on gays serving as adoptive or foster parents. In fact, Dukakis's administration went so far as to remove a child from the home of a gay foster parent over the objections of caseworkers who said it was a successful placement. Eventually, the state supreme court overturned the order, but not before the child was sexually abused while in the care of heterosexual foster parents.[20] In Florida in 1996, the state appeals court ruled that John Ward, who was convicted of murdering his first wife in 1974, was a more fit parent than his ex-wife, Mary, a lesbian.[21] The state supreme court in Missouri left a youth in a home with evidence of spousal abuse rather than grant custody to his openly gay father in California.[22] In Illinois, a judge was reprimanded for trying to block three uncontested adoptions by lesbian parents. The actions for which the judge was rebuked included voiding adoption decrees issued by another judge; grilling the mothers on their sexual history; sending names of the parents and children (considered confidential information) to the conservative Family Research Council (FRC); and appointing the FRC as "secondary guardians" to the children.[23] Lastly, in Indiana, a man who inspired legislation banning gays from adopting children was charged with 10 felony counts of child molestation for allegedly molesting a 9–year-old girl whom he and his wife had adopted.[24] He had previously fought to prevent the girl from being adopted by a gay man who had adopted her three brothers. These and similar incidents indicate that there is much to be done in the way of changing public attitudes and policy in order to recognize and legitimize lesbian- and gay-headed families.

mental health research contradicts common myths[25]

When children of LGB parents are compared with children of straight parents, researchers typically find no difference in psychological or psychosocial development.[26] In repeated attempts, researchers have been unsuccessful in finding differences between children with LGB parents and children with straight parents in intelligence, type or frequency of emotional problems, self-esteem, self-concept, quality of peer relationships, and popularity, sociability, and social acceptance.[27] Furthermore, young people raised by lesbian mothers are as likely to have continued good mental health in adulthood as those raised by straight mothers.[28] One study found, however, that although sons of divorced lesbian and divorced heterosexual mothers did not differ in self-reported popularity, girls did, with daughters of divorced lesbian mothers reporting greater popularity than daughters with heterosexual mothers.[29]

Children with gay or lesbian parents are sometimes teased by their peers because of the sexual orientation of their parents, although there is wide disagreement about how often this actually occurs.[30] Are they, however, teased overall more often or more harshly than other children? Research shows that children of lesbian mothers are no more likely to be teased than children of heterosexual parents.[31]

A wealth of research on the sexual identity of children (most with divorced lesbian mothers) attests to the fact that the overall development of gender identity, gender roles, and sexual orientation of these children falls within normal limits.[32] Sons of LGB parents know they are boys and their sisters know they are girls.[33] And neither the daughters nor their brothers wish to be the other sex or consistently engage in cross-gender behavior.[34] Both children with lesbian or gay parents and those with heterosexual parents prefer toys, games, activities, television programs, and friendships consistent with conventional gender roles. Adult children of lesbians also have been studied[35] and do not differ from adult children of heterosexual parents in their gender role preferences. In studies assessing the sexual orientation of adolescent or adult children of divorced lesbian mothers or gay fathers, the vast majority identify as heterosexual.[36] For example, in the largest study to date of sexual orientation among the offspring of gay fathers,[37] researchers not only found that the majority of sons of gay fathers were heterosexual, but also that the sexual orientation of sons had nothing to do with many aspects of the environment in which the sons were raised. For example, the sexual orientation of sons was not related to the number of years spent living in the gay fathers' households, to the frequency of current contact with gay fathers, or to the rated quality of current father-son relationships.

a variety of ways to parent

Despite the prevailing notion in some public and legal arenas that the traditional family headed by a heterosexual married couple is the "best" family form, many lesbian and gay individuals have made parenting an important part of their lives. There is no way of knowing exactly how many LGB parents there are in the United States; estimates range from 800,000 to 7 million.[38] Many les-

Box 9.1

**LESBIAN AND GAY PARENTING:
A RESOURCE FOR PSYCHOLOGISTS**

The Office of Lesbian, Gay, and Bisexual Concerns and the Committee for Lesbian, Gay, and Bisexual Concerns commissioned Charlotte J. Patterson, Ph.D., of the University of Virginia to critique the published literature relevant to lesbian and gay families. The full report (available at www.apa.org/pi/parent.html) summarizes research findings on lesbian mothers, gay fathers, and their children. It also includes an annotated bibliography of the relevant published psychological literature. The report concludes with the following summary:

> [T]here is no evidence to suggest that lesbians and gay men are unfit to be parents or that psychosocial development among children of gay men or lesbians is compromised in any respect relative to that among offspring of heterosexual parents. Not a single study has found children of gay or lesbian parents to be disadvantaged in any significant respect relative to children of heterosexual parents. Indeed, the evidence to date suggests that home environments provided by gay and lesbian parents are as likely as those provided by heterosexual parents to support and enable children's psychosocial growth.

bians and gay men have had children in the context of heterosexual relationships (often marriage)[39] prior to coming out; increasingly, however, others are becoming parents through adoption, fostering, and the use of alternative reproductive strategies. Even within these broad categories, there is tremendous diversity.[40] There exist families in which the parents divorced when one or both came out as LGB, and families in which one or both of the parents came out but decided not to divorce. A lesbian or gay parent may be either the custodial (with solo or joint custody) or the noncustodial parent. She or he may be single, or have a partner, and the partner may or may not take a stepparenting role with the children.

Lesbians (both singly and in couples) are increasingly giving birth to children[41] through the use of donor insemination. In some cases the donor is known, and in others sperm is obtained from a sperm bank and the donor is unknown. If the donor is known, decisions must be made regarding what role the biological father will have, if any, in the life of the child.

Box 9.2

**CHILDREN'S BOOKS ON GROWING UP
IN NONTRADITIONAL FAMILIES**

Abramchik, L. (1993). *Is your family like mine?* New York: Open Heart, Open Mind.

Bosche, S. (1981). *Jenny lives with Eric and Martin*. London: Gay Men's Press.

Dahl, J. (1989). *River of promise*. San Diego, CA: Luramedia.

Elwin, R., & Meredith, M. (1991). *How would you feel if your dad was gay?* Boston: Alyson.

Greenberg, K. E. (1996). *Zach's story*. Minneapolis, MN: Lerner.

Newman, L. (1989). *Heather has two mommies*. Boston: Alyson.

Newman, L. (1991). *Gloria goes to gay pride*. Boston: Alyson.

Newman, L. (1993). *Saturday is Pattyday*. Boston: Alyson.

Schaffer, P. (1988). *How babies and families are made: There is more than one way*. Berkeley, CA: Tabor Sarah Books.

Skutch, R. (1995). *Who's in a family?* Berkeley, CA: Tricycle Press.

Willhoite, M. (1990). *Daddy's roommate*. Los Angeles: Alyson Wonderland.

Willhoite, M. (1991). *Families: A coloring book*. Boston: Alyson.

Willhoite, M. (1993). *Uncle what-is-it is coming to visit*. Boston: Alyson.

Through donor insemination or through sexual intercourse, some gay men are choosing to biologically father children. They may then parent these children singly, or co-parent with a single woman, a lesbian couple, or a gay male partner.[42] Gay men also are having children through surrogacy arrangements as attested to by the creation of Growing Generations, the world's first company devoted to managing surrogacy exclusively for LGBs, both couples and individuals.[43] These surrogacy arrangements are of two general types: *traditional surrogacy*, in which the surrogate's own egg is used, and *gestational surrogacy*, in which one woman serves as an egg donor and another as the surrogate.

Lastly, gay men and lesbians are becoming parents through foster or adoptive parenting. The most permanent, binding way of becoming a nonbiological parent is by adoption,[44] and adoption agencies report more and more inquires from prospective parents—especially men—who identify themselves as gay.[45] Traditionally, these adoptions have been so-called stranger adoptions in which the child and potential parents had never resided with one another prior to adoption arrangements. The rise in lesbian and gay parenting, however, has produced a rise in co-parent or second-parent adoptions in which a lesbian or gay man adopts the biological or adoptive child of her or his partner.

the legal and policy climate

Custody Decisions

Gay and lesbian parents have often come to the attention of the legal system by way of custody decisions following divorce. Frequently, lesbian and gay parents have been denied or lost custody solely because of their sexual orientation,[46] with judges arguing that exposure to a "homosexual lifestyle" would not be in the child's best interests. (See Box 9.3 for an example.) Increasingly, however, courts are utilizing what is known as the nexus standard by which to adjudicate custody and visitation decisions. In the nexus approach, a parent's sexual orientation is relevant in making custody or visitation decisions only if there is actual evidence that the parent's homosexual behavior has resulted in or will likely result in harm to the child.[47]

Not all courts in all states utilize the nexus standard; some (such as courts in Virginia and North Carolina) still adopt a so-called traditionalist stance in which, in deciding what is in the best interests of the child, judges often interject personal opinion and supposition.[48] Several attorneys and other authors have noted the many opportunities for judges to apply their own moral standards in child custody cases.[49] Expert witnesses and court evaluators present the research findings that are quite clear in their conclusions that children with lesbian and gay parents are as healthy and competent as children with heterosexual parents.[50] However, if a judge is prejudiced or feels pressure from various conservative or religious groups, then she or he can rule against the gay or lesbian parent by taking into account only a part of the evidence or by not taking evidence into consideration at all. The only legitimate justification judges then need to give is the potential for problems, for example, stigma within the society, peer pressure, or possible *future* problems in the child's mental and emotional well-being. In this way, they can claim that their decisions are in the best interests of the children.[51] In cases where gay or lesbian parents are awarded custody of their children or given visitation rights, restrictions often have been set on their relationships such as no displays of affection to same-sex adults in the presence of the child, or no live-in partners.[52]

Outside the courtroom, many gay and lesbian parents abdicate custody or concede to limitations on visitation due to the reluctance of these parents to have their sexual orientation revealed or their sexuality discussed in a public arena. This decision may be made, in part, based on a state's particular track record concerning custody and visitation decisions involving a gay or lesbian parent. According to data provided by Lambda Legal Defense and Education Fund,[53] the most intolerant states with more gay and lesbian parents losing custody or

Box 9.3

THE COURTS CONTINUE TO STRUGGLE

During the 1990s, high courts across the country struggled with the rights of lesbian and gay parents. Wisconsin and Massachusetts courts declared that the nonbiological parent of a child of a same-sex couple has legal rights as a parent even after the couple breaks up, while courts in New York, California, and Texas took actions that did not recognize the rights of co-parents.[54] As the decade came to a close, a Boulder, Colorado, judge awarded full parental rights to both partners in a lesbian couple even though one of the women had no biological ties to the other's then-unborn child.[55] By 2002 a respected authority on child rearing, the American Academy of Pediatrics, announced support for the rights of gay men and lesbians to adopt their partners' children.[56]

In spite of this advice, on February 15, 2002, in a case of a lesbian mother seeking custody of her *own* children, Alabama Supreme Court Chief Justice Roy Moore denounced homosexuality as "detestable and an abominable sin." The Chief Justice wrote:

> Homosexual behavior . . . is a crime in Alabama, a crime against nature, an inherent evil, and an act so heinous that it defies one's ability to describe it.

In this case, Dawn Huber sought to regain custody of her teenage children. According to *The Washington Blade*, "their father admitted to hitting the children with a belt and hanger, forcing one child to ask permission to eat or use electricity and forcing the kids to sit on the family lawn with bags over their heads as punishment for being late."[57]

So, the struggle continues. . . .

visitation rights have included Virginia, North Carolina, Tennessee,[58] Florida, and New Hampshire. Some of the more tolerant states have been California, Ohio, New York, New Jersey, Massachusetts, and Vermont.

Adoption

This tendency toward tolerance or intolerance can clearly be seen as well in a state's laws or statutes regarding adoption by nontraditional families. Some states implement the nexus (or proof of harm) standard in evaluating prospective parents in adoption cases. Others, ostensibly trying to determine what is in the best interests of a child, have taken a more moralistic approach in evaluating the fitness of a parent to adopt.[59] There may be a greater tendency toward conservatism in adoption compared with custody cases, because in a custody case a change of circumstances can be cause for reversing a legal decision; however, in cases of adoption, the order is final when issued.[60]

Laws governing adoption and foster care by lesbian and gay adults vary tremendously from state to state.[61] In 2000 Mississippi joined Florida as states that place a categorical ban on gays or lesbians serving as adoptive parents.[62] Utah has also banned adoption by unmarried couples, including gay and lesbian ones,[63] and Arkansas uses state agency rules to prevent lesbian and gay heads of household from adopting. In 1999 a bill was passed in Oklahoma that prohibits lesbians and gay men from adopting children who are in the custody of the state's Child Protective Services agency.[64] Traditionally adoptions have been awarded solely to married couples, but the inclusion of single adults as adoptive parents has been slowly taking hold in state laws. More resistance has been felt to the decision to include unmarried couples as adoptive parents. For example, conservatives in Congress tried in 1999 to pass legislation barring unmarried couples, including gays and lesbians, from adopting children in Washington, D.C. This measure was defeated by only a two-vote margin.[65] The House passed similar legislation in 1998, but it was later dropped at the insistence of the White House.[66] Currently, in 22 states single gay men and women can be considered as adoptive parents, and in 21 others, lesbians and gay men can adopt as individuals and then petition for a second-parent adoption.[67] The second-parent adoption procedure is costly and time-consuming, however, and is being challenged as discriminatory in several states.[68] Although a few state supreme courts have recognized simultaneous co-parent adoptions by gay or lesbian couples (e.g., Vermont and New Jersey), in some states the appellate courts have ruled that same-sex couples can jointly adopt, and in roughly 20 others, trial courts have made similiar rulings.[69]

The matter of second-parent adoptions also becomes relevant in cases where one gay or lesbian parent is the biological parent of a child (through whatever means) and his or her partner wishes to adopt the child. This situation, too, has been controversial. At the crux of this controversy are the numerous state laws which indicate that (except in the case of a married stepparent) a biological parent must waive all parental rights in order for another adult to adopt the child. In the case of a gay man or lesbian wishing to adopt his or her partner's biological child (often a child he or she has helped raise from birth), this would create a ludicrous circumstance. Second-parent adoptions are usually undertaken by lesbians and gay men in order to provide benefits to a child that he or she would not otherwise legally receive from the second parent, including inheritance, Social Security, and health insurance.[70]

The need to protect and provide benefits to a child is especially evident in cases where a relationship ends. The biological parent is seen as the one with all the rights and responsibilities to make decisions about care for the child; the nonbiological parent has no such rights or responsibilities. Although some state courts may recognize a lesbian or gay man who has helped substantially to raise a child as a de facto parent (parent in fact), most courts are antagonistic to recognizing anyone without a biological relationship to a child as a parent.[71] In a landmark case in Colorado in 1998, a district judge awarded two lesbian mothers joint custody of their daughter, calling one her biological mom and the other her "psychological" mom.[72]

Donor Insemination

Colorado also took the lead in another nontraditional area when a Boulder judge allowed a lesbian couple to place both their names on the birth certificate of a child conceived by one partner through insemination techniques.[73] The ruling made both women legally the child's parents.[74]

Another primary concern among lesbians utilizing donor insemination is if the sperm donor, whether known or unknown, will be recognized as the father of the child at any time. According to the Uniform Parenting Act of 1973,[75] if a woman is married at the time of donor insemination, her husband is considered to be the father, rather than the donor. If a woman is unmarried, as is the case for most lesbian mothers, the donor presumably would be the father.[76] As with many donor insemination issues, the laws and court decisions on this topic vary from state to state.[77] Generally, the issue is most prominent in cases where the donor is known to the recipient; among gay men and lesbians, most arrangements for the role the donor would play in the life of the child have been decided outside the courtroom by all parties involved.

Surrogacy

Parenting by surrogacy methods also involves a great many difficult legal issues. Although the number of gay men using surrogacy to become parents is increasing, some states, including Arizona and New York, still criminalize either surrogacy or paid surrogacy,[78] while surrogacy contracts in a few other states are unenforceable.[79] With surrogacy, as with other parenting methods, one partner in a same-sex couple typically has been recognized as the legal parent. This leaves the other partner in legal limbo or having to resort to second-parent adoption procedures sometime after the child's birth. This situation is improving. California, for example, passed legislation allowing the names of both members of a gay couple to be listed on the birth certificate of a child born through surrogacy, thus eliminating the need for a second-parent adoption.[80] The legislation also terminates the rights of the surrogate prior to the birth of the child.

Regardless of the method used by gay men and lesbians to become or remain parents, it is by no means guaranteed that they will be successful. Public policies, such as those regulating foster care and adoption, often work against LGBs. And though improvements have been seen, the U.S. legal system has long been extremely hostile toward LGBs.[81] Few state courts have argued that sexual orientation per se should be used to restrict parenting options. However, there is still a deeply entrenched sentiment in many courtrooms that children raised by gay fathers or lesbian mothers will somehow be at risk for impaired development. After 25 years of social science research, there is no support for this assumption.

making the system friendlier

Given that researchers have found few differences between children with gay or lesbian parents and children with heterosexual parents, negative attitudes regarding gay- or lesbian-headed families are based on factually inaccurate information. Thus, we must educate policy makers about lesbian- and gay-headed families. In addition, conditions can be improved for lesbian and gay parents and their children through activism by persons both within and outside these families at individual, community, state, and national levels.

Education

Lesbians, gay men, and their children encounter prejudice in part because of a lack of accurate information.[82] There is a tremendous need to dispel myths and impart facts in classrooms, in courtrooms, and in the culture at large.[83]

The curriculum in elementary, junior high, and high schools should include information about nontraditional families and the contributions of LGB persons currently and historically. Incorporation of this material into the school curriculum is challenging, not only in small town America but also in large metropolitan areas. When the superintendent of schools for New York City supported implementation of a "rainbow curriculum" that, among other things, suggested the use of a children's book called *Heather Has Two Mommies*[84] in elementary school classrooms, the move was widely viewed as contributing to his dismissal.[85] A film produced by Women's Educational Media called *It's Elementary: Talking About Gay Issues in School* (the purpose of which is to show teachers how to promote discussion and acceptance of homosexuality in the classroom) encountered tremendous resistance from conservative groups such as Focus on the Family and the Family Research Council. An article in *The New York Post* (an antigay newspaper)[82] published in September 1997 stated that in watching this film, children are

> being drafted as guinea pigs in a massive social engineering experiment designed to strip them of their natural innocence and brainwash them into accepting homosexuality. The film is essentially a whole-sale rejection of family traditions. . . .
> [and] the latest onslaught in the campaign to corrupt the morals of the young in the nation's public schools—and nobody is doing a thing to stop it.

Actually, organizations such as Concerned Women for America are doing a great deal to stop it with "huge, well-oiled fundraising machines bankrolling their efforts to censor 'It's Elementary.'"[87] When actions like this happen, it decreases the likelihood of students understanding or appreciating the true diversity among families.[88]

Another arena in which education can potentially improve conditions for LGB families is the courtroom. Litigators can spend time educating the court on homosexuality, demythologizing and demystifying LGB people and their lives, and helping the court to understand that LGBs are multifaceted and their sexual orientation is just one part of who they are. Of course, first the attorneys themselves must be educated, and other lawyers who are sensitive to homophobia and heterosexism can help in this regard.

Gay and lesbian parents who will be entering the courtroom to determine custody, visitation, or adoption decisions are well advised to select carefully a sympathetic and knowledgeable lawyer who will work for, rather than against, them. The attorney should be not only be gay/lesbian friendly but also gay/lesbian-headed family friendly—these two do not always go hand in hand. Perhaps the best strategies are to find out a lawyer's record in child custody cases (or other cases involving gay or lesbian parents) or to contact one of several legal advocacy groups such as the Lambda Legal Defense and Education Fund in New York City or the National Center for Lesbian Rights in San Francisco for advice and referrals.

Activism

It has been said that the single most important thing that gays and lesbians can do to fight homophobia and heterosexism is to come out[89] and not hide their sexual orientation, thereby forcing the realization that, indeed, "we are everywhere." This is probably no less true for gay and lesbian parents, although caution and good judgment are advised for the safety of their families. Each gay and lesbian parent who discloses his or her sexual orientation in any way, however small, makes a statement about pride and confidence in oneself and serves as a role model for others. Even when seeking to adopt or foster a child, dishonesty is not advised; be willing to confront issues of sexuality head-on.[90]

Lesbian and gay parents whose children are teased or harassed can stress to them that prejudice and discrimination are not caused by the victim; the problem is within society, not within the child. If the harassment occurs at school, parents can talk to the teachers and administrators and let them know that they and their children will not tolerate this situation.[91] When gay and lesbian parents feel safe doing so, they should take each opportunity to counter heterosexism by educating about the existence of gay- and lesbian-headed families. For example, when registering children for school or any of the myriad activities in which children become involved, parents are asked to fill out numerous forms. If these forms ask for the names of "mother" and "father," individuals in charge can be informed that options such as "Parent 1" and "Parent 2" might be more appropriate.

Although partnered gay and lesbian parents are still denied legal rights afforded married heterosexual parents,[92] they should take steps to develop legal documents such as wills, powers of attorney, and joint parenting agreements. These documents will serve to protect couples and their children. They will also provide evidence that they see themselves, and would like others to see them, as legitimate families. Respecting connections even when not based on marriage or biology, and ritualizing relationships through commitment ceremonies, or showers and naming ceremonies when babies arrive, will help other people see families where they might not have seen them otherwise.[93]

conclusion

In the United States today, there are a wide variety of family forms. Most of these families are loving, committed groups of individuals; some of them just happen to be headed by gay or lesbian parents. Research indicates that these parents are raising well-adjusted, "normal" children. Despite the evidence, however, these parents and their families are often the target of vitriolic rhetoric and attitudes from individuals professing to be pro-family. This negativity toward lesbian- and gay-headed families is seen in religious, legal, and legislative venues, and it has been used to deny them countless rights afforded other parents and children.

There are a few glimmers of hope.[94] In 1999 New Hampshire repealed its ban prohibiting lesbians and gay men from becoming adoptive or foster parents, and California dropped its policy of automatically opposing adoptions of foster children by lesbian, gay, and unmarried couples. In March 2000 Connecticut became the second state in the union (behind Vermont) to enact legislation explicitly recognizing second-parent adoptions. And divorcing (and out) lesbian and gay parents are more likely now than at any time in history to be awarded custody of their children. Slowly, courts also are beginning to recognize that loving and committed connections among individuals in families are good for children, even if those connections are not based on biology. With societal education and activism by gay and lesbian parents, their families, and their allies, perhaps one day nontraditional parents and families will be afforded the rights and respect they deserve.

Children born or adopted into a gay or lesbian household are truly wanted.[95] And many children in this country need to be wanted. For example, in 1999 there were 547,000 children in this country in foster care homes and 117,000 waiting to be adopted.[96] The ultimate goal in changing public policy to benefit children, such as those who need parents and those who already have lesbian or gay parents, is to get to the point where one's sexual orientation is not an issue in any venue including the family; and that love, communication, respect, and good parenting skills (and not a particular sexual orientation) are recognized as the necessary ingredients for *family* members to live happy, healthy lives.

what you can do!

- Stay informed. Check websites and news sources for reports concerning lesbian- and gay-headed families.
- Educate others.
  - Dispel myths and stereotypes of gay and lesbian parents and their children.
  - Spread the word that families are groups of individuals who love, support, and provide for one another and that these qualities are not the sole prerogative of heterosexual individuals.
  - Educate through bumper stickers, buttons, workshops, debates, video presentations, and speaking out at public meetings.
- Register and vote to elect LGB-supportive candidates to public office.
  - Encourage others to do the same.
  - Even in jurisdictions where the judges who decide custody and adoption cases are appointed, you can vote for the officials who appoint them.
  - The National Gay and Lesbian Task Force website (www.ngltf.org) provides information on how to register to vote.
- Network with others, locally and nationally, who have an interest in promoting family rights for lesbian and gay individuals. These might include clergy, parents, educators, campus organizations, civil rights groups, and

gay/lesbian organizations as well as the National Organization for Women's Lesbian Rights Program (www.now.org/issues/lgbi)

- Support organizations and businesses that affirm the rights of gay- and lesbian-headed families. For example, write letters to TV and movie producers and directors showing support of positive portrayals of lesbian and gay parents and expressing concern when portrayals are negative.
- Organize a demonstration to protest legislation that will promote discrimination against gay- and lesbian-headed families. Publicize the demonstration (and other events) through newsletters, mailings, flyers, local newspapers, and gay/lesbian publications.
- Write a letter to the editor of your local newspaper. Include personal stories about hardships that are faced by LGB families when they are not recognized by law. The National Organization for Women has a sample letter to the editor on their website (www.now.org/issues/lgbi/events/nfmd99/sample/html).
- Contribute your time and financial support to parent groups, educational organizations, or legal advocacy groups that fight heterosexism. The National Gay and Lesbian Task Force (www.ngltf.org/pi/family/htm) has created a Family Policy program to coordinate research, strategy, and action to protect and promote gay, lesbian, bisexual, and transgendered families.
- Support corporations and businesses that provide protection and support for gay and lesbian parents, and challenge or boycott businesses whose policies embody cultural heterosexism and homophobia. Lists of these companies can be obtained from various sources including *How to Make the World a Better Place for Gays and Lesbians* by Una Fahy (1995).
- Monitor your local schools with respect to education on nontraditional families.
  - Attend school board meetings and know what is in the curriculum.
  - Ask that the school board provide sensitivity training for teachers, guidance counselors, and school administrators and that LGB-affirming resources be available in school libraries.
  - Vote for school board officials who hold attitudes that are LGB-family friendly.
- Applaud the efforts of organizations when they adopt policies, pass resolutions, or lobby in support of gay- and lesbian-headed families. For example:
  - The American Civil Liberties Union (www.aclu.org).
  - The American Psychological Association (www.apa.org).
  - The National Association of Social Workers (www.naswdc.org).
  - The American Bar Association (www.abanet.org).

- The Child Welfare League of American (www.cwla.org).
- The American Academy of Pediatrics (www.aap.org).
- Lobby (call, write, and visit) your local and state elected or appointed officials. Use what you have learned from this chapter to justify support for legislation that will benefit LGB families and to protest discriminatory legislation. Include a copy of *Why We Need Policy to Protect LGB Families* with your letter.

for more information

- Barrett, R. L., & Robinson, B. E. (1990). *Gay fathers.* Lexington, MA: Lexington Books.
- Benkov, L. (1994). *Reinventing the family: Lesbian and gay parents.* New York: Crown.
- Burke, P. (1993). *Family values: A lesbian mother's fight for her son.* New York: Random House.
- Corley, R. (1990). *The final closet: The gay parents' guide to coming out to their children.* Miami: Editech Press.
- Curry, H., & Clifford, D. (1991). *A legal guide for lesbian and gay couples.* Berkeley, CA: Nolo Press.
- Fahy, U. (1995). *How to make the world a better place for gays and lesbians.* New York: Warner Books.
- Gill De Lamadrid, M. (Ed.). (1991). *Lesbians choosing motherhood: Legal implications of donor insemination and co-parenting.* San Francisco: National Center for Lesbian Rights.
- Guggenheim, M., Lowe, A. D., & Curtis, D. (1996). *The rights of families.* Carbondale: Southern Illinois University Press. (An American Civil Liberties Union handbook)
- Jagger, G., & Wright, C. (Eds.). (1999). *Changing family values.* New York: Routledge.
- Martin, A. (1993). *The lesbian and gay parenting handbook.* New York: HarperCollins.
- Morgan, K. B. (1995). *Getting Simon: Two gay doctors' journey to fatherhood.* New York: Bramble Books.
- Patterson, C. (1996). Lesbian and gay parents and their children. In R. C. Savin-Williams & K. M. Cohen (Eds.), *The lives of lesbians, gays, and bisexuals: Children to adults* (pp. 274–304). Fort Worth, TX: Harcourt Brace.
- Rafkin, L. (Ed.). (1990). *Different mothers: Sons and daughters of lesbians talk about their lives.* Pittsburgh, PA: Cleis Press.

WHY WE NEED POLICY TO PROTECT LGB FAMILIES HEADED BY LESBIAN, GAY, AND BISEXUAL PEOPLE

Lesbians and gay men in the United States are becoming parents in growing numbers through various means including adoption, fostering, and the use of alternative reproductive strategies. Lesbian- and gay-headed families, however, are often not seen as legitimate family forms and are at best ignored, and at worst, actively discriminated against in various public and legal arenas. This is particularly evident in the actions of the religious right and political conservatives who target lesbians and gay men as antifamily.

What is a family?

There is no one typical family structure in contemporary American society. The definitions of *parent* and *family* can and should be expanded beyond traditional boundaries to include loving and committed relationships among individuals regardless of individual characteristics. All families should have equal rights and protection under the law.

Does the gender of family caregivers have an impact on children in the family?

Research indicates that two involved, accepting, warm, nurturing caregivers who support each other emotionally and financially are more important in a household than having parents of both genders. The quality of parenting is the most crucial factor in a child's growth and development, not the sexual orientation of the parents.

Studies have consistently shown that children with lesbian or gay parents are as well adjusted socially and psychologically as children with heterosexual parents, and no more likely to be gay or lesbian themselves. This is true when children with single homosexual parents are compared to children with single heterosexual parents; it is also found when comparing children of homosexual couples with children of heterosexual couples.

What are the arguments against families headed by lesbian, gay, and bisexual people?

Conservatives often attack gay men and lesbians with unfounded accusations such as that they are more likely to molest children than are heterosexual individuals. On the contrary, most incidents of child molestation are perpetrated by heterosexual men.

Professional organizations support families headed by lesbian, gay, and bisexual people.

Several professional organizations have adopted policies that support same-sex marriage and alternative family structures. For example, the American Psychological Association has issued a policy statement that "[t]he sex, gender identity, or sexual orientation of natural, or prospective adoptive or foster parents should not be the sole or primary variable considered in custody or placement cases."

---

* The material presented here is discussed in greater detail in *Everyday Activism: A Handbook for Lesbian, Gay, and Bisexual People and Their Allies*, edited by Michael R. Stevenson, Ph.D., and Jeanine C. Cogan, Ph.D., and published by Routledge in 2003.

CHAPTER 10

debunking myths about child abuse[1]

Michael R. Stevenson

In this chapter, you will

- *See how policy makers confuse pedophiles with gay men.*
- *Discover how the media has distorted research about child sexual abuse.*
- *Evaluate research on the relationship between sexual orientation and sexual abuse.*
- *Learn how Megan's Laws may threaten the civil rights of LGBs.*
- *Use sound research to debunk myths about sexual orientation.*

Despite a lack of scientific evidence, some policy makers, activists, and members of the voting public continue to believe that children must be protected from gay people. Furthermore, the belief that gay people recruit others, especially children, through sexual coercion has been used to undermine public support for LGBs as parents, as teachers, and in other capacities where they might develop healthy relationships with children. According to a tabloid published in 1992 by Colorado for Family Values: "Lately, America's been hearing a lot about the subject of childhood sexual abuse. This terrible epidemic has scarred countless young lives and destroyed thousands of families. But what militant homosexuals don't want you to know is the large role they play in this epidemic. In fact, pedophilia (the sexual molestation of children) is actually an accepted part of the homosexual community! . . . Don't let gay militant double-talk hide their true intentions. Sexual molestation of children is a large part of many homosexuals' lifestyle—part of the very lifestyle 'gay-rights' activists want government to give special class, ethnic status! Say no to sexual perversion with children—vote Yes! On Amendment 2!"

Ten years later, according to news reports, at least 225 Catholic priests quit or were suspended between January and June 2002 due to allegations of sexual misconduct, primarily with adolescent boys.[2] During the 1990s the Catholic Church in the United States spent well over a half billion dollars in jury awards, settlements, legal fees, and assessment and therapeutic expenses responding to claims of sexual abuse by priests.[3] Despite this history, church officials were quick to point an accusing finger at gay priests rather than focusing on more glaring problems with church officials' responses to reports of abuse. In fact, news coverage of this scandal did more to link gay men with the abuse of children than any story in decades.[4]

The belief that gay men are prone to abuse children influences policy within the Church and elsewhere. In January 2002 the UN Committee on Non-Governmental Organizations voted against recommending consultative status for the International Lesbian and Gay Association (ILGA) to the UN's Economic and Social Council. Such recognition would give ILGA access to UN meetings and documents and would provide opportunities to lobby UN delegates. According to ILGA's North American regional representative, Dr. Harold Kooden, the countries that voted against ILGA (e.g., China, Ethiopia, Libya, Pakistan, Russia, Senegal, Sudan, and Tunisia) did so because they continue to view LGB people as pedophiles.[5]

Although few doubt the negative consequences of sexual coercion, regardless of the age of the victim, the body of scholarly research that has accumulated demonstrates that LGBs are *not* a threat to children. This chapter describes how activists and policy makers have misused research findings, and it evaluates the scientific evidence concerning these beliefs. The chapter focuses on gay men because lesbians are less often portrayed as having sexual interest in children. As you will see, there is no scientific evidence supporting the claim that children need protection from gay men.

extreme (and unsubstantiated) claims

Antigay activists argue that gay men pose a threat to young boys and are more likely than straight men to perpetrate acts of sexual coercion against children. On the other hand, advocates of "man-boy love" argue that "consensual" sexual interactions between adult men and boys are, for the most part, harmless and may be beneficial to the boy. As the examples in Box 10.1 demonstrate, the belief that gay men seduce boys is apparently widespread among groups who oppose the civil rights of LGB people as well as among those who wish to ban gay men from the priesthood. Furthermore, antigay activists have met with some success by associating advocates of man-boy love with LGB-affirming policy. Both positions often misrepresent research findings and distort psychological constructs to support their beliefs.

Box 10.1

EXTREME CLAIMS

- Anita Bryant's 1977 Save Our Children campaign was based, at least in part, on the belief that "gay men seduce young boys and turn them into queers."[6]

- Don Wildmon of the American Family Association likens same-sex sexual behavior to a variety of serious crimes and endorses the myth that LGBs recruit children: "For the sake of our children and society, we must OPPOSE the spread of homosexual activity! Just as we must oppose murder, stealing, and adultery! Since homosexuals cannot reproduce, the only way for them to 'breed' is to RECRUIT! And who are their targets for recruitment? Children!"[7]

- The National Association for Research and Therapy on Homosexuality (NARTH) champions the idea that sexual orientation can be changed through therapeutic intervention. It claims that gay men are more likely than straight men to engage minors in sexual behavior and declares that large proportions of gay men were essentially "recruited" as children as the result of sexual abuse by older men.[8]

- During their campaign to limit the rights of LGBs through Colorado's Amendment 2, Colorado for Family Values claimed that "pedophilia (the sexual molestation of children) is actually an accepted part of the homosexual community!" and that voting yes on Amendment 2 was saying "no to sexual perversion with children."[9]

- In January 1994 the U.S. Senate unanimously voted to reduce contributions to the United Nations for international organizations unless the president of the UN could certify that it had cut ties to any organization that condones pedophilia. Spearheading this initiative, Sen. Jesse Helms suggested that the UN had granted consultative status to a European international association of which the North American Man-Boy Love Association (NAMBLA) was a member.[10]

- Founded in Boston in 1978, the North American Man-Boy Love Association argues that "consensual" sexual interactions between adult men and boys are harmless and possibly beneficial.[11] In 1983 it called for "the adoption of laws that both protect children from unwanted sexual experiences and at the same time leave them free to determine the content of their own experiences."[12]

- Cardinal Adam Maida of Detroit described the sexual abuse scandal in the Catholic Church as "not truly a pedophilia-type problem but a homosexual-type problem."[13]

- During the papal summit, the meeting called by the pope to discuss the sex abuse crisis, Cardinal Francis George of Chicago indicated, "A definite connection was made between homosexuality and sexual misconduct with minors if the conduct is with minor men . . . it was taken for granted if you have got an adult man having relations with an adolescent boy you have got homosexuality."[14]

Proponents of policies that discriminate against gay men and lesbians, like the National Association for Research and Therapy on Homosexuality (NARTH) and Colorado for Family Values, distort research findings and cite flawed research[15] in support of their arguments. Much of this research fails to meet even the basic criteria of scientific rigor.[16] Biased and unscientific research such as this has been discredited in the scientific arena and is not cited by serious scholars. Unfortunately, however, it continues to have an impact on the development of public opinion and policy.

On the other hand, the North American Man-Boy Love Association (NAMBLA) supports its position statements by selectively citing and distorting excerpts of studies published in well-known academic journals.[17] Although anti-gay activists cite NAMBLA as evidence that pedophilia and child sexual abuse are widely accepted in the gay community,[18] in reality membership in the organization is less than 500 and it has never been widely accepted in the gay and lesbian movement in the United States.[19] In fact, simply being on a NAMBLA mailing list is politically dangerous in the United States.[20]

In addition to political organizations, media personalities have contributed to the distortion of research findings. For example, Laura Schlesinger (a radio personality, popular in the late 1990s, who referred to herself as "Dr. Laura")[21] misused an article that appeared in a publication of the American Psychological Association (APA)[22] by arguing that it provided evidence of a link between homosexuality and pedophilia. The article cited by Dr. Laura was actually the third in a series of related publications.[23] For the article, researchers had analyzed the results of 59 studies of college students who had experienced child sexual abuse. This analysis indicated that college students with a history of child sexual abuse were somewhat less well adjusted than students who reported no history of abuse. However, the authors attributed the adjustment difficulties to conflict, pathology, and lack of support in the home rather than to the sexual abuse per se. The authors argued that child sexual abuse could be viewed as a component of a poor family environment rather than as a direct cause of maladjustment. In addition, based on responses from college students, the authors concluded that the harm caused by child sexual abuse is not as pervasive or intense as is often assumed and that men react less negatively to coercive sexual experiences in childhood than women do.

Following Dr. Laura's lead, Judith Reisman,[24] a nationally known critic of sexuality research, interpreted the publication of these conclusions in an APA journal as evidence that the APA advocated the removal of pedophilia from the official listing of mental disorders,[25] much as homosexuality was removed years ago. At the local level, Richard Lessner,[26] a newspaper columnist, also used this analysis to argue that his local government should maintain a ban on gay adoption based on this erroneous link between pedophilia and homosexuality.

Given the media attention, the APA publication became the target of the Family Research Council and other conservative political organizations. In contrast, NAMBLA celebrated the publication and cited it on their website as further evidence for their position. This process of distortion and the associated media hype eventually drew the attention of members of Congress. A press release from the office of Congressman Tom DeLay, then House majority whip, alleged that the APA "recommends that pedophilia no longer be considered child abuse" when no such recommendation had been made. The associated media firestorm came to a head when both houses of Congress passed resolutions condemning the article.[27]

Given the way it was used by the Family Research Council, Dr. Laura, and others in the media, it is ironic that the original report did not include explicit discussion of research relevant to the presumed associations between child sexual abuse and homosexuality. The studies referred to in the original paper simply did not provide such data!

conceptual confusion

Much of the hoopla surrounding the APA article resulted, at least in part, from a misunderstanding of the difference between sexual orientations and psychiatric diagnoses. Although chapter 3 deals with the distinctions among *sexual orientation*, *sexual identity*, and *sexual behavior* in some detail, understanding research concerning sexual behavior with children requires a clear differentiation between *pedophilia* as a psychiatric diagnosis and *sexual orientation* as an aspect of *sexual identity*.

Mental health professionals have not reached consensus as to why a small percentage of adults seek sexual activity with children. However, a diagnosis of pedophilia refers to adults who are sexually attracted to prepubescent children.[28] Researchers suggest that many men with pedophilia had coercive sexual experiences as children and are shy and introverted.[29] The psychiatric profession[30] believes that these men are typically attracted to children of a particular age range. Although girls are about twice as likely as boys to have experienced sexual coercion,[31] some perpetrators prefer males. Others prefer females, and still others are aroused by both boys and girls. Additional research[32] suggests that regardless of their claimed preferences, their attraction is to the child's immature body type or lack of secondary sex characteristics rather than the child's gender. In any case, their sexual desires are focused on children rather than other adults. Put simply, men with pedophilia are sexually aroused by children. Gay men experience erotic attraction to other adult men.

According to media reports, many young people abused by priests are older youths rather then prepubescent children. In these cases, the abusers would not meet the technical definition of pedophilia. Some mental health professionals use the term *ephebophile* to describe adults who are attracted to adolescent youth who are not yet adults. Unlike pedophilia, ephebophilia is not an official diagnostic category. That is, it does not appear in the *Diagnostic and Statistical Manual*, published by the American Psychiatric Association, the document used by mental health professionals to label and describe symptoms of pathology. Although not an official diagnosis, such a condition can be treated under the label "paraphilia not otherwise specified."[33]

Policy makers generally have assumed that any sexual activity with a *child*[34] should be a punishable offense regardless of a perpetrator's sexual identity or psychiatric diagnosis. In spite of the detractors,[35] most legal codes in the United States agree that it is illegal for an adult to engage in sexual behavior with a youth who has not yet reached the legal age of consent, although the age of consent varies from one state to another. In other words, according to the law, whether perpetrators choose targets based on age or level of maturation is of little significance as long as the victim is under age.[36] The bottom line is that when sexual behavior occurs between an adult and a child of the same sex, we know nothing about the sexual orientation of either party. Furthermore, the sexual orientation of both parties is essentially irrelevant given the illegality of the behaviors in question.

sexual coercion of boys, sexual orientation, and sexual identity development

Contrary to the warnings of antigay crusaders, researchers have demonstrated repeatedly that a gay man is no more likely than a straight man to perpetrate sexual activity with a child.[37] (Relevant evidence is summarized in Box 10.2.) Gay

Box 10.2

WHAT THE RESEARCH SAYS

- "[T]he adult heterosexual male constitutes a greater risk to the under-age child than does the adult homosexual male. . . . Offenders who are sexually attracted exclusively to children show a slight preference for boys over girls, yet these same individuals are uninterested in adult homosexual relationships. In fact, they frequently express a strong sexual aversion to adult males, reporting that what they find attractive about the immature boy are his feminine features and the absence of secondary sexual characteristics such as body hair and muscles." (Groth & Birnbaum, 1978, in *Sexual Assault of Children and Adolescents*, pp. 175, 180)

- "Gay people often have been accused of preying on children. This is a manifestation of a general cultural tendency to portray disliked minority groups (e.g., Jews, Blacks) as threats to the dominant society's most vulnerable members. . . . It appears from these studies that gay men are no more likely than heterosexual men to molest children." (Herek, 1991, in, *Law & Sexuality: A Review of Lesbian and Gay Legal Issues*, pp. 152–153, 156)

- "A review of the literature reveals few references to persons living a homosexual lifestyle [*sic*] and committing child sexual abuse. Clinical experience in the evaluation of sexually abused children would indicate that homosexual individuals are infrequently named as potential perpetrators. . . . Most child abuse appears to be committed by situational child abusers who present themselves as heterosexuals." (Jenny et al., 1994, in, *Pediatrics*, pp. 41–43)

- "Gay men are no more likely than heterosexual men to perpetrate child sexual abuse. Fears that children in the custody of gay or lesbian parents might be at heightened risk for sexual abuse are thus without empirical foundation." (Patterson, 1997b, in, *Advances in Clinical Child Psychology*, p. 246)

- "About one in five of homosexuals in the current series was a perpetrator of [child sexual] abuse, but the rate is significantly higher in those subjects who were not homosexuals, where one in three was a perpetrator." (Glasser et al., 2001, in, *British Journal of Psychiatry*, p. 487) men are not the problem. Therefore, policies intended to prevent contact between gay men and children do not protect children from unwelcome sexual experiences.

The distinction between *legal* and *biological* status as a child[38] may also be relevant to policy concerning the prevention of sexual abuse.[39] Regardless of their biological status, the age at which children legally reach adulthood has varied across history and cultures. In other words, in some contexts, individuals who have not yet attained the legal status of adult may already display secondary sex characteristics, an adult body shape, and, perhaps, even adult thinking skills. It is important to point out that although older than their victims, many males who perpetrate acts that might be considered sexually abusive have not yet reached legal adult status. This is especially true when the victim is also male.

In addition to confusing pedophiles with gay men, proponents of discrimination against gay and lesbian people[40] have argued that boys who experience unwanted sexual behavior perpetrated by men are likely to identify as gay or bisexual in adulthood. This is the scenario antigay crusaders revisit when claiming that gay men seduce children. Let's consider the available research. Some scholars claim, for example, that adult gay men are more likely than straight men to report having had a coercive sexual experience as a child.[41] These studies show that boys who had been coerced into sexual behavior by males were more likely than other boys (those coerced by females and those who had not experienced sexual coercion) to engage in subsequent same-sex behavior.[42] Although it may be tempting to use this finding as evidence supporting the seduction myth, this conclusion is clearly inappropriate. Not all children who have a sexual experience with a same-sex adult grow up to identify as gay. Most gay men do *not* report a history of child sexual abuse.[43] And gay men are no more likely than straight men to have their first same-sex sexual encounter with a man much older than themselves.[44]

So, if homosexual seduction does not explain this phenomenon, why might gay men be more likely to report having had an unwelcome sexual experience as a child? Antigay prejudice plays a role. Boys who turn out to be heterosexual in adulthood may be less willing to report or less likely to remember sexual encounters with older males because of the social stigma against homosexual behavior. Boys who will later develop a gay identity may more likely be the recipients of unwelcome sexual advances from adult men for some unknown reason. Moreover, boys who have experienced unwanted sexual behavior with older males may be more likely to label the experience as homosexual and question their own sexual orientation.[45] In other words, same-sex sexual contact in childhood tells us nothing about a boy's eventual sexual orientation unless the boy comes to understand it in certain ways and/or seeks to repeat it.[46]

Inconsistencies in the assumptions underlying the seduction myth become clear when considering beliefs about lesbianism.[47] If you assume that sexual abuse by men produces homosexuality in boys, then sexual abuse of girls by men should produce heterosexuality rather than erotic interest in women, as is often suggested. Conversely, if girls who have been sexually abused by men become lesbian, then boys who have been sexually abused by men should become heterosexual. These assumptions are further undermined by the realization that sexual orientation is not like a light switch.[48] A person who is "turned off" to women does not automatically "turn on" to men. Research on the impact of childhood sexual abuse,[49] research on the origins of sexual orientation,[50] as well as research on attempts to alter sexual orientation[51] all demonstrate clearly that human sexuality is not that simple.

Another indirect way to look for a relationship between childhood sexual coercion and adult sexual orientation is to ask boys with a history of sexual abuse to describe their own sexual behavior or sexual identity. These data do not allow us to draw conclusions about causes and effects; however, they do suggest that gay men whose first sexual experience was abusive may be less comfortable with their sexuality and may have more difficulties in sexual identity development.[52] Not surprisingly, coercive experiences may complicate the process of sexual identity development regardless of the adolescent's eventual sexual orientation. However, such experiences do not determine to whom an individual will be attracted. Rather than leading to a gay or lesbian identity, early sexual experiences may be related to engaging in a wider array of sexual behaviors in adulthood.[53]

Despite its value, we cannot expect empirical research to produce accurate estimates of the prevalence of sexual behavior between adult men and children. Samples of men who accurately represent the population of gay men and the population of men who have unwanted sexual experiences in childhood are simply impossible for researchers to construct. However, the available data do show that the vast majority of boys do not have sexually abusive experiences.[54] These studies also show that same-sex sexual experiences in childhood do not necessarily lead to a gay identity in adulthood. In fact, for some, same-sex sexual experience is limited to childhood.[55]

attitudes of the general public

Social science research on prejudice shows that members of stigmatized groups tend to be accused of the same misconduct, including rape, child abuse, and the inability to control sexual impulses.[56] The same unsupported rhetoric is reflected in the erroneous assumptions that adult men who sexually abuse boys are gay and that gay men molest children. These prejudiced beliefs need to be viewed in light of the fact that members of minority groups, including African Americans, Jews, Gypsies, and developmentally disabled people, historically have been accused of posing a threat to the health and well-being of women and children.[57]

In the United States, a failure to distinguish between homosexual identity and pedophilia was well established among policy makers at least as early as the 1930s. Yet the myth that the majority of gay men are a threat to young boys was debunked scientifically in the late 1950s and the association between homosexuality and pedophilia began to fade in the law, although perhaps not in public opinion, during the 1960s.[58] Since then antigay activists have attempted to resurrect this myth in order to prevent formal recognition in law of equal rights for LGBs, including the inequality inherent in the Defense of Marriage Act passed by Congress in 1996, which federally defined marriage as a union between a man and a woman, and thus unavailable to same-sex couples. Furthermore, lesbians have apparently been considered much less threatening[59] as they are rarely if ever mentioned in either the legal or theoretical context.

Although some[60] assume that the general public still believes that pedophilia is common among gay men, studies of the extent to which adults in the United States associate homosexuality and pedophilia or child sexual abuse are rare. Of the adults interviewed in a 1970 national survey,[61] approximately 71 percent agreed that "homosexuals try to play sexually with children if they cannot get an adult partner" and about 74 percent agreed that "homosexuals are dangerous as teachers or youth leaders because they try to get sexually involved with children." In contrast, data gathered in 1999 show that the general public no longer subscribes to the myth that gay men are likely to abuse children.[62] Only 19 percent of men in this national survey of 1,335 heterosexual adults believed that most gay men are likely to molest children. An even smaller number, 8.5 percent, expressed this belief about lesbians. Furthermore, far fewer women regarded gay people as child molesters, as only 6.5 percent held this view about lesbians and 9.6 percent believed it to be true of gay men. As this chapter documents, the existing body of psychological research supports the general public's belief that gay men pose no threat to children.

Other potentially relevant findings come from opinion polls concerning the extent to which U.S. adults approve of gay elementary school teachers.[63] These polls are cited on the assumption that opposition to gay teachers is based, at least to some extent, on the belief that gays frequently abuse children. A thorough analysis of public opinion polls[64] showed that support for gay teachers has increased to the point where the majority of adults support hiring and disapprove of firing gay teachers. The most recent available data were gathered in 1996. This research showed that 55 percent supported the hiring and retention of gay and lesbian elementary school teachers and 60 percent supported gay and lesbian people as high school teachers.

child sex offender registration and notification laws[65]

Tracking Convicted Sex Offenders

Megan's Laws, also known as sex offender registration and notification laws, represent one approach to protecting children from sexual coercion. They are aimed at preventing repeat offenses by requiring police departments to track convicted sex offenders and to advertise their presence in the local community.

The Jacob Wetterling Crimes Against Children and Sexually Violent Offender Registration Act, an amendment to the 1994 federal crime law, was named for an 11-year-old Minnesota boy who was abducted from his home and never found. It requires states to register and track convicted sex offenders for 10 years after their release from prison and to notify law enforcement officials when criminal sex offenders move into their communities. This law allows, but does not require, states to make public notification of the whereabouts of paroled sex offenders.[66]

Megan Kanka was a 7-year-old New Jersey girl who was allegedly raped and murdered by a neighbor twice convicted of sexual offenses. Her story sparked state legislators to enact Megan's Law in her memory.[67] This action was followed by federal legislation, of the same name, which requires states and localities to inform communities when dangerous sexual offenders are about to be released from prison.

Since passage of the Jacob Wetterling Act, all 50 states have adopted a registration and tracking system for paroled sex offenders. However, few states have adopted laws that require public notification. The federal version of Megan's Law requires states to publicize information about child molesters and sexually violent offenders. However, it allows local lawmakers to set guidelines on the amount of publicity offenders will receive and how the information will be disseminated. Failure to enact state laws could result in a reduction of federal crime-fighting funds.[68]

Taking this issue further, President Clinton endorsed a Senate proposal to create a national registry of sex offenders. Such a database would make it easier for law enforcement agencies to track offenders across state lines. The Senate bill would have required the FBI to establish a database to track the whereabouts and movement of every person convicted of a criminal offense against a minor, every person convicted of a sexually violent offense, and every person who is considered a sexually violent predator.[69]

Unfortunately, Megan's Laws are based on two unsupported premises. Federal legislators have assumed that convicted sex offenders are a greater threat to children than other classes of people and that sex offenders against children are more likely than others to become repeat offenders. Whether the victim is a child or an adult, someone the victim knows and trusts typically perpetrates coercive sexual behavior.[70] In the case of children, this is most often a member of their family or a close family friend. The majority of these cases are never reported and the perpetrators are not prosecuted.[71] As a result, their names would never appear on a sex offender register. Perhaps more importantly, focusing on convicted offenders shifts the focus of discussion away from incest and may prevent the discovery of the abuse.[72]

Contrary to the data presented to Congress during the debate on these laws, success rates for intensive treatment programs for child abusers can be over 90 percent.[73] Moreover, requiring that convicted child sex offenders register and requiring public release of this information could result in decreased reporting of the crime, decreased participation in treatment, and in the end, increased incidence of the behaviors the laws are intended to deter or punish. These laws may also be ineffective because the risks associated with compliance are far more severe than the penalties for not registering. Furthermore, law enforcement lacks the resources necessary to track compliance.[74]

In addition, state and federal child sex offender registration and notification laws may be challenged in court under the Eighth, Fifth, and Fourteenth Amendments to the U.S. Constitution. The Eighth Amendment prohibits the infliction of cruel and unusual punishment, excessive fines, and excessive bail. The Fifth and Fourteenth Amendments prohibit the government from depriving an individual of life, liberty, or property without due process of law.

Although consensus has not yet been reached,[75] requiring individuals to register with the government can be construed as punishment. Furthermore, the vigilantism and public humiliation that can result from community notification may be deemed cruel and unusual. Finally, community notification may deprive the offender of "liberty." Offenders are rarely provided a hearing. As a result, community notification requirements may lead to the deprivation of liberty without due process. Disclosure of private information, such as the offender's home address and telephone number, and interference with family relations and job opportunities have also been construed by the courts as deprivation of a liberty interest.

When it reviewed the law in 1995, the New Jersey Supreme Court held that the community notification provision in New Jersey's Megan's Law imposed extra punishment on people already sentenced for their crimes and implicated an offender's liberty interest because the law allowed the publication of private information. However, given the criminal context, it ruled that the intent of the law was regulatory rather than punitive and the state's interest in public safety supercedes the individual's right to privacy. In addition, the court granted sex offenders the protections of due process rights.[76]

Regulating Same-Sex Behavior Through Sex Offender Registration Laws

At this point, you may be wondering why such an extensive discussion of Megan's Laws is included in a chapter focused on sexual orientation and child sexual abuse. This is why. In spite of their recent reincarnation, sex offender registration laws predate their modern counterparts by over 50 years. They were first introduced in California to regulate same-sex sexual behavior and were used to harass gay men and lesbians. Although the early laws did not permit community notification, as required by today's Megan's Laws, persons convicted of consensual sodomy or other minor offenses, such as loitering in a public toilet, were often required to maintain registration for life. Again, these early statutes were based, at least in part, on the erroneous belief that homosexual persons were prone to commit crimes against children[77] and they continue to cause concern in LGB communities across the country.

As the examples in Box 10.3 suggest, Megan's Laws in some states require registration for convictions that apply primarily to gay men and have no relevance to protecting children from harm. In some cases convictions for consensual sodomy, solicitation of sodomy, or even attempted sodomy may trigger registration. As late as 1999, Alabama, Idaho, Louisiana, Mississippi, Missouri, and South Carolina required those convicted of consensual sodomy, variously labeled "sexual misconduct," "crime against nature," "unnatural intercourse," or "bug-

Box 10.3

EXAMPLES OF THE MISUSE OF SEX OFFENDER REGISTRATION LAWS[78]

- In Massachusetts, a grandfather in his 60s was required to register as a sex offender for at least 15 years when convicted of placing his hand on the groin of an undercover police officer who had approached him in a wooded area near a rest stop.

- In Arizona, a man was forced to register as the result of a conviction on a public sexual indecency charge when an undercover police officer caught him masturbating in a public restroom.

- In California, a married 90-year-old retirement community resident was required to register for placing his hand on another man's knee in a parked car—a "crime" for which he was convicted in 1944.

gery," to register under Megan's Law. Many states also require registration for convictions for nonviolent behavior that result from police entrapment and decoy techniques.[79] Adolescents, whether gay or straight, whose sexual exploration with a peer was interpreted by guardians or government representatives as sexually abusive may also be at risk for registration under some state laws.[80]

Lawmakers have attempted to modify the application of Megan's Laws in at least two potentially useful ways. Removing crimes like consensual sodomy and solicitation from Megan's Laws would not compromise the stated purpose of these laws. Therefore, there have been attempts to narrow the list of offenses requiring registration. At the federal level, Rep. Charles Schumer introduced legislation in 1997 that would have discouraged states from using Megan's Laws to register people who were convicted solely of consensual sodomy.[81] In Schumer's words, "Countless people are being unfairly added to sexual offender lists nationwide. . . . The law passed by Congress was written to apply to rapists and child molesters. But several states are including people who clearly are not dangerous, had no involvement with children, and pose absolutely no threat to others."[82] Unfortunately, Schumer's attempt to modify the law failed. Sometime later, when such a law was proposed for the District of Columbia, it originally included language that would have required individuals convicted of consensual sodomy (in states where such laws still exist) to register as sex offenders with the police if they chose to move to D.C.[83] While antigay advocates persist in their attempts to include consensual same-sex behavior in these laws, other legislative attempts to limit their scope have been successful.[84]

The courts have also been used to limit the scope of Megan's Laws. In response to concerns about their constitutionality, some states have eliminated retroactive application of the laws. In addition, rather than automatically requiring those convicted to register, in some states hearings are held so that the decision is made on a case-by-case basis. Although not without pitfalls, individual determinations may help to balance the concerns of the community to reduce crime and control the costs of administering the laws while protecting gay men from unnecessary harassment.[85] Although developed in reaction to real pain and sorrow, sex offender registration and notification laws are often misused as a means to criminalize and punish LGBs' sexual behavior and are a threat to the well being and liberty of gay or lesbian youth and adults.

protecting children from sexual coercion

Contrary to the outpourings of radio talk show hosts and newspaper columnists as well as spokespersons for the Catholic Church, basing public policy on the erroneous assumption that children need protection from self-identified gay men or lesbians will do little to harbor children from sexual coercion and will undoubtedly detract attention from more fruitful avenues to enhance child safety. Put simply, knowing that a person is gay or bisexual is of no more use in predicting the perpetration of child sexual abuse than knowing whether that person is right- or left-handed, blue- or brown-eyed, Catholic or Jewish, old or young, lower or middle class, or having any other specific characteristic.[86] In fact, knowing that a person is straight might be more useful, because sexual abuse is most often perpetrated by heterosexual males.[87]

Clearly, sexual contact between adults and children is inappropriate and illegal, regardless of whether the adult is gay, straight, or bisexual; or whether he or she has been given a psychiatric diagnosis such as pedophilia. To be effective, policies should focus on the prevention of behavior rather than confusing behavior with sexual identities and psychiatric diagnoses. Policy makers who are concerned about protecting children from sexual coercion must recognize that the perpetrators of child sexual abuse are more likely to be members or friends of the child's own family than a child's gay teacher or a lesbian child care worker.[88]

Regardless of the point of view being advocated, basing public policies intended to protect children from harm on arguments that distort empirical findings fail in providing children with safe environments free from sexual coercion. Doing so simply exacerbates prejudices that hinder the development of positive relationships between children and adults of any sexual orientation.

Given the rhetoric used by opponents of LGB rights, it appears that they purposefully confuse identity and behavior. They continue to do so, because as a strategy this intentional misrepresentation works. It has prevented LGB-positive policies from being passed into law, and it has garnered support for advocates of discrimination against LGBs. Armed with the ability to clearly distinguish among the concepts presented here, you will be articulate in the fight against policies that have these misrepresentations at their roots.

what you can do!

- Educate your community, your friends, and your family about the myths regarding sexual orientation and child sexual abuse.
  - Respond to letters to the editor when they contain misinformation concerning child sexual abuse.
  - Follow the suggestions in chapter 1 and write an op-ed column for a local publication or your church newsletter.
- Encourage state lawmakers to repeal laws prohibiting consensual sexual behavior between adults and to limit the scope of Megan's Laws.
- Network with others who have an interest in protecting children from sex-

ual abuse. Use the network to advocate for effective legislation that does not scapegoat gay men.

- Hold government officials accountable when they use the myth that gay men are a threat to children as a means to justify antigay policy (such as passing antigay marriage laws).
- Call, e-mail, or write your elected officials. Provide them with a copy of *Homosexuality Has Nothing to Do With Pedophilia.*
- Hold media personalities accountable for propagating these misconceptions.
  - Write to the newspaper, magazine, radio, or TV station that airs these views.
  - Boycott its sponsors.
- Encourage your church or religious organization to become knowledgeable about the difference between sexual orientation, pedophilia, and the abuse of power.

for more information

- Herek, G. M. (1998). Bad science in the service of stigma: A critique of the Cameron group's survey studies. In G. M. Herek (Ed.), *Stigma and sexual orientation: Understanding prejudice against lesbians, gay men, and bisexuals* (pp. 223–255). Thousand Oaks, CA: Sage. (See also psychology.ucdavis.edu/rainbow/html/facts_molestation.html)
- Holmes, W. C., & Slap, G. B. (1998). Sexual abuse of boys: Definitions, prevalence, correlates, sequelae, and management. *Journal of the American Medical Association, 280*(21), 1855–1862.
- Human Rights Campaign. *Fact sheet on sexual orientation and child abuse.* hrc.grassroots.com/family/soandchildabusefact/
- Jacobson, R. L. (1999). Megan's Laws reinforcing old patterns of anti-gay police harassment. *Georgetown Law Journal 87* 2431.
- Jean, L. L. (2002, April 17). *NGLTF: Stop scapegoating gay priests; Catholic cover-up "appalling."* www.ngltf.org/news/release.cfm?releaseID=449
- Renna, C. *A letter from GLAAD news media director.* www.glaad.org/org/relations/reference/index.html
- Rind, B., Tromovitch, P., & Bauserman, R. (1998). A meta-analytic examination of assumed properties of child sexual abuse using college samples. *Psychological Bulletin, 124*(1), 22–53.
- Stevenson, M. R. (1999). Sexual victimization: Responses of the U.S. Congress. In M. Paludi (Ed.), *The psychology of sexual victimization: A handbook* (pp. 171–183). Westport, CT: Greenwood.

Antigay advocates continue to conflate homosexuality with pedophilia despite a large body of research that disproves such misinterpretations. Additionally, they argue that lesbian, gay, and bisexual people are a threat to the safety and well-being of children. Well-respected scientific research shows that this is simply not true.

Clarifying the difference between pedophilia and homosexuality.
Pedophilia is a psychiatric diagnosis. Sexual orientation is not. Sexual orientation refers to an aspect of sexual identity. Individuals with pedophilia are usually heterosexual adult men who are attracted to prepubescent boys and/or girls. If a pedophile engages in sexual behavior with a child of the same sex, this does not make him homosexual. He is attracted to the child's immature body type, *not the gender*. In contrast, gay men desire sexual relationships with other *adult* men.

Are gay men more likely than other men to sexually abuse children?
No. The consensus of well-respected and credible researchers is that gay men are no more likely than heterosexual men to perpetrate sexual abuse of children. In fact, perpetrators of sexual coercion with children are most often *heterosexual male* family members or friends whom the child knows and trusts.

The general public knows that gay men and lesbians are not a threat to children.
Although some continue to argue that gay men and lesbians pose a threat to children, prejudicial attitudes toward lesbian and gay people have lessened dramatically over the past 30 years. A recent national survey shows that only 19 percent of men and 9.6 percent of women believe that most gay men are likely to molest children. Only 8.5 percent of men and 6.5 percent of women expressed this belief about lesbians.

Attempts to protect children from sexual coercion by targeting gay men are misguided.
Inaccurately portraying gay men as child abusers serves as a dangerous decoy and lulls the public into thinking this serious problem is being addressed. If policy makers allow themselves to be influenced by this disproved claim, they lose the opportunity to appropriately address child sexual abuse.

Megan's Laws have been inappropriately used against gay men.
Sex offender and notification laws are aimed at preventing repeat offenses by requiring police departments to track convicted sex offenders and make their names public to communities. Yet these laws have been misused to publicly humiliate gay men for consensual sexual behavior. This violates the spirit of the law, and consequently lawmakers have attempted to modify the application of Megan's Laws so they are not applied to consensual sodomy.

---

* The material presented here is discussed in greater detail in *Everyday Activism: A Handbook for Lesbian, Gay, and Bisexual People and Their Allies*, edited by Michael R. Stevenson, Ph.D., and Jeanine C. Cogan, Ph.D., and published by Routledge in 2003.

- Stevenson, M. R. (2000). Public policy, homosexuality, and the sexual coercion of children. *Journal of Psychology and Human Sexuality, 12*(4), 1–19.
- Stevenson, M. R. (2002). Understanding child sexual abuse and the Catholic Church: Gay priests are not the problem. *Angles, 6*(2). Available at www.iglss.org
- Yang, A. S. (1998). *From wrongs to rights: Public opinion on gay and lesbian equality.* New York: National Gay and Lesbian Task Force.

CHAPTER 11

making schools safe

Karen M. Anderson and Michael R. Stevenson

In this chapter, you will

- *Learn about current sexuality education programs in U.S. public schools.*
- *Encounter the hostile environment LGB teens face daily in their schools.*
- *Discover the legal protections that have been established for LGB students.*
- *Find out how education associations are working to protect LGB students.*
- *Help make schools safer for all students.*

In the United States, the battle for lesbian, gay, and bisexual equality is moving into the K–12 educational system. The news media provide a constant stream of reports focusing on how school districts deal with sexual orientation issues among both students and teachers. Major newspapers like *The Washington Post* and *The New York Times* have published sympathetic stories portraying the lives of LGB youth.[1] And increasingly, the courts are being asked to make judgments about cases involving sexual orientation in the public schools.

This chapter provides some basic information about public schools, including the role of federal, state, and local policy, relevant to improving the climate for LGB students. We also discuss school climate, legal protections for LGB students, and the role of school professionals in dealing with LGB students. The chapter closes with practical recommendations that will assist you in making our nation's schools safer for LGB students.

public education in the united states

Who Finances Public Education?

A basic question in considering how public schools treat LGB issues is, "Who controls what happens in public schools?" A simple answer to this complex question derives from how public schools are funded. The myth is that the federal government—the U.S. Department of Education—is responsible for funding public education. In fact, the federal government funds only 6 to 7 percent of total public school spending. Although the ratio varies from state to state, the vast majority of school funding comes from state and local governments.

From a financial perspective, then, most of the economic power over schools is in the hands of state and/or local policy makers. In fact, the United States has a long-standing emphasis on local control of public schools. At the most basic level, this is demonstrated by local school boards, the vast majority of which are elected by the community.

Sexuality Education in the Schools

Comprehensive sexuality education programs in the schools are the most obvious opportunity to address LGB issues in the K–12 curriculum. Although content related to sexual orientation can be infused into other subjects, debates about students' participation in these sexuality education programs have a direct impact on the lessons students learn about the lives of LGB people, whether in the classroom, in school corridors, or on the playground.

Opt-Out vs. Opt-In. Not surprisingly, the question of how—and whether—schools teach sexuality education has been a source of controversy. One ongoing debate centers on the opt-out vs. opt-in question. Traditionally, schools sent permission slips home to parents alerting them that their child would be exposed to sexuality education. Parents who did not wish their child to participate had to sign and have their child return the slip exempting them from this experience. That is, they allowed their child to opt out of sexuality education.

More recently, however, many schools have moved to an opt-in model. In this case, the child has to return a signed parental permission slip *allowing* his or her participation. Requiring written parental permission for participation in *any* kind of activity means that fewer students actually participate. The result of this policy shift is that fewer children in opt-in schools receive this important information because it requires more effort on the part of parents to ensure their child's participation. Thus, if the goal is to expose children and adolescents to basic information about sexuality and contraception, the opt-out process is clearly preferable.

Abstinence-Only Sex Education. A more recent controversy concerns the promotion of abstinence as the only effective form of contraception. What does the content of sexuality education programs have to do with LGB students? If a school district can only discuss sexuality in terms of abstinence until marriage, then by definition the needs of LGB students will not be met. For example, students will not have access to information about nonprocreative sexual behaviors or information that might protect them from sexually transmitted disease. It may be useful to note that while nearly 80 percent of teachers believe that sexuality education should include discussions of sexual orientation, only 50 percent manage to include such content.[2] Thus, the students who most need high-quality information about sexuality will not receive it in the schools.

While no one would argue that abstaining from procreative behavior during adolescence is a bad message for teens, schools are being encouraged to adopt sexuality education curricula that *only* consider abstinence, rather than provide more comprehensive education. One of the reasons for the increase in abstinence-only programs is the federal Welfare Reform Act of 1996, which explicitly allocated money to states to promote abstinence.

Federal efforts to influence local decisions about sexuality education have apparently been successful. The Alan Guttmacher Institute reported that between 1988 and 1995 the percentage of public school teachers in grades 7–12 who teach abstinence as the only way to prevent pregnancy rose from one in 50 to one in 4.[3] The rationale underlying abstinence-only curricula appears to be the unsupported assumption that if we teach adolescents about responsible sexual activity—such as using condoms to prevent pregnancy, HIV infection, and other sexually transmitted diseases—they will be more likely to actually *participate* in sexual activity.

In reality, denying students access to comprehensive sexuality education does *not* delay the onset of their sexual behavior. In fact, research suggests that the reverse is the case. That is, students who are exposed to comprehensive sexuality education are more likely to delay involvement in procreative activity than are students denied access to this information.[4] There are *no* scientifically rigorous published studies that demonstrate abstinence-only programs work.

In contrast to congressional pressure to limit students' access to information about sexuality, Surgeon General David Satcher released a report in June 2001 encouraging respect for a diversity of sexual values, recognizing what science shows to be effective, and supporting open discussion about sexuality. The report indicates that sexuality education should begin early and be wide-ranging. Although Satcher recommends that abstinence be discussed, the report recognizes that there is no evidence that abstinence-only programs work and encourages a more comprehensive approach to the discussion of disease and pregnancy prevention. Moreover, the report describes the consequences of antigay harassment and argues that we have a responsibility to be supportive and proactive with regard to LGB youth. Unlike federal policy, the report encourages abstinence until people are involved in committed, enduring, and mutually monogamous relationships, which is a much more realistic approach.[5] This inclusive language applies to people regardless of sexual orientation. This is the first report in many

---

Box 11.1

EXCERPTS FROM THE SURGEON GENERAL'S CALL TO ACTION[6]

- "Sexual responsibility should be understood in its broadest sense. While personal responsibility is crucial to any individual's health status, communities also have important responsibilities. Individual responsibility includes understanding and awareness of one's sexuality and sexual development; respect for oneself and one's partner; avoidance of physical or emotional harm to either oneself or one's partner; ensuring that pregnancy occurs only when welcomed; and recognition and tolerance of the diversity of sexual values within any community. Community responsibility includes assurance that its members have access to developmentally and culturally appropriate sexuality education, as well as sexual and reproductive health care and counseling; the latitude to make appropriate sexual and reproductive choices; respect for diversity; and freedom from stigmatization and violence on the basis of gender, race, ethnicity, religion, or sexual orientation."

- "Sexual orientation is usually determined by adolescence, if not earlier, and there is no valid scientific evidence that sexual orientation can be changed. Nonetheless, our culture often stigmatizes homosexual behavior, identity, and relationships. These anti-homosexual attitudes are associated with psychological distress for homosexual persons and may have a negative impact on mental health, including a greater incidence of depression and suicide, lower self-acceptance and a greater likelihood of hiding sexual orientation."

- "Few would disagree that parents should be the primary sexuality educators of their children or that sexual abstinence until engaged in a committed and mutually monogamous relationship is an important component in any sexuality education program. It does seem clear, however, that providing sexuality education in the schools is a useful mechanism to ensure that the Nation's youth have a basic understanding of sexuality."

years by a representative of the federal government that provides a basis for advocacy on behalf of LGB students. We should take full advantage of it.

Who Makes Decisions About Sexuality Education?

From a policy perspective, decisions about how—and whether—a school wants to offer a curriculum module (usually in a social studies or health class) on sexuality are made at the local level. This is often necessarily consistent with state law or policies. The issue of where the decision making should reside regarding sexuality education has, in fact, been a bedrock issue for political conservatives, who rail against federal interference in local schools. However, in practice, the religious right has presented a very different message on the importance of local control. The issue of local control is suddenly unimportant to conservatives if there is federal legislation that supports their positions, even if the federal law would override local decision making in schools.

One classic example of this can be seen in the efforts of conservative Republican senators and members of Congress to impose federal restrictions on the teaching of sexuality education in both public and private schools. In the 1994 reauthorization of the Elementary and Secondary Education Act, two separate amendments were introduced that would have dramatically restricted local control over decisions about sex education. The first amendment, introduced by Rep. John Doolittle (R-Calif.), would have required schools receiving federal funding—that is virtually every public school in the country as well as many private schools—to "continually stress throughout the sex education program and sexual intercourse discussion that abstinence from sexual intercourse is the only protection that is 100 percent effective." The second amendment, offered by Rep. Mel Hancock (R-Mo.), would have restricted schools receiving federal funding from implementing "a program or activity that has either the purpose or effect of encouraging or supporting homosexuality as a positive lifestyle alternative."[7]

In each case, had the amendment passed, the ability of the school district to make decisions about sexuality education programs would have been compromised. And much needed information relevant to LGB sexuality would have been eliminated from the curriculum. In both of these cases, the amendments were strongly supported by organizations representing the religious right.[8]

This situation has been construed by some as an issue of free speech. In fact, 35 prominent national organizations have released a joint statement on abstinence-only education. Organizations representing churches, free speech, sexuality educators, and women, among many others, have joined the National Coalition Against Censorship in this effort. The text of the joint statement and the organizations endorsing it appear in Box 11.2.[9]

Box 11.2

JOINT STATEMENT AGAINST ABSTINENCE-ONLY EDUCATION

- Abstinence-ONLY education is censorship;
- Abstinence-ONLY education affronts the principle of church-state separation;
- Abstinence-ONLY education silences speech about sexual orientation; and
- Censorship of sexuality education is ineffective, unnecessary, and dangerous.

ACT UP/New York
Advocates for Youth
American Bookseller Foundation for Free Expression
American Civil Liberties Union
American Medical Student Association
Americans United for Separation of Church and State
Association of Reproductive Health Professionals
Boston Coalition for Freedom of Expression
Boston Women's Health Book Collective
Catholics for Free Choice
Center for Reproductive Law and Policy
Center for Women's Policy Studies
Feminists for Free Expression Project
International Women's Health Coalition
Justice and Witness Ministries, United Church of Christ
Lambda Legal Defense and Education Fund, Inc.
Mass MIC (Massachusetts Music Industry Coalition)
Mother's Voices
National Abortion and Reproductive Rights Action League
National Coalition Against Censorship
National Education Association
National Network for Youth
National Women's Health Network
NOW Legal Defense and Education Fund
Online Policy Group
People for the American Way
Physicians for Reproductive Choice and Health
Planned Parenthood Federation of America
ProChoice Resource Center
Sexuality Information and Education Council of the United States

Society for the Scientific Study of Sexuality
Third Wave Foundation
Unitarian Universalist Association
World Association of Sexology

school climate

In most respects, the developmental challenges faced by LGB teens are similar to those faced by their heterosexual counterparts. All youth must deal with a range of issues concerning identity, relationships, career options, and sexuality. However, as a report from Human Rights Watch documents, unlike other teens LGB youth often face a school climate filled with harassment and victimization that can affect their emotional and physical health.[10] For example, at school, LGB youth are more likely than others to experience harassment by peers, be threatened with a weapon, and be a victim of violence. As a result, it should not be surprising that LGB youth may also experience emotional distress.[11]

Rather than recognize these outcomes as consequences of hostility and hate, findings regarding risk behaviors, such as attempted suicide,[12] have been used to accuse LGBs of mental dysfunction and to support efforts to limit LGBs' civil rights.[13] As activists, we need to consider carefully how these data are used and ensure that we do not exacerbate an already hostile climate for LGB students.

Given the prevalence of harassment and hate, it is not difficult to understand why LGB students do not perceive their schools to be safe places.[14] The American Civil Liberties Union has reported that LGB students are five times as likely as their peers to skip school out of fear for their own safety![15] Aside from the harassment, violence, and so on, the climate of most schools is hostile to any discussion of LGB issues. A survey of teens listed in *Who's Who Among American High School Students* found that nearly 40 percent of the nation's top-achieving high school students admit to being prejudiced against gays and lesbians. This percentage is far higher than those reporting racial, ethnic, or religious prejudices.[16] Data from Massachusetts indicate that 97 percent of high school students in the state regularly heard antigay comments from their peers. It is most alarming that students also reported hearing these slurs from school staff members.[17] The Gay, Lesbian, and Straight Education Network surveyed students in 32 states and reported that over 90 percent of LGB youth sometimes or frequently heard homophobic comments in their schools.[18] Similarly, a study of gay teens in Indianapolis, Indiana, showed that 26 percent heard derogatory comments against them on a *daily* basis; 34 percent said they had been verbally harassed because of their sexual orientation by school faculty and staff; and 32 percent reported having been physically harassed at school.[19]

Why don't schools do more to protect these students? The results of interviews with 23 school health and mental health professionals indicate that most schools are not supportive of a focus on these issues.[20] For example:

- School health and mental health professionals report knowing very little about LGB students and are uncomfortable having to deal with LGB adolescents.
- School health and mental health professionals report receiving little or no formal professional training in LGB issues.
- The professional journals read by these school personnel have historically published little or no information about LGB health and mental health.
- Interviewees report that this is an extremely politically volatile issue for schools especially in some geographic areas.
- Most of the interviewees reported that their school system had no policies on same-sex relationships.
- And finally, the interviewees reported having fears about parental objections, of being labeled gay themselves, and about losing their jobs if they raised LGB issues in their schools.

Given the inevitable conclusion that the school climate for LGB students is hostile, if not dangerous,[21] schools must address the needs of LGB-identified or questioning students. To support this effort, many education-related organizations and associations have adopted policy statements and created resources to support these efforts. Some of these organizations are presented in Box 11.3 and their associated websites are included in the endnotes.[22] Some school systems are also addressing this issue with new staff positions. For example, in 2001 the Madison, Wisconsin, school district hired Bonnie Augusta, an openly gay educator who had worked for the district for 25 years, as the district's first gay, lesbian, bisexual, transgender, and questioning resource teacher.[23] In addition, the U.S. Department of Education has stated explicitly that schools risk losing their federal funding if discrimination based on sexual orientation leads to the deprivation of educational benefits for these students.

Labor unions are also playing an increasingly important role in protecting teachers and staff.[24] In one example, a grievance was filed by the Michigan Education Association on behalf of a teacher who had created a bulletin board at his middle school about Gay and Lesbian History Month.[25] Similarly, an educator from Massachusetts asked her labor union to intervene when she was fired after making a presentation that included explicit discussion of sexual activity. The presentation had been taped by conservative activists and was released to the media.

Labor unions can also press for change in other ways. In 1996 and again in 2001, the National Education Association (the nation's largest teachers union) adopted a comprehensive resolution on racism, sexism, and sexual orientation discrimination (see Box 11.4). It had been expected to consider, during their 2001 annual meeting, a resolution that aimed to make public schools safer for LGB students. The proposed measure urged the implementation of curricula that would educate all students about LGB history and culture, among other things. However, supporters chose to send the issue to a task force for further study rather than bring it to a vote after antigay protesters gathered outside the convention.[26] In February 2002 the association's board of directors adopted a plan that encourages schools to develop factual, age-appropriate, nonjudgmental materials for classroom discussions on homosexuality. The plan also encourages teachers and staff to report sexual orientation discrimination when they see or experience it.[27] The increased levels of involvement by labor unions in the area of sexual orientation and schools may help move us to a more LGB-friendly environment in the schools.

Box 11.3

EDUCATION ORGANIZATIONS AND ASSOCIATIONS THAT HAVE ADOPTED LGB-AFFIRMING SCHOOL POLICIES[28]

- American Federation of Teachers. (1990). *Educational equity for sexual minorities.*[29]
- American Federation of Teachers. (1994). *Rights of gay, lesbian, and bisexual people.*[30]
- American Federation of Teachers. (1996). *Safety in all schools.*[31]
- American School Counselor Association. (1995). *The professional school counselor and sexual minority youth.*[32]
- American School Health Association. (1994). *Gay and lesbian youth in school.*[33]
- National Association of School Nurses. (1994). *Sexual orientation position statement.*[34]
- National Education Association. (2000). *Racism, sexism, and sexual orientation discrimination.*[35]
- National School Boards Association. (2000). *Non-discrimination belief and policy of the national school boards association.*[36]

Box 11.4

NATIONAL EDUCATION ASSOCIATION RESOLUTION ON RACISM, SEXISM, AND SEXUAL ORIENTATION DISCRIMINATION

The National Education Association believes in the equality of all individuals. Discrimination and stereotyping based on such factors as race, gender, immigration status, disability, ethnicity, occupation, and sexual orientation must be eliminated.

The Association also believes that plans, activities, and programs for education employees, students, parents/guardians, and the community should be developed to identify and eliminate discrimination and stereotyping in all educational settings. Such plans, activities, and programs must:

a. Increase respect, understanding, acceptance, and sensitivity toward individuals and groups in a diverse society composed of such groups as American Indians/Alaska Natives, Asians and Pacific Islanders, Blacks, Hispanics, women, gays, lesbians, bisexuals, transgendered people, and people with disabilities

b. Eliminate discrimination and stereotyping in curricula, textbooks, resource and instructional materials, activities, etc.

c. Foster the dissemination and use of nondiscriminatory and non-stereotypical language, resources, practices, and activities

d. Eliminate institutional discrimination

e. Integrate an accurate portrayal of the roles and contributions of all groups throughout history across curricula, particularly groups who have been underrepresented historically

f. Identify how prejudice, stereotyping, and discrimination have limited the roles and contributions of individuals and groups, and how these limitations have challenged and continue to challenge our society

g. Eliminate subtle practices that favor the education of one student over another on the basis of race, ethnicity, gender, disability, or sexual orientation

h. Encourage all members of the educational community to examine assumptions and prejudices, including, but not limited to, racism, sexism, and homophobia, that might limit the opportunities and growth of students and education employees

i. Offer positive and diverse role models in our society, including the recruitment, hiring, and promotion of diverse education employees in our public schools

j. Coordinate with organizations and concerned agencies that promote the contributions, heritage, culture, history, and special health and care needs of diverse population groups

k. Promote a safe and inclusive environment for all.

The Association encourages its affiliates to develop and implement training programs on these matters. (1996, 2001) www.nea.org/resolutions/01/01b-9.html

legal protections for LGB students

Both federal and state courts have established precedents that school districts are legally liable to protect LGB students and to ensure a safe climate for all students, irrespective of sexual orientation.

Federal Law

The first such case to be brought under federal law occurred in Ashland, Wisconsin, in 1996 when a former student named Jamie Nabozny sued his school district for failing to protect him against antigay harassment. He won his case and the school district was forced to pay more than $900,000 in damages.[37] This case demonstrates that school officials can be held liable for lack of action—that is, for failing to intervene to help a student who was in constant physical danger at school because of his sexual orientation.

Nabozny based his case on Title IX, the federal statute prohibiting sex discrimination in schools. Title IX cases typically involve ensuring that men's and women's sports programs are supported in an equitable fashion. However, a growing number of students and former students are suing their school districts under Title IX by arguing that sex and sexual orientation are inseparable. For example, six former students in Morgan Hill, California, sued their school board and school administrators because the district failed to protect them from being taunted, teased, and sometimes beaten because their classmates believed they were gay or lesbian. In Fayetteville, Arkansas, William Wagner won a case against the Fayetteville public schools under Title IX arguing that the district had failed to protect him from same-sex harassment by his fellow students. A number of other districts, including Kent, Washington, and Pleasant Hill, Missouri, have agreed to out-of-court settlements.

Several other federal statutes have relevance to LGB issues in schools. For example, the 1984 Equal Access Law focuses on the right of noncurricular groups to use public schools for meetings. Ironically, this law resulted from the efforts of those who wanted access to school facilities for student-led Bible study. The law states that schools that allow any non–curriculum related group to meet must allow all such groups to meet. This means that districts must permit the presence of gay-straight alliances (GSAs) in schools.

Not all school districts, however, have cooperated with students wanting to form a GSA.[38] The best known case involved the Salt Lake City, Utah, school district, where in late 1995 a group of students at East High School started a GSA. In response to these efforts, the school board banned all noncurricular clubs. This action prevented the formation of an official GSA and prohibited the students from meeting on campus. A similar situation occurred at El Modena High School in Orange County, California, when the school board voted to deny a student-proposed GSA.[39]

State Law

Although a number of states have broad antidiscrimination laws that implicitly include sexual orientation, only a handful have a law or language in the state administrative code that explicitly prohibits antigay harassment in public schools. These include California, Connecticut, Rhode Island, Massachusetts, New Jersey, Minnesota, Pennsylvania, Wisconsin, and Vermont.

In 1993 Massachusetts was among the first to take legislative action to explicitly protect gay and lesbian students. With the support of Republican governor William Weld, the state was the first to add sexual orientation to the state's education code. Additionally, the legislation established the Governor's Commission on Gay and Lesbian Youth, which led to the establishment of gay-straight alliances across the state and eventually across the country. The commission also produced a widely cited report and set the stage for additional research by the Massachusetts Department of Education. This work provided important data to support LGB-positive programs.[40] More recently, in 1999, after a 5-year effort by state representative Sheila Kuehl,[41] California passed legislation that bans discrimination based on sexual orientation in schools.

Some states—primarily western states—have given citizens the right to place a measure on a state election ballot simply by acquiring the requisite number of voter signatures. In essence, this allows voters to bypass the state legislative process as long as enough signatures can be collected. A variety of ballot initiatives related to sexual orientation have been attempted in these states.

Sexual orientation ballot measures at the state level began to develop in the 1970s. For example, the Briggs Initiative in California would have prohibited LGBs from being public school teachers. Similarly, same-sex marriage has been addressed by ballot measures in several states.[42] Recently, however, the use of ballot initiatives to address the role of LGB issues specifically in the school setting has intensified.

In the 2000 election, Oregon's state ballot included an initiative that would have restricted schools from "sanctioning" homosexuality. Although the initiative failed, conservative groups in other states may imitate this strategy. Additionally, conservative groups in Oregon are already working on another ballot proposition with a similar mission and a potentially misleading title: The Student Protection Act. LGB activists must build opposition to such initiatives and consider opposing this process as a way to enact public policy more generally.

Local Law

The fact that many states have addressed sexual orientation in the schools has led a number of local municipalities to follow suit. For example, when the state of California passed the inclusion of sexual orientation in its nondiscrimination policy, many school districts added sexual orientation to their district's antidiscrimination policies. Rather than being based on more noble motives, it is important to note that districts may do this to avoid potential lawsuits such as that brought by Jamie Nabozny.[43]

Cities and municipalities have also formally included sexual orientation in their antidiscrimination laws. However, when they exist, most policies relating explicitly to LGB youth in schools are created at the school board level.[44] When Hawaii (which is unique in that the school district covers the entire state) first grappled with this issue, the school board was sharply divided. Eventually, in November 2000, the board passed the inclusion of sexual orientation by a vote of eight to three with two abstentions.[45]

In educational institutions, battles over the inclusion of sexual orientation in antidiscrimination policies play out in different ways. Some policies are written broadly so that they implicitly cover a broad range of characteristics, including sexual orientation. Adopting such a policy could avoid explicit debates about sexual orientation yet offer LGB youth the needed protections. Other policies develop over time in much the same way as hate crimes laws.[46] That is, sexual orientation and other characteristics are explicitly added to existing policies as awareness of these issues is raised and support for the change grows. Which approach advocates choose will depend a great deal on the state and local climate surrounding this issue.

what can you do![47]

- Discover your local school district's policy regarding sexuality education in the schools.

- If the policy emphasizes abstinence until marriage, the needs of LGB students will not be met.
- Fight against abstinence-only policies.
- Encourage your local school district to adopt an antiharassment policy that covers and protects all students. In addition, encourage schools to implement antidiscrimination policies that cover teachers and other school staff.
  - Ensure that any such policy also includes procedural guidelines to be implemented if the policy is violated.
  - The formation of an oversight or monitoring committee can also serve as a mechanism for solving problems.
- Encourage your school system to provide services for LGB staff and families as well as students.
  - A gay-straight alliance (GSA) sends a message of tolerance to everyone in the school setting. The Gay, Lesbian, and Straight Education Network (GLSEN)[48] estimates that there are currently about 750 such groups in high schools across the country.
- Monitor school board elections.
  - Become a candidate for your local school board.
  - Attend candidate forums.
  - Be informed of candidates' views with regard to LGB issues.
- Be aware of your school district's relationship with the Boy Scouts of America. Because the Boy Scouts ban gays from participation, several school districts have decided that they will no longer sponsor Boy Scout troops in their institutions.[49]
- Determine whether local school and public libraries have relevant resources and materials that might be beneficial to LGB youth. If such materials do not exist, purchase and donate these materials and ensure that they are made readily available.
- Monitor ballot initiatives for anti-LGB language. Antigay ballot initiatives can bring harm to LGBs even when they are eventually defeated.
- Lobby your state lawmakers for a state-level antidiscrimination policy that includes sexual orientation. Effective state laws make it easier to create similar local policies.
- Involve your local community in discussions of the needs of LGB students.
  - Emphasize school safety.
  - Advocate the prevention of risky behaviors.
  - Found a LGB task force in your local Parent-Teacher Association.
  - Develop allies among community members.
- Educate elected officials on the importance of safe schools. Provide them

No safe haven: Schools are dangerous for lesbian, gay, and bisexual youth.
According to survey research 97 percent of high school students regularly hear antigay comments from their peers and school staff. One in four gay teens hears derogatory comments *daily*. When such slurs go unnoticed and unpunished they often escalate into violence. In fact, one in three students is physically harassed at school for being gay.

Unsafe schools hurt LGB students.
The hostile climate of many schools has a direct impact on students, such as a decreased sense of physical safety, social isolation, lowered academic performance, greater absenteeism, and increased emotional stress.

Schools are responsible for protecting all students.
Schools are required to protect all students from harm. A growing number of court cases have established a legal precedent that school districts are legally liable if they fail to protect LGB students from discrimination and harassment. Yet school staff are often untrained in how to respond appropriately to LGB harassment and/or fear losing their jobs if they raise LGB issues in their schools.

Curriculum is absent of LGB information.
A number of states have restricted their public schools' sex education curriculum in ways that prevent the discussion of issues relevant to LGB students. Two examples are (1) the requirement for parents to send a signed permission slip to allow the student to participate (this opt-in process decreases the number of students who receive sex education) and (2) a focus on abstinence, which often eliminates the possibility of discussing information that would be helpful for LGB students.

The solution: How can policy protect LGB students?
Local, state, and federal policies are necessary to ensure a safe school environment for LGB students. Possible solutions include the following:
1. The passage of laws that explicitly prohibit antigay harassment (this has already occurred in a number of states).
2. As is increasingly typical of colleges and universities, school districts could volunteer or be required by law to include sexual orientation in antidiscrimination policies.
3. Removing the obstacles to a comprehensive sex education curriculum.

---

* The material presented here is discussed in greater detail in *Everyday Activism: A Handbook for Lesbian, Gay, and Bisexual People and Their Allies*, edited by Michael R. Stevenson, Ph.D., and Jeanine C. Cogan, Ph.D., and published by Routledge in 2003.

with a copy of *Why We Need Policies That Ensure a Safe Environment for Lesbian, Gay, and Bisexual Youth in Schools.*

for more information

- Casper, V., & Schultz, S. (1996). Lesbian and gay parents encounter educators: Initiating conversations. In R. C. Savin-Williams & K. M. Cohen (Eds.), *The lives of lesbians, gays, and bisexuals: Children to adults* (pp. 305–330). Fort Worth, TX: Harcourt Brace.
- Casper, V., & Schultz, S. (1999). *Gay parents/straight schools: Building communication and trust.* Winston, VT: Teachers College Press.
- Griffin, P., & Ouellett, M. L. (2002). Going beyond gay-straight alliances to make schools safe for lesbian, gay, bisexual, and transgender students. *Angles, 6*(1). Available at www.iglss.org
- Harbeck, K. M. (Ed.). (1991). *Coming out of the classroom closet: Gay and lesbian students, teachers, and curricula.* New York: Harrington Park Press.
- Lambda Legal Defense and Education Fund. (1998). *Stopping anti-gay abuse of students in public schools: A legal perspective.* Available at www.lambdalegal.org.
- Lipkin, A. (2000). *Understanding homosexuality, changing schools.* Boulder, CO: Westview Press.
- Sears, J. T. (1993/1994). Challenges for educators: Lesbian, gay, and bisexual families. *The High School Journal, 77,* 138–156.
- Victor, S., & Fish, M. C. (1995). Lesbian mothers and their children: A review for school psychologists. *School Psychology Review, 24,* 456–479.
- Youth Pride, Inc. (1997). *Creating safe schools for lesbian and gay students: A resource guide for school staff.* (For a copy, e-mail ypi@ma.ultranet.com)

APPENDIX

web resources

Jennifer M. Hoag and Lisa M. Schmidt

The Advocate
www.advocate.com/html/gaylinks/resources.asp
This well-known news and entertainment magazine provides links to LGB-related websites around the world through the resources page of its website.

American Civil Liberties Union
www.aclu.org/issues/gay/hmgl.html
The Gay and Lesbian Rights page of the ACLU site provides updates on ACLU's efforts on behalf of LGBs. It tracks LGB issues in the U.S. Congress and provides access to informational electronic resources and newsletters.

American Psychoanalytic Foundation
www.cyberpsych.org/homophobia/
This website focuses on homophobia, a "permissible" prejudice. It summarizes a Public Forum meeting of the American Psychoanalytic Association in conjunction with its Committee on Issues of Homosexuality.

American Psychological Association, Lesbian, Gay, and Bisexual Concerns Office
www.apa.org/pi/lgbc/
The LGB Concerns office at the APA provides policy analysis, supports APA policy development, and advocates APA policy on LGB concerns in psychology. The site provides access to a multitude of resources published by the APA, including *amicus* briefs filed by the APA in state and federal court cases.

American Veterans for Equal Rights, Inc.

www.glbva.org/

American Veterans for Equal Rights, Inc. (AVER) was formerly Gay, Lesbian, and Bisexual Veterans of America, Inc. As described on the site, "AVER is a non-profit, chapter-based association of active, reserve and veteran servicemembers dedicated to full and equal rights and equitable treatment for all present and former members of the U.S. Armed Forces."

Children of Lesbians and Gays Everywhere

www.colage.org

COLAGE is the only national and international organization specifically supporting young people with LGB parents. The site provides information about chapter activities and resources for advocates who wish to lobby on behalf of LGB families.

Congress Online

www.congress.org/

Offers information on representatives in your area. Also provides information on current legislation, bill status reports, and association and advocacy groups that assemble rankings for representatives on issues of interest.

Couples National Network, Inc.

www.couples-national.org/

Couples National Network, Inc. is a nonprofit organization that provides a social, educational, and humanitarian forum for gay and lesbian couples. It promotes the validity of same-gender relationships. You can find information on affiliates of the network as well as learn how to become an affiliate.

Current Events in Law and Civil Rights

law.about.com/library/weekly/topicsubcrit.htm

Provides information about current events in law and civil rights. Allows users to contact their community about current issues, signup for free newsletters, and become part of discussion forums about events and civil rights.

Dignity/USA

www.dignityusa.org/

Dignity/USA is the United States' largest and most progressive organization of LGBT Catholics. It serves as a proactive voice for reform in the church and society. The site provides links to many news articles about Dignity/USA; it provides brief descriptions of several committees and projects along with people to contact for more information.

Electronic Activist

www.berkshire.net/~ifas/activist

The Electronic Activist is a service of the Institute for First Amendment Studies, focusing on the separation of church and state. The database currently contains contact information for U.S. senators and representatives, governors, and some state legislatures.

Family Pride Coalition

www.familypride.org/

Family Pride seeks to advance the well-being of LGBT parents and their families. You can find a list of family pride events, local parenting groups, links to books and articles, along with links to other online resources.

Feberal Web Locator

www.infoctr.edu/fwl

The Federal Web Locator is a service provided by the Center for Information Law and Policy. It offers links to the legislative, judicial, and executive branches of the federal government as well as to other federal agencies, corporations, and committees.

Firstgov: Your First Click to the U.S. Government

firstgov.gov

This is a one-stop site for federal information. It allows users to browse the U.S. government by topic. It features a very large database and an index of all federal webpages.

Freedom to Marry Collaborative

www.geocities.com/evanwolfson

Developed by Evan Wolfson, director of the Marriage Project for the Lamda Legal Defense and Education Fund, the Freedom to Marry Collaborative explains the rationale behind the fight for legalizing same-sex marriage.

Gay and Lesbian Activists Alliance

www.glaa.org

GLAA is an all-volunteer, nonpartisan, nonprofit political organization providing information, resources, and projects promoting the equal rights of gay men and lesbians.

Gay and Lesbian Advocates and Defenders
www.glad.org
GLAD is a nonprofit, public interest legal organization whose mission is to achieve full equality and justice for New England's lesbian, gay, bisexual, and HIV- or AIDS-affected individuals. Provides information about LGB legal issues and HIV/AIDS legal issues, referrals for individuals affected by these issues, a hotline, marriage bulletins, and information about speakers and upcoming events.

Gay and Lesbian Alliance Against Defamation
www.glaad.org
Not to be confused with the regional group (GLAD), GLAAD is a national organization that has had considerable impact on the way LGBs are portrayed in the media. The site provides up-to-date information on media coverage of LGB issues.

Gay and Lesbian Medical Association
www.glma.org
GLMA combats homophobia within the medical profession and in society at large and promotes quality health care for LGBT and HIV-positive people. Using the site's free referral service, you can find an LGBT or LGBT-friendly health care provider. The site also describes programs in health research, support groups for HIV-positive people, and increasing lesbian and gay visibility at medical association meetings.

Gay and Lesbian Victory Fund
www.victoryfund.org/
The Gay and Lesbian Victory Fund is a national political organization that recruits, trains and supports openly LGBT candidates and officials. The site provides a list of candidates for public offices who are endorsed by the Gay and Lesbian Victory Fund as well as those currently in office. If you are looking for someone in particular, people and events can be searched by state.

Gay, Lesbian, and Straight Education Network
www.glsen.org
GLSEN strives to assure that each member of every school community is valued and respected, regardless of sexual orientation. This site provides information for students interested in sexual orientation issues and describes how to get involved in student pride activities.

Gay Parent Magazine

www.gayparentmag.com

Gay Parent Magazine provides information for LGBs who are or wish to be parents. It also provides gay-friendly resources for creating and nurturing families of all sorts.

Gay Today

www.gaytoday.badpuppy.com/topstory.htm

Advertised as a "global site for daily gay news," Gay Today is updated daily. It provides access to a wide variety of news stories, interviews, and editorials.

Gay Vote

www.gayvote.com

Gay Vote provides information about gay candidates, voter information for any state, and access to a forum about selected issues concerning elections.

Gender Education and Advocacy, Inc.

www.gender.org/

GEA is a nonprofit, national organization that seeks to educate and advocate for all human beings who suffer from gender-based oppression.

Human Rights Campaign

www.hrc.org

HRC offers information about renewing America's commitment to fighting HIV/AIDS, ending workplace discrimination, launching a rapid response to antigay hate legislation, and focusing attention on lesbian health issues. The site provides the text of current LGBT-relevant legislation, talking points, action alerts, and sample letters that can be used to lobby members of Congress.

House of Representatives

www.house.gov

This site provides addresses for members' homepages for the House of Representatives.

International Gay and Lesbian Human Rights Commission

iglhrc.org

IGLHRC's mission is to protect and advance the human rights of those subject to discrimination or abuse on the basis of sexual orientation, gender identity, or HIV status. The website will help advocates keep informed about LGB-related human rights abuses around the globe. It also includes a variety of resources for those seeking asylum in the United States based on issues related to sexual orientation.

Lambda Legal Defense and Education Fund

www.lambdalegal.org

Lambda is a legal organization working for the civil rights of LGBs and PWAs. The site provides information on current legal cases, special events around the country, and other resources about these issues.

Lesbian and Gay Immigration Rights Task Force

www.lgirtf.org

LGIRTF focuses on the needs of three overlapping groups: binational couples, immigrants with HIV/AIDS, and sexual orientation–based asylum seekers. Their website provides access to relevant resources including *The Status Report*, a newsletter that includes up-to-date information on changes in immigration law.

LLEGÓ

www.llego.org/

LLEGÓ is The National Latina/o Lesbian, Gay, Bisexual, and Transgender Organization. The site provides information on upcoming events, programs for Latina/o LGBTs, and jobs within LLEGÓ's organization. It also provides links to relevant news articles as well as links to various resources for Latina/o LGBTs (e.g., youth, coming-out issues, and mental health).

Log Cabin Republicans

www.lcr.org/

Log Cabin Republicans (LCR) is the nation's largest gay and lesbian Republican organization, with more than 50 chapters across the country. This site offers the opportunity to subscribe to the newsletter, and make a donation. You can find local chapters as well as a listing of the board of directors, the National Advisory Board, and other personnel.

The Mautner Project for Lesbians with Cancer

www.mautnerproject.org/

The Mautner Project is a national organization dedicated to lesbians with cancer, their partners, and caregivers. The site offers information on support and community services, and resources and referrals.

Members of Congress

bioguide.congress.gov

This site provides access to biographical information on members of Congress.

National Center for Lesbian Rights

www.NCLRights.org

NCLR is a national legal resource center committed to advancing the rights and safety of lesbians and their families through litigation, public policy advocacy, free legal advice and counseling, and public education. It also provides representation and resources to LGBT individuals on key issues that also advance lesbian rights.

National Coalition for Lesbian, Gay, Bisexual, and Transgender Health

www.lgbthealth.net.

The National Coalition for Lesbian, Gay, Bisexual, and Transgender Health is committed to improving the health and well-being of lesbian, gay, bisexual, and transgender individuals and communities through public education, coalition building, and advocacy that focuses on research, policy, education, and training. They were a significant force in shaping the *Healthy People 2010*, a document that will guide federal policy development and encourage the inclusion of LGBT concerns in federal programs.

National Lesbian and Gay Law Association

www.nlgla.org/

NLGLA is a national association of legal professionals, law students, and affiliated LGBT legal organizations. The site allows you to download NLGLA newsletters, find out about different regional and local events (e.g., writing competitions) sponsored by NLGLA, get information on becoming a member, and contact executive members.

National Gay and Lesbian Task Force

www.ngltf.org

NGLTF is a national activist organization. It serves as a national resource center for grassroots LGBT organizations that are facing a variety of battles at the state and local levels. The site includes resources relevant to combating antigay violence, battling radical right antigay legislative and ballot measures, advocating an end to job discrimination, working to repeal sodomy laws, demanding an effective governmental response to HIV, reforming the health care system, and much more.

National Gay Pilots Association

www.ngpa.org/

NGPA is a national organization of gay and lesbian pilots and other aviators from around the country. Find out how to become a member and about the benefits you would receive. You can find a listing of both future and past events, links to related websites, information on becoming a pilot, and scholarship opportunities.

National Organization of Gay and Lesbian Scientists and Technical Professionals

www.noglstp.org/

NOGLSTP is a national, nonprofit educational organization of LGBT people (and their advocates) either employed or interested in scientific or technology fields. Access to selected articles from the *NOGLSTP Bulletin* is available for reference, a list of members is available for networking purposes, and you can read about past meetings.

National Prevention Information Network

www.cdcnpin.org/hiv/start.htm

Formerly referred to as the National AIDS Clearinghouse, this website is maintained by the Centers for Disease Control. The HIV/AIDS section of this site provides access to information and resources on HIV and AIDS. It allows users to subscribe to electronic newsletters and search back issues. It also provides synopses of key scientific articles and media reports.

National Stonewall Democratic Federation

www.stonewalldemocrats.org

The federation provides information about mobilizing voters through a national grassroots network of gay and lesbian Democratic clubs. It works to advance gay and lesbian civil rights and supports the nomination of Democratic candidates who will fight bigotry. It also educates voters on the vast difference that exists between the two major parties on LGB issues.

National Youth Advocacy Coalition

nyacyouth.org/

The NYAC advocates for LGBT and questioning youth to improve their lives. The site offers the opportunity to write elected officials, contact national and local media, read press releases, and find out about upcoming events. The site also provides summaries and status information about key bills and key congressional roll call votes, tips about communicating with members of Congress, and general information about Capital Hill staffers and the legislative process.

Parents, Family, and Friends of Lesbians and Gays

www.pflag.org

PFLAG promotes the health and well-being of LGBTs and their families and friends through support, to cope with an adverse society; education, to enlighten an ill-informed public; and advocacy, to end discrimination and to secure equal civil rights. PFLAG provides opportunities for dialogue about sexual orientation and gender identity, and works to create a society that is healthy and respectful of human diversity.

Partners Task Force for Gay and Lesbian Couples

www.buddybuddy.com/toc.html

Partners Task Force focuses on issues of concern to same-sex couples, including legal marriage and sources of support. The site provides extensive information on ceremonial marriage and parenting, relationship tips, legal marriage essays and data, and links to other resources.

People for the American Way

www.pfaw.org

PFAW conducts research and supports legal and educational work. It also monitors the Religious right movement and its political allies. This site provides vital information about civil right issues for policy makers, scholars, and activists nationwide.

Political Resources on the Net

www.agora.stm.it/politic

This site provides listings of political sites available on the Internet sorted by country, with links to parties, organizations, governments, media, and more from around the world.

Pride at Work, AFL-CIO

www.prideatwork.org/

Pride at Work is a constituency group of the AFL-CIO (American Federation of Labor and Congress of Industrial Organizations). Its purpose is to mobilize mutual support between the organized labor movement and the LGBT community around issues of social and economic justice.

Project Vote Smart

vote-smart.org/

This website provides quick references to questions about government at various levels, and the people involved. It provides information on different government offices, including state, local, and city offices. It allows you to track the status of legislation and appropriation bills. Information is also available on broad government issues, such as briefs and voter registration. Links to information on current elections are also available.

Proud Parenting

www.proudparenting.com/

Formerly known as Alternative Family Magazine, Proud Parenting addresses the needs of LGBT parents and their families. On a state-by-state basis, the site provides links to resources on parenting groups; camps; reproduction, adoption, and fostering; and national and international organizations.

Queer Resources Directory

www.qrd.org

This electronic library contains more than 20,000 files about LGB issues. Worldwide information is also available. Specific subjects can be searched by date or users can rely on general subject headings.

Servicemembers Legal Defense Network

www.sldn.org

SLDN is a legal aid, watchdog, and policy organization for service members harmed by "Don't Ask, Don't Tell, Don't Pursue, Don't Harass." SLDN has directly assisted 2,600 service members and obtained 30 changes in military policy and practice related to "Don't Ask, Don't Tell, Don't Pursue, Don't Harass" since 1993. The website features a law library that includes relevant congressional testimony, court cases, Department of Defense memoranda and reports, executive orders, law journal articles, and various other useful resources.

Stop the Hate

stop-the-hate.org

This site focuses on how to stop hate crimes. It documents the stories of those who have endured hate crimes and provides many other resources and links concerned with prejudice.

Teaching Tolerance

www.tolerance.org

Teaching Tolerance is a project of the Southern Poverty Law Center. It encourages people from all walks of life to "fight hate and promote tolerance." The sister website TeachingTolerance.org provides access to a wealth of materials for use in the classroom by K-12 teachers. Users can also subscribe to a free magazine and contribute their own ideas.

Thomas: Legislative Information on the Internet

thomas.loc.gov

Thomas provides information about legislation, congressional records, committee information, bill status, and summaries.

Turn Out

www.turnleft.com/out

Turn Out features an extensive list of links to organizations and people involved in the political process, and information specific to the LGBT community. As of publication, the site has not been updated, but the links provide a good start for anyone researching LGB politics online.

United States Senate

www.senate.gov

Senate.gov provides addresses for U.S. senators' homepages. You will find a calendar of the day's activities for the Senate. You can search by number or keyword for a bill, or get general information about the Senate and legislative activities as well as contact information for senators.

Unity Through Diversity

www.geocities.com/westhollywood/castro/3212

This site focuses on gay youth and school issues and LGBT issues. It provides information on who to contact about school issues and links to other sites promoting safe schools.

White House

www.whitehouse.gov

This site provides easy access to government information. It also provides insight into the president's policy perspectives and includes government reports relevant to high-profile legislation.

NOTES

Introduction

1. A wide variety of terms have been used to refer to members of the lesbian, gay, and bisexual communities. We use the abbreviation *LGB* when we wish to refer to lesbian, gay, and bisexual people as a group. For example, we refer to LGB servicemembers and LGB youth or simply LGBs rather than use a more cumbersome phrase. Rather than a political statement, this is simply a matter of economy and style.

2. See chapters 1 and 5 for additional information.

3. Gay appointees of the Clinton administration. (2001, January 19). *The Washington Blade*, p. 17.

4. The full text of the bill passed by the Vermont House and Senate and a summary of the Civil Union Law are accessible from the website for the Vermont Freedom to Marry Task Force (www.VTFreetomarry.org).

5. Evelyn Hooker first established this finding in 1957.

6. Carey, A. R., & Lynn, G. (2000, May 9). Fortune tellers? *USA Today*, p. 1.

7. Greenberg, A. (1999, May 14). Public opinion makes better sense without the opinion makers. *Chronicle of Higher Education*, pp. B8–B9.

8. Ikenberry, S. O., & Hartle, T. W. (1998). *Too little knowledge is a dangerous thing: What the public thinks and knows about paying for college*. Washington, DC: American Council on Education.

9. Psychologists have been particularly active in this area through the advocacy activities of the American Psychological Association and the efforts of its policy savvy members and leaders. See Bjork, R. (2000, December). Giving away and selling the behavioral sciences. *APA Monitor*, p. 27. DeLeon, P. H. (2000, March). The critical importance of public policy involvement. *APA Monitor*, p. 5. Smith, D. (2000, October). Is there a better way to influence policy? *APA Monitor*, p. 41.

10. Keen, L. (1999, April 16). Federal court: Transsexual status "private and intimate." *The Washington Blade*, p. 25.

11. See the Human Rights Campaign at www.hrc.org.

12. Fox, K. (2001, July 20). Rhode Island adds transgender protections to law. *The Washington Blade*, p. 12.

13. British court voids transsexual's marriage. (2001, July 27). *The Washington Blade*, p. 26.

14. Malaysia denies gender recognition request. (2001, July 27). *The Washington Blade*, p. 26.

15. See APHA policy number 9933: The need for acknowledging transgendered individuals within research and clinical practice. Available at www.apha.org/legislative/policy/99policy.pdf

16. The National Institutes of Health issued a program announcement on *Behavioral, Social, Mental Health, and Substance Abuse Research with Diverse Populations* (PA-01–096) in 2001. Researchers were encouraged to submit research proposals that included transgendered people for this program. The official announcement was published in the NIH guide at grants.nih.gov/grants/guide/pa-files (click on PA-01–096).

17. The June 2001 issue of the *American Journal of Public Health* focused explicitly on LGBT health. Articles from that issue have been compiled with others from past issues of the journal in *Lesbian, Gay, Bisexual, and Transgender Health: Selections from the American Journal of Public Health.* Further information about the volume is available at www.apha.org.

18. Andrea L. Solarz, Ph.D., directed the National Academy of Sciences Institute of Medicine Committee on Lesbian Health Research Priorities. The study was funded by the National Institutes of Health Office of Research on Women's Health, and the Centers for Disease Control and Prevention Office of Women's Health.

19. For example, Cochran, S. D., Keenan, K., Schober, C., & Mays, V. M. (2000). Estimates of alcohol use and clinical treatment needs among homosexually active men and women in the U.S. population. *Journal of Consulting and Clinical Psychology, 68* (6), 1062–1071. See also Freiberg, P. (2001, January 12). Study: Alcohol use more prevalent for lesbians—Gay men measure about the same as heterosexuals, while straight women drink far less. *The Washington Blade*, p. 21.

20. Readers interested in additional information are encouraged to read the original report. It is available at www.nap.edu/catalog/6109.html.

21. Fox, 2001 (see note 12); The report, *Healthy People 2010*, will guide federally funded research through 2010. It can be retrieved from the National Coalition for LGBT Health at www.lgbthealth.net.

22. See the official announcement for the program at grants.nih.gov/grants/guide/pa-files (click on PA-01–096); see also Fox, 2001.

23. Additional sources of support for LGB health research can be located through the National Coalition for GLBT Health at www.lgbthealth.net

24. The IOM is a prestigious independent organization chartered by Congress to examine policy matters pertaining to public health.

25. The report is available at www.nap.edu/catalog/6109.html

26. A more detailed discussion of the roundtable meeting, and analysis of the politics surrounding this event, is presented in Plumb, M. (2000). *The politics of lesbian health policy: A critical review of the politics that created and shaped the Institute of Medicine's Report on Lesbian Health.* Manuscript submitted for publication.

27. Plumb, M. (1997, July 24). *Invited statement of the Gay and Lesbian Medical Association.* Presented to the IOM Committee on Lesbian Health Research Priorities, Washington, DC. See also Plumb, 2000.

28. Plumb, 1997. See also Stachelberg, W. (1996, Spring). Advancing the lesbian health agenda. *Human Rights Campaign Quarterly.* Retrieved August 22, 2001, from www.hrc.org/publications/hrcq/hrcq96sp/pg14.asp

29. Plumb, 1997. See also Plumb, 2000.

30. Plumb, 1997.

31. This conference, which took place in September 1999, was sponsored by the National Institute of Mental Health, the National Institute on Drug Abuse, the NIH Office of Behavioral and Social Sciences Research, the NIH Office of Research on Women's Health, and the American Psychological Association.

32. The Scientific Workshop on Lesbian Health was held in Washington D.C., in March 2000. It was sponsored by the DHHS Office on Women's Health as well as a number of other federal offices and outside advocacy organizations.

33. O'Bryan, W. (2001, April 6). Not just lip service: Dutch couples join in wedlock. *The Washington Blade*, pp. 1, 12.

34. Tokyo gays first in Asia to be covered. (2001, January 19). *The Washington Blade*, p. 10.

35. Romania gets legislation to protect gays. (2000, September 22). *The Washington Blade*, p. 12.

36. European Union to grant gays work protections. (2000, December 8). *The Washington Blade*, p. 12.

37. Same-sex Kiwi couples to get property rights. (2000, December 8). *The Washington Blade*, p. 12.

38. Gay partners take senior political posts. (2000, April 28). *The Washington Blade*, p. 32.

39. O'Bryan, W. (2001, March 9). China changes guidelines for gay psychiatry. *The Washington Blade*, p. 10.

40. Wright, K. (2001, April 28). Saudi men sentenced to lashes for "deviance": Gay Muslim group plans embassy protest. *The Washington Blade*, p. 34. Krisberg, K. (2002, January 4). Saudis beheaded for sodomy: Men convicted of "extreme obscenity, ugly acts" under nation's Islamic law. *The Washington Blade*, pp. 1, 14.

41. Namibian leader calls for arrest of gays (2001, March 23). *The Washington Blade*, p. 10. O'Bryan, W. (2001, April 13). Namibia's president bans gay foreigners. *The Washington Blade*, pp. 1, 14. Namibian official calls for police to "eliminate" gays. (2002, September 6). *The Washington Blade*, p. 23.

42. Malaysian sodomy case brings 9 yrs. (2000, August 11). *The Washington Blade*, p. 10. Court upholds sodomy law and conviction. (2000, June 9). *The Washington Blade*, p. 14.

43. In December 2000 the Clinton administration provided greater recognition and better treatment for the domestic partners of foreign service workers. The Bush State Department decided to leave the new rules in place in 2002. Chibbaro, L., Jr. (2002, April 12). Foreign service DPs treated like spouses: Bush administration leaves in place last-month Clinton policy. *The Washington Blade*, pp. 1, 12. O'Bryan, W. (2000, January 21). Foreign Service's union pushes for gay benefits: "Unique circumstances" of job demands cited. *The Washington Blade*, p. 24.

44. Advocate poll. (1999, October 12). *The Advocate*, p. 6.

45. See the ACLU website for updates at www.aclu.org/action/permanentpartner107.html

46. See www.lgirtf.org/issues.html for the most recent information.

47. Chibbaro, L., Jr. (2001, October, 27). Gore's comments on immigration draw praise: Candidate says gay foreigners should have same rights as married heterosexuals. *The Washington Blade*, p. 20. O'Bryan, W. (2001, January 5). Pro-gay immigration bill left untouched by Congress. *The Washington Blade*, p. 21.

48. O'Bryan, W. (2000, March 3). Seeking refuge: S.F. resolution seeks to assist same-sex binational couples. *The Washington Blade*, pp. 1, 18.

49. Web addresses for these organizations appear in the Appendix.

50. Hughes, J. (2001, Spring). Torn apart: Immigration bill would give binational, same-sex couples a fair shake. *HRC Quarterly*, pp. 10–11.

51. Wright, K. (1999, March 19). Mapping persecution: U.S. report excludes many gay cases. *The Washington Blade*, pp. 1, 10.

52. Chibbaro, L. (1998, January 23). "You cannot imagine the fear": Man's application for political asylum details persecution in Iran. *The Washington Blade*, p. 5.

53. Savage, T. (1999, September 14). Give me your tired, your poor, your gay . . . more and more gay foreigners turn to the United States for refuge. *The Advocate*, pp. 26–27.

54. Keen, L. (2000, September 8). Mexican male gets chance for asylum. *The Washington Blade*, p. 23. Savage, 1999.

55. *Crimes of Hate, Conspiracy of Silence: Torture and Ill-Treatment Based on Sexual Identity.*

56. O'Bryan, W. (2001, June 29). Persecution targeted: Lantos resolution looks for global solution. *The Washington Blade*, p. 22.

57. Bullock, M. (2001). Science and foreign policy—The State Department reaches out! *Psychological Science Agenda, 14*(4), 4.

58. Smith, D. (2000, October). Is there a better way to influence policy? *APA Monitor*, p. 41.

Chapter 1

1. This chapter is based on Cogan, J. C., & Preston, C. (2002). Women, federal policy, and social change: Bringing a feminist presence to Capitol Hill. In L. H. Collins, M. R. Dunlap, & J. C. Chrisler (Eds.). *Charting a new course for feminist psychology*. (pp. 348–366) Westport, CT: Praeger.

2. As chapter 8 describes in detail. The full text of DOMA is available online through the Thomas website: TP://Thomas.loc.gov/CGI-BIN/Query/z?c104:H.R.3396.ENR.

3. See chapter 8 for how members of Congress voted.

4. These issues are discussed in detail in chapter 5.

5. See chapter 5 for how members voted.

6. See chapter 4 for more information.

7. American Psychological Association. (1995). *Advancing psychology in the public interest: A psychologist's guide to participation in federal policy making*. Washington, DC: Author.

8. Wells, W. G. (1996). *Working with Congress: A practical guide for scientists and engineers*. Washington, DC: American Association for the Advancement of Science.

9. Lorion, R. P., & Iscoe, I. (1996). Reshaping our views of our field. In R. P. Lorion, I. Iscoe, P. H. DeLeon, & G. R. VandenBos (Eds.), *Psychology and public policy* (pp. 1–19). Washington, DC: American Psychological Association. Truman, D. B. (1987). The nature and functions of interest groups: The governmental process. In P. Woll (Ed.), *American government: Readings and cases* (pp. 255–262). Boston: Little, Brown.

10. Ceaser, J. W., Bessette, J. M., O'Toole, L. J., & Thurow, G. (1995). *American government: Origins, institutions, and public policy* (4th ed.). Dubuque, IA: Kendall/Hunt.

11. Nickels, I. B. (1994). *Guiding a bill through the legislative process* (Congressional Research Service Report for Congress, 94–322 GOV). Washington, DC: Library of Congress.

12. Key, V. O. (1987). The nature and functions of interest groups: Pressure groups. In P. Woll (Ed.), *American government: Readings and cases* (pp. 266–273). Boston: Little, Brown.

13. American Psychological Association, 1995 (see note 7). Wells, 1996 (see note 8).

14. Drew, E. (1987). A day in the life of a United States Senator. In P. Woll (Ed.), *American government: Readings and cases* (pp. 487–497). Boston: Little, Brown. Vincent, T. A. (1990). A view from the Hill: The human element in policy making on Capitol Hill. American Psychologist, 45(1), 61–64.

15. American Psychological Association, 1995.

16. Wells, 1996.

17. Rundquist, P. S., Schneider, J., & Pauls, F. H. (1992). *Congressional staff: An analysis of their roles, functions, and impacts* (Congressional Research Service Report for Congress, 92–90S). Washington, DC: Library of Congress.

18. Redman, E. (1987). Congressional staff: The surrogates of power. In P. Woll (Ed.), *American government: Readings and cases* (pp. 452–461). Boston: Little, Brown. Rundquist, Scheidner, & Pauls, 1992.

19. Vincent, T. A., 1990, p. 61 (see note 14).

20. Bevan, W. (1996). On getting in bed with a lion. In R. P. Lorion, I. Iscoe, P. H. DeLeon, & G. R. VandenBos (Eds.), *Psychology and public policy* (pp. 145–163). Washington, DC: American Psychological Association. Nissim-Sabat, D. (1997). Psychologists, Congress, and public policy. Professional Psychology: Research and Practice, 28(3), 275–280. Wells, 1996 (see note 8).

21. This is the rationale for including briefing memos throughout this book.

22. I wrote this example of a briefing memo specifically for the purposes of this chapter. The material is based on my advocacy work in the Public Policy Office at the American Psychological Association.

23. For example, Wilson, D. K., Purdon, S. E., & Wallston, A. (1988). Compliance to health recommendations: A theoretical overview of message framing. *Health Education Research, 3,* 161–171.

24. Adapted from unpublished matierals originally drafted by William Baily, American Psychological Association.

25. I wrote this as an example of a good constituent letter. The Tiahrt amendment was introduced to the D.C. appropriations bill in 1997. Although it was elimiated, a similar amendment had been introduced every year since.

26. American Psychological Association, 1995 (see note 7). For more information on how to write an effective letter, the reader is referred to the information brochure written by the APA titled: Calkins, B. J. (1995). *Psychology in the public interest: A psychologist's guide to participation in federal policy making.* Washington, DC: APA. Available at www.apa.org/ppo/grassroots/sadguide.html

27. Text adapted from Fairness and Accuracy in Reporting (FAIR) at www.fair.org/

28. Text adapted from PFLAG at www.pflag.org/

Chapter 2

1. Delaware Senate mulls gay civil rights bill. (2002, February 8). *The Washington Blade,* p. 12.

2. Krisberg, K. (2002, February 1). Asylum can be luck of the draw: Cases hinge on INS officers' discretion, advocates say, bringing success to some and frustration to others. *The Washington Blade,* p. 24.

3. Black, D., Gates, G., Sanders, S., & Taylor, L. (2000). Demographics of the gay and lesbian population in the United States: Evidence from available systematic data sources. *Demography, 37*(2), 139–154.

4. *Gay* can be used to refer to either men or women, but *lesbian* refers only to women.

5. The conventions we currently use to distinguish between people of different sexual orientations are based on the assumption that there are two discrete sexes. They also assume that being male or female is based on biological differences in genitalia or other biological markers. However, recent scholarship and activism by and about people who are transgendered or intersexed is leading scientists to reexamine this basic assumption. Kessler, S. J. (1998). Lessons from the intersexed. Brunswick, NJ: Rutgers University Press. Rottnek, M. (Ed.). (1999). *Sissies and tomboys: Gender nonconformity and homosexual childhood.* New York: New York University Press. As awareness of these issues increases, policy makers and the general public may come to very different conclusions about what constitutes good public policy.

6. See Bohan, J. S., & Russell, G. M. (1999). *Conversations about psychology and sexual orientation.* New York: New York University Press.

7. For example, Blanchard, R., & Dickey, R. (1998). Pubertal age in homosexual and heterosexual sexual offenders against children, pubescents, and adults. *Sexual Abuse: A Journal of Research and Treatment, 10*(4), 273–282.

8. For example, Reisman, J. A. (1999, March 26). *The APA's: Academic pedophile advocates.* Retrieved from Available at www.worldnetdaily.com/bluesky_excomm/19990326_xex_the_apas_aca.shtml

9. Stevenson, M. R. (2000). Public policy, homosexuality, and the sexual coercion of children. *Journal of Psychology and Human Sexuality, 12*(4), 1–19.

10. Laumann, E. O., Gagnon, J. H., Michael, R. T., & Michaels, S. (1994). *The social organization of sexuality: Sexual practices in the United States*. Chicago: University of Chicago Press.

11. For example, Cameron, P., & Cameron, K. (1996). Do homosexual teachers pose a risk to pupils? *Journal of Psychology, 130*, 603–613. Cameron, P., & Cameron, K. (1998). What proportion of newspaper stories about child molestation involves homosexuality? *Psychological Reports, 82*, 863–871.

12. Laumann, Gagnon, Michael, & Michaels, 1994.

13. See chapter 3 for in depth discussion of the so-called ex-gay movement. See also Pietrzyk, M. E. (2000). Pathology of the ex-gay movement. *The Gay & Lesbian Review, 7*(3), 32–37.

14. Leap, W. (1999a). *Public sex and sustainable gay community*. Remarks prepared for a Safeguards-sponsored Gay Men's Heal Forum, Philadelphia.

15. Sedgewick, E. (1993). The epistemology of the closet. In H. Abelove, M. Barale, & D. Halperin (Eds,), *The lesbian & gay studies reader* (pp. 45–61). London: Routledge.

16. Pryce, A. (1996). Researching eros: Revisiting ethnographic chronicles of male sex in public places. *Sexual and Marital Therapy, 11*(3), 321–334.

17. Ambady, N., Hallahan, M., & Conner, B. (1999). Accuracy of judgments of sexual orientation from thin slices of behavior. *Journal of Personality and Social Psychology, 77*(3), 538–547.

18. Renna, C. (2000, January 29). How do we know they're gay. *The Washington Post*, p. A19.

19. D'Augelli, A. R. (1994). Lesbian and gay male development: Steps toward an analysis of lesbian's and gay men's lives. In B. Greene & G. M. Herek (Eds.), *Lesbian and gay psychology: Theory, research, and clinical applications* (pp. 118–132). Thousand Oaks, CA: Sage.

20. Herman, D. (1997). *The antigay agenda: Orthodox vision and the Christian right*. Chicago: University of Chicago Press. Omoto, A. (1999). Lesbian, gay, and bisexual issues in public policy: Some of the relevance and realities of psychological science. In J. S. Bohan & G. M. Russell (Eds.), *Conversations about psychology and sexual orientation* (pp. 165–182). New York: New York University Press.

21. Omoto, 1999. Aguero, J., Block, L., & Byrne, D. (1984). The relationship among sexual beliefs, attitudes, experience, and homophobia. *Journal of Homosexuality, 10*, 95–107. Whitley, B. E., Jr. (1990). The relationship of heterosexuals' attributions for the causes of homosexuality to attitudes toward lesbians and gay men. *Personality and Social Psychology Bulletin, 16*, 269–377. Bohan & Russell, 1999a (see note 6).

22. Berke, R. L. (1998, August 2). Chasing the polls on gay rights. *The New York Times*, p. 3.

23. Omoto, 1999.

24. Kitzinger, C., & Wilkinson, S. (1995). Transitions from heterosexuality to lesbianism: The discursive production of lesbian identities. *Developmental Psychology 31*, 95–104.

25. Omoto, 1999.

26. Russell, G. M., & Bohan, J. S. (1999). Implications for public policy. In J. S. Bohan & G. M. Russell (Eds.), *Conversations about psychology and sexual orientation* (pp. 139–164). New York: New York University Press.

27. Kauth, M. R., & Kalichman, S. C. (1995). Sexual orientation and development: An interactive approach. In L. Diamant & R. D. McAulty (Eds.), *The psychology of sexual orientation, behavior, and identity: A handbook* (pp. 81–103). Westport, CT: Greenwood.

28. Bower, B. (1993). Genetic clue to male homosexuality emerges. *Science News, 144*(3), 37. Hamer, D. H., & Hu, S. (1993). A linkage between DNA markers on the X chromosome and male sexual orientation. *Science, 261*(5119), 321–327. Rice, G., Anderson, C., Risch, N., & Ebers, G. (1999). Male homosexuality: Absence of linkage to microsatellite markers at Xq28. *Science, 284*(5414), 665–667. Travis, J. (1995). X chromosomes again linked to homosexuality. *Science News, 148*(19), 295. Wickelgren, I. (1999). Discovery of "gay gene" questioned. *Science, 284* (5414), 571.

29. Auditory functioning: McFadden, D., & Pasanen, E. G. (1998). Comparison of the auditory systems of heterosexuals and homosexuals. *Proceedings of the National Academy of Science, 95*(5),

2709–2713. Left-handedness: Lalumière, M. L., Blanchard, R., & Zucker, K. J. (2000). Sexual orientation and handedness in men and women: A meta-analysis. *Psychological Bulletin, 126*(4), 575–592. Finger-length patterns: Williams, T. J., & Pepitone, M. E. (2000). Finger-length ratios and sexual orientation. *Nature, 404*(6777), 455.

30. Savin-Williams, R. C. (1998). *". . . And then I become gay": Young men's stories*. New York: Routledge. Savin-Williams, R. C., & Cohen, K. M. (Eds.). (1996). *The lives of lesbians, gays, and bisexuals: Children to adults*. Fort Worth, TX: Harcourt Brace.

31. D'Augelli, 1994 (see note 19).

32. Diamant, L., & McAnulty, R. D. (1995). *The psychology of sexual orientation, behavior, and identity: A handbook*. Newport, CT: Greenwood.

33. Gonsiorek, J. C. (1995). Gay male identities: Concepts and issues. In A. R. D'Augelli & C. J. Patterson (Eds.), *Lesbian, gay, and bisexual identities over the lifespan* (pp. 24–47). New York: Oxford University Press.

34. For example, Cameron & Cameron, 1996 (see note 11). See also Herman, 1997 (see note 20).

35. Kahn, S. (2000). The "ex-gays": Anatomy of a fraud. *The Gay & Lesbian Review, 7*(3), 29–32. Pietrzyk, 2000 (see note 13).

36. From "I like it," which appeared in McNaught, B. (1981). *A disturbed peace: Selected writings of an Irish Catholic homosexual* (pp. 122–123). Washington, DC: Dignity.

37. Pietrzyk, 2000.

38 See the 2001 Surgeon General's *Report on Sexual Health* at www.surgeongeneral.gov/library/sexualhealth

39. Leap, W. (Ed.). (1999b). *Public sex/gay space*. New York: Columbia University Press. Laumann, Gagnon, Michael, & Michaels, 1994 (see note 10).

40. Diamond, L. M. (2000). Sexual identity, attractions, and behavior among young sexual-minority women over a 2–year period. *Developmental Psychology, 36* (2), 241–250. Pietrzyk, 2000.

41. Haldeman, D. C. (1999). The pseudo-science of sexual orientation conversion therapy. *Angles, 4*(1), 1–4. Available at www.igliss.org/iglss/pubs/angles/angles_4–1_p1.html. Lawrence, A. (1999). Changes in the sexual orientation of six heterosexual male-to-female transsexuals: Comment. *Archives of Sexual Behavior, 28*(6), 581–583. Yarhouse, M. A. (1998). Group therapies for homosexuals seeking change. *Journal of Psychology and Theology, 26*(3), 247–259.

42. Herman, 1997, pp. 75–76 (see note 20).

43. Schneider, R., Jr. (2000). "The people gay" and the 10% debate. *The Gay & Lesbian Review, 7*(2), 4, 61–62.

44. Russell & Bohan, 1999 (see note 26).

45. Black, Gates, Sanders, & Taylor, 2000 (see note 3).

46. Kinsey, A. C., Pomeroy, W. B., & Martin, C. E. (1948). *Sexual behavior in the human male*. Philadelphia: W. B. Saunders.

47. Butler, A. (2000). Trends in same-sex partnering, 1988–1998. *Journal of Sex Research, 37*(4), 333–343.

48. Black, Gates, Sanders, & Taylor, 2000.

49. Schneider, 2000 (see note 43).

50. Black, Gates, Sanders, & Taylor, 2000. See www.hrc.org/newsreleases/2001/census/010711graph_hi.asp for the most recent U.S. Census figures.

51. Schneider, 2000.

52. Exit polls are surveys taken at the exits of polling places after people have cast their votes in elections.

53. Schneider, 2000.

54. Black, Gates, Sanders, & Taylor, 2000.

55. Butler, 2000.

56. Dutch official wed almost 2,000 same-sex couples. (2001, December 21). *The Washington Blade*, p. 33.

57. Some states go further, outlawing such things as *gross lewdness* and *gross indecency*.

58. American Civil Liberties Union. (1999). *Status of U.S. sodomy laws*. Available at www.aclu.org/issues/gay/sodomy.html. SIECUS. (1999). Courts instrumental in shaping sexual rights: Sodomy laws. *Advocates Report, 6*(2), 1–2.

59. Hyman, D. (1999). *Sodomy laws: Are they constitutional?* Available at www.utexas.edu/courses/phl347/papers/hyman.html

60. Cain, P. A. (1993). Litigating for lesbians and gay rights. *Virginia Law Review, 79*(1551), 1587–1641.

61. Leap, 1999b (see note 39).

62. American Civil Liberties Union, 1999.

63. Chibbaro, L., Jr. (2000, July 14). LA court upholds sodomy law: Ruling calls oral and anal sex "an injury against society itself." *The Washington Blade*, p. 13.

64. For recent updates, visit websites maintained by the National Gay and Lesbian Task Force (www.ngltf.org) or the ACLU (www.aclu.org).

65. For additional examples, visit the ACLU website (www.aclu.org/issues/gay/sodomy.html).

66. Same-sex acts remain illegal in 82 countries. (1999, April 30). *The Washington Blade*, p. 10.

67. Cain, P. A. (2000). *Rainbow rights: The role of lawyers and courts in the lesbian and gay civil rights movement*. Boulder, CO: Westview.

68. Family Research Institute. (1992). *Medical consequences of what homosexuals do*. Washington, DC: Author.

69. Hyman, 1999 (see note 59).

70. Stader, J. K. (1993). Constitutional challenges to the criminalization of same-sex sexual activities: State interest in HIV-AIDS issues. *Denver University Law Review, 70*(2), 337–357.

71. Lewis, T. P. (1993). *Commonwealth v. Wasson*: Invalidating Kentucky's sodomy statute. *Kentucky Law Journal, 81*, 423–448.

72. Hyman, 1999.

73. American Civil Liberties Union, 1999 (see note 58).

74. Leap, W. (1999c). *Studying gay city: Lesbian/gay studies as applied anthropology*. Paper presented at the meeting of the Society for Applied Anthropology, Tucson, AZ.

75. Pryce, 1996 (see note 16).

76. Leap, 1999b (see note 39).

77. Leap, 1999a (see note 14).

78. Leap, 1999b.

79. Leap, 1999c.

80. Humphreys, L. (1970). *Tearoom trade*. London: Duckworth.

81. Leap, 1999b.

82. Leap, 1999a. Leap, W. (1999d). *Public sex/gay space: How this book came to be, issues which it explores, and (some of the) larger questions which it raises*. Remarks prepared for a reading from *Public sex/gay space*, D.C. Arts Centers, Washington, DC.

83. Leap, 1999b.

84. Leap, 1999d, p. 15 (see note 82).

Chapter 3

1. The authors would like to acknowledge Riley Morgan for assistance with this chapter.

2. Khan, S. (1998a). *Calculated compassion: How the ex-gay movement serves the right's attack on democracy* (p. 17). Somerville, MA: Political Research Associates.

3. Gudel, J. P. (1992, Summer). Homosexuality: Fact and fiction. *Christian Research Journal,* 30–41. Available at iclnet93.iclnet.org/pub/resources/text/cri/cri-jrnl/crj0107a.txt

4. Cited in People for the American Way. (1999). *Hostile climate: Report on anti-gay activity.* Washington, DC: People for the American Way Foundation. See also www.pfaw.org/pfaw/general/default.aspx?oiv=2041

5. Gonsiorek, J. C. (1991). The empirical basis for the demise of the illness model of homosexuality. In J. C. Gonsiorek & J. D. Weinrich (Eds.), *Homosexuality: Research implications for public policy* (pp. 115–136). Newbury Park, CA: Sage. Herek, G. M. (1991a). Myths about sexual orientation: A lawyer's guide to social science research. *Law & Sexuality: A Review of Lesbian & Gay Legal Issues, 1,* 133–172.

6. Hooker, E. (1957). The adjustment of the male overt homosexual. *Journal of Projective Techniques, 21,* 18–31.

7. For reviews of this research, see Gonsiorek, 1991; Rothblum, E. D. (1994). I only read about myself on bathroom walls: The need for research on the mental health of lesbians and gay men. *Journal of Consulting and Clinical Psychology, 62,* 213–220. Otis, M. D., & Skinner, W. F. (1996). The prevalence of victimization and its effect on mental well-being among lesbian and gay men. *Journal of Homosexuality, 30,* 93–121.

8. Gonsiorek, 1991.

9. Conger, J. (1975). Proceedings of the American Psychological Association, Incorporated, for the year 1974: Minutes of the annual meeting of the Council of Representatives. *American Psychologist, 30,* 620–651, p. 633.

10. Howe, R. G. (1994). The myths of homosexuality. In *Homosexuality in America: Exposing the myths* (p. 11). Tupelo, MS: American Family Association. Available at www.afa.net/homosexual_agenda/homosexuality.pdf

11. Socarides, C. W. (1994). The erosion of heterosexuality: Psychiatry falters, America sleeps. In *Homosexuality in America: Exposing the myths.* Tupelo, MS: American Family Association. Available at www.afa.net/homosexual_agenda/homosexuality.pdf

12. Links to all resolutions and policies are found at www.apa.org/pi/lgbc/policies/html. Information from the APA website (www.apa.org) can be found from the Lesbian, gay, and Bisexual Concerns Office of the Public Interest Directorate at www.apa.org/pi/lgbc/homepage. html. *Answers to your questions about sexual orientation and homosexuality* can be found at www.apa.org/pubinfo/answers.html

13. *Division 44/Committee on Lesbian, Gay, and Bisexual Concerns Joint Task Force on Guidelines for Psychotherapy With Lesbian, Gay, and Bisexual Clients,* 2000. Available at www.apa.org/pi/lgbc/publications/guidelines.html

14. American Psychiatric Association (undated). Gay and Bisexual Lesbian Issues, *FactSheet* (p. 4), Washington, DC: Author. Available at www.psych.org/public_infor/gaylesbianbisexualissues22701.pdf

15. Available at ww.aglbic.org.bradley.htm. See also www.counseling.org.

16. See www.socialworkers.org/diversity.lgb.reparative.asp

17. Available at www.apsa. org/pubinfo/homosexuality.htm

18. American Academy of Pediatrics. (1993, October). Policy statement: Homosexuality and Adolescence (RE 9332). *Pediatrics, 92*(4), 631–634. Available at www.aap.org/policy/05072.html.

19. Herman, J. L. (1992). *Trauma and recovery.* New York: Basic Books.

20. American Psychiatric Association. (2000, February). *FactSheet* (p. 1). Washington, DC: Author.

21. Amercian Psychological Association. (1998). *Answers to your question about sexual orientation and homosexuality.* Washington, DC: Author. Available at www.apa.org/pubinfo/answers.html

22. Diamond, S. (1989). *Spiritual warfare: The politics of the Christian right.* Boston: South End Press.

23. From an undated Family Research Council brochure titled *We can still win the war! FRI: Scientists defending traditional values.*

24. Brief of Amicus Curiae the Family Research Institute in support of the Apellee, in the District Court of Appeal, First District, State of Florida, Mary Frank Ward, Appellant vs. John Andrew Ward, Appellee. Case No.: 95–04184.

25. "Clearly, when investigators have a vested interest in the outcome of their research, considerable caution in accrediting their conclusions is prudent." Brief of *amicus curiae* by the Family Research Institute (see note 24).

26. Nicolosi's *What is "cure"* is available at www.narth.com.

27. Howe, 1994, p. 12 (see note 10).

28. Nicolosi, J. (1993). *Insight*. Family Research Council, IS93G2HS. Available at www.frc.org/insight/is93g2hs.html

29. Drescher, J. (1998). I'm your handyman: A history of reparative therapies. *Journal of Homosexuality, 36,* 19–42. Haldeman, D.C. (1994). The practice and ethics of sexual orientation conversion therapy. *Journal of Consulting and Clinical Psychology, 62,* 221–227.

30. Haldeman, 1994.

31. From an undated Family Research Council brochure entitled *We can still win the war! FRI: Scientists defending traditional values.*

32. Satinover, J. (1996). *Homosexuality and the politics of truth.* Grand Rapids, MI: Baker Books. Quoted in Khan, 1998a (see note 2).

33. Khan, 1998a.

34. Ibid.

35. For reviews of this research, see Haldeman, 1994. Herek, G. M. (1998). Bad science in the service of stigma: A critique of the Cameron group's survey studies. In G. M. Herek (Ed.), *Stigma and sexual orientation: Understanding prejudice against lesbians, gay men, and bisexuals* (pp. 223–255). Thousand Oaks, CA: Sage. Tozer, E. E., & McClanahan, M. K. (1999). Treating the purple menace: Ethical considerations of conversion therapy and affirmative alternatives. *Counseling Psychologist, 27,* 722–742.

36. For further discussion, see chapter 2.

37. Institute for the Scientific Investigation of Sexuality (ISIS). (1984). *What causes homosexuality and can it be cured?* [ISIS Brochure]

38. Howe, 1994, p. 12 (see note 10).

39. Khan, S. (1998b). *Challenging the ex-gay movement: An information packet.* Somerville, MA: Political Research Associates.

40. Ibid., p. 4.

41. Ibid., p. 3.

42. American Psychological Association, 1998 (see note 14); see also www.apa.org/pubinfo/answers.html

43. Khan, 1998b, p. 9.

44. Anthony Falzarano, executive director of P-FOX, 1996, Family Research Council, www.frc.org

45. ISIS, 1984 (see note 37).

46. Available at www.messiah.edu and www.exodusnorthamerica.org/aboutus/

47. American Psychiatric Association. (2000, February). *FactSheet* (p. 1) Washington, DC: Author.

48. Tozer & McClanahan, 1999 (see note 28).

49. Haldeman, 1994 (see note 22).

50. Morris, J. F., & Rothblum, E. D. (1999). Who fills out a lesbian questionnaire: Years out, disclosure of sexual orientation, sexual experience with women, and participation in the lesbian community. *Psychology of Women Quarterly, 23,* 537–557.

51. Khan, 1998b (see note 39); also see Human Rights Campaign's Ray of Light Project at www.hrc.org

52. Chin, J. (1995). Saved: Our reporter survives the Ex-Gay Ministries. *The Progressive*, 32–35. Mills, K. I. (1998). *Mission impossible: Why reparative therapy and the ex-gay ministries fail.* Washington, DC: Human Rights Campaign.

53. St. Pierre as quoted at www.hrc.org

54. Darrell Gingrich, Human Rights Campaign, as quoted at www.hrc.org

55. For more details, see Kahn, 1998a, p. viii (see note 2).

56. Serra, R. (2000). The continued struggle of civil rights in the gay community. *Journal of Psychology and Christianity, 20*, 168–175. This quotation is from pp. 168 and 174.

57. Khan, 1998a, p. 19.

58. Khan, 1998a; Mills, 1998 (see note 52).

59. Anthony Falzarano, national leader of P-FOX, in a letter to the editor of the *Free Lance-Star*, Fredricksburg, VA, April 24, 1998. In Kahn, 1998b, p. 17 (see note 39).

60. *The Colorado Springs Gazette.* (2000, October 5).

61. Family Research Council. (2000, October 19). *Culture facts.* [FRC Brochure]

62. Khan, 1998a, p. vii.

63. Khan, 1998b, p. 17.

64. Goldberg, C. (1998, February 12). Maine voters repeal a law on gay rights. *The New York Times*, p. A1.

65. *Bangor Daily News.* (1998, February 7).

66. Kahn, 1998b, p. 19.

67. www.family.org

68. Kahn, 1998b.

69. *Omaha World-Herald.* (2000, October 11).

70. York, F., & Knight, R. H. (1998). *Homosexual teens at risk: Victims of "homophobia" or self-destructive behavior?* Family Research Council. Available at http://www.frc.org/fampol/fp98fcu.html

71. Family Research Council, 1996. (October 16). Available at www.frc.org

72. LaBarbera, P. (1999). *Insight.* Family Research Council, IS99F4HS. Available at www.frc.org/insight/is99f4hs.html

73. LaBarbera, P. (1994). *Gay youth suicide: Myth is used to promote homosexual agenda.* Family Research Council. Available at www.frc.org/insight/is94b3hs.html

74. Blake, S. M., Ledsky, R., Lehman, T., Goodenow, C., Sawyer, R., & Hack, T. (2001). Preventing sexual risk behaviors among gay, lesbian, and bisexual adolescents: The benefits of gay-sensitive HIV instruction in schools. *American Journal of Public Health, 91*, 940–946. Fergusson, D. M., Horwood, J., & Beautrais, A. L. (1999). Is sexual orientation related to mental health problems and suicidality in young people? *Archives of General Psychiatry, 56*, 876–880. Garofalo, R., Wolf, C., Wissow, L. S., Woods, E. R., & Goodman, E. (1999). Sexual orientation and risk of sucide attempts among a representative sample of youth. *Archives of Pediatric Adolsecent Medicine, 153*, 487–493. Bagley, C., & Tremblay, P. (1997). Suicidal behaviors in homosexual and bisexual males. *Crisis, 18*, 24–34. Remafedi, G., French, S., Story, M., Resnick, M. D., & Blum, R. (1998). The relationship between suicide risk and sexual orientation: Results of a population-based study. *American Journal of Public Health, 88*, 57–60. Russell, S. T., & Joyner, K. (2001). Adolescent sexual orientation and suicide risk: Evidence froma national study. *American Journal of Public Health, 91*(8), 1276–1281.

75. Garofalo, Wolf, Wissow, Woods, & Goodman, 1999; Remafedi, French, Story, Resnick, & Blum, 1998.

76. Savin-Williams, R. C. (2001). A critique of research on sexual-minority youths. *Journal of Adolescence, 24*, 5–13.

77. Nicolosi, 1993 (see note 28).

78. Retrieved from www.oregoncitizensalliance.org

79. Ibid.

80. York & Knight, 1998 (see note 70).

81. Faulkner, A. H., & Cranston, K. (1998). Correlates of same-sex sexual behavior in a randon sample of Massachusetts hight school students. *American Journal of Public Health, 88*, 262–266. Russell & Joyner, 2001 (see note 74). Sauwyc, E. M., Bearinger, L. H., Heinz, P. A., Blum, R. W., & Resnick, M. D. (1998). Gender differences in health and risk behaviors among bisexual and homosexual adolescents. *Journal of Adolescent Health, 23*, 181–188. Savin-Williams, 2001 (see note 76).

82. Savin-Williams, R. C. (1994). Verbal and physical abuse as stressors in the lives of lesbian, gay male, and bisexual youths: Associations with school problems, running away, substance abuse, prostitution, and suicide. *Journal of Consulting and Clinical Psychology, 62*, 261–269.

83. O'Leary, D. (2001, February 5). *Gay teens and attempted suicide.* Available at www.narth.com

84. Garofalo, R., & Katz, E. (2001). Health care issues of gay and lesbian youth. *Current Opinion in Pediatrics, 13*, 298–302. Russell & Joyner, 2001 (see note 74). Savin-Williams, 1994.

85. Garofalo & Katz, 2001.

86. Safren, S. A., & Heimberg, R. G. (1999). Depression, hopelessness, suicidality, and related factors in sexual minority and heterosexual adolescents. *Journal of Consulting and Clinical Psychology, 67*, 852–866.

87. Blake et al., 2001 (see note 74).

88. These issues are also considered in chapter 11.

89. David LaFontaine's summary of the Mission and History of the Massachusetts Governor's Commission on Gay and Lesbian youth is available at www.state.ma.us/gcgly/. The full text of the law is available on the website for the Massachusetts Governor's Commission on Gay and Lesbian Youth at www.state.ma.us/gcgly/TheGayandLesbianStudentsRightsLaw.html

90. People for the American Way, 1999 (see note 4).

91. Ibid.

92. Ibid.

93. According to Robert Knight, author of California's Proposition 22 (the Knight Initiative), "Homosexuals typically have [a] shorter life expectancy. They are also more likely to display risky, self-destructive behavior such as alcoholism and drug abose," See Knight, R. H., & Garcia, D. S. (1994). *Insight.* Family Research Council. Available at www.frc.org/insight/is94e3hs.html

Chapter 4

1. Jenness, V., & Broad, K. (1997). *Hate crimes: New social movements and the politics of violence.* New York: Aldine de Gruyter.

2. Ibid.

3. States that did not have a hate crimes law of any kind as of September 2002 include Arkansas, New Mexico, South Carolina, and Wyoming.

4. U.S. Department of Justice. (1995). *National bias crimes training for law enforcement and victim assistance professionals.*

5. As of September 2002, according to NGLTF at www.ngltf.org/issues/issue.cfm?issueid=12

6. Whereas the broad-based coalition of organizations lobbying members of Congress for the passage of the HCSA were advocating for the inclusion of gender, it was not included in the final language of the bill. In fact, gender was more difficult to include as a category of hate crimes than any other category, including sexual orientation. A common question that gets raised regarding gender is, "Does this mean every rape is a hate crime?" And legislators feared what would happen if the answer to that question was yes.

7. Hate Crimes Statistics Act, Pub. L. N. 101–275 104 Stat. 140, (1990).

8. Chapter 3 provides information on how to counteract such myths.

9. Federal Bureau of Investigation, U.S. Department of Justice. (1996). Hate Crime Statistics of 1996. In *Uniform Crime Reports.*

10. Human Rights Campaign website at www.hrc.org

11. American Sociological Association. (1999). *Hate crime in America: What do we know?* [Briefing sheet].

12. Jacobs, J., & Potter, K. (1998). *Hate crimes: Criminal law and identity politics.* New York: Oxford Press.

13. American Psychological Association. (1998). *Answers to your questions about sexual orientation and homosexuality.* Washington, DC: Author. Available at www.apa.org/pubinfo/answers.html

14. Herek, G. M., Gillis, J. R., & Cogan, J. C. (1999). Psychological correlates of hate crime victimization among lesbian, gay, and bisexual adults. *Journal of Consulting and Clinical Psychology, 67*(6), 945–951.

15. This information was adapted from the New York City Gay and Lesbian Anti-Violence Project (AVP) at www.avp.org

16. Ibid.

17. This information was adapted from Stop the Hate at www.stopthehate.org/get_involved/law/empower/crimes_vs_incidents.php

18. Human Rights Campaign website at www.hrc.org

19. Ibid.

20. Ibid.

21. Herek, Gillis, & Cogan, 1999 (see note 14).

22. Dunbar, E. (1997). *Hate crime patterns in Los Angeles County: Demographic and behavioral factors of victim impact and reporting of crime.* Washington, DC: American Psychological Association. (Testimony at a congressional briefing on hate crimes.)

23. In their criticisms, Jacobs and Potter (1998) (see note 12) are critical of the data that suggest hate crimes are at epidemic levels and therefore argue that hate crimes legislation is unwarranted.

24. Herek, Gillis, & Cogan, 1999 (see note 14).

25. This information was adapted from the victim information section of the New York City Gay and Lesbian Anti-Violence Project at www.avp.org and LAMBDA at www.lambdalegal.org

26. Franklin, K. (2002). Good intentions: The enforcement of hate crime penalty enhancement statutes. *American Behavioral Scientist, 46*(1), 154–172.

27. American Psychological Association. (1997). Testimony on the Juvenile Justice and Delinquency Act submitted to the Education and Workforce Committee, Early Childhood, Youth and Families Subcommittee of the U.S. House of Representatives, May 21, 1997.

28. Ezekiel, R. S. (2002). An ethnographer looks at neo-nazi and klan groups: The racist mind revisited. *American Behavioral Scientist, 46*(1), 51–70.

29. U.S. Department of Justice. (1998). *OJJDP annual report.* Office of Juvenile Justice and Delinquency Prevention.

30. Ibid.

Chapter 5

1. Additional examples of discrimination against LGBs can be found in *Documenting Discrimination*, a report that includes more than 130 stories of antigay discrimination in the workplace. The report is available online at www.hrc.org.

2. In this chapter, the terms *job discrimination, employment discrimination*, and *workplace discrimination* refer to illegal practices with regard to race, color, religion, sex, or national origin under the 1964 Civil Rights Act, 42 U.S.C. 2000e-2, and sexual orientation under the proposed Employment Non-Discrimination Act. These practices include "to fail or refuse to hire, or to discharge any individual, or otherwise to discriminate against any individual with respect to the compensation, terms, conditions, or privileges of employment." 1964 Civil Rights Act 703(a)(1), 42 U.S.C. 2000e-2(a)(1); H.R. 2355 (4)(a)(1); S. 1276 (4)(a)(1).

3. *Dillion v. Frank*, 58 Fair Empl. Prac. Cas. (BNA) 144 (6th Cir. 1992). *Jantz v. Muci*, 976 F.2d 623 (10th Cir. 1992). Cunningham, M. (1992). Queer/straight. *Mother Jones, 17*, 60–68. Shepard, B. (1992, March 29). Not just fired, but fired up. *Atlanta Journal Constitution*, p. 7; *Blain v. Golden State Container, Inc.*, See also *Arizona Republic*, December 7, 1994.

4. Lazarus, R. S., & Folkman, S. (1984). *Stress, appraisal, and coping*. New York: Springer.

5. Meyer, I. (1995). Minority stress and mental health in gay men. *Journal of Health Sciences and Social Behavior, 36*, 38–56.

6. Waldo, C. R. (1999). Working in a majority context: A structural model of heterosexism as minority stress in the workplace. *Journal of Counseling Psychology, 46*(2), 1–15. Persons with disabilities also typically have parents who do not share their child's minority status. Job discrimination against people with disabilities is now illegal under the Americans With Disabilities Act, 42 U.S.C. 12101–12213 (Supp. V 1993).

7. Laumann, E. O., Gagnon, J. H., Michael, R. T., & Michaels, S. (1994). *The social organization of sexuality: Sexual practices in the United States*. Chicago: University of Chicago Press. Levine, M. P. (1979). Employment discrimination against gay men. *International Review of Modern Sociology, 9*(5–7), 151–163. Even the mainstream media realize that "polling gays is notoriously tricky." Leland, J. (2000, March 20). Shades of gay. *Newsweek*, pp. 46–49.

8. Levine, M. P., & Leonard, R. (1984). Discrimination against lesbians in the work force, *Signs, 9*(4), 700–710. Levine, 1979.

9. Friskopp, A., & Silverstein, S. (1995). *Straight jobs, gay lives: Gay and lesbian professionals, the Harvard Business School, and the American workplace*. Croteau, J. M., & Von Destinon, M. (1994). A national survey of job search experiences of lesbian, gay, and bisexual student affairs professionals. *Journal of College Student Development, 35*(1), 40–45.

10. Badgett, M. V. L., Donnelly, C., & Kibbe, J. (1992). *Pervasive patterns of discrimination against lesbians and gay men: Evidence from surveys across the United States*. Washington, DC: National Gay and Lesbian Task Force.

11. Herek, G. M., Gillis, J. R., Cogan, J. C., & Glunt, E. K. (1997). Hate crime victimization among lesbian, gay, and bisexual adults: Prevalence, psychological correlates, and methodological issues. *Journal of Interpersonal Violence, 12*(2), 195–215.

12. Waldo, 1999 (see note 6).

13. Levine, 1979 (see note 7). Badgett, M. V. L. (1996, August). *Tolerance or taboos: Occupational differences by sexual orientation*. Paper presented at the annual meeting of the American Psychological Association, Toronto, Ontario, Canada.

14. Day, N. E., & Schonerade, P. (1997). Staying in the closet versus coming out: Relationships between communication about sexual orientation and work attitudes. *Personnel Psychology, 50*, 147–163.

15. Waldo, 1999. Powers, B. (1996). The impact of gay, lesbian, and bisexual workplace issues on productivity. In A. L. Ellis & E. D. B. Riggle (Eds.), *Sexual identity on the job: Issues and services* (pp. 79–90). New York: Harrington Park Press/Haworth Press.

16. Klawitter, M. M., & Flatt, V. (1998). The effects of state and local antidiscrimination policies for sexual orientation. *Journal of Policy Analysis and Management, 17*(4), 658–687. Black, D., Gates, G., Sanders, S., & Taylor, L. (2000). Demographics of the gay and lesbian population in the United States: Evidence from available systematic data sources. *Demography, 37*(2), 139–154.

17. Klawitter & Flatt, 1998

18. Badgett, M. V. L. (1995). The wage effects of sexual orientation discrimination. *Industrial and Labor Relations Review, 48*(4), 726–739. Three other studies put the income disparity at 4–7 percent. Badgett, M. L. V. (2000). The myth of gay and lesbian affluence. *The Gay & Lesbian Review, 7*(2), 22–25. Badgett, M. V. L. (2001). *Money, myths, and change: The economic lives of lesbians and gay men.* Chicago: University of Chicago Press. The evidence is less convincing for an income disparity for single lesbians. See also Klawitter & Flatt, 1998; Black, Gates, Sanders, & Taylor, 2000 (see note 16).

19. Black, Gates, Sanders, & Taylor, 2000; specifically, 80% of married couples, 60% of partnered gay men, and 65% of partnered lesbians.

20. Leland, 2000 (see note 7). Laumann, Gagnon, Michael, & Michaels, 1994 (see note 7). Results of poll. (1989, June 6). *San Francisco Examiner,* June 6, 1989, pp. A-19, A-20. Badgett, 2000. Edelman, M. J. (1993). Understanding the gay and lesbian vote in '92. *Public Perspectives, 8.* Elliot, S. (1994, June 9). A sharper view of gay consumers. *New York Times,* pp. D1, D17.

21. Leland, 2000. This percentage has remained consistently high in recent years. Yang, A. S. (1998). *From wrongs to rights: Public opinion on gay and lesbian equality.* New York: National Gay and Lesbian Task Force. See also Newport, F. (1999, March 1). Some change over time in American attitudes towards homosexuality, but negativity remains. *Gallup News Service,* p. 3 (83% support "equal rights in terms of job opportunities").

22. See Kessler, F., & Gilmore, G. (1970). *Contracts: Cases and materials.* Boston: Little Brown, p. 11. Friedman, L. (1965). *Contract law in America.* Madison: University of Wisconsin Press, p. 24.

23. Council on the Role of the Courts. (1984). *The role of the courts in American society.* St. Paul, MN: West.

24. Council on the Role of Courts, 1984.

25. Feinman, J. M. (1976). The development of the employment at will rule. *American Journal of Legal History, 20,* 118–126. The frequency of such cases increased once more in the late 20th century. Leonard, A. (1988). A new common law of employment termination. *North Carolina Law Review, 66,* 631–650.

26. Finkin, M. (1986). The bureaucratization of work: Employer policies and contract law. *Wisconsin Law Review,* 733–746. The seminal case is *Martin v. New York Life Ins. Co.,* 148 N.Y. 117, 42 N.E. 416 (1895).

27. However, California has provided statutory protection for the political activities of private sector workers. See Cal. Lab. Code 1101–02 (1989).

28. Leonard, 1988. The principal exception is Montana's Wrongful Discharge From Employment Act, MT Code Ann. 39–2–901 to -914 (1987).

29. AFL-CIO. (2001, September). *Workers' rights in America: What workers think about their jobs and employers.* (Peter D. Hart), Available at www.aflcio.org/rightsinamerica/index.htm

30. Taylor, H. (2001, June 13). *The Harris Poll* #27. Available at www.harrisinteractive.com. Forty-two percent of respondents believed that federal law already prohibits sexual orientation job discrimination; 33% admitted they didn't know. Even among LGBs, only 47% realized they lack legal protection under federal law.

31. For example, comments of Sen. Dan Coats, Senate floor debate on the proposed Federal Employment Non-Discrimination Act, Cong. Rec. 22469 (September 10, 1996). Comments of presidential candidate G. W. Bush (2000, October 12). *The New York Times,* (transcript of second presidential debate). Family Research Council. (1997, April 24). *Pro-family America will fight the ENDA agenda of putting sex into the workplace* [Press release].

32. See Comments of Sen. Don Nickels, Senate floor debate on the proposed Federal Employment Non-Discrimination Act, Cong. Rec. 22475 (September 10, 1996): "under Federal employment laws as written every heterosexual, homosexual, or bisexual person is treated equally."

33. The slogan "No Special Rights" also makes sense only if one ignores the protection a sexual orientation job bias law would provide to heterosexuals. Heterosexuals who can suffer job discrimination because of an employer's mistaken impression as to their sexual orientation, or even because of their employer's preference for gay or lesbian employees (see the case of Carolyn O'Neill, a heterosexual waitress fired when her employer decided to market primarily to gay customers, first reported in Human Rights Campaign, *Documenting discrimination*, 1994). Riccucci, N. M., & Gossett, C. W. (1996). Employment discrimination in state and local government: The lesbian and gay male experience. *American Review of Public Administration, 26*(2), 175–200 (reporting a case in which a heterosexual employee, under an antidiscrimination provision, alleged harassment based on sexual orientation by a lesbian supervisor).

34. Leonard, 1988 (see note 25).

35. Epstein, R. (1984). In defense of the contract at will. *University of Chicago Law Review, 51*, 947.

36. Bureau of Labor Statistics, U.S. Department of Labor, 1999.

37. Cox, Bok, Gorman, R. (2001). *Labor Law*. Mineola, NY: Foundation Press.

38. See Challenging sexual preference discrimination in private employment, 41 *Ohio State Law Journal* (1980). 501, 520–522.

39. Leonard, 1988.

40. Gould, W. B., IV. (1986). The idea of the job as property in contemporary America: The legal and collective bargaining framework. *Brigham Young University Law Review, 6*, 885–887.

41. See *Joachim v. AT&T Information Systems*, 793 F.2d 113 (5th Cir. 1986); *Sabetay v. Sterling Drug, Inc.,* 69 N.Y.2d 329, 506 N.E.2d 919, 514 N.Y.S.2d 209 (1987); Leonard, 1988.

42. 42 U.S.C. 12211 (Supp. V 1993).

43. See *Baehr v. Lewin*, 74 Hawaii 530, 852 P.2d 44 (1993); Editors of the *Harvard Law Review*, (1989) *Sexual orientation and the law*, Cambridge, MA: Harvard Univesity Press. Law, S. (1998). Homosexuality and the social meaning of gender. *Wisconsin Law Review, 187*, 218.

44. *Faraca v. Clements*, 506 F.2d 956 (5th Cir. 1975). See also *Loving v. Virginia*, 388 U.S. 1 (1967) (finding racial discrimination in law forbidding blacks and whites from intermarrying).

45. Developments in the law—Employment discrimination, 109 *Harvard Law Review*, 1568, 1632 (1996); see *DeSantis v. Pacific Telephone & Telegraph Co.*, 608 F.2d 327 (9th Cir. 1979); *Smith v. Liberty Mutual Ins. Co.*, 569 F.2d 325 (5th Cir. 1978): see also EEOC Decision 76–75, 19 Fair Empl. Prac. Cas. (BNA) 1823, 1824 (1975).

46. For information on East Lansing, see Fletcher, L. Y. (1992). *The first gay pope*. Boston: Alyson. "At the dawn of the 21st Century, the strength of the GLBT movement is at the state and local level." Urvashi Vaid, director of the National Gay and Lesbian Task Force Policy Institute, quoted in NGLTF (2000, January 3). *Nondiscrimination laws now cover 100 million Americans, new report finds*. [Press release].

47. National Gay and Lesbian Task Force Policy Institute. (2000). *Legislating equality: A review of laws affecting gay, lesbian, bisexual, and transgendered people in the United States*. Washington, DC: NGLTF Policy Institute. Developments in the law—Employment discrimination, 109 *Harvard Law Review* 1568, 1626 (1996).

48. For cities and counties banning sexual-orientation, see National Gay and Lesbian Task Force Policy Institute, 2000; Note, Constitutional limits on anti-gay-rights initiatives, 106 *Harvard Law Review* (1993). 1905, 1923–1925. The *Harvard Law Review* calls the enactment of statewide job bias laws covering sexual orientation "one of the quiet labor law revolutions of the 1990s." Developments in the law—Employment discrimination, 109 *Harvard Law Review*, 1568, 1625 (1996). Human Rights Act, 1977, D.C.L. 2–38, D.C. Code 1–2541(c) (1977).

49. For cities and counties with executive orders concerning discrimination, see National Gay and Lesbian Task Force Policy Institute, 2000. For the federal government's policies see Further Amendment to Executive Order 11478 EEO (May 28, 1998). On the inconsistent and sometimes

illusory protections provided to public sector workers by executive orders or administrative regulations, see Riccucci & Gossett, 1996 (see note 33).

50. For example, *Norton v. Macy*, 417 F.2d 1161 (D.C. Cir. 1969) (federal agency covered by civil service must show rational nexus between job and sexual orientation). See Hunter, N. D., Michaelson, S. E., & Stoddard, T. B. (1992). *The rights of lesbians and gay men: The basic ACLU guide to a gay person's rights*. Carbondale: Southern Illinois University Press. But see *Shahar v. Bowers*, 114 F.3d 1097 (11th Cir. 1997) (state attorney general can refuse employment based on sexual orientation), cert. denied, 118 S. Ct. 693 (1998).

51. See H.R. 2692 & S. 1284 (107th Congress) introduced July 31, 2001.

52. Executive Order No. 83–64 (December 1983). See *Columbus Dispatch*, January 13, 2000. *Cincinnati Enquirer*, January 13, 2000.

53. By contrast, administrative agencies cannot change their own regulations without "reasoned analysis." See *Motor Vehicle Mfrs. Ass'n v. State Farm Automobile Ins. Co.*, 463 U.S. 29, 42 (1983).

54. See, for example, *Rendell-Baker v. Kohn*, 457 U.S. 830 (1982).

55. Bureau of Labor Statistics, U.S. Department of Labor, 1999.

56. An attorney correctly advised Cheryl Summerville that any legal action she filed would suffer the same fate.

57. Most of the empirical arguments against job discrimination laws covering sexual orientation resemble those made against job discrimination laws covering other criteria. Fiss, O. (1971). A theory of fair employment laws. *University of Chicago Law Review, 38*, 235–263.

58. See for example, Sex, lies, and civil rights: A critical history of the Massachusetts gay civil rights bill, 26 *Harvard Civil Rights-Civil Liberties Law Review*, 549, 572 (1991).

59. Ibid.

60. This box is based on material provided by the Human Rights Campaign and in Chibbaro, L., Jr. (2001, August 3). Legislators focus on 'unfinished business': Kennedy predicts ENDA vote in Senate. *The Washington Blade*, pp. 1, 12. Updates can be retrieved from the HRC website (www.hrc.org).

61. Calabresi, G. (1970). *The costs of accidents: A legal economic analysis*. New Haven: Yale University Press. With regard to accident prevention, Judge Calabresi calls preventive costs "primary." What this chapter calls "remedial costs," Judge Calabresi calls "secondary" and "tertiary" costs.

62. Barnard, T. H. (1990). The Americans with Disabilities Act: Nightmare for employers and dream for lawyers? *St. John's Law Review, 64*, 229–252. Stuhlbarg, S. F. (1991). Reasonable accommodation under the Americans with Disabilities Act: How much must one do before hardship turns undue? *University of Cincinnati Law Review, 59*, 1311–1320. Neither the ADA nor the proposed Employment Non-Discrimination Act applies to private businesses with fewer than 15 employees. See 42 U.S.C. 12111(5)(A) (Supp. V 1993); H.R. 2692 & S. 1284 (3)(4)(A) (107th Congress) (introduced July 31, 2001).

63. See *Report to Congress on the Job Accommodation Network* by Barbara Judy, Americans with Disabilities Forum, Senate Subcommittee on Disability Policy, July 26, 1995.

64. Comments of Sen. Paul Coverdell, Senate floor debate on the proposed Federal Employment Non-Discrimination Act, Cong. Rec. 22264 (September 6, 1996). Comments of Sen. Nancy Landon Kassebaum, at 22248, 2265 (September 6, 1996) ("prolonged litigation"). Comments of Senator Orrin Hatch, at 22251, 22264 (September 6, 1996), 22470 (September 10, 1996) ("a litigation bonanza"). Comments of Sen. Trent Lott, at 22474 (September 10, 1996) ("a guarantee of multiple lawsuits").

65. Sex, Lies, and Civil Rights, 1991 (see note 58). Thirteen years after enactment of the Massachusetts gay rights law, MCAD funding had risen to $4,199,455. Massachusetts Commission Against Discrimination. (2002). *Annual report*.

66. Barnard, 1990 (see note 60). Fitzpatrick, R. B. (1993, June 3). Reasonable accommodation and undue hardship under the ADA: Selected issues. In *Employment Discrimination & Civil Rights Actions in Federal & State Courts*, 267, 282 (ALI-ABA Course of Study). McGraw, E. J. (1993). Compliance costs of the Americans with Disabilities Act. *Delaware Journal of Corporate Law*, *18*, 521–541.

67. See Developments in the law—Employment discrimination, 109 *Harvard Law Review* 1568, 1617–18 (1996).

68. Reno, J., & Thornburgh, D. (1995, July 26). ADA—Not a disabling mandate. *The Wall Street Journal*, p. A12.

69. Riccucci & Gossett, 1996 (see note 33).

70. For additional discussion, see chapters 6 and 11 of this volume.

71. Vermont Human Rights Law, Vt. Stat. Ann. tit. 21, 495 (1994).

72. Comments of Sen. James Jeffords, Senate floor debate on the proposed Federal Employment Non-Discrimination Act, Cong. Rec. 22251 (September 6, 1996).

73. General Accounting Office. (2000, April 28). *Sexual-orientation-based employment discrimination: States' experience with statutory prohibitions since 1997* (GAO/OGC-00–27R). Comments of Sen. Edward M. Kennedy, Senate floor debate on the proposed Federal Employment Non-Discrimination Act, Cong. Rec. 22323 (September 9, 1996).

74. See General Accounting Office, 2000.

75. Riccucci & Gossett, 1996.

76. Massachusetts Gen. Laws, Chapter 151D, 3–4 (West 1995).

77. See Sex, Lies, and Civil Rights, 1991 (see note 58) for comments on HIV and passage of the Massachusetts law. For further discussion on child sexual abuse, see chapter 10 this volume. When made, this claim usually focuses on gay men. Lesbians rarely are accused of having sexual interest in children. This claim resembles, but is distinct from, the claim, treated in the next portion of this chapter, that gay role models will influence young people to adopt a gay or lesbian sexual orientation.

78. However, opponents made neither argument in the 1996 Senate floor debate on the proposed Federal Employment Non-Discrimination Act. See Cong. Rec. 22245–66 (September 6, 1996), 22320–24, 22331–36, & 22355–56 (September 9, 1996), 22439–40, 22458, & 22467–77 (September 10, 1996). Senator John Ashcroft at one point did ground his opposition to ENDA in the need to keep children "protected." Id. at 22261 (September 6, 1996). But in context he clearly meant "role model considerations" and "send[ing] the right signals" rather than direct sexual predation. See also comments of Sen. Ashcroft at 22260 (expressing concern about "role models" for "young men" in "transition" from "boyhood to manhood"). This chapter covers the "role model" argument in the next subsection, as a matter of morals rather than health.

79. *AIDS facts and statistics*. Available at www.healthnews.com/aids.html See *Citizens for Responsible Behavior v. Superior Court*, 2 California Reporter 2d 648, 658–69 (Court of Appeal 1992) (calling fear of AIDS, as a basis for antigay discrimination, unconstitutionally irrational).

80. Schneider, M. (1993). Educating the public about homosexuality. *Annals of Sex Research, 6*, 57–66. Martin, A. D. (1988). The stigmatization of the gay or lesbian adolescent. In M. Schneider (Ed.), *Often invisible: Counseling gay and lesbian youth* (pp. 59–69). Toronto; Central Toronto Youth Services. Nevertheless, the child-abuse allegation led the successful advocates of the Massachusetts law to accept an amendment qualifying the term "sexual orientation," whenever it appears, specifically to exclude "those persons whose sexual orientation involves minor children as a sex object." See Sex, Lies and Civil Rights, 1991 (see note 58).

81. See chapter 10 of this volume.

82. Becker, J. V., Alpert, J. L., BigFoot, D. S., Bonner, B. L., Geddie, L. F., Henggeler, S. W., Kaufman, K. L., & Walker, C. E. (1995). Empirical research on children abuse treatment: Report by the child abuse and neglect treatment working group, American Psychological Association.

Journal of Clinical Child Psychology, 24(Suppl.), 23–46. Jenny, C., Roesler, T. A., & Poyer, K. L. (1994). Are children at risk for sexual abuse by homosexuals? *Pediatrics, 94*, 41–44.

83. Gebhard, P. H., & Johnson, A. B. (1979). *The Kinsey data: Marginal tabulations of the 1938–1963 interviews conducted by the Institute for Sex Research*. Philadelphia: Saunders.

84. Comments of Sen. Orrin Hatch, Senate floor debate on the proposed Federal Employment Non-Discrimination Act, Cong. Rec. 22251–52 (September 6, 1996). Comments of Sen. Dan Coats, id. at 22469 (September 10, 1996).

85. Formulations include "homosexuality is a sin": Peyser, M., & Lorch, D. (2000, March 20). High school controversial. *Newsweek*, pp. 54–55. Newport, F. (1998, July 25). "Homosexual behavior is morally wrong," *Gallup News Service*, Americans remain more likely to believe sexual orientation due to environment, not genetics, reported in R. L. Berke (Ed.), (1998, August 2). Chasing the polls on gay rights. *The New York Times*, p. 3. "homosexual relationships between consenting adults are morally wrong," and "sexual relations between two adults of the same sex are always wrong": Yang, 1998 (see note 21). Even polls conducted by the same polling organization in the same month can have different wordings. Compare Newport, p. 3 (see note 21) ("homosexuality should be considered an acceptable alternative lifestyle" poll conducted February 8–9, 1999), with Gillespie, M. (1999, April 7). Americans support hate crimes legislation that protects gays. *Gallup News Service*, p. 5 ("homosexual behavior should be considered an acceptable lifestyle" poll conducted February 19–21, 1999).

86. Yang, 1998.

87. Peyser & Lorch, 2000 (46%); Newport, 1999 (50%); Gillespie, 1999 (52%); Newport, 1998 (5990).

88. See Comments of Sen. Bob Kerrey, Senate floor debate on the proposed Federal Employment Non-Discrimination Act, Cong. Rec. 22255 (September 6, 1996) (calling sexual orientation a "benign" trait). Comments of Sen. Don Nickles, id. at 22475 (September 10, 1996) (ENDA would make sexual orientation "irrelevant" in the workplace). This argument led the successful proponents of the Massachusetts gay rights law to accept an amendment providing that nothing in the law would "be construed as an approval or endorsement" of homosexuality. See Sex, Lies, and Civil Rights, 1991 (see note 58).

89. Posner, 1992; Posner argues that allowing employers to discriminate will not inhabit same-sex behavior. As a result, even if one thinks same-sex sexual behavior is immoral, there is no moral cost to laws against job discrimination. See also Sex, Lies, and Civil Rights, 1991 (see note 58).

90. See, for example, Comments of Sen. John Ashcroft, Senate floor debate on the proposed Federal Employment Non-Discrimination Act, Cong. Rec. 22260, 22261 (September 6, 1996). Comments of Sen. Don Nickles, at 22258, 22333 (September 9, 1996), 22473 (September 10, 1996). Public support for job bias protection is weakest for occupations involving children. Yang, 1998; Gillespie, 1999 (see note 85).

91. Comments of Sen. Orrin Hatch, Senate floor debate on the proposed Federal Employment Non-Discrimination Act, Cong. Rec. 22253, 22264 (September 6, 1996), 22470 (September 10, 1996).

92. See Comments of Sen. Dianne Feinstein, Senate floor debate on the proposed Federal Employment Non-Discrimination Act, Cong. Rec. 22259 (September 6, 1996).

93. Comments of Sen. John Ashcroft, Senate floor debate on the proposed Federal Employment Non-Discrimination Act, Cong. Rec. 22260 (September 6, 1996).

94. See Comments of Sen. Don Nickles, Senate floor debate on the proposed Federal Employment Non-Discrimination Act, Cong. Rec. 22333 (September 9, 1996) (claiming that "'Bisexual' by definition means promiscuous") and at 22473 (September 10, 1996) (claiming that western religions teach that "homosexuality is wrong").

95. See Sex, Lies, and Civil Rights, 1991 (see note 58).

96. See Comments of Sen. Orrin Hatch, Senate floor debate on the proposed Federal Employment Non-Discrimination Act, Cong. Rec. 22264 (September 6, 1996). Comments of Sen. Don Nickles, at 22333 (September 9, 1996). Opponents sometimes add the assertion that any federal law protecting conduct would do so "for the first time in our history." Comments of Sen. Dan Coats, at 22469 (September 10, 1996). This assertion is patently false. See 1964 Civil Rights Act 701(j) & 703(a)(1), 42 U.S.C. 2000e(j) & 2000e-2(a)(1) (requiring that employers "reasonably accommodate" an employee's "religious observance or practice"), *Trans World Airlines, Inc. v. Harbison*, 432 U.S. 63 (1977).

97. See Comments of Sen. Don Nickles, Senate floor debate on the proposed Federal Employment Non-Discrimination Act, Cong. Rec. 22333 (September 9, 1996): "'Bisexual' by definition means promiscuous."

98. See chapter 2 for further discussion of this distinction.

99. *Webster's New Collegiate Dictionary* (8th ed., 1977), p. 809.

100. Laumann, Gagnon, Michael, & Michaels, 1994 (see note 7).

101. Klein, F. (1993). *The bisexual option* (2nd ed., pp. 29–37). Binghamton, NY: Harrington Park Press.

102. Riccucci & Gossett, 1996 (see note 33).

103. Batchelor, E., Jr. (Ed.). (1980). *Homosexuality and ethics* (pp. 149–167, 235–243). New York: Pilgrim Press.

104. Murphy, J. G. (1971). Involuntary acts and criminal liability. *Ethics, 51*, 332–342.

105. Yang, 1998. Whitley, B. E., Jr. (1990). The relationship of heterosexuals' attributions for the causes of homosexuality to attitudes toward lesbians and gay men. *Personality and Social Psychology Bulletin, 16*, 269–377.

106. Schneider, W., & Lewis, I. A. (1984, February–March). The straight story on homosexuality and gay rights. *Public Opinion*, 16–20, 59–60. Aguero, J., Block, L., & Byrne, D. (1984). The relationship among sexual beliefs, attitudes, experience, and homophobia. *Journal of Homosexuality*, 10, 95–107.

107. Haldeman, D. C. (1999). The pseudo-science of sexual orientation conversion therapy. *Angles, 4*(1), 1–4. Lawrence, A. A. (1999). Changes in the sexual orientation of six heterosexual male-to-female transsexuals: Comment. *Archives of Sexual Behavior, 28*(6), 581–583. Yarhouse, M. A. (1998). Group therapies for homosexuals seeking change. *Journal of Psychology and Theology, 26*(3), 247–259. See also chapters 2 and 3 this volume.

108. Yang, 1998 (see note 21). Herek, G. M. (1984). Beyond "Homophobia": A social psychological perspective on attitudes toward lesbians and gay men. *Journal of Homosexuality, 10*, 1–21. Herek, G. M., & Capitanio, J. P. (1995). Black heterosexuals' attitudes toward lesbians and gay men in the United States. *Journal of Sex Research, 32*, 95. Herek, G. M., & Glunt, E. K. (1993). Interpersonal contact and heterosexuals' attitudes toward gay men: Results from a national survey. *The Journal of Sex Research, 30*, 239–244.

109. To the extent a job discrimination law encourages self-disclosure, it could thus also indirectly affect public perceptions of the moral irrelevance of sexual orientation.

110. See Sex, Lies, and Civil Rights, 1991 (see note 58).

111. Green, R. (1978). Sexual identity of 37 children raised by homosexual or transsexual parents. *American Journal of Psychiatry, 135*, 692–693. Patterson, C. J. (1992). Children of lesbian and gay parents. *Child Development, 63*, 1025–1042. Patterson, C. J. (1997). Children of lesbian and gay parents. In T. H. Ollendick & R. J. Prinz (Eds.), *Advances in Clinical Child Psychology, 19*, 235–282. See also chapter 9 this volume.

112. Quoted in Comments of Sen. Edward M. Kennedy, Senate floor debate on the proposed Federal Employment Non-Discrimination Act, Cong. Rec. 22335 (September 9, 1996).

113. Yang, 1998 (see note 21).

114. Berke, 1998 (see note 85).

115. Kirk M., & Madsen, H. (1989). *After the ball: How America will conquer its fear and hatred of gays in the nineties.* New York: Plume.

116. Successful advocates of the comprehensive Massachusetts gay rights law avoided any direct engagement on the moral issues. See Sex, Lies, and Civil Rights, 1991. Sherrill, K. (1998). Introduction. In A. Yang, *From wrongs to rights: Public opinion on gay and lesbian equality* (p. iii). New York: National Gay and Lesbian Task Force ("progress can be achieved [on] tangible issues while it may remain slower on more abstract or symbolic issues").

117. It also explains how 59% could find "homosexual behavior" immoral whereas 70% supported President Clinton's executive order barring sexual orientation discrimination in federal employment (Berke, 1998); and how polls can show African Americans, compared with white Americans, both more disapproving of gays and lesbians and more supportive of equal employment rights (Yang, 1998).

118. In a recent poll, 75% supported inclusion of sexual orientation under a state hate crimes law. Gillespie, 1999 (see note 85).

119. See Sex, Lies, and Civil Rights, 1991.

120. Gillespie, 1999. Yang, 1998.

Chapter 6

1. Leonard, A. (1994). Lesbian and gay families and the law: A progress report. *Fordham Urban Law Journal, 21*, 927. Rubenstein, W. B. (1997). *Sexual orientation and the law.* St. Paul: West.

2. *Braschi v. Stahl Associates*, 74 N.Y.2d 201; 543 N.E.2d 784; 1989 LEXIS 877 (1989).

3. Leonard, 1994. See also Rubenstein, 1997, n. 5, p. 779.

4. Rubenstein, 1997, n. 6, p. 780.

5. Rubenstein, 1997, n. 1, p.779.

6. *Levin v. Yeshiva University*, 180 Misc. 2d 829; 691 N.Y.S.2d 280; 1999 N.Y. Misc. LEXIS 205.

7. Lambda Legal Defense supported the litigation brought by the two lesbian medical students and their partners in their efforts to gain access to affordable university housing for couples. Sara Levin and Maggie Jones, both of whom were students at Yeshiva University's Albert Einstein College of Medicine in the Bronx, were denied housing for themselves and their partners solely because the two couples are not legally married. They sued Yeshiva University, alleging that the housing policy has a disparate impact on gay people, and thus violates New York City's law prohibiting sexual orientation discrimination in housing. In addition, they argued that the policy violates state and local laws prohibiting discrimination based on marital status. In an important victory in June 2001, New York's highest court reversed the trial court's order dismissing the sexual orientation claims. Dismissal of the marital status claim was, unfortunately, upheld. The case was remanded to the trial court for further proceedings. Lambda filed an *amicus* brief with the Court of Appeals arguing that New York's law against marital status discrimination prohibits this type of housing discrimination. The ACLU Lesbian and Gay Rights Project is litigating this case. Lambda's brief, written by Stephen Scarborough, was filed on behalf of Lambda, NOW Legal Defense and Education Fund, and People for the American Way Foundation. See Lambda Legal Defense and Education Fund, Update of November 13, 2001. Available at www.lambdalegal.org/cgi-bin/iowa/cases/record?record=159

8. See, for example, Aberson, C., Swan, D., & Emerson, E. (1999). Covert discrimination against gay men by U.S. college students. *The Journal of Social Psychology, 139*(3), 323–234. Lark, J. (1998). Lesbian, gay and bisexual concerns in student affairs: Themes and transitions in the development of the professional literature. *NASPA Journal, 35*, 157–168.

9. Lambda Legal Defense. (1997, October 2). Victory! Petition for US Supreme Court review denied [press release]. Available at www.lambdalegal.org/cgi-bin/pages/cases/record?record=26 SMITH v. FAIR EMPLOYMENT AND HOUSING COMMISSION, 12 Cal. 4th 1143; 913 P.2d 909; 51 Cal. Rptr. 2d 700; 1996 Cal. LEXIS 1389 (Supreme Court of California, 1996); US cert. denied 1997 US LEXIS 4211.

10. *Thomas v. Anchorage Human Rights Commission*, 165 F. 3d 692 (9th Cir. 1999).

11. *McCready v. Hoffius*, 459 Mich. 1235 (1999), 593 NW2d 545, 1999 Mich. LEXIS 694 (1999); see also Rubenstein, W. B. (1999). *Supplement of cases and materials on sexual orientation and the law*. St. Paul, MN: West, n. 9, p. 780.

12. Lerblance, P. (1994). Legal redress for disability discrimination: Bob, Carol, Ted, and Alice encounter AIDS. *Golden Gate University Law Review, 24*, 307–356.

13. The Federal Housing Amendments Act, 42 U.S.C.S. 3604 *et seq.* (2001).

14. The Americans with Disabilities Act, 42 U.S.C.S. 12102 *et seq.* (2001).

15. The Rehabilitation Act, 42 U.S.C.S. 701 *et seq.* (2001).

16. Lerblance, 1994, p. 345.

17. Aids Action Council. (1999). *Why do people with AIDS need housing?* Available at www.aids-action.org/policy/housing/body.html

18. Press release available online from Lambda Legal Defense and Education Fund at www.lambdalegal.org./cgi-bin/pages/documents/record?record=575

19. Housing Opportunities for People with AIDS, 42 U.S.C.S. 12901 *et seq.* (2001).

20. The Ryan White CARE Act, 42 U.S.C.S. 300ff *et seq.* (2001).

21. AIDS Action Council. (1999). Available at www.aidsaction.org/appropriations.

22. Van der Meide, W. (2000). *Legislating equality: A review of laws affecting gay, lesbian, bisexual and transgendered people in the United States*. Washington, DC: National Gay and Lesbian Task Force Policy Institute. See especially map and table showing details of 11 states with protections for gays in housing starting at p. 83.

23. Ibid.

24. Press release of Speaker Villaraigosa, California State Assembly, October 2, 1999, Available at www.assembly.ca.gov/defaulttext.asp

25. Van der Meide, 2000.

26. 24 C.F.R. 812.2(d)(1)(1977), as quoted in Rubenstein, 1997, n. 7, p. 780 (emphasis added) (see note 1).

27. 123 Cong. Rec. 19076 (1977). See also Rubenstein, 1997, n. 7, p. 780.

28. For a more comprehensive discussion of these cases, see Rubenstein, 1997, n. 7, p. 780.

29. See, for example, *Silver v. Starret*, 674 NYS 2nd 915 (1998); Rubenstein, 1999, n. 2, p. 762 (see note 11).

30. Excerpted with permission from Smith, C. W. (1999). The gay and lesbian couple's guide to home buying. Available at www.gfn.com.

31. See *Sexuality at mid-life and beyond*, a joint publication of SIECUS and the Kinsey Institute, Statement of Terry Kaebler, Executive Director SAGE, Indiana University Press [publication expected September 2003].

32. Johnson, S. (1998, April 16). Developers plan communities for gay, lesbian retirees. *Tacoma Morning News Tribune*.

33. Blotcher, J. (2000, March 12). For gay and lesbian elderly, a paper of their own. *The New York Times*, p. 9.

34. Cart, J. (1998, July 16). In retirement, gays and lesbians forging new communities. *The Los Angeles Times*, p. 5.

35. For more information on lesbian and gay retirement communities:
Our Town, 415–566–4100, www.ourtownvillages.com/
Metropolitan Community Homes Inc., 415–453–5653.

Gay and Lesbian Association of Retiring Persons Inc.,
310–966–1500, www.gaylesbianretiring.org/
Palms of Manasota, 941–722–5858, www.prideworks.com/palms.htm

36. As quoted in Cart, 1998, p. 5.

37. For information about the National Association of Lesbian, Gay, Bisexual, and Transgender Community Centers, see www.nalgbtcc.org See also www.gaycenter.org/natctr

38. National Gay and Lesbian Task Force. (1984). *Anti-gay/lesbian victimization.* New York: NGLTF Policy Institute. Remafedi, G. (1987). Male homosexuality: The adolescent's perspective. *Pediatrics, 79,* 326–330.

39. Ryan, C., & Futterman, D. (1998). *Lesbian and gay youth care and counseling* (pp. 24–25). New York: Columbia University Press.

40. Wolfson, J. (1998). Safety GLASS for gay students leaves most unprotected. *The Education Digest, 64*(4), 50–55.

41. Excerpted with permission from *Gay and Lesbian Seniors: Unique Challenges of Coming Out Later in Life,* by Carolyn Altman, C.S.W., Clinical Director, Senior Action in a Gay Environment (SAGE), New York, as published in *The SIECUS Report,* February 1999.

42. Ibid.

43. GLASS is headquartered at 650 N. Robertson Blvd., Ste. A, West Hollywood, CA 90069 (phone: 310–358–8727). The Green Chimney Gramercy Residence is on Manhattan's East Side, at 327 East 22nd St., New York, NY 10010 (phone: 212–677–7288). For information regarding youth issues in housing, and to locate a lesbian, gay, bisexual, and transgender youth–friendly facility near you, contact the National Youth Advocacy Coalition in Washington, D.C., at www.nyacyouth.org, or Advocates for Youth, also in the nation's capital, at www.advocatesforyouth.org

44. Walters, A. S. (1999). HIV prevention in street youth. *Journal of Adolescent Health, 25*(3), 187–198.

45. Chauncey, G. (1994). *Gay New York.* New York: Basic.

46. Moss, M. (1997). Reinventing the central city as a place to live and work. *Housing Policy Debate, 8*(2), 471–490.

47. Ibid. See also Dewitte, K. (1994, September 6). Gay presence leads revival of declining neighborhoods. *The New York Times,* p. A14. Collins, A. (1996). *Gay guide to the USA.* New York: Fodor's.

48. Bailey, R. (1999). *Gay politics, urban politics.* New York: Columbia, p. 51.

49. Moss, 1997, pp. 480–481.

50. Bailey, 1999, p. vii.

51. Posner, R. A. (1992). *Sex and reason* (p. 302). Cambridge, MA: Harvard University Press.

52. Knox, P. (1995). *Urban social geography* (p. 191). New York: Wiley.

Chapter 7

1. Hackett, T. (2000, March 2). The execution of Pvt. Barry Winchell: The real story behind the "don't ask, don't tell" murder. *Rolling Stone,* p. 80.

2. Ibid.

3. *Policy concerning homosexuality in the Armed Forces: Hearings before the Committee on the Armed Services, Senate,* 103rd Cong., 2nd Sess. 707 (1993).

4. Policy Concerning Homosexuality in the Armed Forces, 10 U.S.C.S. § 654 (LEXIS 2000).

5. Ibid.

6. DOD Enlisted Administrative Separation Directive, 1332.14 (1994). DOD Separation of Regular Commissioned Officers Directive, 1332.30 (1994).

7. "[H]omosexuals have privately served well in the past and are continuing to serve well today." *Policy concerning homosexuality in the Armed Forces: Hearings before the Committee on the Armed Services, Senate,* 103d Cong., 2d Sess. 707 (1993) (testimony of General Colin Powell).

8. Policy Concerning Homosexuality in the Armed Forces, 10 U.S.C.S. § 654 (LEXIS 2000). "Sexual orientation is considered a personal and private matter, and homosexual orientation is not a bar to continued service unless manifested by homosexual conduct." DOD Enlisted Administrative Separation Directive, 1332.14, encl. 3 H.1.a (1994); DOD Separation of Regular Commissioned Officers Directive, 1332.30, encl. 2.C (1994).

9. Homosexual conduct includes homosexual acts, statements that demonstrate propensity or intent to engage in homosexual acts, or same-sex marriage or attempted marriage. Policy concerning Homosexuality in the Armed Forces, 10 U.S.C.S. § 654 (LEXIS 2000). DOD Enlisted Administrative Separation Directive, 1332.14 (1994). DOD Separation of Regular Commissioned Officers Directive, 1332.30, (1994).

10. President Clinton pledged that the policy would provide for "a decent regard for the legitimate privacy and associational rights of all service members." Text of remarks announcing the new policy. (1993, July 20). *The Washington Post,* p. A12. Senator William Cohen stated that the "small amount of privacy under the current policy was intended to prevent the military from prying into people's private lives." *Policy concerning homosexuality in the Armed Forces: Hearings before the Committee on the Armed Services, Senate,* 103d Cong., 2d Sess. 788 (1993).

11. "We will not witch hunt. We will not chase. We will not seek to learn orientation." *Policy concerning homosexuality in the Armed Forces: Hearings before the Committee on the Armed Services, Senate,* 103d Cong., 2d Sess. 709 (1993) (testimony of General Colin Powell).

12. "[The new policy] provides that investigations into sexual misconduct will be conducted in an evenhanded manner, without regard to whether the alleged misconduct involves homosexual or heterosexual conduct." Aspen, L. (1993, December 21). *Memorandum for Secretaries of the military departments, Subject: Implementation of the DOD policy on homosexual conduct in the Armed Forces.*

13. "The Armed Forces do not tolerate harassment or violence against any service member, for any reason." Addendum to DOD Directive Qualification Standards for Enlistment, Appointment, and Induction: Applicant Briefing Item on Separation Policy, 1304.26 (1993).

14. Kozaryn, L. D., & Garamone, J. (1999, December 29). Cohen adds "don't harass" to homosexual policy, says it can work. *American Forces Press Service.*

15. The incidence of violations of the policy are based on the reports received by the Servicemembers Legal Defense Network, an independent legal aid and watchdog organization devoted to the protection of the civil rights of LGB people in the U.S. military. This chapter includes material adapted from the seven annual reports that the SLDN has published since 1995. See Osburn, C. D., & Benecke, M. M. (1995). *Conduct unbecoming continues: The first year under "Don't Ask, Don't Tell, Don't Pursue."* Washington, DC: Servicemembers Legal Defense Network. Osburn, C. D., & Benecke, M. M. (1996). *Conduct unbecoming: The second annual report on "Don't Ask, Don't Tell, Don't Pursue" violations.* Washington, DC: Servicemembers Legal Defense Network. Also see the third annual report (1997), the fourth annual report (1998), the fifth annual report (1999), the sixth annual report (2000), and the seventh annual report (2001), all Washington, DC: Servicemembers Legal Defense Network.

16. Burns, R. (2000, February 2). Military sets new rules on antigay threat. *The Boston Globe,* p. A4.

17. U.S. DOD Office of the Inspector General—Audit. (2000, March 16). *Report on the military environment with respect to the homosexual conduct policy* (Audit and Evaluation Report No. D-2000–101). Arlington, VA: Author.

18. U.S. DOD Working Group. (2000, July 21). *Anti-harassment action plan.*

19. The military is finally facing the flaws in the policy on homosexuals. (2000, February 7). *Albany Times Union,* p. A6. "Don't ask, don't tell" policy doesn't work. (1999, December 15). The

Arizona Republic, p. B8. Enforcing "Don't Harass." (2000, February 7). *The Boston Globe*, p. A14. Reviving "Don't Ask, Don't Tell." (2000, February 4). *Chicago Tribune*, p. 20. Don't lie: Clinton admits "don't ask don't tell" is a policy failure; the answer is to lift the ban on homosexuals in the military. (1999, December 21). *Cleveland Plain Dealer*, p. B8. Military's gay policy: Time to get real. (1999, December 15). *Dayton Daily News*, p. A14. Gays in military: Clinton admits "don't ask, don't tell" is a failure. (1999, December 20). *Houston Chronicle*, p. 34. Other similar articles were published in news sources around the country at that time.

20. For further discussion of these issues, see chapter 3.

21. Bérubé, A. (1990). *Coming out under fire: The history of gay men and women in World War II*. New York: Free Press.

22. DOD Directive 1332.14(H)(1)(a), 32 C.F.R. part 41, App. A.

23. Crittenden, S. H., Captain. (1957). *Report of the board appointed to prepare and submit recommendations to the Secretary of the Navy for the revision of policies, procedures, and directives dealing with homosexuals: 21 December 1956–15 March 1957*. Washington, DC: U.S. Navy. McDaniel, M. A. (1989). *Preservice adjustment of homosexual and heterosexual military accessions: Implications for security clearance suitability*. Monterey, CA: Defense Personnel Security Research and Education Center. Sarbin, T. R. (1991). *Homosexuality and personnel security*. Montery, CA: Defense Personnel Security Research and Education Center.

24. Executive Order No. 12968 3.1(c), (d), 60 Fed. Reg. 40245 (1995).

25. The new regulations stated, in part, that the mere presence of LGB service members adversely affected the ability of the military to achieve the following objectives: foster mutual trust and confidence among service members; ensure the system of rank and command; facilitate assignment and worldwide deployment of service members who frequently must live and work under close conditions affording minimal privacy; recruit and retain members of the military services; and maintain public acceptability of military service.

26. Department of Defense Directives 1332.14 and 1332.30, 32 C.F.R. part 41, App. A, adopted on January 29, 1991.

27. U.S. General Accounting Office. (1992a). *Defense force management: DOD's policy on homosexuality* (Document GAO/NSIAD-92–98). Washington, DC: Author.

28. Office of the Under Secretary of Defense (Personnel and Readiness) (1998, April). *Report to the Secretary of Defense: Review of the effectiveness of the application and enforcement of the Department's policy on homosexual conduct in the military*.

29. Office of Assistant Secretary of Defense (Public Affairs). (1999, December 13). *Secretary of Defense directs assessment of extent of harassment*.

30. U.S. DOD Office of the Inspector General—Audit, 2000 (see note 17).

31. McVeigh v. Cohen, 983 F. Supp. 215 (D.D.C. January 26, 1998).

32. Two years after the witch hunt, a Pentagon review weighed in against the use of pretrial agreements to obtain information about consensual sexual conduct. U.S. DOD Office of Under Secretary of Defense (Personnel and Readiness). (1998, April). *Report to the Secretary of Defense: Review of the effectiveness of the application and enforcement of the department's policy on homosexual conduct in the military*. No action has been taken to make amends to the former service members who were targeted in this witch hunt or to discipline the errant prosecutors.

33. Jury acquits Air Force Major accused of lesbian affair. (1996, August 17). *The New York Times*, p. L7.

34. Caplan, L. (1994, June 13). "Don't Ask, Don't Tell"—Marine style. *Newsweek*, p. 5.

35. Hugick, L. (1992, June). Public opinion divided on gay rights. *Gallup Poll Monthly*, pp. 2–6. Yang, A. S. (1997). The polls: Trends: Attitudes toward homosexuality. *Public Opinion Quarterly, 61*, 477–507.

36. Yang, 1997. See also www.gallup.com/poll/release/PR010604.asp

37. The military is finally facing the flaws in the policy on homosexuals, 2000; "Don't ask, don't tell" policy doesn't work, 1999; Enforcing "Don't Harass," 2000; Reviving "Don't Ask, Don't Tell," 2000; Don't lie: Clinton admits "don't ask don't tell" is a policy failure, 1999; Military's gay policy: Time to get real, 1999; Gays in military: Clinton admits "don't ask, don't tell" is a failure, 1999 (see note 19). Verdict is in for "Don't Ask." (2000, February 4). *Los Angeles Times*, p. B10; Sheldon, D. P. (1999, December 16). Don't expect a change in "Don't Ask . . ." *Newsday*, p. A65; Bigotry in the military. (1999, August 30). New York Times, p. A22.

38. Moskos, C. (1998). *Miller/Moskos nonrandom surveys of Army personnel*. Evanston, IL: Northwestern University. Survey responses based on the question, "How do you feel about the proposal that gays and lesbians should be allowed to enter and remain in the military?"

39. See statements by Gen. Barry Goldwater, USAF (Ret.) (*Washington Post*, June 10, 1993); Gen. Benjamin O. Davis, USAF (Ret.) (*Buffalo News*, December 2, 1993); Maj. Gen. Vance Coleman, U.S. Army (Ret.) (*MacNeil/Lehrer Newshour*, March 29, 1993); Brig. Gen. Evelyn P. Foote, U.S. Army (*San Francisco Chronicle*, April 6, 1993); Capt. Lawrence Korb, USN (Ret.) (Assistant Secretary of Defense for Readiness and Manpower under President Reagan); (*Atlanta Journal and Constitution*, November 22, 1992); Capt. William K. Yates, USN (Ret.) (*New London Day*, June 2, 1993); Col. Ronald C. Anderson, U.S. Army (Ret.) (May 13, 1993, letter to Senate Armed Services Committee); Col. Karl Kropsey, U.S. Army (Ret.) (*Kansas City Star*, May 30, 1993); Col. Lucian Truscott III, U.S. Army (Ret.) (*Los Angeles Times*, April 30, 1993); Col. Sam J. Turnbull, U.S. Army (Ret.) (June 10, 1993, letter to members of Congress); Col. Joseph B. Holt, USAF (Ret.) (*Chicago Tribune*, May 11, 1993) ; Commr. William R. Bryant, USN (Ret.) (May 16, 1993, letter to Senate Armed Services Committee); Lt. Col. Charles H. Mixon, USAF (Ret.) (*International Herald Tribune*, June 25, 1993); Capt. Thomas W. Ratliff, USAF (May 14, 1993, letter to Sen. Sam Nunn); Lt. David Zeni, USN (Ret.) (May 19, 1993, letter to Sen. Joseph Lieberman); Lt. George Cooper, USN (Ret.) (National Public Radio, February 24, 1993).

40. U.S. General Accounting Office. (1992b). *Defense force management: Statistics related to DOD's policy on homosexuality* (Document GAO/NSIAD-92-98S). Washington, DC: Author.

41. Suro, R. (2000, September 21). Army ads open new campaign: Finish education. *The Washington Post*, p. A3.

42. Binkin, M., Eitelberg, M., Schexnider, A. J., & Smith, M. M. (1982). *Blacks and the military*. Washington, DC: Brookings Institution. Kauth, M. R., & Landis, D. (1996). Applying lessons learned from minority integration in the military. In G. M. Herek, J. B. Jobe, & R. M. Carney, (Eds.), *Out in force: Sexual orientation and the military* (pp. 86–105). Chicago: University of Chicago Press. MacGregor, M. J. (1981). *Integration of the armed forces, 1940–1965*. Washington, DC: U.S. Army Center of Military History.

43. Binkin, M., & Bach, S. J. (1977). *Women and the military*. Washington, DC: Brookings Institution. Stiehm, J. H. (1989). *Arms and the enlisted woman*. Philadelphia: Temple University Press. Thomas, P. T., & Thomas, M. D. (1996). Integration of women in the military: Parallels to the progress of homosexuals? In G. M. Herek, J. B. Jobe, & R. M. Carney, (Eds.), *Out in force: Sexual orientation and the military* (pp. 65–85). Chicago: University of Chicago Press.

44. U.S. Air Force Academy. (1984). The military family. In *Proceedings of the ninth biennial psychology in the Department of Defense symposium*. Colorado Springs, CO: Author.

45. Goffman, E. (1963a). *Behavior in public places: Notes on the social organization of gatherings*. New York: Free Press.

46. Janowitz, M. F., & Little, R. D. (1965). *Sociology and the military establishment*. New York: Russell Sage Foundation.

47. Bérubé, 1990 (see note 21).

48. Examples include Petty Officer Keith Meinhold, Sergeant Justin Elzie, and Colonel Margarethe Cammermeyer. See Anderson, C. A., & Smith, R. S. (1993). Stigma and honor: Gay, lesbian, and bisexual people in the U.S. military. In L. Diamant (Ed.), *Homosexual issues in the*

workplace (pp. 65–89). Washington, DC: Taylor & Francis. Bérubé, 1990. Gibson, E. L. (1978). *Get off my ship: Ensign Berg vs. the U.S. Navy.* New York: Avon. Harry, J. (1984). Homosexual men and women who served their country. *Journal of Homosexuality, 10*(1–2), 117–125. Hippler, M. (1989). *Matlovich: The good soldier.* Boston: Alyson. Humphrey, M. (1990). *My country, my right to serve: Experiences of gay men and women in the military, World War II to the present.* New York: Harper Collins. Murphy, L. R. (1988). *Perverts by official order: The campaign against homosexuals by the United States Navy.* New York: Haworth. Williams, C. J., & Weinberg, M. S. (1971). *Homosexuals and the military: A study of less than honorable discharge.* New York: Harper & Row.

49. Gade, P. A., Segal, D. R., & Johnson, E. M. (1996). The experience of foreign militaries. In G. M. Herek, J. B. Jobe, & R. M. Carney, (Eds.), *Out in force: Sexual orientation and the military* (pp. 106–130). Chicago: University of Chicago Press. Koegel, P. (1996). Lessons learned from the experience of domestic police and fire departments. In G. M. Herek, J. B. Jobe, & R. M. Carney, (Eds.), *Out in force: Sexual orientation and the military* (pp. 131–153). Chicago: University of Chicago Press.

50. Lyall, S. (2001, February 10). Gays in the British military: Ask, tell, and then move on. *The New York Times*, p. A1.

51. U.S. General Accounting Office, 1992a (see note 27). Gordon, R. (1993, January 30). S.F. top cop praises gays to Colin Powell. *San Francisco Examiner*, p. A13. Sarbin, T. R., & Karols, K. E. (1988). *Nonconforming sexual orientations and military suitability.* Monterey, CA: Defense Personnel Security Research and Education Center.

52. Henderson, W. D. (1985). *Cohesion: The human element.* Washington, DC: National Defense University Press. MacCoun, R. J. (1993). What is known about unit cohesion and performance. In National Defense Research Institute, *Sexual orientation and U.S. military personnel policy: Options and assessment* (pp. 283–321). Santa Monica, CA: Rand. MacCoun, R. J. (1996). Sexual orientation and military cohesion. In G. M. Herek, J. B. Jobe, & R. M. Carney (Eds.), *Out in force: Sexual orientation and the military* (pp. 157–176). Chicago: University of Chicago Press.

53. Festinger, L. (1950). Informal social communication. *Psychological Review, 57*, 271–282. Festinger, L., Schachter, S., & Back, K. (1950). *Social pressures in informal groups: A study of human factors in housing.* Stanford, CA: Stanford University Press.

54. Policy Concerning Homosexuality in the Armed Forces, S. Rep. No. 112, 103d Cong., 1st Sess 307 (1993) (testimony of Col. William Darryl Henderson, retired research fellow at the National War College).

55. Id. at 308. Testimony of Dr. David H. Marlowe of the Walter Reed Army Institute of Research.

56. Moskos, C. (1992, March 30). Why banning homosexuals still makes sense. *Navy Times*, p. 27.

57. Goffman, E. (1963b). *Stigma: Notes on the management of spoiled identity.* Englewood Cliffs, NJ: Prentice-Hall.

58. Herek, G. M. (2000). The psychology of sexual prejudice. *Current Directions in Psychological Science, 9*(1), 19–22.

59. Herek, G. M. (1996a). Social science, sexual orientation, and military personnel policy. In G. M. Herek, J. B. Jobe, & R. M. Carney (Eds.), *Out in force: Sexual orientation and the military* (pp. 3–14). Chicago: University of Chicago Press. Herek, G. M. (1996b). Why tell if you're not asked? In G. M. Herek, J. B. Jobe, & R. M. Carney, (Eds.), *Out in force: Sexual orientation and the military* (pp. 197–225). Chicago: University of Chicago Press.

60. Herek, 2000.

61. Herek, 1996a, 1996b.

62. Eagly, A., & Chaiken, S. (1993). *The psychology of attitudes.* Fort Worth, TX: Harcourt Brace Jovanovich.

63. Bandura, A. (1997). *Self-efficacy: The exercise of control.* New York: Freeman.

64. Benistant, S. J. H., & Thuijsman, C. J. (1990). *Policy plan on homosexuality in the Royal Netherlands Navy* (Document SWO-1990–5). The Hague, The Netherlands: Directorate of Personnel, Royal Netherlands Navy, Social Science Research Department.

65. U.S. General Accounting Office, 1992a (see note 27).

66. Benistant & Thuijsman, 1990. U.S. General Accounting Office, 1992a. Gade, Segal, & Johnson, 1996 (see note 45). Koegel, 1996 (see note 49).

67. See note 9.

68. See notes 10–13.

69. Kozaryn & Garamone, 1999 (see note 14).

70. U.S. DOD Under Secretary of Defense Rudy de Leon. (1999, August 12). *Memorandum to Secretaries of the military, Subject: Guidelines for investigating threats against or harassment of service members based on alleged homosexuality.* August U. S. DOD Office of Assistant Secretary of Defense (Public Affairs), U.S. DOD Office of Assistant Secretary of Defense (Public Affairs). (1999, December 13). Secretary of Defense directs assessment of extent of harassment.

71. Policy Concerning Homosexuality in the Armed Forces, 10 U.S.C. § 654.

Chapter 8

1. American Psychological Association. (1996). *The American Psychological Association answers to frequently asked questions regarding the Defense of Marriage Act (DOMA) H.R. 3396, S. 1740.* Washington, DC: Author.

2. Smith, D. M., & Gates, G. J. (2001). *Gay and lesbian families in the United States: Same-sex unmarried partner households.* Washington, DC: Human Rights Campaign.

3. American Psychological Association, 1996.

4. Peplau. A. L. (1991). Lesbian and gay relationships. In J. C. Gonsiorek & J. D. Weinrich (Eds.), *Homosexuality: Research implications for public policy* (pp. 177–196). Newbury Park, CA: Sage. p. 195.

5. Freiberg, P. (2001, March 16). Couples study shows strengths: Heterosexual pairs "may have a lot to learn from Gays." *The Washington Blade*, pp. 1, 19.

6. American Psychological Association, 1996. It is also important to note that 6 to 14 million children are being raised in gay- or lesbian-headed households. (See Kendell, K. (1998). Lesbian couples creating families. In R. P. Cabaj & D. W. Purcell (Eds.), *On the road to same-sex marriage: A supportive guide to psychological, political, and legal issues* (pp 41–57). San Francisco: Jossey-Bass.) As a result, unless eligible for second-parent adoptions or domestic partner benefits, nonbiological parents are unable to provide health insurance for their children, may be unable to visit their children in the hospital, and may have no right to visitation should the parental relationships dissolve. Further, these children are ineligible for child support by the nonbiological parent. For further discussion of these issues, see chapter 9.

7. O'Bryan, W. (2001, April 6). Not just lip service: Dutch couples join in wedlock. Washington Blade, pp. 1, 12.

8. Belgium takes step toward equal marriage. (2001, July 13). *The Washington Blade*, p. 10. DiversityInc.com. (2003, February 6). *Diversity factoid: Gay marriages.* Retrieved from www.diversityinc.com/public/4417.cfm

9. See chapters 5 and 6.

10. For a review of the history of antimiscegenation laws in the United States, see Tong, L. (1998). Comparing mixed-race and same-sex marriage. In R. P. Cabaj & D. W. Purcell (Eds.), *On the road to same-sex marriage: A supportive guide to psychological, political, and legal issues* (pp 109–127). San Francisco: Jossey-Bass. Washington, J. R. (1970). *Marriage in black and white.* New York: University Press of America.

11. *Loving v. Virginia*, 388 U.S. 1 (1967).

12. *Baker v. Nelson*, 191 N.W.2nd 185 (Minn. 1971), *appeal dismissed*, 409 U.S. 810 (1972).

13. *Jones v. Hallahan*, 501 S.W.2s 588 (Ky. 1973).

14. *Singer v. Hara*, 11 Wn. App. 247, 522 P.2d 1187, *review denied*, 84 Wn.2d 1008 (1974).

15. *Thorton v. Timmers.* (Ohio, 1974)

16. *Adams v. Howerton.* 1486 F.2d 1036, 9th Circuit, 1982.

17. *Baehr v. Lewin*, 852 P.2d 44 (Hawaii 1993).

18. *Baker v. State of Vermont*, No. 1009–97CnC.

19. O'Bryan, 2001, (see note 7).

20. Sorransson, L. (1998). International trends in same-sex marriage. In R. P. Cabaj & D. W. Purcell (Eds.), *On the road to same-sex marriage: A supportive guide to psychological, political, and legal issues* (pp. 165–189). San Francisco: Jossey-Bass.

21. *M. v. H. & Ontario.* 2 S. C. R. 3, 1999.

22. *Loving v. Virginia*, 388 U.S. 1, 1967.

23. American Psychological Association. (1998). *Answers to your questions about sexual orientation and homosexuality.* Washington, DC: Author. Available at www.apa.org/pubinfo/answers.html

24. Kohn, S. (1999). *The domestic partnership organizing manual for employee benefits.* Washington, DC: National Gay and Lesbian Task Force.

25. Herrschaft, D., & Mills, K. I. (2000). *The state of the workplace for lesbian, gay, bisexual, and transgendered Americans 2000.* Washington, DC: Human Rights Campaign Foundation.

26. See www.hrc.org/worknet/cei/index.asp for details.

27. Winfeld, L., & Spielman, S. (1995). *Straight talk about gays in the workplace: Creating an inclusive, productive environment for everyone in your organization.* New York: American Management Association.

28. See www.hrc.org/worknet/cei/index.asp for details.

29. See www.allianceformarriage.org for details.

30. International Society of Certified Employee Benefit Specialists. (1995, May). *Domestic partner benefits.* Brookfield, WI: Author. The Segal Company. (1993). *Executive letter, 17*(1 & 2). Towers Perrin. (1996, November 20). *Interest in domestic partner benefits growing.* New York: Author. Winfeld & Spielman, 1995.

31. National Lesbian and Gay Journalists Association. (1997). *Domestic partner benefits: A trend toward fairness.* Washington, DC. Winfeld & Spielman, 1995.

32. Hewitt Associates. (1997, January). *Update to 1994 study of domestic partner benefits.* Lincolnshire, IL.

33. As cited in Winfeld & Spielman, 1995, p. 101.

34. Kohn, 1999 (see note 22).

35. Coles, M. A. (1996). *Try this at home: A do-it-yourself guide to winning lesbian and gay civil rights policy.* New York: New Press.

36. Ibid.

Chapter 9

1. U.S. Census Bureau, 2002. www.census.gov/Press-Release/www/2002/cb02–19.html

2. Simmons, T., & O'Neill, G. (2001). *Households and families 2000: Census 2000 brief.* Retrieved February 10, 2002 from the U.S. Census Bureau at www.census.gov/prod/2001pubs/c2kbr01–8.pdf

3. National Center for Health Statistics, 2000. www.cdc.gov/nchs/releases/00facts/nonmarit.htm

4. Simmons & O'Neill, 2001.

5. Ibid.

6. Human Rights Campaign. (2001). *Census figures show lesbian and gay families are integral part of American society.* Retrieved February 11, 2002, from www.hrc.org/familynet/chapter.asp? article=340

7. Ibid.

8. Herman, D., cited in Millbank, J. (1996). "Which, then, would be the 'husband' and which the 'wife'?": Some introductory thoughts on contesting "the family" in court. *Murdoch University Electronic Journal of Law, 3.* Retrieved October 31, 1999, from www..murdoch.edu.au/elaw/ issues/v3n3/millbank.html

9. For example, see various articles and speeches written by Robert H. Knight, director of cultural studies for the Family Research Council (a conservative think tank) that can be accessed at www.frc.org

10. Millbank, 1996.

11. Eshleman, R. E., Jr. (1999, February 16). Adoption court to rule on same-sex parents. *Philadelphia Inquirer.* Retrieved October 31, 1999, from www.gaylawnet/ne_child.html

12. Family Research Council. www.frc.org/insight/is94e3hs.html.

13. Family Research Institute. (1999). *Family Research Institute education pamphlets.* Retrieved February 11, 2002, www.familyresearchinst.org/FRI_Educational_Pamphlets.html

14. See, for example, Herek, G. M. (2002a). *The Cameron group's survey studies: A methodological critique.* Retrieved February 11, 2002 from psychology.ucdavis.edu/rainbow/html/facts_ cameron_survey.html. Herek, G. M. (2002b). *Paul Cameron bio and fact sheet.* Retrieved February 11, 2002, from psychology.ucdavis.edu/rainbow/html/facts_cameron_sheet.html See also chapter 2 in this book.

15. For example, A. Nicholas Groth, director of the Sex Offender Program at Connecticut's Department of Correction, accused Cameron of misrepresenting Groth's research to advance his own homophobic views. See Mark Pietrzyk's exposé "Paul Cameron, Professional Sham: Queer Science" in the October, 3, 1994, *New Republic.* Available at www.familyresearchinst.org/ NewRepublic100394_pietrzyk.html

16. Colker, D. (1993, February 22). Statistics in "gay agenda" questioned videotape: Critics say figures on sex practices cited by doctor are not reliable. *Los Angeles Times,* p. 16.

17. American Sociological Association, 1987, p. 14.

18. See Mark Pietrzyk's exposé in the October 3, 1994, *New Republic.* Paul Cameron, professional Sham: Queer Science. Available at www.familyresearchinst.org/NewRepublic100394_ pietrzyk.html

19. *Baker v. Wade,* 106 Federal Rules Decisions 526, N.D. Texas, 1985.

20. Kantrowitz, B. (1996, November 4). Gay families come out. *Newsweek,* pp. 50–56. Note: Over 99 percent of child sexual abuse in foster/adoptive care is committed by heterosexual parents—see Tafel, R. (1999). Adoption, foster card [*sic*], and gay parents. Retrieved October 3, 1999, from Georgia Log Cabin Republicans at www.lcrga.com/archive/199907281648.shtml

21. Paul Cameron's Family Research Institute argued for the father by submitting an *amicus* brief in this case stating that although the father had significant flaws, the child was endangered by spending time with her lesbian mother. Scheer, R. (1996, December 10). A Warped view of what's fit as family life. *Los Angeles Times.* Available at http://www.robertscheer.com/1_ natcolumn/96_columns/121096.htm

22. Branson, R. (1999, February 9). High court: Home with abuse better than gay father's. *Commercial Appeal.* Retrieved October 31, 1999, from www.gaylawnet/ne_child.html

23. *Chicago Tribune.* (1999, June 2). Panel rebukes adoption judge. Retrieved October 31, 1999 from *GayLawNews,* on-lone news digest, on the World Wide Web: http://www.gaylawnet/ne_ child.html

24. Indiana legislation won't be dropped. (2000, March/April). *Alternative Family Magazine, 3,* 8.

25. This research has been conducted mostly with children of lesbian mothers; information concerning children of gay fathers is included where available. For more detailed reviews, see Barret, R. L., & Robinson, B. E. (1994). Gay dads. In A. E. Gottfried & A. W. Gottfried (Eds.), *Redefining families: Implications for children's development* (pp. 157–170). New York: Plenum Press. Falk, P. J. (1994). The gap between psychosocial assumptions and empirical research in lesbian-mother child custody cases. In A. E. Gottfried & A. W. Gottfried (Eds.), *Redefining families: Implications for children's development* (pp. 131–156). New York: Plenum Press. Patterson, C. J. (1995). Lesbian and gay parenthood. In M. H. Bornstein (Ed.), *Handbook of parenting: Vol. 3. Status and social conditions of parenting* (pp. 255–274). Mahwah, NJ: Lawrence Erlbaum. Patterson, C. J., & Chan, R. W. (1997). Gay fathers. In M. E. Lamb (Ed.), *The role of the father in child development* (3rd ed.) (pp. 245–260). New York: John Wiley & Sons.

26. However, see Stacey, J., & Biblarz, T. J. (2001). (How) does the sexual orientation of parents matter? *American Sociological Review, 66*, 159–183, for a critique of this "no difference" interpretation and a discussion of the ways in which heterosexism hampers research and analysis. Available at www.asanet.org/pubs/stacey.pdf

27. Intelligence: Flaks, D. K., Ficher, I., Masterpasqua, F., & Joseph, G. (1995). Lesbians choosing motherhood: A comparative study of lesbian and heterosexual parents and their children. *Developmental Psychology, 31*, 105–114. Green, R., Mandel, J. B., Hotvedt, M. E., Gray, J., & Smith, L. (1986). Lesbian mothers and their children: A comparison with solo parent heterosexual mothers and their children. *Archives of Sexual Behavior, 15*, 167–184. Kirkpatrick, M., Smith, C., & Roy, R. (1981). Lesbian mothers and their children: A comparative survey. *American Journal of Orthopsychiatry, 51*, 545–551. Emotional problems: Flaks, Ficher, Masterpasqua, & Joseph, 1995. Gottman, J. S. (1990). Children of gay and lesbian parents. *Marriage and Family Review, 14*, 177–196. Green, Mandel, Hotvedt, Gray, & Smith, 1986. Kirkpatrick, Smith, & Roy, 1981. Patterson, C. J. (1994). Lesbian and gay couples considering parenthood: An agenda for research, service, and advocacy. *Journal of Lesbian and Gay Social Services, 1*, 33–55. Self-esteem: Huggins, S. L. (1989). A comparative study of self-esteem of adolescent children of divorced lesbian mothers and divorced heterosexual mothers. In F. W. Bozett (Ed.), *Homosexuality and the family* (pp. 123–135). New York: Harrington Park Press. Self-concept: Patterson, 1994. Peer relationships: Golombok, S., Spencer, A., & Rutter, M. (1983). Children in lesbian and single-parent households: Psychosexual and psychiatric appraisal. *Journal of Child Psychology and Psychiatry, 24*, 551–572. Green, Mandel, Horvedt, Gray, & Smith, 1986. Hotvedt, M., & Mandel, G. (1982). Children of lesbian mothers. In W. Paul, J. Weinrich, J. Gonsiorek, & M. Hotvedt (Eds.), *Homosexuality: Social, psychological, and biological issues* (pp. 275–285). Beverly Hills: Sage. Social acceptance: Green, Mandel, Hotvedt, Gray, & Smith, 1986.

28. Tasker, F. L., & Golombok, S. (1997). *Growing up in a lesbian family: Effects on child devlopment.* New York: Guilford.

29. Hotvedt & Mandel, 1982.

30. See, for example, Green, R. (1982). The best interests of the child with a lesbian mother. *Bulletin of the AAPL, 10*, 7–15. Riddle, D., & Arguelles, M. (1981). Children of gay parents: Homophobia's victims. In I. Stuart & L. Abt (Eds.), *Children of separation and divorce: Management and treatment* (pp. 174–197). New York: Van Nostrand Reinhold. Sears, J. T. (1993/1994). Challenges for educators: Lesbian, gay, and bisexual families. *The High School Journal, 77*, 138–156. Susoeff, S. (1985). Assessing children's best interests when a parent is gay or lesbian: Toward a rational custody standard. *UCLA Law Review, 32*, 852–903.

31. Tasker, F., & Golombok, S. (1995). Adults raised as children in lesbian families. *American Journal of Orthopsychiatry, 65*, 203–215.

32. According to Green, 1982, gender identity is the psychological awareness of self as male or female; gender roles consist of the behaviors deemed appropriate for males and females in our cul-

ture; and sexual orientation is one's emotional and sexual attraction to members of the same or other gender.

33. Patterson, C. J. (1992). Children of lesbian and gay parents. *Child Development, 63,* 1025–1042.

34. Tasker & Golombok, 1995, p. 204.

35. For example, Gottman, 1990 (see note 27).

36. Bozett, F. W. (1980). Gay fathers: How and why they disclose their homosexuality to their children. *Family Relations, 29,* 173–179. Bozett, F. W. (1982). Heterogeneous couples in heterosexual marriages: Gay men and straight women. *Journal of Marital and Family Therapy, 8,* 81–89. Bozett, F. W. (1987). Children of gay fathers. In F. W. Bozett (Ed.), *Gay and lesbian parents* (pp. 39–57). New York: Praeger. Bozett, F. W. (Ed.). (1989). *Homosexuality and the family.* New York: Harrington Park Press. Golombok, S., & Tasker, F. (1996). Do parents influence the sexual orientation of their children? Findings from a longitudinal study of lesbian families. *Developmental Psychology, 32,* 3–11. Gottman, 1990; Huggins, 1989 (see note 27). Miller, B. (1979). Gay fathers and their children. *Family Coordinator, 28,* 544–552.

37. Bailey, J. M., Bobrow, D., Wolfe, M., & Mikach, S. (1995). Sexual orientation of adult sons of gay fathers. *Developmental Psychology, 31*(1), 124–129.

38. Patterson L. J., & Freil L. V., cited in Stacey & Biblarz, 2001 (see note 26).

39. Green, G. D., & Bozett, F. W. (1991). Lesbian mothers and gay fathers. In J. C. Gonsiorek & J. D. Weinrich (Eds.), *Homosexuality: Research implications for public policy* (pp. 197–214). Newbury Park, CA: Sage.

40. As described in Patterson, C. J. (1997a). Children of lesbian and gay parents. In T. H. Ollendick & R. J. Prinz (Eds.), *Advances in Clinical Child Psychology, 19,* 235–282.

41. Ibid.

42. Ibid.

43. Gideonse, T. (1999, June 22). Baby by proxy. *The Advocate,* p. 83.

44. Sultan, S. L. (1995). The right of homosexuals to adopt: Changing legal interpretations of "parent" and "family." *Journal of the Suffolk Academy of Law, 10.* Retrieved October 31, 1999, from www.tourolaw.edu/publications/Suffolk/vol10/part3_txt.htm

45. Kantrowitz, B. (1996, November 4). Gay families come out. *Newsweek,* pp. 50–56.

46. Bohan, J. (1996). *Psychology and sexual orientation: Coming to terms.* New York: Routledge. Green, & Bozett, 1991 (see note 39).

47. Price, J. R. (Summer, 1999). A search for justice: Homosexuality in custody cases. *Alternative Family Magazine,* pp. 20–25.

48. Ibid.

49. Duran-Aydintug, C., & Causey, K. A. (1996). Child custody determination: Implications for lesbian mothers. *Journal of Divorce and Remarriage, 25,* 55–74. Rivera, R. R. (1987). Legal issues in gay and lesbian parenting. In F. W. Bozett (Ed.), *Gay and lesbian parents* (pp. 199–227). New York: Praeger. Sears, 1993/1994 (see note 30).

50. See later in this chapter or Patterson, C. J. (1996). Lesbian and gay parents and their children. In R. C. Savin-Williams & K. M. Cohen (Eds.), *The lives of lesbians, gays, and bisexuals: Children to adults* (pp. 274–304). Fort Worth, TX: Harcourt Brace, for review.

51. Duran-Aydintug & Causey, 1996.

52. These restrictions are made despite the findings that children in two-parent homes, regardless of the gender of the parents, have better emotional health than those raised by single parents (e.g., Mandel, J. B., & Hotvedt, M. E. (1980). Lesbians as parents. *Huisarts and Praktyk, 4,* 31–34), and that one of the best predictors of parent and child happiness in gay-headed stepparent families is the full inclusion and integration of the parent's partner into the family. Crosbie-Burnett, M. and Helmbrecht, L. A. (1993). Descriptive empirical study of gay male stepfamilies. *Family Relations, 42,* 256–262.

53. Reported in Gover, T. (1996, November 26). Fighting for our children. *The Advocate*, pp. 22–30.

54. Keen, L. (1999, July 2). Massachusetts co-parent's rights acknowledged: State's high court says nonbiological lesbian mom is part of "child's nontraditional family." *The Washington Blade*, p. 25.

55. Lowe, P. (1999, October 26). Lesbian couple ruled parents: Judge's decision allows both women's names on birth certificate. *Denver Post*, p. B-01.

56. Goode, E. (2002, February 4). Group backs gays who seek to adopt a partner's child [Electronic version]. *The New York Times*.

57. Douglas-Brown, L. (2002, February 22). Gay is 'inherent evil': Homosexuality makes gays unfit to have children, Ala. Chief justice rules. *The Washington Blade*, 1, 20. quotation pg 1.

58. However, in an important recent case, the Tennessee Supreme Court overturned an appeals court decision that barred a woman from having her female partner in their home during overnight visits with the woman's daughter. The Tennessee Supreme Court reaffirmed the principle that there must be evidence of harm to the child before a parent's visitation can be restricted. (See www.nclrights.org/cases.html.) Richard E. LADD v. Julia Edith ELDRIDGE. Supreme Court of Tennessee Eastern Section at Knoxville. No. E-1999-02583-SC-R11-CV.

59. Sultan, 1995 (see note 44).

60. Ibid.

61. Patterson, C. J. (1995). Adoption of minor children by lesbian and gay adults: A social science perspective. Originally printed 1995, *Duke Journal of Gender Law and Policy*, 191–205.

62. Gay Adoption Poll. Retrieved November 30, 2002 from uspolitics.about.com/library/blgayadoptpoll.htm?terms=gay

63. Utah-state brief defends ban on adoption by unmarried couples. (2000, March/April). *Alternative Family Magazine, 3*, 6.

64. Human Rights Campaign. (2002). *Adoption laws in your state*. Retrieved February 11, 2002, from Human Rights Campaign FamilyNet at www.hrc.org/familynet/adoption_laws.asp

65. *The Advocate*. (1999, July 31–August 2). House rejects anti-gay adoption motion. Retrieved October 31, 1999, from www.gaylawnet/ne_child.html

66. Lowy, J. (1999, February 24). Child adoptions by homosexuals ignite legislative fights. *Scripps Howard News Service*. Retrieved October 31, 1999, from http://www.gaylawnet/ne_child.html

67. Datalounge. (2002). *Adoption*. Retrieved February 11, 2002, www.datalounge.com/datalounge/issues/index.html?storyline=217

68. Ibid.

69. Gideonse, 1999 (see note 43).

70. Branson, 1999 (see note 22).

71. Crary, D. (1999, October 17). Lesbian moms left in legal limbo. Retrieved October 27, 1999 from Yahoo! NewTop Stories Headlines: www.dailynews.yahoo.com/h/ap/19991917/us/when_lesbinas_divorce_1.html

72. The term *psychological parent* refers to a person not necessarily related to a child by genetics or adoption but with whom the child has an important bond. (Lowry, 1999). It is a vague legal concept and has not been frequently used in legal arenas, although its use may be increasing. In April 2000 the Supreme Court of New Jersey also ruled that a lesbian mother was a "psychological parent" and entitled to visitation with twins she helped raise with her ex-partner (*V.C. v. M.J.B.*, A-111, A-126 September Term 1998, SUPREME COURT OF NEW JERSEY, 163 N. J. 200; 748 A.2d 539; 2000 N. J. LEXIS 359, October 25, 1999, Argued, April 6, 2000, Decided, Certiorari Denied October 10, 2000, Reported at: 2000 U.S. LEXIS 6634). Goldstein, J., Freud, A., & Solnit, A. J. (1979). *Beyond the best interests of the child*. New York: Free Press.

73. McCullen, K. (1999, October 28). Boulder judge grants legal rights to lesbians. *Rocky Mountain News*. Retrieved October 31, 1999, from www.gaylawnet/ne_child.html

74. Yahoo! News: Colorado Headlines (1999, October 26). Gay activists celebrate ruling. Retrieved October 27, 1999 from: www.dailynews.yahoo.com/headlines/loc...ory.html?s=v/rs/19991026/co/index_2.html

75. Cited in Pagliocca, Melton, Weisz, & Lyons, 1995.

76. Ibid.

77. Rubenstein, W. B. (Ed.). (1993). *Lesbians, gay men, and the law.* New York: New Press.

78. iVillage.com: The Women's Network. (2002). *Legal info: Surrogacy FAQs.* Retrieved February 11, 2002 from pages.ivillage.com/cl-ags2b/SurroFAQS/id8.html

79. Gideonse, 1999 (see note 43).

80. Vorzimer, A. W., & Meyers, L. S. (1999, July 5). Pre-birth legal judgments and the recognition of same-sex parental rights. *Gay Parent Magazine.* Retrieved October 31, 1999, from GayLawNews, online news digest, at www.gaylawnet/ne_child.html

81. Rivera, R. R. (1991). Sexual orientation and the law. In J. C. Gonsiorek & J. D. Weinrich (Eds.), *Homosexuality: Research implications for public policy* (pp. 81–100). Beverly Hills, CA: Sage.

82. Gottman, 1990 (see note 27).

83. Bigner, J., & Bozett, F. (1990). Parenting by gay fathers. In F. Bozett & M. Sussman (Eds.), *Homosexuality and family relations* (pp. 155–175). New York: Haworth Press.

84. Newman, L. (1989). *Heather has two mommies.* Los Angeles: Alyson Wonderland.

85. Barbanel, J. (1993, February 8). Political miscalculations threaten Fernandez's job. *The New York Times*, sec. 1B, p. 2. Dillon, S. (1993, February 11). Board removes Fernandez as New York schools chief after stormy 3–year term. *The New York Times*, sec. 1A, p. 6.

86. Fahy, U. (1995). *How to make the world a better place for gays and lesbians.* New York: Warner Books.

87. Women's Educational Media, personal communication, April 3, 1998.

88. Sears, 1993/1994 (see note 30).

89. Fahy, 1995.

90. Walker, C. (1999, June 22). Adopting a strategy: Several steps to help simplify the adoption process. *The Advocate.* Retrieved December 5, 2002, from www.advocate.com/html/stories/0699B/0699_adoption.asp

91. Fahy, 1995.

92. For further discussion, see chapter 8.

93. Witkowski, T. (1997, April). *Not in a family way: If homosexual marriage isn't legal, what kind of rights does a gay parent have?* Retrieved October 31, 1999, from www.phx.com/archive/1in 10/97/04/PARENT_RIGHTS.html

94. Logue, P. M. (2002). *The rights of lesbian and gay parents and their children.* Retrieved February 11, 2002, from Lambda Legal Defense and Education Fund at www.lambda.org/cgi-bin/iowa/documents/record?record=990 (Originally prepared for fall 2001, *American Academy of Matrimontial Lawyers*). National Center for Lesbian Rights. (2000). *Lesbians and gay men as adoptive and foster parents: An information sheet.* Retrieved February 11, 2002, from www.nclrights.org/publications/pubs_adoptive-information.html

95. Gallagher, J. (1995, May 30). Gay . . . with children. *The Advocate*, pp. 28–33.

96. www.nclrights.org/publications/pubs_adoptive-information.html

Chapter 10

1. These issues are addressed in more detail in Stevenson, M. R. (2000). Public policy, homosexuality, and the sexual coercion of children. *Journal of Psychology and Human Sexuality, 12*(4), 1–19. Portions of this chapter are based on that publication.

2. Grossman, C. L. (2002, June 12). Bishops resign; scandal widens. *USA Today*, p. 1.

3. Cozzens, D. B. (2000). *The changing face of the priesthood*. Collegeville, MN: Liturgical Press.

4. Fox, K. (2002, May 3). Gays resist link to abuse scandal. *The Washington Blade*, p. 38. For further discussion of this scandal, see Stevenson, M. R. (2002). Understanding child sexual abuse and the Catholic Church: Gay priests are not the problem, *Angles 6*(2), 1–7. This report is also available online from the Institute of Gay and Lesbian Strategic Studies, www.iglss.org.

5. U.N. panel rejects ILGA status: Decision criticized as "a playing-out of global politics." (2002, February 1). *The Washington Blade*, pp. 1, 25.

6. Thorstad, 1990, p. 253 (see note 19).

7. www.pfaw.org/issues/right/rtvw.antigay.shtml#molester

8. www.narth.com/docs/pedophNEW.html

9. Colorado for Family Values, 1992, p. 2 (see note 18).

10. Abrams, J. (1994, January 29) Senate demands U.N. end ties with NAMBLA. Retrieved November 30, 2002 from qrd.tcp.com/qrd/orgs/NAMBLA/senate.demands.un.oust.nambla

11. Technically, people who have not yet reached the legal age of consent cannot "consent" to anything in the legal sense; therefore, it is not surprising that NAMBLA advocates for lowering the age of consent or abolishing such laws altogether.

12. This position was adopted December 4, 1983. Additional excerpts of NAMBLA position papers are located at qrd.tcp.com/qrd/orgs/NAMBLA/nambla.replies.to.ilga.secretariat. The NAMBLA website is located at www.NAMBLA.org. Its statement of purpose can be found at qurd.tcp.com/qurd/orgs/NAMBLA/statement.of.purpose. For further information, see Freierman, 1990 (see note 20), and Thorstad, 1990.

13. Smith, R. (2002, April 26). Homosexual atmosphere blamed by Catholic leaders: US Cardinals meet with pope on sex abuse scandal, but blame heaped on gay priests. *The Washington Blade*, pp. 1, 24.

14. Lieblich, J. (2002, April 24). "An appalling sin," pope says: Vatican session with cardinals on sex abuse also opens debate on homosexuality in priesthood. *Chicago Tribune*, p. 1.

15. For example, Cameron, P., & Cameron, K. (1996). Do homosexual teachers pose a risk to pupils? *Journal of Psychology, 130*, 603–613. Cameron, P., & Cameron, K. (1998). What proportion of newspaper stories about child molestation involves homosexuality? *Psychological Reports, 82*, 863–871. Cameron, P., Proctor, K., Cobrun, W., Forde, N., Larson, H., & Cameron, K. (1986). Child molestation and homosexuality. *Psychological Reports, 58*, 327–337.

16. See Herek, G. M. (1998). Bad science in the service of stigma: A critique of the Cameron group's survey studies. In G. M. Herek (Ed.), *Stigma and sexual orientation: Understanding prejudice against lesbians, gay men, and bisexuals* (pp. 223–255). Thousand Oaks, CA: Sage. Herek's careful critique produced a long list of serious flaws, including failure to adequately describe their sampling methodology, generalizing from nonrepresentative samples, performing analyses on subsamples that were far too small to produce reliable results, omitting checks for internal consistency, and asking questions in a way that made them confusing, alienating, and difficult to answer.

17. The *Journal of Homosexuality* and the *Journal of Sex Research* are frequently cited.

18. Colorado for Family Values. (1992). *Equal rights—Not special rights*. Colorado Springs, CO: Author.

19. Thorstad, D. (1990). Man/boy love and the American gay movement. *Journal of Homosexuality, 20*, 251–274.

20. Feierman, J. R. (1990). *Pedophilia: Biosocial dimensions*. New York: Springer-Verlag.

21. Schlesinger, L. (1999). *Psychology is NOT a science: Dr. Laura comments on the pedophilia study*. Retrieved from www.drlaura.com

22. Rind, B., Tromovitch, P., & Bauserman, R. (1998). A meta-analytic examination of assumed properties of child sexual abuse using college samples. *Psychological Bulletin, 124*(1), 22–53.

23. See also Bauserman, R., & Rind, B. (1997). Psychological correlates of male child and adolescent sexual experiences with adults: A review of the nonclinical literature. *Archives of Sexual Behavior*, 26(2), 105–141. Rind, B., & Tromovitch, P. (1997). A meta-analytic review of findings from national samples on psychological correlates of child sexual abuse. *Journal of Sex Research*, 34(3), 237–255.

24. Reisman, J. A. (1999, March 26). *The APA's: Academic pedophile advocates*. Retrieved from www.worldnetdaily.com/bluesky_excomm/19990326_xex_the_apas_aca.shtml

25. The *Diagnostic and Statistical Manual (DSM)* is the official compendium used by mental health professionals to describe and diagnose psychological disorders. Published by the American Psychiatric Association, it is revised periodically and is currently in its fourth edition. Homosexuality was removed from the *DSM* in 1973.

26. Lessner, R. (1999, March 26). We are now on the cusp of re-paganizing our culture. *Manchester Union Leader*.

27. Burling, S. (1999, November 17). Despite stir, sex-abuse study won't be reviewed. *The Philadelphia Inquirer*, p. A20. Farberman, R. K. (1999, December). AAAS declines to review controversial child-sexual abuse study. *APA Monitor*, p. 7.

28. Although some perpetrators of sexual behavior with children are female: Holmes, W. C., & Slap, G. B. (1998). Sexual abuse of boys: Definitions, prevalence, correlates, sequelae, and management. *Journal of the American Medical Association, 280*(21), 1855–1862, suggested that they are most likely to be adolescent baby-sitters. Adult lesbians are rarely accused of having sexual interest in children (Weinrich, J. (1994). Homosexuality. In V. L. Bullough & B. Bullough (Eds.), *Human sexuality: An encyclopedia* (pp. 277–283). New York: Garland) and cases of perpetration of sexual behavior with a prepubescent child by an adult lesbian are virtually nonexistent (Gebhard, P. H., & Johnson, A. B. (1979). *The Kinsey data: Marginal tabulations of the 1938–1963 interviews conducted by the Institute for Sex Research*. Philadelphia: Saunders). (See also American Psychiatric Association. (1994). *Diagnostic and statistical manual of mental disorders* (4th ed.). Washington, DC: Author.)

29. Ames, M. A., & Houston, D. A. (1990). Legal, social, and biological definitions of pedophilia. *Archives of Sexual Behavior, 19*(4), 333–342.

30. *DSM-IV*, 1994

31. Rind & Tromovitch, 1997 (see note 23). Rind, Tromovitch, & Bauserman, 1998 (see note 22).

32. Freund, K. (1965). Erotic preference in pedophilia. *Behavioral Research and Theory, 3*, 229–234. Freund, K., & Kuban, M. (1993). Deficient erotic gender differentiation in pedophilia: A follow-up. *Archives of Sexual Behavior, 22*(6), 619–628. Howell, K. (1979). Some meanings of children for pedophiles. In M. Cook & G. Wilson (Eds.), *Love and attraction* (pp. 519–526). New York: Pergamon. See also Ames & Houston, 1990.

33. American Psychiatric Association. (2000). *Diagnostic and statistical manual of mental disorders* (4th ed.–text revision). Washington, DC: Author.

34. That is, an individual who has not reached the legal age of consent.

35. Thorstad, 1990 (see note 19).

36. Some research in this area also fails to distinguish incest from other forms of potentially harmful childhood sexual experience. Although the relationship of the perpetrator to the victim is undoubtedly relevant to the child's subsequent well-being, this too is less salient in the policy arena.

37. Barret, R. L., & Robinson, B. E. (1994). Gay dads. In A. E. Gottfried & A. W. Gottfried (Eds.), *Redefining families: Implications for children's development* (pp. 157–170). New York: Plenum Press. Becker, J. V., Alpert, J. L., BigFoot, D. S., Bonner, B. L., Geddie, L. F., Henggeler, S. W., Kaufman, K. L., & Walker, C. E. (1995). Empirical research on children abuse treatment: Report by the child abuse and neglect treatment working group, American Psychological Association. *Journal of Clinical Child Psychology, 24*(Suppl.), 23–46. Groth, A. N. (1978). Patterns of sexual assault against children and adolescents. In A. W. Burgess, A. N. Groth, L. L. Holmstrom, & S. M. Sgroi (Eds.), *Sexual assault of children and adolescents* (pp. 3–24). Lexington, MA: Lexington

Books. Groth, A. N., & Birnbaum, H. J. (1978). Adult sexual orientation and attraction to under-age persons. *Archives of Sexual Behavior, 7*(3), 175–181. Herek, G. M. (1991a). Myths about sexual orientation: A lawyer's guide to social science research. *Law and Sexuality: A Review of Lesbian and Gay Legal Issues,* 1, 133–172. Jenny, C., Roesler, T. A., & Poyer, K. L. (1994). Are children at risk for sexual abuse by homosexuals? *Pediatrics, 94,* 41–44. Patterson, C. J. (1995). Adoption of minor children by lesbian and gay adults: A social science perspective. *Duke Journal of Gender Law and Policy,* 191–205. Sarafino, E. P. (1979). An estimate of nation-wide incidence of sexual offenses against children. *Child Welfare, 58,* 127–134.

38. That is, the absence of secondary sex characteristics and mature body shape.

39. Ames & Houston, 1990 (see note 20).

40. For example, Cameron et al., 1986; Cameron & Cameron, 1996 (See noe 6.).

41. Bell, A., Weinberg, M., & Hammersmith, S. K. (1981). *Sexual preference: Its development among men and women.* Bloomington: Indiana University Press. Finkelhor, D. (1979). *Sexually victimized children.* New York: Free Press. Finkelhor, D. (1984). *Child sexual abuse: New theory and research* (pp. 150–170). New York: Free Press. Johnson, R. L., & Shrier, D. K. (1985). Sexual victimization of boys: experience at an adolescent medicine clinic. *Journal of Adolescent Health Care, 6,* 372–376. Johnson, R. L., & Shrier, D. K. (1987). Past sexual victimization by females of male patients in an adolescent medicine clinic population. *American Journal of Psychiatry, 144,* 650–652. Laumann, E. O., Gagnon, J. H., Michael, R. T., & Michaels, S. (1994). *The social organization of sexuality: Sexual practices in the United States.* Chicago: University of Chicago Press. Paul, J. P., Catania, J., Pollack, L., & Stall, R. (n.d.) *Understanding childhood sexual coercion as a predictor of sexual risk-taking among men who have sex with men: The urban mens health study.* Manuscript submitted for publication. Shrier, D., & Johnson, R. L. (1988). Sexual victimization of boys: An ongoing study of an adolescent medicine clinic population. *Journal of the National Medical Association, 80*(11), 1189–1193.

42. Johnson & Shrier, 1985, 1987; Shrier & Johnson, 1988.

43. Doll, L. S., Joy, D., Bartholow, B. N., Harrison, J. S., Bolan, G., Douglas, J. M., Saltzman, L. E., Moss, P. M., & Degado, W. (1992). Self-reported childhood and adolescent sexual abuse among adult homosexual and bisexual men. *Child Abuse and Neglect, 16,* 865–876. Weinrich, 1994 (see note 28).

44. Bell, Weinberg, & Hammersmith, 1981; Weinrich, 1994.

45. Beitchman, J. H., Zucker, K. J., Hood, J. E., daCosta, G. A., Akman, D., & Cassavia, E. (1991). A review of the long-term effects of childhood sexual abuse. *Child Abuse and Neglect, 16,* 101–118. Finkelhor, 1984 (see note 41). Holmes & Slap, 1998 (see note 28). Johnson & Shrier, 1985 (see note 41). Lisak, D. (1994). The psychological impact of sexual abuse: Content analysis of interviews with male survivors. *Journal of Traumatic Stress, 7*(4), 525–548. Rogers, C., & Terry, T. (1984). Clinical intervention with boy victims of sexual abuse. In I. Stewart & J. Greer (Eds.), *Victims of sexual aggression* (pp 91–104). New York: Van Nostrand Reinhold. Simari, C. G., & Baskin, D. (1984). Incestuous experiences within lesbian and male homosexual populations: A preliminary study. *Child Psychiatry Quarterly, 17*(1/2), 21–40.

46. Bell, Weinberg, & Hammersmith, 1981, p. 102 (see note 41).

47. Brown, L. S., Schneider, M., & Glassgold, J. (2001). *Implementing the resolution on appropriate therapeutic responses to sexual orientation: A guide for the perplexed.* Unpublished paper. Glassgold, 1999, personal communication. Posner, R. A. (1992). *Sex and reason.* Cambridge, MA: Harvard University Press.

48. This issue is discussed in some detail in chapter 2.

49. Bauserman, R., & Rind, B. (1997). Psychological correlates of male child and adolescent sexual experiences with adults: A review of the nonclinical literature. *Archives of Sexual Behavior, 26*(2), 105–141. Rind & Tromovitch, 1997 (see note 23). Rind, Tromovitch, & Bauserman, 1998 (see note 22)

50. D'Augelli, A. R., & Patterson, C. J. (Eds). (1995). *Lesbian, gay, and bisexual identities over the lifespan: Psychological perspectives*. New York: Oxford University Press. Stein, E. (1999). *The mismeasure of desire: The science, theory, and ethics of sexual orientation*. New York: Oxford University Press. These issues are also discussed in chapter 2.

51. Haldeman, D. C. (1999). The pseudo-science of sexual orientation conversion therapy. *Angles, 4*(1), 1–4. Lawrence, A. A. (1999). Changes in the sexual orientation of six heterosexual male-to-female transsexuals: Comment. *Archives of Sexual Behavior, 28*(6), 581–583. Yarhouse, M. A. (1998). Group therapies for homosexuals seeking change. *Journal of Psychology and Theology, 26*(3), 247–259.

52. Bartholow, B. N., Doll, L. S., Joy, D., Douglas, J. M., Jr., Bolan, G., Harrison, J. S., Moss, P. M., & McKirnan, D. (1994). Emotional, behavioral, and HIV risks associated with sexual abuse among adult homosexual and bisexual men. *Child Abuse and Neglect, 18*(9), 747–761.

53. Laumann, Gagnon, Michael, & Michaels, 1994 (see note 41). Paul, Catania, Pollack, & Stall, submitted (see note 41).

54. Risin, L., & Koss, M. (1987). The sexual abuse of boys: Prevalence and descriptive characteristics of childhood victimizations. *Journal of Interpersonal Violence, 2*(3), 309–323.

55. Laumann, Gagnon, Michael, & Michaels, 1994.

56. Martin, A. D. (1982). The minority question. *et cetera. 39*(1), 22–42. Martin, A. D. (1988). The stigmatization of the gay or lesbian adolescent. In M. Schneider (Ed.), *Often invisible: Counseling gay and lesbian youth* (pp. 59–69). Toronto: Central Toronto Youth Services. Schneider, M. (1993). Educating the public about homosexuality. *Annals of Sex Research, 6*, 57–66.

57. Herek, G. M. (1991b). Stigma, prejudice, and violence against lesbians and gay men. In J. C. Gonsiorek & J. D. Weinrich (Eds.), *Homosexuality: Research implications for public policy* (pp. 60–80). Newbury Park, CA: Sage.

58. Pratt, J. (1998). The rise and fall of homophobia and sexual psychopath legislation in postwar society. *Psychology, Public Policy, and Law, 4*(1/2), 25–49. Wolfenden, J. (1957). *Report of the Committee on Homosexual Offences and Prostitution*. London: Command 247.

59. Weinrich, 1994 (see note 28).

60. For example, www.ReligiousTolerance.org

61. Levitt, E. E., & Klassen, A. D., Jr. (1974). Public attitudes toward homosexuality: Part of the 1970 national survey by the institute for sex research. *Journal of Homosexuality, 1*, 29–43.

62. Herek, G. (2002). Gender gaps in public opinion about lesbians and gay men. *Public Opinion Quarterly, 66*(1), 40–66.

63. Herek, 1991a. (see note 37).

64. Yang, A. S. (1998). *From wrongs to rights: Public opinion on gay and lesbian equality*. New York: National Gay and Lesbian Task Force.

65. The material presented in this section is based in part on Stevenson, M. R. (1999). Sexual victimization: Responses of the U.S. Congress. In M. Paludi (Ed.), *The psychology of sexual victimization: A handbook* (pp. 171–183) Westport, CT: Greenwood.

66. Gray, J. (1996, May 10). Senate approves measure requiring states to warn communities about sex offenders. *The New York Times*, p. A28. Harris, J. F. (1996, June 23). President endorses sex offender registry: Reno to report on a national tracking system. *The Washington Post*, p. A19.

67. See Todd Whitman, C., & Farmer, J. J. (2000, March). *Attorney General guidelines for law enforcement for the implementation of sex offender registration and community notification laws*. (Prepared by the Attorney General of New Jersey and available at www.ojp.usdoj.gov/BJA/html/megan1.pdf)

68. Gray, 1996. Ingram, C. (1996, June 12). Bill to publicize locations of sex offenders gains; Children: State senate panel approves version of federal "Megan's law." Failure to enact legislation could lead to loss in crime-fighting funds. *The Los Angeles Times*, p. A3.

69. Amendment to H.R. 1533.

70. Jenny, Rosesler, & Poyer, 1994 (see note 37). Jinich, S., Paul, J., Stall, R., Acree, M., Kegeles, S., Hoff, C., & Coates, T. (1998). Childhood sexual abuse and HIV risk-taking behavior among gay and bisexual men. *AIDS and Behavior, 2*(1), 41–51. Johnson & Shrier, 1985, 1987 (see note 32). Paul, Catania, Pollack, & Stall, submitted (see note 41). Risin & Koss, 1987 (see note 41). Schneider, M. (1993). Educating the public about homosexuality. *Annals of Sex Research, 6*, 57–66. Shrier & Johnson, 1988 (see note 41).

71. Burgess, A. W., Groth, A. N., Holmstrom, L. L., & Sgroi, S. M. (Eds.). (1978). *Sexual assault of children and adolescents*. Lexington, MA: Lexington Books. Risin & Koss, 1987. Shrier & Johnson, 1988.

72. Earl-Hubbard, M. L. (1996). The child sex offender registration laws: The punishment, liberty deprivation, and unintended results associated with the scarlet letter laws of the 1990s. *Northwestern University Law Review, 90*(2), 788–862, 852.

73. Allam, J. M. (1998). Evaluation community-based treatment programs for men who sexually abuse children. *Child Abuse Review, 71*, 13–29; Marques, J. K. (1999). How to answer the question, does sex offender treatment work? *Journal of Interpersonal Violence, 14*(4), 437–451; Polizzi, D. M., MacKenzie, D. L., & Hickman, L. J. (1999). What works in adult sex offender treatment? A review of prison- and non-prison-based treatment programs. *International Journal of Offender Therapy and Comparative Criminology, 43*(3), 357–374.

74. Earl-Hubbard, 1996, p. 861.

75. Fein, B. (1995). Community self-defense laws are constitutionally sound. *ABA Journal, 81*, 38. Martone, E. (1995). Mere illusion of safety creates climate of vigilante justice. *ABA Journal, 81*, 39.

76. Van Natta, D. (1996, March 22). Law tracking sex offenders faces setback. *The New York Times*, p. B1. Trivits, L. C., & Reppucci, N. D. (2002). Application of Megan's law to juveniles. *American Psychologist, 57*(9), 690–704.

77. Jacobson, R. L. (1999). Megan's Laws reinforcing old patterns of anti-gay police harassment. *Georgetown Law Journal, 87*, 2431.

78. Jacobson, 1999 (see note 77).

79. Ibid.

80. Trivits & Reppucci, 2002.

81. See discussion of so-called sodomy laws in chapter 2.

82. American Civil Liberties Union. (1997, September 9). *ACLU urges Congress to curb reach of Megan's Law to exclude consensual sodomy*. [Press release]. See also www.aclu.org

83. Chibbaro, L. (1999, July 2). Megan's Law clause called mistake: D.C. sex offender bill won't include convictions of consensual sodomy. *The Washington Blade*, p. 5.

84. Jacobson, 1999 (see note 77).

85. Ibid.

86. Newton, D. E. (1978). Homosexual behavior and child molestation: A review of the evidence. *Adolescence, 13*(49), 29–43, 35.

87. Glasser, M., Kolvin, I., Campbell, D., Glasser, A., Leitch, I., & Farrelly, S. (2001). Cycle of child sexual abuse: Links between being a victim and becoming a perpetrator. *British Journal of Psychiatry, 179*, 482–494.

88. Jenny, Roesler, & Poyer, 1994 (see note 37). Jinich et al., 1998 (see note 70).

Chapter 11

1. For example, Stepp, L. S. (2001, June 19). A lesson in cruelty: Anti-gay slurs common at school. *The New York Times*, p. A1. Egan, J. (2000, December 10). Lonely gay teen seeking same: How Jeffrey found friendship, sex, heartache—and himself—online. *New York Times Magazine*, pp. 110–117, 128.

2. Darroch, J. E., Landry, D. J., & Singh, S. (2000). Changing emphasis in sexuality education in U.S. public secondary schools, 1988–1999. *Family Planning Perspectives, 32*(5), 204–211, 265. See also Dailard, C. (2001, February). *Sex education: Politicians, parents, teachers, and teens. The Guttmacher Report on Public Policy.* Retrieved from www.agi-usa.org/pubs/ib_2–01.html It is difficult to determine from these data what sexuality educators actually say about sexual orientation when they cover the topic. To include such a discussion does not ensure that nonheterosexual orientations will be portrayed in a positive fashion.

3. Dailard, 2001. See also www.agi-usa.org/pubs/ib_2–01.html

4. See surgeongeneral.gov/library/sexualhealth/ for a discussion of this research.

5. The report is available at surgeongeneral.gov/library/sexualhealth/

6. Excerpts from *The Surgeon General's call to action to promote sexual health and responsible sexual behavior,* 2001 (pp. 1, 5, 12). The full report is available online at www.surgeongeneral.gov/library/sexualhealth/call.htm

7. The full text of the Doolittle amendment is available through the Thomas website at Thomas.loc.gov/CGI-BIN/Query/F?r103:1:./Temp?~R103UDVSIN:E55984. The full text of the proposed Hancock amendment is available through the Thomas website at Thomas.loc.gov/CGI-BIN/Query/F?r103:2:./Temp/~r103nbx5d2:e1183.

8. Chapter 3 discusses the rhetoric of the religious right in greater depth.

9. The joint statement and supporting documentation are available at www.ncac.org/issues/abonlypresskit.html

10. Human Rights Watch. (2001). *Hatred in the hallways: Violence and discrimination against lesbian, gay, bisexual, and transgendered students in U.S. schools.* Retrieved from www.hrw.org/reports/2001/uslgbt.

11. Valleroy, L. A., MacKellar, D. A., Karon, J. M., Rosen, D. H., McFarland, W., Shehan, D. A., Stoyanoff, S. R., LaLota, M., Celentano, D. D., Koblin, B. A., Thiede, H., Katz, M. H., Torian, L. V., & Janssen, R. S. (2000). HIV prevalence and associated risks in young men who have sex with men. *Journal of the American Medical Association, 284*(2), 198–204. Saewyc, E. M., Bearinger, L. H., Heinz, P. A., Blum, R. W., & Resnick, M. D. (1998). Gender differences in health and risk behaviors among bisexual and homosexual adolescents. *Journal of Adolescent Health, 23*, 181–188. Resnick, M. D., Bearman, P. S., Blum, R. W., Bauman, K. E., Harris, K. M., Jones, J., Tabor, J., Behring, T., Sieving, R. E., Shew, M., Ireland, M., Bearing, L. H., & Uldry, J. R. (1997). Protecting adolescents from harm: Findings from the National Longitudinal Study on Adolescent Health. *Journal of the American Medical Association, 278*(10), 823–832. Remafedi, G., French, S., Story, M., Resnick, M. D., & Blum, R. (1998). The relationship between suicide risk and sexual orientation: Results of a population-based study. *American Journal of Public Health, 88*, 57–60. Ryan, C., & Futterman, D. (1998). *Lesbian and gay youth care and counseling.* New York: Columbia University Press. See also the Healthy Lesbian, Gay, and Bisexual Students Project at www.apa.org/ed/hlgh.html

12. McDaniel, J. S., Purcell, D., & D'Augelli, A. B. (2001). The relationship between sexual orientation and risk for suicide: Research findings and future directions for research and prevention. *Suicide and Life-Threatening Behavior, 31*(Suppl. 1), 84–105. Russell, S. T., & Joyner, K. (2001). Adolescent sexual orientation and suicide risk: Evidence from a national study. *American Journal of Public Health, 91*(8), 1276–1281. www.wsw.soton.ac.uk/gay-youth-suicide/01–gay-bisexual-male-suicide.htm. See also sources listed in note 11.

13. See chapter 3 for further discussion of these issues.

14. For recent news stories on student discrimination and harassment visit the Gay, Lesbian, and Straight Education Network website at www.glsen.org/templates/issues/indexhtml?subject=7

15. Retrieved from www.aclu.org/issues/gay/safe_schools.html

16. The report is available at www.eic-whoswho.com/highschool/frame.html

17. Massachusetts Governor's Commission on Gay and Lesbian youth. (1993). *Making schools*

safe for gay and lesbian youth: Report of the Massachusetts Governor's Commission on Gay and Lesbian Youth. 1993.

18. Gay, Lesbian, and Straight Education Network. (1999). *GLSEN's national school climate survey.* Retrieved from www.aclu.org/issues/gay/statistics.html

19. *Indiana Youth Group Education for all? A report on homophobic hatred in greater Indianapolis schools.* (2001). The report is available from Indiana Youth Group, Inc., P.O. Box 20716, Indianapolis, IN 46220–0716.

20. Healthy Lesbian, Gay, and Bisexual Students Project, 2001, is available online at www.apa.org/ed/hlgbreport.html.

21. For further evidence see Garofalo, R., Wolf, C., Kessel, S., Palfrey, J., & DuRant, R. H. (1998). The association between health risk behaviors and sexual orientation among a school-based sample of adolescents. *Pediatrics, 101*, 895–902. Ryan, & Futterman, 1998 (see note 11). Sears, J. T. (1992). Educators, homosexuality, and homosexual students: Are personal feelings related to professional beliefs? In K. Harbeck (Ed.), *Coming out of the classroom closet* (pp. 29–79). New York: Harrington Park Press. For a summary of statistics on LGB youth in schools, consult www.aclu.org/issues/gay/statistics.html

22. For additional resources, consult www.apa.org/ed/hlgbreport.html

23. Gay teacher. (2001, June 15). *The Washington Blade*, p. 18.

24. For additional examples of teacher/staff discrimination and harassment visit the Gay, Lesbian, and Straight Education Network website at www.glsen.org/templates/issues/index.html?subject=8

25. *Detroit News*, September 26, 2000.

26. Smith, R. (2001, July 6). NEA drops pro-gay resolution: Task force to study issue of protecting, educating students. *The Washington Blade*, p. 16.

27. Teachers union asks schools to protect gay students and staff. (2002, February 15), *The Washington Blade*, p.14.

28. Adapted from www.apa.org/ed/hlgbreport.html

29. www.aft.org/human/resource/download/keeping.pdf

30. www.aft.org.human/resource/download/keeping.pdf

31. www.aft.org.human/resource/download/keeping.pdf

32. www.schoolcounselor.org/ethis/standards.htm

33. www.ashaweb/org/resolution1.html#familylife

34. www.nasn.org/position/orientation.htm

35. www.nea.org/resolutions/00/00b-9.html

36. www.nsba.org/about/beliefs.htm#ArticleII

37. Associated Press. (1996, November 20). Retrieved from www.youth.org/loco/PERSONProject/Alerts/Old/Nabozny.html

38. GSA's across the nation: A calm after the storm (2001, Spring). *Respect, 5*, 12–13.

39. Friedman, M. (2000, Spring). Orange County gay students win historic ruling in favor of club. *People for the American Way News, 6*(1), 4, 8.

40. Massachusetts Department of Education. (1999). *Massachusetts youth risk behavior survey.* Massachusetts Governor's Commission on Gay and Lesbian Youth, 1993 (see note 17).

41. Kuehl, S. (2001, Spring). How to pass safe schools legislation: Five lessons. *Respect, 5*, 22–23.

42. These issues are discussed in more detail in chapter 8.

43. *Antelope Valley Press*, March 21, 2000.

44. School boards are the locally elected bodies that set policy for a school district.

45. *Honolulu Advisor*, November 3, 2000.

46. See chapter 4 for details.

47. Teachers may also wish to consult *Responding to Hate at School*, which provides guidance on how to respond promptly to individual expressions of intolerance as well as to schoolwide emergencies. These materials were developed by Teaching Tolerance, a project of the Southern Poverty Law Center. They can be retrieved at www.splcenter.org/teachingtolerance/tt-index.html. Additional resources for making schools safe for every student can be retrieved from the ACLU website, www.aclu.org/issues/gay/safe_schools.html

48. www.GLSEN.org

49. Frankfurt, K. (2001, Spring). Badge of dishonor. *Respect, 5*, 8–11.

BIOGRAPHICAL NOTES

Clinton W. Anderson is on staff at the American Psychological Association, where his program area is lesbian, gay, and bisexual concerns. He is currently enrolled in a doctoral program in psychology at the University of Maryland, Baltimore County. His current research focuses on fear and avoidance of homosexuality as aspects of masculinity.

Karen M. Anderson is senior research associate at Howard University. She earned her Ph.D. in psychology from the University of Pittsburgh. Karen was formerly director of the Center for Psychology in School and Education and assistant executive director in the Education Directorate at the American Psychological Association. She is also the project co-director of the Healthy Lesbian, Gay, and Bisexual Students Project (funded by the Centers for Disease Control). Dr. Anderson also worked as director of Policy Research for the National School Boards Association and as senior legislative assistant for Rep. Jolene Unsoeld in the U.S. House of Representatives.

Robin A. Buhrke is staff psychologist and assistant clinical professor in psychiatry and behavioral sciences at Duke University. She served in the office of Sen. Paul Wellstone as a 1997–1998 APA Senior Congressional Science Fellow. She is past president of the Society for the Psychological Study of Lesbian, Gay, and Bisexual Issues (APA Division 44) and past chair of the APA Committee on Lesbian, Gay, and Bisexual Concerns (CLGBC).

Jeanine C. Cogan completed her Ph.D. at the University of Vermont. As a Congressional Science Fellow working in the office of a congresswoman, she wrote a federal bill that passed into law in 2000. She also successfully lobbied for increased research funding addressing the problem of hate crimes. As a result of her success, she was awarded Fellow status in the SPSSI, a division of APA. She founded Cogan Consulting, which focuses on organizational development, motivational speaking, designing mentoring programs, and successfully working with members of Congress.

Stacey Hart received a Ph.D. from the University of Southern California and completed a National Institute of Mental Health Postdoctoral Fellowship at Stanford University School of Medicine. She was invited by the Department of Health and Human Services and the Office on Women's Health to participate in the first Scientific Workshop on Lesbian Health, which provided recommendations on how to implement the Institute of Medicine's report on improving lesbian health research.

Jennifer M. Hoag is a doctoral student in the clinical/school psychology program at Hofstra University. Her interests include child psychopathology, child assessment and intervention, the role of psychopharmacological drugs in the development of children, and psychotherapy in the geriatric population.

Beverly R. King earned a Ph.D. in developmental psychology from Purdue University. She is a member of the psychology department at South Dakota State University. Currently, she is planning research to investigate the development of prejudice in children and young adults.

Jessica F. Morris is a licensed psychologist with an independent practice. Her work focuses on the psychology of lesbians including the coming out process, mental health, and ethnicity, as well as psychological testing and forensic evaluation.

C. Dixon Osburn co-founded Servicemembers Legal Defense Network (SLDN) in 1993 with Michelle Benecke. He has earned both an M.B.A. and a J.D. from Georgetown University. He has published seven annual reports on "Don't Ask, Don't Tell, Don't Pursue, Don't Harass" and the *Survival Guide*, a handbook to assist service members with the rules of survival under the policy. In 1998, Osburn was named by *The Advocate* magazine as one of the top 10 national gay leaders.

Christopher J. Portelli earned his J.D. from New York Law School. As a Ph.D. candidate in public and urban policy at The New School, he is focusing on the impact that large communities of lesbians and gay men have had on the development of policy in major urban centers. He has served as the director of information for the Sexuality Information and Education Council of the United States (SIECUS) in New York City, and was the founding executive director of the National Lesbian and Gay Health Association in Washington, D.C.

Lisa M. Schmidt graduated in 2002 from Ball State University with her master's degree in clinical psychology. Her interests range from forensic pathology and legal applications of psychology to behavioral analysis.

David C. Sobelsohn has served as counsel to the Michigan House Judiciary Committee and to U.S. Rep. John Conyers Jr. (D-Mich.). As chief legislative counsel of the Human Rights Campaign (HRC) from 1994 to 1995, he prepared the first draft of the Employment Non-Discrimination Act (ENDA), helped organize Senate hearings on ENDA in July 1994, and initiated HRC's Documenting Discrimination project.

Andrea L. Solarz received her Ph.D. from Michigan State University. While at the National Academy of Sciences Institute of Medicine (IOM), she directed the study on lesbian health and a study on genetics, health, and behavior. She also served as assistant director for science policy in the Public Policy Office of the American Psychological Association, as a policy analyst in the U.S. Congress Office of Technology Assessment health program, and as a Congressional Fellow in the Senate Subcommittee on the Handicapped. She is currently working as a health policy consultant.

Michael R. Stevenson is currently director of the Diversity Policy Institute and professor of psychological science at Ball State University. As a Senior Congressional Fellow (1995–1996), he served as science advisor to Sen. Paul Simon (D-Ill.) where he was instrumental in the passage of the National Gambling Impact Study Commission Act. In 2000 he was awarded Fellow status by the Society for the Teaching of Psychology and the Society for the Psychological Study of Lesbian, Gay, and Bisexual Issues (both divisions of the American Psychological Association). His current work focuses on diversity policy in higher education and the application of research findings in the development of public policy.

INDEX